The transmission of Ch

This is the first time that an ethnographer has studied three different forms of medical education simultaneously. Conducting extensive fieldwork in Kunming in the People's Republic of China, Elisabeth Hsu became the disciple of a *qigong* healer, who taught her his esoteric arts by imitation and repetition only. She also attended seminars of a senior Chinese doctor who plunged his followers into studying arcane medical classics, and she took the regular courses for Chinese students at the Yunnan College of Traditional Chinese Medicine, where the standardised knowledge of official Chinese medicine is inculcated. Dr Hsu compares these different medical traditions and shows how the same technical terms may take on different meanings in different contexts. This is a fascinating insider's account, which brings out the way in which the context of instruction shapes knowledge.

ELISABETH HSU is a teaching and research fellow in the history of Chinese science at the University of Cambridge. She has published in scholarly journals and is co-editor of *Naxi and Moso Ethnography* (1998) and editor of *Chinese Medicine: Innovation, Convention and Controversy* (forthcoming).

Cambridge Studies in Medical Anthropology 7

Medical anthropology is the fastest growing specialist area within anthropology, both in North America and in Europe. Beginning as an applied field serving public health specialists, medical anthropology now provides a significant forum for many of the most urgent debates in anthropology and the humanities. It includes the study of medical institutions and health care in a variety of rich and poor societies, the investigation of the cultural construction of illness, and the analysis of ideas about the body, birth, maturity, ageing, and death.

This series includes theoretically innovative monographs, state-of-the-art collections of essays on current issues, and short books introducing main themes in the subdiscipline.

1. Lynn M. Morgan, *Community Participation in Health: The Politics of Primary Care in Costa Rica*
2. Thomas J. Csordas (ed.), *Embodiment and Experience: The Existential Ground of Culture and Health*
3. Paul Brodwin, *Medicine and Morality in Haiti: The Contest for Healing Power*
4. Susan Reynolds Whyte, *Questioning Misfortune: The Pragmatics of Uncertainty in Eastern Uganda*
5. Margaret Lock and Patricia Kaufert, *Pragmatic Women and Body Politics*
6. Vincanne Adams, *Medical Science and Democratic Truth: Doctors and Revolution in Nepal*

The transmission of Chinese medicine

Elisabeth Hsu

University of Cambridge

CAMBRIDGE
UNIVERSITY PRESS

PUBLISHED BY THE PRESS SYNDICATE OF THE UNIVERSITY OF CAMBRIDGE
The Pitt Building, Trumpington Street, Cambridge, United Kingdom

CAMBRIDGE UNIVERSITY PRESS
The Edinburgh Building, Cambridge CB2 2RU, UK,
http://www.cup.cam.ac.uk
40 West 20th Street, New York NY 1011–4211, USA
http://www.cup.org
10 Stamford Road, Oakleigh, Melbourne 3166, Australia

First published 1999

Printed in the United Kingdom at the University Press, Cambridge

Typeset in 10/12pt Plantin [GC]

A catalogue record for this book is available from the British Library

Library of Congress cataloguing in publication data

Hsu, Elisabeth.
The transmission of Chinese medicine / Elisabeth Hsu.
    p.   cm. – (Cambridge studies in medical anthropology; 7)
Includes bibliographical references.
ISBN 0 521 64236 1 (hardback). – ISBN 0 521 64542 5 (paperback)
1. Medicine, Chinese – Study and teaching – China.   2. Medical
anthropology – education, medical – China.   I. Title.   II. Series.
R601.H697   1999
610'.951—dc21   98–50700   CIP
ISBN 0 521 64236 1 hardback
ISBN 0 521 64542 5 paperback

For Manu

Contents

Acknowledgements

This book has gone through many stages, and I would like to thank all those who have contributed to its completion; it would be impossible to acknowledge them all here. The book is based on my Ph.D. thesis, 'Transmission of Knowledge, Texts, and Treatment in Chinese Medicine' (1992), which was conducted under the supervision of Gilbert Lewis. My first and foremost thanks go to him for his trust in me at that stage of my studies in anthropology and for his insights which continue to give me guidance. But a thesis makes no book, and Sir Geoffrey Lloyd not only encouraged me but also gave me vital advice on how to refine my work. In addition, I thank the Press's four anonymous reviewers and the style editor. The book would not have taken its present form without their comments.

The research was funded by the Swiss National Foundation, the Wenner–Gren Foundation for Anthropological Research, the National Science Foundation of the United States who provided a Research Fellowship at the Needham Research Institute, and the Chiang Ching-kuo Foundation for a post-doctoral Teaching and Research Fellowship in the History of Chinese Science and Technology at the Faculty of Oriental Studies of the University of Cambridge where the manuscript was completed. I should also mention the British Council, Clare Hall College, the Overseas Research Scholarship, and the Zürich City Council who in the beginning of my researches provided relatively small but decisive support. The contact between the sister cities Zürich and Kunming was crucial for favourable fieldwork conditions.

Above all, I wish to express my gratitude to the people in Kunming, in and outside the Yunnan Traditional Chinese Medical College. I would like to thank my teachers Wu Zongbo and Yan Yuwei who really cared that I acquire a comprehensive training and Zhou Yongsheng who arranged my stay at the college with a warm-hearted concern. Thanks also to *qigong* master Qiu and Jade Blossom who made me feel so much at home, and to all the friends, patients, students, and doctors on whose cooperation this research depended.

Note on Chinese terms

Chinese words are all rendered in *pinyin*, the official transliteration system of the People's Republic of China (PRC), even in quotations from works in which other transcription systems have been used. Chinese medical terms have all been approximated by an English term, but where these need to be understood in a special sense I have used initial capital letters to identify them. Blood (*xue*), for instance, is not in all respects equivalent to the English term 'blood'. These terms have been translated into English previously, but the Chinese medical terminology varies greatly between different authors. In the context of the government-promoted Chinese medicine, I have used primarily the *Revised Outline*, partially translated by Sivin (1987), and Wiseman's (1990) comprehensive *Glossary of Chinese Medical Terms and Acupuncture Points*. However, since I worked in different social contexts, style and register had to be adjusted, and therefore the same Chinese term has been translated differently in different contexts in approximation of the speaker's understanding of its connotations. Some terms clearly have changed their connotations over time, and they are treated accordingly in translation. The precise interpretation of these terms will of course continue to be subject to debate.

The glossary concerns medical and philosophical terms and includes a synopsis of the various translations given by Manfred Porkert, Paul Unschuld and Nathan Sivin.

Translations are my own if not otherwise indicated. Personal names and certain biographical details have for reasons of discretion been disguised.

Introduction: ways of learning

Chinese medicine is grounded in medical practice and in texts – in experience and in its transmission from one generation to another. It changes over time as its social and historical contexts change, but these changes do not occur uniformly. This book explores variations of key terms in Chinese medicine and examines ways in which they are understood in different social contexts. In particular, it concerns the extent to which the understanding and social significance of these terms depend on the way in which they are transmitted and learnt.

Why should the understanding of specific concepts depend on the way in which they are learnt? Knowledge is generally assumed to depend on what one has learnt, regardless of how one has learnt it. This study contests the idea that there are contents of knowledge that can be transmitted and learnt regardless of how the actors involved, in their social relationship to each other, relate to knowledge. It shows that styles of knowing differ according to one's perception of and attitudes to knowledge, and that the meaning of the same term may change as the ways change in which one perceives, expresses, uses, credits, orders, and applies knowledge. The underlying question in this book is thus how far the way in which one learns these terms determines the way in which one knows them or, simply, how different ways of learning relate to different styles of knowing.

Modes of transmission

Central to this study are the ways in which Chinese medical knowledge and practice were transmitted and learnt in three different social settings. These different modes of transmission may be called 'secret', 'personal', and 'standardised', terms which refer primarily to the observed relationships between the medical practitioners and their acolytes, while simultaneously accounting for overall features of the settings in which the transmission of medical knowledge and practice took place. The 'secret', 'personal', and 'standardised' modes do not describe idealised

1

types; they were not starting assumptions nor hypotheses I set out to test, but have arisen from an interpretation of ethnographic data and correspond, in that sense, to the conclusion of the study.

'Secret knowledge' is much discussed in the anthropological literature, although it is in fact the process of transmission that is secret. This secretly transmitted knowledge is not to be confused with 'tacit knowledge' that refers, in contexts in which knowledge is proclaimed to be open and accessible to anyone, to those aspects of a practice that are transmitted without being explicitly mentioned. Secretly transmitted knowledge is intentionally made secret, and this is crucial for the social relationship of those involved. It may very well consist of explicit statements which may be the same as those transmitted in other ways, but the ways in which one knows them – their powers and dangers – differ significantly.

The personal transmission of knowledge and practice tends to be subsumed under the secret transmission of knowledge but my fieldwork observations call for singling it out: it depends critically on the personalities of mentor and follower and their choice to maintain a personal relationship of mutual trust within which the follower acquires medical knowledge and practice. The historical and crosscultural perspectives underline the relevance of these observations: the personal transmission of knowledge, as observed in ethnographic fieldwork, shares several features with the way in which Chinese medicine, according to textual records, was practised and transmitted among the literate elite in Imperial times, and some of its features are also found among the traditional elite in India and other parts of the Far East, the Hellenistic and Islamic world, and medieval Europe.

The standardised mode of transmission is generally considered a form of 'Westernisation', 'modernisation', or 'professionalisation', although it is in no way specific either to Western culture or to modernisation. Particularly in China and probably also in other highly stratified societies with a literate elite, government efforts to standardise medical knowledge and practice have a long history. In the People's Republic of China (PRC), *guifanhua*, 'to standardise', is the word with which many doctors in government institutions describe their endeavours. The notion of standardisation that I use as a meta-category for ordering ethnographic material is thus derived from the actors' point of view.

Styles of knowing

This study was designed to avoid discussing Chinese medical terms decontextualised from social practice, as is so common in textbooks and textbook-like monographs. The aim was to focus not on words and concepts but on utterances and verbal reasoning in social practice. Moreover, I declined to approach this reasoning in terms of Western philosophical categories, valuable as such studies have been (e.g. Hutchins 1980; D'Andrade 1996:193–9).[1] Instead, I intended to become immersed in it, much as Duden ((1987)1991) leads the reader into a world of flows and stagnations – the monthly blood being 'stubborn', wind coming out of the ears, milk flowing off through the stomach, being excreted as the very same white fluid, and sweat smelling like the elderberry juice just drunk – which all give rise to women's illnesses, thereby revealing how a doctor of the early eighteenth century reasoned about mind–body processes.[2]

While historians like Duden must be content with an archaeology of textual fragments, anthropologists can observe the actual incidences of reasoning as social practice. The aim of my research on Chinese medical reasoning was to focus on the situation in which it took place, to account for the actors involved – it went without saying that their social positions determined much of the significance of their assertions – and I was attentive to the variation and variability of access to specialised knowledge and practice. Concepts are not shared to the same degree among the members of a group; some know things others do not know, and some can say things improper for others to say. A statement is not the same if uttered by a child or an elder. Depending on the audience, things otherwise not mentioned can be said. Individuals differ: 'Some people are quick to see the point of a joke, others are slow. Some see a suggestiveness about it which others miss. Some have fertile, inventive and daring imaginations; others, more stolid, remain earthbound, literal, and poetry is lost on them' (Lewis 1980:6). Dispositions change: 'We differ in our preoccupations, our moods, the state of our desires, in our readiness to see something' (p. 116). Reasoning is a creative act. Utterances are not propositions. They have pitch and intonation underlining the mood and modality in which they are uttered. They may be more expressive than descriptive and have a 'speech appeal' (Bühler (1934) 1982:28–9). They may represent an 'illocutionary' or 'perlocutionary' act (Austin 1962:109). They need not be well-formed to be understood, and people attribute different values to them depending on the actors and the occasion.

[1] Hutchins (1980) has provided a formal analysis of how the Trobriand Islanders, deemed incapable of intentional and causal reasoning, did in fact make logical inferences during disputes concerning land ownership.
[2] Duden claims that these recordings reflect the women's own perceptions, but this is difficult to know. They certainly are not to be mistaken for representing the scholarly Galenic traditions.

Verbal reasoning, just like ritual, can be over-intellectualised. In Chinese medicine, we are often confronted with concepts comparable to 'empty notions' such as *evur* (witchcraft power) among the Fang (Boyer 1990:24–45). Boyer has convincingly contested the structuralist and intellectualist approaches to such *mana* concepts, which consider them either as central cultural symbols marked by a so-called 'semantic vacuity' (postulated by Claude Lévi-Strauss) or as 'theoretical principles' comparable to laws in the modern Western sciences (postulated by Robin Horton). The more viable approach to such empty notions, according to Boyer (1990:30), is to 'distinguish between several interrelated "registers" or "styles" of discourse'. He distinguishes between 'common discourse' which is generalising, not related to any precisely defined source of knowledge, and willingly inconclusive; 'gossip' which is very definite, centred on singular cases, and of no use in the contexts in which truths are supposedly expressed; and 'experts' utterances', which are definite, focused on singular cases, and fairly reliable. This study concerns almost exclusively experts' utterances. We will see that registers of discourse or, rather, 'styles of knowing' will vary even among experts, and the so-called 'empty notions' of Chinese medicine will be shown to vary accordingly.[3]

The notion of 'style' in the idiom 'styles of knowing' alludes to the aesthetic in art and literature, and in this sense it may also be used to refer to ways of doing science or medicine. When Fleck ((1935)1980) coined the term *Denkstil* (thought style), he spoke of 'style' in a slightly different way. A certain *Denkstil* belonged to a certain *Denkkollektiv* (thought collective): 'The force of explanation was dependent on the possibility of relating a term to other *stylistically matched* terms' (p. 51, italics added). While this aspect of Fleck's notion of 'style', which stresses the socially approved within a collective, should not be overlooked, I shall use the word 'style' more in Hacking's (1992) sense, emphasising fluidity and individualistic endeavour: 'Every style comes into being by little *microsocial* interactions and negotiations' (p. 10, italics added). 'Style' may be 'generalised' or 'personalised': 'There is a Balzacian style and there is Balzac's style. Equally, in swimming, there is the Australian crawl and freestyle, as opposed to the style of Patti Gonzalez, that can be imitated but is inimitably hers. It is entirely natural to talk of the style of an individual scientist, research group, programme or tradition' (Hacking 1992:2). I have investigated the styles

---

[3] According to Boyer (1990) all three registers of discourse together give the actors an idea of what is meant by *evur*. However, the Chinese actors discussed in this monograph had access to only one style of knowing.

of three individuals; whether these styles can be generalised remains to be seen.

The notions of 'reasoning' and 'discourse' refer to verbal interaction, while 'knowing' involves, in addition, the non-verbal aspects of social interaction in an instance of medical reasoning, including knowing through the intellect, through feelings and intuitions, and through bodily automatisms or, as Csordas (1993) put it, 'somatic modes of attention'. Knowing is meant to emphasise that the instances of medical reasoning are instances of doing all kinds of things in addition to engaging in intellectual communication.[4] Although neither verbal reasoning nor knowing are likely to reach the same salience and emotional arousal as ritual performances, they are a form of action which Lewis (1980:118), with regard to ritual, describes as: 'A way of doing, making, creating, showing, expressing, arousing – a complex form of stimulus to which people respond.'

Knowing Practice

In *Knowing Practice*, Farquhar (1994a) has emphasised the concept of 'knowing Chinese medicine' as opposed to 'knowledge of Chinese medicine'. She does not define 'knowing', but it appears that 'knowing Chinese medicine' has something to do with the particular way in which Chinese medical knowledge is applied to Chinese medical practice. Examining the clinical encounter, Farquhar suggests that Chinese medical discourse has the peculiarity of moving along a gradient from more 'concrete' to more 'verbose' idioms and back again. In the process of what she calls 'looking at the illness' (*kan bing*), a doctor transforms concrete 'signs' (*zheng*1, complaints of the patient) into less concrete 'symptoms' (*zheng*2, the doctor's notations in Chinese medical terms) and then into verbose 'syndrome-therapies' (*zheng*3, also called Distinguishing Patterns), which I was taught generally consisted of a four-word phrase such as *feng shi tou teng* (a Wind Dampness Headache). In the process of 'syndrome differentiation and therapy determination' (*bianzheng lunzhi*), the verbose 'syndrome-therapies' are translated into more concrete 'formulae' (*fangji*) which are in turn composed of specific 'drugs' (*yao*).

Although Farquhar calls her book *Knowing Practice*, her model provides an idealisation of the clinical encounter rather than an account of

---

[4] Hacking (1992:3) makes a similar point: 'Reasoning is done in public as well as in private: by thinking, yes, but also by talking and arguing and showing.' Reasoning in Hacking's sense, like knowing in this sense, is a form of action.

observed ways of 'knowing practice'. The model nicely reflects the claim of doctors in government-run institutions, namely, that they have a step by step way of coming from signs to symptoms to syndromes,[5] although we do not know exactly how Chinese medical doctors get from patients' complaints to the prescription of specific drugs. Farquhar's book reflects the information presented to students in the more advanced courses on the *Diagnostics of Traditional Chinese Medicine* (*Zhongyi zhenduanxue*) and the *Formularies* (*Fangjixue*). It contains translations of seminal texts by leading figures in Traditional Chinese Medicine and textbook passages with which most practitioners are familiar. It aims at a comprehensive account of the clinical encounter throughout the PRC, but this aim has its disadvantages; Farquhar attributes more authority to written texts than to fieldwork observations, anecdotes of which tend to be recorded only in footnotes.

This monograph, by contrast, is intended to provide an ethnographic account for a particular place and time: three settings in Kunming city between September 1988 and December 1989. It discusses key concepts of Chinese medicine embedded in an ethnography of social practice, whether in a healer's consultation room, in the seminars of a self-constituted reading group, or in college classrooms. It aspires not to comprehensiveness but to accuracy and fidelity to what was observed and experienced. It is intended to provide an understanding of Chinese medicine that complements and sometimes calls into question the understanding derived from textbooks and the view that one gains from a focus on texts (Porkert 1974; Sivin 1987; Farquhar 1994a). It is meant to contextualise earlier accounts by medical anthropologists (Ots (1987)1990 and Farquhar 1994a) in that it is not limited to the medicine taught and practised in government institutions, and takes an approach Unschuld ((1980)1985) has long advocated by naming his book *Medicine in China*, which calls for abandoning the idea of a monolithic doctrine and practice of Chinese medicine.

TCM

The context of learning Chinese medicine that deserves particular attention, not least because it is the most discussed in the Western literature (see above), is the traditional medicine that is promoted on

---

[5] Farquhar's model strikes me as being so much in tune with the intentions of TCM textbook compilers that it would not be surprising to find it incorporated in their future teaching materials.

a nationwide scale in colleges, hospitals, and clinics. Its legitimation in the PRC, which took place only in the late 1950s and early 1960s, has led to a reforging that is driven by many different interests – among them nationalism, Confucian values, humanitarian ideals, reformist and 'Enlightenment' movements, the pragmatic politics of a party in pursuit of power, and economic considerations of how to allocate manpower and scarce resources.[6] This medicine is here called 'Traditional Chinese Medicine' and abbreviated to TCM. TCM, when used by Chinese authors in translation, implicitly refers to Chinese medicine in general. This study, however, proposes to narrow its sense down to refer to the government-promoted medicine only and use the more general term 'Chinese medicine' (inclusive of TCM) to refer to what in Chinese is called *zhongyi*.[7] Although there is no specific term for TCM in Chinese, there was among the people I worked with a tendency to recognise it on a conceptual level.

TCM, in spite of being called 'traditional' (*chuantong*), is generally referred to as the 'modernised' (*xiandaihuade*), 'scientific' (*kexuehuade*), 'systematic' (*xitonghuade*), and 'standardised' (*guifanhuade*) Chinese medicine. In awareness of how ideology-laden these attributes were, one doctor called TCM the 'school of the colleges' (*xueyuanpai*), which implied that it was just one of many 'schools' of Chinese medicine. However, government officials, if not aiming at its monopoly, advocated its predominance. TCM, like the professionalised Ayurvedic medicine in India (Leslie 1976a) or Kanpo in Japan (Lock 1980:109–54; Ohnuki-Tierney 1984:91–122; Oberländer 1996), can be regarded as the professionalised Chinese medicine.

Considering how intertwined Chinese medical practice is with shamanic (Kleinman 1980), temple-based (Gould Martin 1975), divinatory (Topley 1976), fortune-telling (Smith 1991), home-based 'herbal drug' (*caoyao*), and other practices, we may agree that 'it is unlikely that before 1949 TCM was a particularly discrete unit for the majority of practitioners' (Farquhar 1994a:15). Currently, however, TCM can be identified as such by investigating the educational scheme, its organisation of knowledge, its textual presentation in textbooks, and verbal reasoning in classrooms and clinics.[8] TCM knowledge is no longer represented as a

---

[6] A history of Chinese medicine in the PRC has yet to be written. Croizier (1968) and Lampton (1977) still provide most detailed information. On Chinese medicine in the Republican period, see Croizier (1968), Ma et al. (1993), and Andrews (1996).
[7] See also Farquhar (1994a:15) and Sivin (1995d:197). Sivin (1995c), however, speaks of 'Traditional Chinese Medicine' with reference to what I would call 'Chinese medicine'.
[8] On variations of TCM practice, see Scheid (1998).

medical 'doctrine', and in this respect differs from Chinese medical learning, which for many centuries ingeniously combined book learning with medical practice.

TCM is distinct also in respect of its institutional setting: the colleges, hospitals, and clinics are all institutions of the Chinese socialist state, so-called 'work units' (*gongzuo danwei*). It is within such socialist institutions that Chinese medicine has been modernised, Westernised, standardised, and made scientific. However, the modernisation of everyday life has affected all medical practices within and outside government institutions, often closely interrelated with a certain Westernisation, and 'science' or 'scientific' is a ubiquitously found attribute for any therapy. It is only in government institutions that the aim of standardising Chinese medical learning has been formulated and pursued. Comparison of this government-promoted medicine with other Chinese therapeutics will allow us to identify both strengths and limitations of the standardisation of medicine.

The settings

The settings for my investigation of the above-mentioned ways of learning and styles of knowing were selected from a wide range of therapeutics in Chinese urban society (see table I.1). My choice took into account that urban spaces were readily divided into 'work units' (*gongzuo danwei*) established by the government in the 1950s as separate cells of urban production and consumption, and the spaces outside them, which included residential areas as well as areas of 'private' or 'individual' enterprise (*getihu*) and 'collectives' (*jitihu*).[9] The government promoted the standardised mode of transmission in the work units. The other two modes of transmission, which were tolerated but not promoted, were overtly practised in the private and collective spaces outside the government institutions (see fig. I.1 on p. 14).

As setting for studying the standardised mode of transmission I chose a TCM college, the Yunnan TCM College (*Yunnan zhongyi xueyuan*). Enrolled between September 1988 and December 1989 as its first foreign student, I was treated with particular care and assigned two excellent tutors, one of whom was teacher Tao. A separate room was prepared for me in a newly built dormitory for 'minority nationalities cadres' (*minzu ganbu*), able medical doctors from the periphery of the province

---

[9] These urban spaces outside work units were never completely abolished in the PRC, and they significantly gained in importance as areas of functional specialisation during the reforms of the 1980s.

Table I.1. *Different medical practitioners in a Chinese urban setting (not comprehensive)*

temple praying monks	fortune tellers	herbalists (*caoyi*)[10]	*qigong* healers[11]	Chinese medical doctors (*zhongyi*)[12]				Western medical doctors (*xiyi*)[13]
				massage (*anmo*)	acumoxa (*zhenjiu*)[14]	Chinese medical doctors (*zhongyi*)	TCM doctors (*zhongyi*)[15]	
	(Qiu)	(Qiu)		(Qiu and Zhang)	(Zhang)	(Zhang)		(Tao)
practise in temples		practise mostly outside government clinics 'folk-medicine'		practise outside and inside government clinics and hospitals				practise mostly inside government clinics and hospitals

[10] 'Herbal medicine' (*caoyi*) was practised by doctors with no formal training or official recognition, and often consisted of applying home-based remedies with 'herbal drugs' (*caoyao*) made up mostly of various parts of plants collected in the hills around the city. The term 'herbalist' (*caoyi*) had in the PRC of the late 1980s a rather restricted sense whereas Topley (1975:243) had earlier observed in Hongkong that: 'All traditional practitioners are thus "herbalists". No traditional practitioner may call himself "doctor" (*yisheng*); this privilege is restricted to qualified, registrable Western-trained physicians. He may call himself *zhongyi* in Chinese . . . but in its English translation . . . he must include the term "herbalist".' In the PRC of the 1980s a Chinese doctor could call himself *yisheng*.

[11] *Qigong* is a compound word composed of two terms, *qi* and *gong*. *Qi* designates a dynamic force and quality in constant flux and flow. It is comparable to *pneuma* in Greek or *prana* in Indian philosophy. English renderings such as 'pneumatic stuff', 'air', 'vapour', and 'breath' all approximate to its meaning, but unsatisfactorily. *Gong* means effect, discipline, capability, achievement, and merit. *Qigong* (workings with the breath) refers to practices of nurturing and conducting the *qi* which enhance the efficiency of *qi* in the body.

[12] *Zhongyi*, a term coined in the last century in response to the presence of the West in China (Croizier 1976:361), comprises many more subdisciplines. Those mentioned here are directly relevant for situating the three main actors in this monograph. *Zhongyi* functions as a superordinate, referring to both government-promoted and government-tolerated Chinese medicine, but it can also refer to the government-promoted TCM alone.

[13] 'Western biomedicine' (*xiyi*) is generally contrasted with Chinese medicine, *zhongyi*. The Western medicine practised by these doctors is neither homeopathy nor scholastic medicine, but biomedicine. Frankenberg (1993:220) rightly draws attention to the 'customary social science conflation of the biological and medical concealed within the term biomedicine, which seems to embody an ideological assumption and a rhetorical claim that need to be explored rather then uncritically accepted'. The term 'biomedicine' is used here precisely because there are basic ideological differences between the Western life sciences and the notion of life and death in Chinese therapeutics.

[14] 'Acumoxa' (*zhenjiu*) comprises both therapies of 'needling' (*zhen*) and 'moxibustion' or 'moxa' (*jiu*), and is throughout this monograph used in place of the term 'acupuncture'. Porkert (1976:1242) coined the term 'Aku-moxi Therapien'.

[15] 'TCM' (*zhongyi*) refers to the standardised medicine that has been promoted at government colleges since the 1950s. The term is used in a narrower sense here than is usually adopted in PRC journals, where TCM is the English term for the Chinese word *zhongyi*.

who had been recruited during the Cultural Revolution and were enrolled for brush-up courses. The sanitary installations were supposed to be better there than elsewhere, and the room was, 'for safety reasons', not easily accessible. I was registered as a first-year student in 'acumoxa and massage' (*zhenjiu tuina*), which was a three-year course that had just begun to be offered by the college for training 'specialists' (*zhuankesheng*), but I also attended classes at higher levels with 'regular students' (*benkesheng*) enrolled in a five-year course on TCM (*zhongyi*). A special curriculum and timetable were set up for me at the beginning of each term, two lectures in different courses every (other) morning.[16] After six months I spent every other morning and after a year every morning at an acumoxa clinic with students who were in their year of clinical practice.

Considering that Yunnan is a 'frontier area' (*bianjiang*) in the southwesternmost corner of the PRC, one may wonder about the representativeness of my experiences at college. College education was largely subject to nationwide policies, and the curriculum, textbooks, and examinations were supposed to accord with the national standards set up in 1984. The architecture and general setup of the work unit also followed the nationwide model. The living conditions in this particular unit were, however, among the worst in Yunnan's provincial capital.[17] College members repeatedly referred to it as the smallest, financially least supported, and academically least respected of all of Yunnan's institutions of higher learning,[18] and this low status is perhaps not characteristic of all TCM colleges in the PRC.

I had chosen to specialise in acumoxa rather than herbal medicine because I considered it important to feel comfortable in delivering the medical treatment about which I was to write after only eighteen months of fieldwork, and herbal medicine appeared to me too vast a subject. As the number of acu-points (*xuewei*) is limited, comprising three to

---

[16] Namely: TCM Fundamentals (*Zhongyi jichu lilun*), Classical Chinese for Medics (*Yiguwen*), Interpretation of the Inner Canon (*Neijing jiangyi*); and [The Study of] Acumoxa [for TCM regular students] (*Zhenjiuxue*), TCM Diagnostics (*Zhongyi zhenduanxue*), Acumoxa Loci (*Shuxue*), Tracts and Links (*Jingluoxue*), Needling and Moxa Techniques (*Zhenfa jiufaxue*), Acumoxa Therapy (*Zhenjiu zhiliaoxue*).

[17] This changed in the late 1980s, when the college acquired land in a southern suburb of the city. In 1996 some of the staff was lodged in a new compound, and the Department of Traditional Chinese Pharmaceutics (*zhongyaoxi*) was in course of being transferred there.

[18] One exception was Prof. Zeng Yulin of the Department of Traditional Chinese Pharmaceutics who was rewarded for his research on extracting the pure and active substances from traditional herbs of some of Yunnan's ethnic minorities. The Yunnan TCM College had apparently enjoyed higher recognition in the 1960s, before excellent staff left or died in the Cultural Revolution (Zhang 1989).

five hundred at most, and the range of disorders known to be successfully treated by acumoxa fairly narrow, learning this skill was not too
ambitious an enterprise. And, indeed, during the last six months of
my training I began to experience that I could alleviate the symptoms
of some patients. Acumoxa has only a few hundred years of history in
this province (Tian 1987:61), and because its promulgation by the
government is quite recent my investigations can be considered fairly
comprehensive.

The setting in which I explored the personal mode of knowledge was
a reading seminar under a 'senior Chinese doctor' (*laozhongyi*), Zhang,
to whom colleagues at the college, when responding to my saying that
I wanted to learn 'real' Chinese medicine, introduced me in April 1989.
Zhang, an acupuncturist whose treatment included herbal medicine
and occasionally massage, already had experience with foreigners, and
was particularly welcoming to me as a foreigner with whom he could
speak without an interpreter. After a few private reading classes, some
of the employees of his collective joined us, and eventually our seminars
consisted of a group of seven. This self-selected group, instigated on
my initiative, was an artificial setting within which Zhang lectured, but
study groups of this kind do not seem to be unusual among Chinese
doctors (Farquhar 1996a:248). We met once or twice a week from
April to December 1989, reading various texts from the *Basic Questions*
(*Su wen*) and *Divine Pivot* (*Ling shu*), the two books that constitute the
Yellow Emperor's Inner Canon (*Huang di nei jing*), and the *Book of Changes*
(*Yi jing*). Since I observed similar approaches to classical texts among
other senior doctors,[19] my discussion of Zhang's modes of interpretation, though selective, may nevertheless be fairly representative. His
attitude and approach to medical texts appear to correspond to those
of the 'scholar doctors' (*ruyi*) of Imperial China (Lu and Needham
(1966)1970:391; Hymes 1987; Wu 1993–4; Cullen 1993; Y. P. Chen
1995) and also have affinities with learned doctors of other Asian medicines (Leslie 1976a; Leslie and Young 1992; Bates 1995).

I spent considerably less time in Zhang's practice than in the other
settings of medical learning and have therefore not systematically recorded his and his followers' treatment of patients. Zhang had only a
few patients; they were almost always 'old friends' (*laopengyou*) who
would engage in long conversations with him while being treated. Sometimes, when he explained a problem to his follower, he would invite me
to join them; sometimes he would show me a successfully treated case.

---

[19] Regular visits to a senior Chinese doctor in a county town near Kunming from August
1989 onward provided particularly interesting information that put Zhang's and also
Qiu's practice into perspective.

In general, however, I felt that my presence at the bedside was intrusive. This fieldwork experience in itself may be telling about the personal transmission of medical practice: the maintenance of a harmonious personal relationship between doctor and client had priority over the transmission of knowledge between the mentor and a follower as tenuously linked to him as I was.

The setting in which I explored the secret mode of transmission was a private practice of a healer, Qiu, specialised in *qigong* (workings with the breath). I was strolling with my bicycle through a back street that appeared promising for finding a private acumoxa practice and had stopped to study his advertisement, when he struck up a conversation: 'Where are you from?' he asked. 'Xinjiang', I replied with a twinkle in my eye. 'Really! That's way up in the northwest, quite far from here. It must still be quite warm there?' Xinjiang was in his mind the land of deserts where grapes and raisins came from. He wanted to know more about it. Which town exactly did I come from? What business brought me to the south? Evidently he considered me Chinese and when I eventually revealed that I was from Europe (*Ouzhou*), he did not understand until his elder brother shouted: 'She's a foreigner, can't you see?'

Qiu accepted me as his disciple after treating an unspecific fatigue that weakened me during the first three months of fieldwork. He later explained that his older brother had urged him to teach me *qigong*, not only to cure me, but also to let me make him known to the world. His wife, Jade Blossom, soon became best friends with me and took me as an ally in her struggles with her in-laws. She had managed to cross the boundary between rural and urban China by means that she did not wish to reveal, which made her suspect, particularly to Qiu's brothers. During the first two months after their wedding in September 1988, Qiu and Jade Blossom alternately confided family problems to me. Later, particularly after Jade Blossom gave birth to a son in June 1989, family relations improved; Jade Blossom agreed at last to call her mother-in-law 'mama' and was, reciprocally, now more accepted by her in-laws.

While the setting within which Qiu worked as a private practitioner was fairly characteristic of back-street environments in the late 1980s, it is difficult to tell how representative his practice was. Comparisons with contemporaries of Qiu who called themselves *qigong* masters revealed discrepancies, but texts on self-cultivation practices in historical times contained descriptions of practices Qiu either performed or described to me (Engelhardt 1987; Kohn 1989; Despeux 1994).

Since I intended to compare different modes of transmission with corresponding styles of knowing, it would have been ideal to work with Chinese medical doctors in all three settings. The hazards of fieldwork led me to a *qigong* healer's instead of a Chinese medical doctor's family practice. In retrospect, the decision to work with a *qigong* healer turned out to have several advantages. First, *qigong*, like the martial arts, is veiled in secrecy, often more conspicuously than Chinese medicine, and in studying it I was therefore much more exposed to social practice characteristic of the secret transmission of knowledge and practice than I would have been otherwise. Secondly, because the skills and knowledge of a *qigong* healer differ from those of a Chinese medical doctor while sharing much of the Chinese medical terminology, I was able to learn about Chinese medical concepts from a different angle, in a therapeutic context that is, strictly speaking, not one of Chinese medicine. Thirdly, when I eventually became friends with a Chinese medical doctor who had, together with his wife, a family practice in a county town near Kunming, my experiences in the *qigong* healer's family practice enabled me to recognise common features of social practice that are related to the secret transmission of knowledge and practice, regardless of whether they pertain to *qigong* or Chinese medicine.

If one were to interpret the medical pluralism in urban China according to Leslie's (1976b:361) well-known diagram of the spectrum of therapeutics in a stratified society like India, the three doctors I worked with would best be compared to popular or folk practitioners (*qigong* master Qiu), learned traditional culture Ayurvedic and Yunani physicians (senior Chinese doctor Zhang), and professionalised Ayurvedic and Yunani physicians (TCM professional Tao). In terms of Kleinman's (1980:50) model of health sectors, the two practitioners working outside the work units, Zhang and Qiu, would belong to the folk sector, and the Chinese medical doctors in the work units, like Tao, would belong to the professional health sector, which apart from TCM comprised all kinds of other organised healing professions.[20] In the PRC, the number of practitioners like Zhang and Qiu may be insignificant, but their practices and explanations seemed relevant because they shared features reminiscent of those described by historians of Chinese medicine. It may not be coincidence that they found a niche in the realm outside government units in which they could survive in Socialist China, although this realm seems to be increasingly populated by TCM-trained doctors (interview with Provincial Health Ministry, December 1989).

---

[20] Zhang did not consider himself part of the folk sector. This contradiction is easily resolved by pointing out that the anthropologist's viewpoint need not completely coincide with the insider's (Frankel and Lewis 1989:2). Zhang's view raises, however, the question of whether the model of the three health sectors is appropriate for complex societies in which the traditional elite set up well-organised state-controlled institutions of health care.

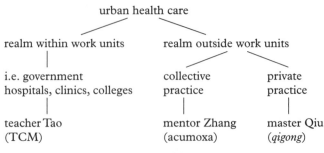

Figure I.1   The three settings of fieldwork

In all three settings the written word was at the core of medical practice and knowledge. They all exemplified a literate tradition of medical practice. Qiu's *qigong* therapy was said to be grounded in the correct pronunciation of the written word in incantations from the *Daoist Canon* (*Dao zang*), and had thus features of word magic. In the two other cases, which concerned Chinese medicine, the written word – frequently a phrase from the *Inner Canon* (*Nei jing*) – was used to justify and explain medical practice.

However, the economic conditions of these settings differed, as did also the social relations of the doctors and healers – among each other, with regard to their recruits, and in respect of their clients. The economic conditions would be classified in Chinese terms as those of a private practice in the case of Qiu's family practice, a collective in Zhang's case, and a government work unit in the case of teacher Tao at the TCM college. The social relations between the senior expert and the junior aspiring to expertise were in the first case a relationship between kin, in the second one between personal acquaintances, and in the third one between citizens of a Socialist state. The three contexts thus involved different micro-economic bases of income (*getihu, jitihu, danwei*), social relations (kinship, friendship, citizenship), and religious practice (though notoriously difficult to circumscribe, here approximated as folk-Buddhism/Daoism, an idiosyncratic form of Confucianism, secularism).

It must be kept in mind that practices varied widely within each context. Structuring ethnographic material around the practice of three individuals in three markedly different settings does not do justice to this variation. Moreover, these contexts cannot be considered separate and homogeneous units; they were mutually interdependent. This study is not a sociological survey of medical pluralism in urban China. Rather, these three settings were chosen for in-depth study of three different ways of learning Chinese medical knowledge and practice.

Approaches to the field

Fieldwork in the PRC is notoriously difficult to arrange.[21] Enrolled as a student at a TCM college and several TCM hospitals, I attended classes or clinics in the mornings. The afternoons were at my disposal. Every other day I spent several hours in and around the private practice of the *qigong* healer, and one or two afternoons a week I spent with the senior Chinese doctor. Common to all these settings was the unusual position in which I performed fieldwork: I was not only a 'participant observer', but also learning specific, technical knowledge and practice. My approach to the field can thus be described as intending to engage in 'participant experience'. My position as student, follower, and disciple placed the doctors and healers I interacted with in the position of 'teacher' (*laoshi*), 'mentor' (*xiansheng*), or 'master' (*shifu*). Well aware that anthropologists are still nowadays in a position comparable to missionaries, backed by an overwhelming military, economic, and political power (Van der Geest 1990), I thereby hoped to modify the unequal relation which prevails between the informant and the anthropologist. Additionally, I believed, an anthropologist who has learnt the specifics of a practice in a foreign culture may help to encourage understanding of it in her own culture.

The anthropologist who decides to be simultaneously fieldworker and apprentice is cast in roles that are not always compatible. First, the topics of interest do not always coincide, and even when activities are of interest to both the fieldworker and the student the problem arises of what to pay attention to. For instance, the student engaged in practical training may want to focus on specific technical details while the participant observer may prefer to observe the interpersonal exchanges between teacher and students. These two roles also posed problems for some people I worked with. Not knowing whether they were relating to a fieldworker or to a student evoked an uncomfortable reserve in some of my teachers and colleagues at the TCM college. Interestingly, neither Zhang nor Qiu who worked outside the realm of work units were much disturbed by my dual role. They clearly welcomed the attention they were receiving from a foreigner and were much less suspicious about

[21] Arranging the fieldwork of 1988–9 was a long process. It began in March 1985 with exploring fieldwork conditions mostly in Chengdu and continued in October 1987 in Kunming. One of the main difficulties was to avoid being put into a special course for foreigners. The Yunnan TCM College first arranged private tutorials, but I insisted that my research was all about learning Chinese medicine in the Chinese way. Finally, one of the two lecturers who had been dispensed from teaching to give private tutorials agreed to teach the main subjects of the introductory course to an entire class of acumoxa and massage specialists.

my role as a social scientist. Given that their practice was only tolerated by the government, they were probably concerned with its legitimation; regular visits by a foreigner were likely to increase its prestige.

At the same time, I would never have obtained the knowledge and insights I did if I had not been accepted as a student, follower, and disciple, particularly in the contexts of esoteric learning outside the college. Moreover, my own attitude to what I learnt by engaging in medical practice myself is likely to be different from that of an observer. A researcher who has learnt to operate within another conceptual framework is likely to gain a more comprehensive understanding of it than someone who is content with the detached observations of an onlooker. My experience was that Chinese medical concepts became more immediate to me after using them, particularly when I found that I was able to achieve therapeutic effects. The fieldworker who has experienced in person the complexities of providing medical treatment – including the rapport with the patient, the recognition of signs and symptoms known from book learning only, the skills of examining the Pulse (*mai*), the Tongue (*she*), and the Complexion (*se*), the synthesis of these different data into a Chinese medical 'diagnosis' (*zhenduan*), the choice of the 'maxims of treatment' (*zhize*), and the selection of acu-points and application of different needling techniques – may be more aware of the problems involved when she is observing other doctors and healers engaging in this process. However, simultaneous practice and critical assessment of that practice invariably leads to a dilemma: the shaman Quesalid began his apprenticeship as a sceptic, intent on exposing the tricks of other shamans, but after learning them he used them himself (Lévi-Strauss (1958)1963). Can he still be a sceptic, if he applies the practice himself?

It might have looked methodologically sound to have conducted surveys, but it is easily forgotten that the evaluation of statistical data is just as much based on the researcher's sensitivity and judgement as on rendering an account of a very particular setting. Nevertheless, partly to prevent potential worries, partly out of curiosity, and mostly because I thought it was an appropriate method for the college setting, I employed more formalised methods for investigating the standardised transmission of knowledge, including semi-structured interviews with 12 assistant teachers, questionnaires administered to 60 undergraduates, questionnaire letters sent to 120 graduates and cross-checked through interviews with 14 of them, and interviews with representatives of the college administration, the Provincial Health Department, and the City Health Bureau. Most respondents were curious and eager to be questioned, but the precision of their answers varied considerably. Some results brought to light problems which I had not anticipated, but in general these formal enquiries only corroborated my subjective impressions. The reward was not overwhelming, if one considers that the carrying-out, the statistical assessment, and the evaluation of this formalised inquiry demanded much time and effort.

Working in the field

Exploring experts' knowledge and reasoning demands considerable linguistic competence. There was, of course, a language barrier. I had studied modern standard Chinese in my late teens in Beijing, ten years before I started fieldwork on Chinese medicine in Kunming, and the local dialect was soon comprehensible to me. I never tried to adopt it, however, which imposed a certain formality on all our conversations.

In addition there were obstacles to smooth communication associated with the perception of the anthropologist's position and the way in which I was seen by those I wished to understand. On the one hand, my Chinese origins gave us common ground. My grandparents, aunts, uncles, and cousins had suffered from the same events as my teachers, colleagues, and friends. The experiences of the reforms of the early 1950s, the disaster that brought many to the edge of starvation during the Great Leap Forward (1958–61), and the violence and cruelty of the Cultural Revolution and the period of the Gang of Four (1966–76) are essential to understanding the attitudes and tastes of the late 1980s in the PRC. I need not render detailed life stories here; they are in kind similar to those recorded by Kleinman (1986) in *Social Origins of Distress and Disease*.

Nevertheless, I almost always remained the 'foreigner' (*waiguoren*), despite my Chinese origins: the TCM teachers considered me as 90 per cent a foreigner, and foreigners were, as one of them half jokingly declared, difficult to handle: first because of the already mentioned language problem (*yuyan butong*), second because foreigners had 'no understanding for Chinese medicine' (*budong zhongyi*), and third because, on top of all this, they were 'very demanding' (*yaoqiu gao*). The senior doctor Zhang said that I was outside Western but inside Chinese. The *qigong* healer had not encountered foreigners personally, and seems to have seen me more as some kind of a stranger than as a 'foreign student' (*liuxuesheng*). The few times I was not recognised as a foreigner were at the hospital during practical training, when I wore a white coat and cap. Being categorised as a foreigner had a decisive impact on the information I elicited. For instance, I came to realise that when a TCM doctor used biomedical terms in my presence he might well have been accommodating to me, the foreigner. College doctors built on former encounters with foreigners in the clinic and tended to view me as a

'Western doctor' (*xiyi*), but my knowledge of biomedical pathology was severely limited, despite having graduated in biology, and biomedical terminology in modern Chinese was not always immediately intelligible. With time, my counterparts altered their explanations according to their perception of my progress in understanding.

Finally, Chinese medical concepts, like symbols in ritual action, are notoriously vague and polysemous.[22] Lewis (1986), pointing to the 'look of magic', has repeatedly emphasised that anthropological research on these domains of human behaviour demands particular caution and circumspection. It is easy to impute one's own meanings to them, sometimes without bothering to ask the people what they say about them and sometimes outrightly dismissing what people know about them. Some practices were considered 'feudalistic' (*fengjiande*) and 'backward' (*luohou*), and people were reluctant to talk about them. Just as the statement that someone was bewitched became less assured as the social distance between the speaker and the alleged victim of witchcraft decreased (Lewis 1976), the information elicited about such 'feudalistic' and 'backward' practices changed depending on the situation in which it was communicated.

I put much time, thought, and also feeling into maintaining the few important rapports I had. The establishment of close links that enable the anthropologist to learn about key concepts and cosmology is not unusual – one recalls Griaule's ((1948)1966) conversations with Ogotemmeli or Turner's ((1960)1967) with Muchona – but there are many reasons for avoiding this approach. One has already been mentioned, namely, that the anthropologist creates an artificial situation for eliciting information by the direction of her questions and the informants accommodate their responses to their perception of the foreigner. Moreover, the question arises to what extent the ideas the anthropologist grasps from these individuals are representative of the entire culture, to what extent of a certain school of thought, and to what extent of idiosyncrasies of fringe figures. The human mind is creative, and ideas and thoughts, like any piece of art, dance, song, or ritual

---

[22] A lexical item is 'vague' (and not 'ambiguous') when it is not precisely defined. Kempson (1977:124–8) distinguishes four types of vagueness: (a) referential vagueness (e.g. is 'city' or 'town' the right word to describe a place like Salisbury?); (b) indeterminacy of meaning (e.g. what does 'good' mean?); (c) lack of specification (e.g. the word 'neighbour' does not indicate sex, age, ethnic identity of a person); and (d) disjunction in the specification of meaning (e.g. different uses of the conjunction 'or'). Chinese medical terms are almost always referentially vague (to the uninitiated) and indeterminate in meaning. They can sometimes be quite specific in meaning, and in those cases they tend to be not vague but polysemous.

A lexical item is 'polysemous' when its meaning 'is not constant but varies from context to context' (Kempson 1977:80). 'Polysemy' is a kind of lexical ambiguity (Lyons 1977:550).

performance, are expressions of the people who communicate them. Finally, the very fact that an 'informant' becomes a 'friend' puts the anthropologist in a dilemma between precision and discretion. This is especially difficult in a country that is haunted by political struggles. Doing fieldwork in three different settings was not always easy. I often felt that I had just missed crucial events in one place while working in another. Yet it was the comparison of different social contexts that brought to light the distinctive features of the learning situations and styles of knowing. Since these contexts were very different, the methodological-cum-theoretical approach had to be modified accordingly, with the result that, depending on the setting, certain topics received closer attention than others. Medical practice, for instance, was observed in all three settings, but case histories will be presented only with regard to *qigong*.[23] Again, the political events of the so-called 'prodemocracy movement' in May and June 1989 were an issue of major concern at the TCM college, while they had little impact on the course of daily life in the area where the *qigong* healer worked.

The structure of the book

The three settings of Chinese medical learning structure the book as three sets of two chapters each. In each set, the first chapter presents the context in which medical knowledge and practice was transmitted. Therefore, chapters 1, 3, and 5 may be of particular interest to the reader wishing to learn about daily life in urban contexts of the PRC during the late 1980s. The second chapter of each set, namely chapters 2, 4, and 6, discuss key concepts that figured prominently in each context of learning, among them *qi* (Breath or 'basic stuff' 'that makes things happen' and 'in which things happen') (Sivin 1987:46–7), *yinyang*, *wuxing* (Five Phases), *shen* (Spirit), and various other notions that refer to change.

Qi, central to the *qigong* master's medical reasoning and practice, was also at the core of reasoning in the two contexts of Chinese medical learning.[24] TCM distinguishes four *qi*: the Primordial *qi* (*yuanqi*), which is considered synonymous with the Original *qi* (*yuanqi*) and the True *qi* (*zhenqi*), the Gathering *qi* (*zongqi*),[25] the Nurturing *qi* (*yingqi*), and the

[23] For TCM case histories as recorded by a participant observer, see Ots ((1987)1990), Hammes and Ots (1996), and Scheid (1998). For translation and analysis of published case material, see Farquhar (1991; 1992; 1994a:46–55).

[24] *Qi* also occurs in colloquial conversation. The notions of *qi* I focused on were always those of medical specialists.

[25] Translation based on Wiseman (1990:349), who also provides the literally more correct term Ancestral *qi*. In the classroom *zongqi* was presented as the *qi* that comprised all the many *qi* coming from different organs and from the outside world (due to

Protective *qi* (*weiqi*).[26] However, the ethnographic account of *qi* will diverge significantly from text-based systematic presentations.

Yinyang was another concept frequently encountered in all three settings, and in the acumoxa wards of TCM clinics and hospitals it was on everyone's lips. Sivin (1987:203–8) renders *yinyang* very much as taught in TCM: *yinyang* (and the Five Phases) are presented as 'spontaneous, naive, materialist theories that also contain elementary dialectic ideas' (p. 203). This understanding of *yinyang* calls for a critical analysis based on the explanations of a teacher lecturing on *yinyang* in the classroom. In the contexts of medical learning outside the TCM college, the political overtones of the term were less marked.

Wuxing (Five Phases) are well documented in recent literature.[27] In TCM, they are closely associated with the so-called Five Organs (*wuzang*) and in the West, reasoning in terms of the Five Phases is generally well understood. However, the *qigong* master Qiu hardly ever reasoned in terms of the Five Phases, and discussion of them has intentionally been kept minimal.

Notably, neither Sivin (1987), Ots ((1987)1990), nor Farquhar (1994a), who have all written substantial monographs about TCM, say much about *shen* (Spirit), which I encountered in all three settings. Not only the semantics of *shen* but also what I propose to call its 'performative significance' varied between these different social contexts: the term *shen* was 'socialised' into these different contexts because it performed certain roles that were significant for the way in which the doctors established their authority in social interaction.

Chinese medical terms will be shown to vary to such an extent in connotation, language use, and performative significance in different social contexts that one hesitates to assume that they refer to one and the same concept. These variations will be shown to depend on different styles of knowing. Given that styles of knowing may determine and be determined by the different ways in which one learns a technical terminology, the findings of this monograph are bound to have implications for the professionalisation of any traditional or alternative medicine.

---

respiration), and therefore it has been translated as the Gathering *qi*. In the *Revised Outline*, *zongqi* is mentioned together with *zhongqi* (Medial *qi*) under the heading of '*Qi* of the Visceral Systems' (Sivin 1987:238).

[26] *TCM Fundamentals* (Yin 1984:57–8). Reproduced in Sivin (1987:237–40) and Ots ((1987)1990:47). Porkert (1974:167–76) contains a useful but ahistorical listing of different *qi*.

[27] *TCM Fundamentals* (Yin 1984:18–27, 28–53). Reproduced in Sivin (1987:208–12, 213–36) and Ots ((1987)1990: particularly 44–5). See also Porkert (1974:43–54).

1   The secret transmission of knowledge and practice

Qigong, which became very popular under Deng Xiaoping's leadership in the 1980s, has been jokingly referred to as the 'fifth modernisation' (*di wuge xiandaihua*). In many instances *qigong* refers to the reinterpretation of Daoist practices under the impact of modern medicine, but the wide range of practices called *qigong* renders a precise definition of this term impossible. *Qigong* is nowadays known mostly as a meditative practice with life-maintaining and therapeutic effects (Kohn 1989, N. N. Chen 1995), but opera singers, calligraphers, and other artists also use it to enhance their performance skills (Ma 1983:8). One can practise *qigong* alone or in groups; or it can be applied from a *qigong* master to his or her clients, in which case effects can be evoked similar to those of a hypnotist (Sundararajan 1990). Telepathy, clairvoyance, psychokinesis, and other phenomena that are studied in the West under the rubric of parapsychology are often said to result from the practice of *qigong*. The ability to achieve the latter effects, called 'extraordinary *qigong*' (*teyi qigong*), is said to depend on a person's *xiantian* (constitution), while health status and artisitic ability are considered to be improved in anyone through *qigong* meditation.

The word *qigong* has only recently been used in this sense. It occurred earlier in texts on self-cultivation as a technical term with another meaning, supposedly for the first time in a text of the Jin dynasty (AD 265–420) (Despeux 1988:9). Although it was already being used in its modern sense during the Republican period (1911–49),[1] it was only in the struggle for the legitimation of Chinese medicine after the Communist revolution that it became more widely known. The goals of this revival of Chinese medicine and with it the promulgation of *qigong* are reflected in its English translation: instead of a 'self-cultivation practice' it is currently called a 'breathing technique'.

---

[1] Apparently, Dong Hao acknowledged *qigong* for its therapeutic effects in 1936 (Despeux 1988:10).

21

The practice of self-cultivation is age-old. The earliest-known written records of ancient traditions of meditation are on bronze inscriptions of the Warring States period (475–221 BC), in the manuscripts excavated from the Mawangdui tombs (168 BC), and in chapters 36–8 of the *Guan zi*, a compilation from the fourth century BC (Harper 1990b). In the literature of the past two thousand years meditation practices of this kind have been referred to by terms such as *yangxing* (to nurture one's Nature), *yangsheng* (to nurture one's life), *daoyin* (to guide and lead (the *qi*)), and *xiushen* (to cultivate oneself). Present day *qigong* practices are in general new versions – often complete transmutations, of former Daoist meditation traditions, sometimes including elements of Buddhist meditation practices. Since *wushu* (unarmed combat) masters were least affected by efforts at modernisation, the meditative practices widespread today under the name of *qigong*, are mainly derived from *wushu* traditions (Wen Linjun, p.c.).[2] Formerly, I was told, all 'Chinese doctors' (*zhongyi*) engaged in meditative practices for self-cultivation, engaging in what a modern *qigong* healer would call 'soft *qigong*' (*ruan qigong*) as opposed to the *wushu* masters' 'hard *qigong*' (*ying qigong*).[3] The former practice strengthened one's Inner *qi* (*neiqi*), the latter one's Outer *qi* (*waiqi*).

The practice of soft *qigong* was in general valued more highly since it enabled one to attain healing and other somewhat supernatural capabilities. *Xiang*, 'having a pleasant smell', like chocolate, orange blossoms, or soap, was one of these faculties. A student I knew at the college had already attained it after two weeks of training: he could make the palm of his hand smell of chocolate – admittedly for seconds only, so that an uncooperative person had difficulty in smelling it. *Fu*, 'levitating', was another, but it was purely a subjective feeling experienced by the meditator (although rumours circulated that it was possible to see *qigong* masters levitate during meditation). *Toushi*, 'having a penetrating vision' (x-ray vision), was a third. Stories were told of *qigong* masters who were able to tell the name, the age, and the work unit of a person on first sight because they could read the person's concealed identity card. Some *qigong* masters were sought out to help find lost objects; others were said to work as spies for the defence ministry in Beijing because they could see through walls.

Training in hard *qigong* strengthened one's Outer *qi* to such an extent that one could become invulnerable to slaps and kicks or capable of

---

[2] Certain forms of *wushu* have become known in the West as kungfu and karate (Lu and Needham 1980:302ff.). On the history of *wushu*, see Matsuda (1984) and Xi (1985).
[3] 'The term for martial practice, *yinggong* (hard *qigong*), was defined in 1978 ... Until very recently most people in China associated *qigong* with these martial techniques' (Miura 1989:342).

tolerating great weight or heavy blows to the body (e.g. trucks rolling over a platform supported by one's body or the splitting of bricks balanced on one's head). Moreover, it enabled one to give performances of eating glass and spitting fire. It was said to be easily learnt and results were guaranteed after only a few months' training. It is apparent that *qigong* includes a wide range of meditative practices found in many social contexts, from the secluded chamber of the Neo-Confucian scholar immersing himself in meditative 'self-cultivation' (*xiushen*)[4] to marketplace performances of wandering jugglers and magicians demonstrating tricks to a crowd of curious gapers.

When the practice of *qigong* became more widely known in the 1950s, it was promoted in the context of public health care: in 1955 the first *qigong* rehabilitation centre was established in Tangshan, and patients suffering from gastro-intestinal disorders were taught Inner Nurture *qigong* (*neiyanggong*). In 1956 a course was set up in Beidaihe to train a first group of professional *qigong* practitioners. In 1957 a rehabilitation centre which monitored *qigong* therapies with scientific methods was established in Shanghai. *Qigong* was thereafter taught in several rehabilitation centres all over the country. It was promoted as a breathing technique particularly effective for the cure of chronic hepatitis, high blood pressure, heart palpitations, tuberculosis, asthma, neurasthenia, diabetes, glaucoma, and toxaemia (Ma 1983:44–6). The new name *qigong* for the old meditation practices emphasised its therapeutic merits, merits that were often proved by biomedical evidence. Health was conceived to result from a form of physical training rather than meditative spirituality.

Qigong was discredited as 'superstition' (*mixin*) during the Cultural Revolution (1966–76) but despite lingering reservations in many circles, it was revived in the late 1970s and the 1980s. In 1988–9 it was no longer limited to improving the health condition of patients in rehabilitation centres but regularly practised by women as well as men; state employees, pensioners, and unemployed youth. *Qigong* was not only practised by individuals at home or in a quiet corner of a park; associations started to flourish which organised '*qigong* meetings' (*qigong jiangzuo*) with famous *qigong* masters in sport stadiums and university auditoriums. During these meetings *qigong* masters were believed to provide therapeutic and life-maintaining benefits to their audience by the act of speaking alone. Short-term *qigong* courses for limited numbers of participants were advertised on posters in the streets and in pamphlets circulated in work

---

[4] *Xiushen* is generally translated as 'self-cultivation' and strongly associated with Neo-Confucian endeavours. I use the word self-cultivation elsewhere in a wider sense, synonymous with the expression 'longevity techniques' in Kohn (1989).

units. Private *qigong* practices promising a sure and safe cure prolifer-
ated in and around the city. In Kunming, the entirety of the regulations
of 1987 made *qigong* therapy in a private enterprise possible. In November 1989, however, when the Communist Party tightened its control
after the June 4th crackdown in Tiananmen Square, new regulations
were set up which allowed only those who passed the exams for 'regular
practitioner' (*yishi*) to open private *qigong* practices (interview with the
City Health Bureau, December 1989).

Reasons for the revival of *qigong* in the 1980s were, as so often
happens in China, attributed to the head of state. Rumour had it that
Deng Xiaoping was treated by a *qigong* healer and therefore promoted
its revival. This saying paralleled the one that made Mao Zedong's
personal experience with Chinese medicine in Yan'an responsible for
policies favourable to TCM in the 1950s (Lampton 1977:62). Without
denying the importance of a leader's promotion for mass movements in
China, additional reasons are needed to explain the recent nationwide
popularity of *qigong*.

'*Qigong* indicates a social problem', a young state employee who
practised it said during a discussion. The policies of the 1980s that had
allowed an economic boom in the private sector and the concession of
increased decision-making to state enterprises had given rise to more
substantial and visible corruption among government officials. Admittedly, the majority of the urban population – state employees in the
work units – simultaneously experienced an improvement in their living
standards, but this improvement was minimal compared with the profits
of private entrepreneurs and the 'gifts' received by government officials.
In Kunming, there was consensus among state employees that soaring
inflation had caused a decline of living standards since 1987, and that
the prospects for changes in employment and acknowledgement of
personal merit were as non-existent as ever. In late 1989, for instance,
students were reluctant to spend 0.3 *yuan* fortnightly for a cinema
ticket or to buy tangerines on the free market where they were about
three times as expensive as apples from the department store. In several
work units cadres were forced to forgo immediate payment of one of
their monthly salaries as a ten-year loan to the state. In this light,
'*qigong* fever' may have indicated a general disillusionment with politics,
a 'crisis of faith' resulting in individual withdrawal. It may have been a
form of resistance to ongoing processes in society that were more than
once described to me as 'chaotic' (*luan*), the term with which political
periods like the Cultural Revolution (1966–76) were characterised.
Whereas the esoteric quest of mystery seems to have played an important role in the spread of *qigong* in the West, as far as I can tell, it was

insignificant in the PRC. It is, however, possible that through *qigong*, introspection, and the discovery of one's own body and self, new values are brought to the individual.

Nowadays many styles of *qigong* are public while the practice of other *qigong* healers is still veiled in secrecy. I discuss one such secret tradition of *qigong* because secrecy was, and for certain families still is, one of the most important features of Chinese medical knowledge. The mode in which a *qigong* healer transmitted his secret knowledge and practice to his disciple may point to features of Chinese medical knowledge and practice secretly transmitted within a family. Most of my observations of *qigong* were made in a private practice of the *qigong* healer Qiu, thirty-two years old, his wife Jade Blossom, twenty-four years old, an acupuncturist, and her younger brother Qiudi, nineteen years old, who was Qiu's disciple.

The setting

The *qigong* healer Qiu's private practice was in a neighbourhood of petty enterprise in a narrow side street of old houses, sheltered from the traffic. This street began in a very crowded free market in front of the former city gate where a bridge crossed one of Kunming's main canals and ended half a mile north at the drum tower, where there was another free market. Situated outside the former city wall, the houses were low-roofed and poorly built; the street was called 'the street of the poor' (*pinminjie*). Indeed, in the teahouse near Qiu's practice there were all kinds of characters, many of them in old, worn-out Mao suits and a few even in rags. Pedestrians coming from the bus station would pass through this street on their way to the city centre. It was effervescent with small-scale business, and cyclists had to step down from their bikes to join the rhythm of the crowd. Private and collective shops, taverns, and inns flourished, and several 'private enterprises' (*getihu*) offered medical care. From the market bridge to Qiu's consultation room one passed three of them: a bone setter, a Chinese herbalist, and a biomedical doctor specialising in paediatrics. Beyond Qiu's practice on the way to the drum tower, one could count another four: two private pharmacies for Western biomedical drugs, an 'integrated Western–Chinese medical' (*zhongxiyi jiehe*) family practice, and, newly installed in January 1989, a small private hospital with between ten and twenty beds. In the mornings the latest mainland hits pounded out from huge Japanese tape recorders, while old men with water pipes and bird cages by their sides played chess in a corner near the teahouse. But in the evenings, there were the long, drawn-out phrases of an *erhu* (a Chinese stringed instrument) and the hoarse voice of an old woman which sounded plaintively through the night. It was in this motley community of petty enterprise and households of partly marginalised city inhabitants that Qiu had established his practice of acumoxa, massage, and *qigong*.[5]

Social networks and private enterprise

Officially Qiu had the status of a *qigong* practitioner; on our first encounter, he showed me the document that certified it. In 1988 he was 'bound by contract' (*chengbao*) to his former work unit, the Third City Hospital, where he had been employed for five years as a *qigong* healer, but in 1989, after his wife had passed the examinations for opening a private 'acumoxa' (*zhenjiu*) practice, he gave up this contract and she applied to one of the city's 'district health bureaus' (*qu weishengju*) for official recognition. The contract had guaranteed them employment by their work unit if their enterprise failed, but it had obliged them to pay 200 *yuan* monthly whereas the monthly taxes to the city district health authorities were only 10–20 *yuan*.[6]

Qiu also had permission from the same district health bureau to sell 'Chinese medical drugs' (*zhongyao*), but in his medical practice he generally used 'herbal drugs' (*caoyao*). He bought dried plants in large quantities at a low price from itinerant 'herbalists' (*caoyi*) which he and his disciple ground in their entirety (with stems, leaves, and often also their roots) into a powder that was prescribed to his clients in portions, small enough to be thrown into the mouth and ingested with a sip of water. He also had some 'ready made Chinese medical drugs' (*zhongchengyao*) against 'common colds' (*ganmao*), 'stomach aches' (*futeng*), and 'coughs' (*kesou*), but mostly stocked 'invigorating drugs' (*buyao*) like extracts of ginseng (*renshen*) or royal jelly (*wangjiang*). He did not risk buying drugs that he could not use himself for fear that he would not sell them. His inventory of Western biomedical drugs was minimal; it comprised pain killers, aspirin, and some antibiotics for primary health care.

Family practices of specialists like Qiu played an important role in health care at the grassroots level. Those seeking specialist proficiency

---

[5] By 1992 the southern parts of this neighbourhood were transformed by the construction of the Yuantong bridge; the northern parts, including the drum tower, were demolished in 1996 because of road construction works.

[6] Exchange rates for the *yuan* fluctuated considerably in 1988/9. Its value is best assessed in light of the monthly salary of work unit members like the TCM teachers, which varied between 76 and 135 *yuan*. See table 5.1.

such as Qiu's *qigong* therapy were prepared to pay large sums for their treatment. The healer's family's livelihood was thus ensured by his speciality. However, as Qiu's inventory of drugs reveals, he had other clients as well. They usually came from the neighbourhood with a cut finger, a fever, or a headache. Although the Red Cross Hospital was only a ten minutes' walk away, they generally sought Qiu's assistance. His *qigong* practice thus fulfilled important functions of primary health care.

No private enterprise in the PRC can survive with official recognition alone. Beneficial non-official contacts are indispensable. Friends and colleagues need to be fostered as 'good connections' (*hao guanxi*). Qiu had many visitors. He was a pleasant person, a good healer, and most of all, known in certain circles as one of the most powerful *qigong* masters in town. Some of his visitors were former patients who had become friends with their healer in the course of their convalescence; others were members of the *Qigong* Association of Kunming City and still others were would-be *qigong* practitioners who hoped to be initiated into Qiu's secrets. One of the visitors, for instance, came almost daily throughout a period of several months. He was often invited to stay for supper, as demanded by Chinese hospitality, but Jade Blossom thoroughly disliked him, suspecting that he was trying to get her husband's secret knowledge. Qiu, instead of being annoyed with him, got angry with her: 'She doesn't understand how our society functions' (*ta bu dong shehui*). It was good to have many friends and even better to attract them with admiration for the secret.

Apart from such visitors, a wealthy entrepreneur for whom Qiu had worked as a carpenter in his youth made Qiu known in Buddhist circles. In 1988 Qiu was summoned to heal a renowned monk belonging to an important temple about thirty miles outside of Kunming – he was proud to tell me that he had been taken there in the temple authority's new minibus. In 1989, when he took part in a Buddhist festivity at another temple, it was again this friend who introduced him to the temple's oldest monk. The first time Qiu had been asked to cure a cancer, but he was called for only a few days before the monk's death; the second time, he was asked to treat a common headache, and apparently did so to the monk's satisfaction.

When pressed, Qiu said he was a Daoist and a Buddhist, but he did not attach much importance to it. He did not have much reason to call himself a Buddhist; he participated in Buddhist festivities very erratically and seemed to do so more for social reasons than out of religious conviction. By contrast, his mother was a devoted Buddhist who had kept her domestic shrine even during the Cultural Revolution. She went regularly to the nearby temple (for her half-hour walk), sometimes alone, sometimes with other women from the neighbourhood. She stuck to the habit that dishes at meals were vegetarian on the first and fifteenth of the lunar month.[7] It was probably in order to maintain this dietary practice that the days were counted according to the lunar calendar in Qiu's family.[8]

Qiu also cultivated contacts with herbalists, one of whom was a neighbour who had no private practice but a few private patients. Lao Yi, a retired worker, claimed to have learnt Chinese medicine on his own, by reading books only.[9] Since he was a widower, he often stayed for lunch with Qiu's family. Qiu was mainly interested in this old man's knowledge of the herbal drugs, their habitats, and their locations in the environs of the city. In the summer and autumn of 1989 the two undertook at least five outings into the nearby hills, usually to gather a specific species for one of Qiu's or Lao Yi's patients. Qiu was eager to learn to recognise and collect medicinal plants so that he would not have to depend on the herbalists for them.

Informal 'contacts' (*guanxi*) – Qiu's friends and colleagues, his Buddhist connection, and his contact with herbalists – were indispensable for running his business. Later, I discovered that he also had two 'bond brothers' (*xiongdi*) when I asked him about a tattoo of a sword on his left arm. The three had become bond brothers shortly after the death of Qiu's master in 1978. Their brotherhood meant pledging to support each other in hardship and to keep their master's knowledge secret. Perhaps it was coincidence, perhaps a reflection of a more general pattern, that these bond brothers and former close friends later became vicious rivals.

Brotherhood and dangers of knowledge

One of Qiu's bond brothers, Luo, had twice tried to kill Qiu, Jade Blossom told me on their way home from a dinner that Qiu had given

---

[7] Qiu said that his mother was vegetarian, which did not mean that she ate vegetarian daily but only on those two days of a month. For a similar pattern of vegetarian diets among sect members, see Naquin (1976:47).

[8] The Gregorian calendar (*yangli*) is used by the administration and city inhabitants and the lunar calendar (*yinli*) mainly in the countryside. In some county towns the market days fall on the first, fifth, eleventh, fifteenth, twenty-first, and twenty-fifth of the Gregorian calendar month, a pattern supposedly related to the lunar calendar.

[9] Qiu spoke of Lao Yi as a *caoyi*, but Lao Yi called himself for reasons of prestige a *zhongyi*. In biographies of Chinese doctors, it is a *topos* to have learnt medicine mainly by reading books, without (*Shi ji* 105 (Sima 1959:2785)) or with the guidance of a master (*Shi ji* 105 (Sima 1959:2796)). This belief in an independent learning from texts, without any mentor's guidance, stands in stark contrast to the principles of the secret transmission of knowledge.

in honour of Luo and his family. Shortly after their master's death, Luo had entrusted to Qiu a particularly powerful *gongfa* (method/efficacy of *qigong*) that consisted of a minimal diet and walking for several hours at night. Qiu, walking off his legs, had become thinner and thinner until one of his older friends, aware of Qiu's grief over his master's death, had made enquiries into the matter and brought him back to his senses. Several years later, Jade Blossom continued, when Qiu was known citywide and asked to go for scientific trials on *qigong* to Beijing, Luo confidentially recommended that he take drugs which instantly induced stomach cramps and put Qiu into a coma. Only immediate intervention at a biomedical hospital had saved him from lethal poisoning by his bond brother. Hesitating to believe this, I looked at Qiu who had been accompanying us silently: he did not say anything but nodded.

Qiu was reluctant to speak ill of Luo who was his master's son. He called him *erge*, second older brother, and tried to treat him like one. Most of Qiu's friends avoided Luo, and therefore he could not invite him to his wedding banquet, but he felt obliged to invite him and his master's entire family to a separate dinner three weeks later. Despite the alleged murder attempts, Qiu showed respect for his master's son, and on *qingming* day,[10] when Qiu planned to visit the grave of his master with his disciple, and I, the foreigner, wanted to join them, he did not fail to invite his master's son to join us.

The other bond brother, Long, was, unlike Qiu and Luo, tall and well-built; most impressive in stature. His father was a high government official and this had probably determined most of the circumstances of Long's life. In 1978 Luo had taught Long his late father's meditation practices and even lent him his father's notebooks, probably with the purpose of establishing a connection with an influential person. In 1982 Long had managed to be called with Qiu to Beijing for trials of *qigong*. In 1988 he had set up a private *qigong* hospital. It was an impressive enterprise, installed in a building of seven storeys which advertised itself by the expensive but prestigious means of television spots. Long had employed a staff of more than ten *qigong* healers as well as Western biomedical and TCM doctors. Thanks to his father, he enjoyed enough credibility to take out enormous bankloans. But when these had proved insufficient, he had approached his bond brother Qiu, so I was told, offering him the position of vice-director and asking for financial support. Qiu had refused participation but claimed to have advanced three thousand *yuan* because of their brotherhood. Less than six months later the hospital went bankrupt. His bond brother changed his address and

---

[10] The fifth day of the fourth lunar month, the day of the commemoration of the dead.

rumour went that he had left the province. It was clear that Qiu would never see a penny of that money again.

The amount of money and life-threatening rivalry involved make the above stories sound fabulous. The dramatic scale of Luo's deception and Long's fraud reflect the prestige and power attributed to *qigong*, and the danger of envy. Danger was, moreover, believed to be inherent in the practice of *qigong* meditation itself. Stories were told of students who had gone mad because they had tried to learn *qigong* by consulting books only. They had put *qi* out of place (for instance, into the arm instead of the Cinnabar Field (*dantian*)), and *qi* permanently out of place resulted in dementia or even in death. Guidance by a master was indispensable, misguidance fatal. With this belief in the need of a master for learning *qigong*, control over knowledge was secured by those who possessed it.

Family bonds and the ethics of knowledge

Qiu had been weak and sickly in his early childhood. His grandfather, who was a Chinese herbal doctor, had sent the five-year-old boy once a week to an old friend in the suburbs who was a *wushu* master. Later he had had him learn medicine and meditation from his neighbour who was a 'senior Chinese doctor' (*laozhongyi*). Qiu told me that his grandfather had not taught his father medicine because he had not thought much of that son's character.[11] For similar reasons his master, Luo, had been reluctant to teach his second son, Qiu explained, but since that son was weedy and weak, the father felt obliged to provide the son a means of livelihood and equip him with his knowledge. *Qigong* meditation not only strengthened the bodies of these physically weak children; the knowledge of *qigong* gave them power and social prestige.

Episodes of Qiu's life pointed to a strong sense of 'filial piety' (*xiao*). His mother told me once at supper that as a child Qiu had refused to eat for several days. He was a toddler, she said, but strong-minded, he had wanted his mother to listen to his advice. Her husband's income had been insufficient to nourish their six children, and therefore she had worked for one *yuan* per day for a neighbour who was a vegetable merchant. Seeing her exploited, 'I always told her not to work for him', Qiu said and continued: 'I left primary school after only five years because I wanted to protect the family.' 'Because your school records

[11] Qiu's father was a 'worker' (*gongren*) of a nearby factory who was in early retirement and spent most of his days sitting in and around Qiu's practice. He never recovered from his nervous breakdown during the Cultural Revolution; the paternal authority tended to be with Qiu's elder brothers rather than with him.

were not good enough', his wife chided. 'That was the only way to get out', Qiu insisted. In his early twenties he had been offered work with an overseas Chinese in Singapore. He maintained that he had not accepted the offer because he wanted to look after his parents. During my fieldwork he lived in his parents' home and gave them one hundred *yuan* per month, since his father's pension was only forty *yuan*. Jade Blossom often complained about this, although it was, according to Qiu, less than a tenth of their income.

An 'upright mind' (*zhengxin*) and a clear conscience were repeatedly cited as preconditions for finding the concentration to meditate. Purity of mind was paralleled by purification through washing the entire body, cleansing the meditation room, respecting food taboos, and abstaining from sexual intercourse. The meditation was to take place regularly at a precise time of the day, during the *zi* hours around midnight (11 p.m. – 1 a.m.). The seating during meditation, the altar, and the taboos had features common to both Daoist and Buddhist traditions, but Qiu's incantations were exclusively Daoist, and with much veneration he kept hidden a portrait of Taishang Laojun.[12] The incantations contained verses of harmful magic, although Qiu and all the other *qigong* masters I met maintained that any kind of harm or disturbance directed at another person would damage one's *gongfa*. According to a story circulating at the time in Kunming, the nationally known *qigong* master Yan Xin once undertook to cure a patient suffering from 'oedema' (*shuizhong*) in her legs. During the following two hours his two disciples repeatedly had the urge to urinate, and as a result the patient's swelling was reduced. 'They were his disciples', was the comment. If the master had inflicted the disturbance he had caused in his disciples on another person, his *gongfa* would have ceased. He could disturb his disciples in this way only because master and disciple were very close. *Qigong* masters were believed to be extremely powerful, and if they refused to perform certain manipulations, it was often on ethical grounds.

Guarding the secrecy of his knowledge was a virtue Qiu admitted to have lacked. In his youth he had made the mistake of teaching his friends. One of his earlier lovers, for instance, had managed to learn from him many aspects of his secret knowledge, and when she left him, she set up her own practice somewhere in town. Her competition was no threat to him, and the broken relationship did not seem to disturb him as much as the regret that he had spilled out so much of the secret knowledge that his beloved master had chosen to give only to him.

---

[12] The highest divinity of Daoist folk religion, Laozi. He was first made the head of the Daoist pantheon and later dubbed Taishang Laojun (Day 1969:135). See also Kohn (1989:134, 154, 155, 167).

Young and inexperienced as he had been in his twenties, he had also made a fool of himself by teaching someone who claimed to be his friend the 'ten precious movements' that formed the beginning of each meditation session. That 'friend' had later written an introductory book on *qigong* containing the sequence of movements that Qiu had taught him.[13]

Discipleship: imitation and repetition

After Qiu and Jade Blossom had signed the civil marriage contract,[14] she asked to be initiated into his esoteric knowledge as evidence of his love. A few months later, shortly before their public wedding, she became pregnant, making the practice of *qigong* too strenuous for her, and in any case forbidden. Her younger brother, who had just graduated from middle school and was unemployed, came from her home province to stay with her, however, and Qiu, in recognition of his affinal ties, was obliged to teach him.

Jade Blossom's younger brother Qiudi was very silent, if not by nature, by his social status and age. He was a newcomer to the extended family, which included Qiu's parents and one of his elder brothers who was not employed by a work unit. As a disciple, Qiudi was expected to assist his master in every aspect of his life. In addition, as the youngest adult member in the household, he was also expected to be helpful and dutiful to his sister's in-laws. He washed the dishes, cleaned the consulting room in the evenings, and did most of the very strenuous labour of grinding the medicinal herbs into powder; he was sent here and there for his sister and her husband. And if something went wrong it was his fault.[15] He was treated in such a way not out of malice, but as a matter of habit. Nobody felt that it was necessary to justify it. Qiudi had been in training for several months when I became friendly with Qiu's family, and given my interest in *qigong*, frequently asked him about his latest progress. Qiu and especially Jade Blossom constantly scolded him for being lazy. During an outing of the three on National Day (October 1), Qiu urged his disciple to take his training more seriously. Jade Blossom confided this to me on a shopping trip during one of the

[13] Almost all the movements in a slightly different sequence are recorded in Wang Zuyuan's ((1834)1956:47–58) *Illustrated Exegesis on Inner Alchemy (Nei gong tu shuo)*: the twelve illustrations of the *Canon for Supple Sinews (Yi jin jing)*.

[14] Civil marriage contracts are signed without general publicity. In the late 1980s they were easily and frequently dissolved. A marriage is, in general, acknowledged only after the wedding banquet (Croll 1981:110).

[15] On the hardly bearable conditions of an apprentice, see Cooper (1980:23–33).

following days. It seemed as if the anthropologist's interest in *qigong* had enlivened theirs and possibly intensified Qiudi's training.

To become a healer, it was most important to cultivate one's Inner *qi* and practice soft *qigong*, Jade Blossom explained. She wanted her brother to become a healer, but since he was a strong young man Qiu had insisted that he undergo the severe training of hard *qigong*. Whereas the practice of soft *qigong* consisted mainly in 'meditation in tranquillity' (*jinggong*) as opposed to 'meditation by movement' (*donggong*),[16] hard *qigong* practices included hitting sacks filled with gravel, tree trunks, and stone walls with one's bare hands, and beating oneself with a sackful of gravel. Apart from that, they included long series of quick movements that could only be performed when the body was in excellent condition.

In autumn 1988, Qiudi was temporarily working in a collective that sold and repaired simple electronic equipment. In the evening after supper and early in the morning he would regularly go for meditation to the nearby park. Qiudi had already been taught the 'ten precious movements', now he was to proceed to meditation in tranquillity. This consisted mainly of several hours of conscious but natural breathing while seated with crossed legs, soles up, after a few introductory incantations and movements. It was probable that one night a bright Light (*guang*) – red, white, or blue-green – would suddenly appear. Novices were taught that it was important not to be frightened by this and to continue to breathe regularly.

Descriptions of a Light or Glow were given to me by most of those who practised *qigong* seriously. An often-described sensation was a warm golden Glow that travelled on the Minor Cosmic Circulation (*xiao zhoutian*), and this description is also found in the rapidly expanding popular literature. A warm sensation was first felt in the region of the Cinnabar Field (*dantian*) just beneath the navel.[17] That Glow was easily transmitted from there to the lower back area of the Gate Pass (*lüguan*).[18] The next step was to make the Glow circulate. This was difficult, for while one could easily let the Glow wander along certain sections of the spine it would usually halt in between them, in passages called the

---

[16] The term *jinggong* can be found in *Zhuang zi* 26 (Miura 1989:345); *donggong* is a form of *qigong* that has, for ideological reasons, been promoted in the PRC (p. 334).

[17] Compare with Yang Xuancao's comments on a phrase in *Nan jing* 66 (translated by Unschuld 1986b:567): 'As to the moving *qi* beneath the navel and between the kidneys, it is the *dantian*', followed by a long discussion of its features. See also footnote 20.

[18] In the literature known as the *weilüguan*, rendered as the Caudal Narrow Pass by Despeux (1994:81). The *locus classicus* is *Zhuang zi* 17: the *weilü* is associated with the place at which the waters of the sea are continuously discharged.

Three Passes (*sanguan*).[19] Once the Glow had reached the top of one's head it would wander downward to the area in which it had originated, the Cinnabar Field. 'The Minor Cosmic Circulation is connected' (*xiaozhoutian tong*) was the expression for this sensation. Some beginners could not bring the Glow to circulation at all and gave up *qigong*, but most arrived at it after several meditation sessions. Once the Minor Cosmic Circulation had been connected, the Glow would easily continue to circulate. The meditator was rewarded with a feeling of relaxation, lightness, and weightlessness that was 'very delightful' (*hen shufu*). This direct emotional reward after persistent repetition of the same movement needs to be stressed.

'There are as many ways of practising *qigong* as there are masters', Qiu replied when I asked his opinion on the experiences described above. His *gongfa* did not make reference to the Minor Cosmic Circulation; he spoke of a Light which originated between his eyebrows at the *yintang*.[20] His disciple Qiudi experienced this Light in front of his forehead too. 'He saw the Red Light (*ta jian hongguangle*)', Jade Blossom told me proudly and I took it that this expression indicated a stage comparable to connecting the Minor Cosmic Circulation. It was clear that Qiudi had made an important step in his training. The problem now was to manipulate this Light for healing purposes.

Qiudi started working as a healer under Qiu's guidance in mid-October. The client with whom they worked was a woman in her fifties who suffered severe shoulder pain. Ma was an unusual patient because of her high social status (she was a physics teacher who had graduated from Beijing University), her vivacious cooperation (talkative, encouraging, and readily influenced), and her health-seeking behaviour (marked by persistence in seeking relief from her symptoms). When the pain in her shoulder had started with sudden onset four months earlier, she had gone to Kunming's most prestigious hospital, the People's Provincial Hospital, like many state-educated and state-employed cadres turning first to Western biomedicine. The doctor she had consulted there, however, had sent her to the acumoxa department of the hospital. She was treated for two or three weeks at a cost of a treatment cycle of ten consultations of two *yuan* each, without tangible improvement. By then she had heard that acupuncturists working in TCM hospitals had better training, but the treatment she subsequently received at the City

---

[19] For a brief account of the Three Passes (*sanguan*), see Despeux (1994:80–7).

[20] The *dantian* (Cinnabar Field) is occasionally referred to as upper, middle, and lower *dantian*, located between the eyebrows (corresponding acu-point *yintang*), between the nipples (corresponding acu-point: *danzhong*), and in the area which is about the breadth of a hand below the navel. Qiu said no more (but see Despeux 1994:74–80).

TCM Hospital had not proved much more successful. The pain continued to keep her from sleeping at night. The masseurs of an itinerant medical service group stationed near the hospital had promised her a definite cure, and for thirty-two *yuan*, paid in advance, she had been guaranteed daily treatment until the pain was gone. That treatment had worsened the pain so that she could hardly lift her arm. She had then turned to *qigong*.

The director of the private *qigong* hospital she had attended, Qiu's bond brother, had recommended Qiu to her. When Qiu heard that his bond brother had refused to commit himself to her healing, he expressed doubt about being able to make her well. She was, however, anxious to receive his treatment and pointed out that he had just cured a client before her eyes in a single session. 'Everyone is different', he replied; 'you have to be "predestined" (*yuanfen*) for *qigong*.' When he eventually agreed to try, he proposed to deliver, in addition to acumoxa, 'cupping' (*huoguan*), fire massage,[21] and *qigong* treatment, so-called 'remote-effect-*qigong*' (*yuan qigong*) – simultaneous meditation in tranquillity by sender and receiver – in their homes on opposite sides of the city. This meant that Qiudi's way of learning to become a healer consisted first of remote-effect-*qigong* sessions; then, after a week, of delivering several *qigong* sessions together with his master; and after two weeks, of performing his first *qigong* healing session entirely on his own.

On Monday 17 October, Ma, accompanied by her husband, came for her first treatment. Jade Blossom delivered acumoxa and cupping treatment, each of about twenty minutes duration, Qiu then administered a half-hour of fire massage, which was extremely painful for the client. Lastly he gave a concentrated *qigong* session of half an hour. Thereafter, he asked Ma to raise her arm, and to the surprise of everyone she did, up to 45 degrees.

Two days later, during the Wednesday treatment after the first remote-effect-*qigong* session, Ma declared that the pain had increased so much that she could not sleep. Qiu's wife was concerned. Firstly, her husband had been unable to lift his shoulder during the remote-effect-*qigong* session the night before, and she knew that he could develop such empathy for his patients that he would take on their ailments during the process of healing, particularly if the problem was very difficult to solve.

---

[21] In fire massage the bottom of a jar is covered with a medicinal alcohol which is saturated with several herbal drugs. With a piece of burning cotton stuck onto scissors, the alcohol is lit and applied to the patient's painful areas with the left hand. The right hand, with which he performs massage, suffocates the flame and rubs the alcohol into the skin. This method, which I observed to alleviate pain and reduce swelling, was generally not practised in government hospitals. Qiu commented: 'It is very hard work.'

Secondly, the x-ray that Qiu had asked Ma to have at a hospital showed physical damage: the sixth neck vertebra was dislocated. When Ma's husband came to accompany his wife home, he started chatting with Qiu, and it was then that Qiu learnt that his bond brother had recommended him. Sensing complications, he declared that he would give her just seven days of treatment, and if there was no improvement she would have to return to his bond brother for treatment. 'She'll come back', he told me later, 'but it's better to let her go than to try to keep her with me.' Obviously he wanted her to be completely committed. During the following hour of her acumoxa and cupping treatment, he told stories of his and others' successes in healing or in predicting death. Before she left he told her what his intentions were for the next remote-effect-*qigong* session; he wanted her to have the sensation of a feeling of 'distension' (*zhang*) in the head.

On the following evening, Qiu, Jade Blossom, and Qiudi cycled to Ma's home and delivered a *qigong* session during the *zi* hour, when '*yin* is deepest' (*yin zui shen*) and *qigong* most efficient. Jade Blossom told me on the following day that the session had been unsuccessful because Ma had not been able to calm down. The only sensation she had had was a prickling in her hands.

The next session was scheduled for Saturday evening after dinner, the treatment of other evening clients being postponed. On this evening, the three healers and the clients were strikingly cordial to each other. While Ma was being acupunctured she expressed her enthusiasm for *qigong*. Qiu now showed her and her husband the photo album of his trip to Beijing, his favourite piece of evidence of his *qigong* powers. He had been twenty-four at that time, a *qigong* healer employed by a hospital of Kunming city. He had had the capability of penetrating vision and after having proved himself in research trials set up by Yunnan University, he had been to Beijing for further trials which he claimed had been arranged by the national secret police. But after being exposed to the stress of the trials in the metropolis, the highly sensitive person from the provinces had lost his extraordinary capability of penetrating vision. He nevertheless remained a capable healer as was evident from the wealth of cases he successfully treated.

Excitement pervaded in the group as the healing session began. Ma sat on the bed with crossed legs, Qiudi behind her, and Qiu in front of her, facing the two of them. Qiu murmured incantations and made a few introductory gestures for meditation, thus imposing silence upon the participants in the room, who were all told to shut their eyes. The necessary concentration was not achieved; in the adjacent room a heated dispute was taking place, and once that had subsided the noise from the street was distracting. At last, after about half an hour, when a heavy lorry came rattling down the street, Qiu gave up: 'That's it. It didn't work.'

The following minutes were critical for us to agree on what had happened. I opened my eyes, feeling numb. Qiudi was soaked in sweat. Ma was numb, too, her eyes were swimming. Her husband, however, sat straight and smiling, he had obviously been peeking at the session. When Qiu sprang off the stool and put on his shoes, Jade Blossom broke the silence, complaining of a headache. Indeed, the air in the room was stale and sticky. Qiudi opened the door, lit a cigarette, and offered me one while Qiu and Jade Blossom worked on Ma's arm. They pressed with both hands against her shoulder and told her to lift her arm rhythmically. It was obvious that she could lift the arm higher than before, but in a few minutes she was tired. Now all of us started to talk about our sensations during the concentration phase. 'He doesn't know how to heal yet, but after half a year of training he has already seen the Light', said Qiudi's sister. 'How big is a Light?' Ma's husband asked. Qiudi held his hands in front of his chest as if he were holding a basketball. 'I would have caught his Light and led it up the arm to the area of the shoulder', Qiu's explanation was followed by a silence. His interpretation was instantly accepted as correct. I asked Qiu how it had been for him. 'Half, half', he replied. Qiu maintained that he had achieved the state of seeing a Light, in spite of the noise, but he had not seen Qiudi's Light. He explained that one person alone was not powerful enough to cure the shoulder. Since the two had to join forces, he had stopped emitting the Light and waited for Qiudi's which, however, had not appeared. If it worked, Qiu explained, *qigong* could make a patient lift his or her arm. Oh, yes, Ma agreed, she had seen such *qigong* performances on television. She was the most excited of all. She had experienced a sensation which she had already had once before but much more clearly this time. It had felt like an insect crawling, first twice above her eyebrow then downwards to a corner of her nose. Thereafter, a prickling feeling had ascended her arm towards the shoulder but then descended again towards her fingers, where it had originated. 'Look, I can even lift my arm to a horizontal position', she exclaimed. But Qiu corrected her; she was twisting her body. Ma then suggested settling her account, since she had now been under treatment for almost a week. Jade Blossom advanced slowly toward the desk. She glanced at Qiu who was carefully buttoning his coat in silence. 'We're friends', she said. So Ma proposed that we all spend Sunday together, but because I was unavailable, the invitation was postponed.

The session that Qiu and Qiudi delivered on Sunday evening at Ma's home was successful. 'Ma sleeps well now and has no pain in the shoulder', Jade Blossom told me the next day; Qiudi had seen the Red Light (*hongguang*) and even bones of the shoulder in it.

On Wednesday evening the party met again, this time in a pavilion in the nearby park. The pavilion was open and airy and the air a bit chilly. Only a few visitors were still strolling in the dusk. It was silent except for the regular sneezes of nearby *qigong* exercisers. Qiudi looked more self-assured; he had obviously received further instructions. After a period of concentration, he started moving his open palms up and down behind Ma's back without touching her. Then Qiu took Ma's hand and put his palms on hers. It looked as if he meant to transmit his *qi* to her. After the concentration phase, Qiu and Qiudi pressed her arm and made her lift it rhythmically, which she did for five to ten minutes.

There was no doubt that *qigong* had worked this time. Qiu was the first to say so. He had seen a White Light (*baiguang*). Ma said that she had felt heat running from the left to the right shoulder and that her hands were unusually warm; she let me confirm this by touching them. She even declared that she had also seen a White Light. The White Light was not as effective as the Red one, Qiu explained; he had tried to let the Light penetrate the blockage in the shoulder five times, but had succeeded only once. Ma nodded; she had felt the prickling feeling ascending and descending her arm before she had the heat sensations between the shoulders. When I asked Qiu how big the Light had been he drew a huge circle in the air with outstretched arms; when I asked Qiudi, he said it had been a ball similar in appearance to the flickering on a television screen. Qiu did not seem to appreciate systematic en-quiries and interrupted me; the treatment had worked for everyone, and that was important. He always emphasised that he did not know why, but it obviously worked. Qiudi was by now, at least, convinced of the effects of his *qigong* and his own *gongfa*.

Two days later Qiudi looked excited and happy. The night before he had seen the 'eight trigrams' (*bagua*) very clearly, and during the morn-ing meditation he had also seen Taishang Laojun. Qiu was surprised that his disciple had made such rapid progress but showed familiarity with the symptoms. He asked Qiudi whether the images had threatened him or simply vanished. When Qiudi reported that the latter was the case, he said: 'If ever they threaten you, do not be afraid, they may become bigger and bigger, but you need not fear them. When they come, tell them to go; when they swell, tell them to shrink.' He assured Qiudi that his spiritual force would be stronger than these images. He was to beware of wild animals, but if he were to see a little man he was to report it to Qiu.

On Sunday, the four of us went to Ma's home. She served us many delicious dishes and after lunch took us to the nearby park. Towards evening she was expecting to receive treatment. For the past three days she had taken Qiu's herbal drug potions three times a day. She had also meditated during the *zi* hours in order to receive treatment by remote-effect-*qigong*. Qiu said that he was tired and told his disciple to treat her in the adjacent room. Forty minutes passed in silence. Eventually Qiu interrupted their session by knocking on the door. He found Ma bursting with enthusiasm. She had had the same sensations as on Wednesday in the park, and this time this was due to Qiudi's *gongfa* alone. Everyone was surprised and delighted. This meant that Qiudi had a very powerful *gongfa*. Later I asked Qiu what the patient was expected to feel during such a successful session. She should feel pain, he answered; if it did not hurt her, it was just like having a rest or falling asleep.

Qiudi slowly opened his eyes, looking a bit dazed. He was expected to say something, but he did not. Instead, his sister immediately started speaking on his behalf: 'He can't express what he experienced. He does not understand it himself, he doesn't know any anatomy.' Later she added that if she could 'emit Red Light' (*fa hongguang*), given her knowledge of anatomy, she would have been able to cure Ma in a few days. Qiu, too, began to offer explanations. It was as if Jade Blossom and Qiu did not want to give Qiudi a chance to put his experiences into words. I tried to get him to speak for himself, but he just repeated what his sister had said: 'It's so difficult to put your experience into words.'

Qiu showed with a gesture of his hand that a blockage – a tight passage – had been opened up so that the *qi* could flow through it. Qiudi had murmured something about going all the way up the arm and from one shoulder to the other. This made Jade Blossom wonder whether there was no blockage in the spine, which would contradict the biomedical information derived from the x-ray. Indeed, Qiu and Jade Blossom had closely inspected the spine and shoulder before Qiudi began the *qigong* session. They had searched for a rash on the surface of the skin, induced by their drug treatment, which would reflect an inner blockage, but had found none.

On the way back I approached Qiudi again, but when he started to talk – 'the Red Glow, well, with that Red Light, I go up the arm' – we were interrupted again. This episode clearly showed what earlier episodes had indicated: the disciple was not asked to express his experience; instead his experience 'difficult to put into words' as it was, was described and labelled by his master. He spoke of his disciple's experiences as if he had had the experience himself. Long before Qiudi had seen the Light, his master had talked about it. Then, after the concentration phase, still overwhelmed by his own new experience, the disciple was told what it was; the master labelled it for him.

Ma did not come again except to pay her bill: about two hundred *yuan*, covered by her work unit's health insurance. During the following year she and her husband occasionally passed by. Her shoulder still hurt, and she could not lift it much higher, but she put up with it and said she had not consulted other healers.

The next step in Qiudi's training was to meditate for forty-nine days, every night during the *zi* hours and two hours early in the mornings, in a private room. From now on he was to eat vegetarian food, sleep regularly, and abstain from sex and alcohol. Moreover, he was to learn a series of Daoist incantations for the cure of the different illnesses by heart.

In mid-December Qiu left for a meeting of the National *Qigong* Association in Beijing, and Jade Blossom went to see her parents in her home village near Chengdu, the capital of Sichuan province. Qiu joined her in early February to spend the Chinese New Year there. Qiudi stayed in Kunming and transformed the consulting room into his meditation room. During the day, he continued to work in the collective, but night and morning he meditated. I visited him once in January. Fumes of incense filled the room, a meditation mat was on the floor, a picture of Guanyin[22] on the wall in front of the mat, flanked by incense sticks. Qiudi looked much thinner; his hands were wounded and swollen and he told me that his whole body was 'sore and painful' (*suanteng*). Obviously, he was practising hard *qigong* too. His notebook, which was on the table, was tiny but filled with drawings of Daoist *fu* (signs)[23] and incantations copied from various books. As well as that, he seemed to have taken the urgings of his sister seriously; an anatomy booklet lay on the bed.

When Qiu and Jade Blossom resumed their practice at the end of February, Qiudi started to work regularly with them and gave up his job at the collective. Qiu taught him the particular incantations and gestures of *qigong* for curing some illnesses, but he was only rarely told to perform *qigong*. Usually he had to deliver the massage treatment, the most strenuous work. The few times I saw Qiudi deliver *qigong* was for curing chronic illnesses or serious diseases which did not promise success for the healer.

---

[22] An autochthonous female deity of the earth and fertility which was merged with the male boddhisattva Avalokitaresh after Buddhism spread in China (Needham 1956:407). Nowadays Guanyin is venerated as a *pusa* (boddhisattva) in Buddhist temples. She is very popular and still fulfils the functions of a fertility deity.
[23] A Daoist charm, see Schipper (1982:287).

For example, in May and June 1989 a woman from the neighbour-hood in her sixties took regular treatment for headache and blurred vision, which Jade Blossom attributed to 'high blood pressure' (*gaoxueya*). She was treated with acumoxa, *qigong*, herbal drugs taken three times a day, and with the therapeutic method of covering the patient's eyes with two fresh, light green mulberry leaves. In spite of daily treatment, her condition did not improve much, nor did the regularly measured blood pressure sink perceptibly. Qiudi was allowed to treat her. As taught, he murmured the incantations and performed the prescribed gestures of *qigong* healing, which included several *fu* drawn in the air before her eyes. Once he delivered a session for almost three-quarters of an hour. In the more public part of the room, Qiu had first treated a hearing-impaired old man from the neighbourhood and then sat chat-ting with his patients. He eventually turned to this woman, seated her on a stool in the middle of the room, and delivered another five-to-ten-minute-long *qigong* performance. After this short session, the woman looked delighted, and when Qiu asked her how she felt she answered that she had had strange sensations of a prickling on her eyelids. In five minutes he had achieved what his disciple had not achieved in the hour before. Seen in contrast to his disciple, he seemed even more of a master. Qiudi sat on the bench, exhausted and silent. I wondered to what extent the master was exploiting his disciple's preparatory work of concentration.

In August, an old man in his seventies came from a distant county for a month of treatment. He was partly paralysed on one side because of a stroke and could hardly walk. His daughter's friend whom Qiu had cured of a uterine tumour had recommended him to her. When his daughter had visited Qiu in his practice to find out whether he would treat her father, he, as usual, told many stories of successful treatment but said that he had to see the patient in order to judge his prospects for recovery. Accordingly, father and mother made the trip into the provincial capital and took a room in one of the many private inns opposite Qiu's practice. After first inspection, Qiu made no promises. Although he did not say so, even when I later asked him in private, he obviously was reluctant to commit himself to this treatment. Instead, he sent Qiudi at least once and sometimes twice a day to perform the massage and *qigong* treatment. Jade Blossom provided acumoxa treat-ment while Qiu prepared the herbal drugs. He only occasionally went to see this patient to deliver *qigong*. I saw Jade Blossom scolding her husband several times during that month, accusing him of neglecting this patient who had come from so far away. The patient's wife and daughter did not scold him, but they were full of praise for Qiudi. They said that the disciple was more helpful and kinder and even delivered better *qigong* treatment than his master. Jade Blossom was very proud of her brother when she told me this. But Qiu did not lose face: when the patient returned home after a month, he was still in the same deplorable state.

In October, Bao, a middle-school teacher in his fifties, sought Qiu for treatment of liver cancer. He had come from the neighbouring province of Guizhou in July to receive treatment that only the hospitals of a provincial capital could supply. During the first few months he and his wife had stayed with his relatives. Biomedical treatment at several hospitals of Kunming had proved incapable of halting the deterioration of his health, and he had turned to *qigong* as a last resort. He reported feeling considerably better after the first series of ten *qigong* sessions. In November Qiu was introduced by a friend to a herbalist who knew a herbal drug, the root of a shrub, which was said to cure liver cancer. Another friend, who was a chauffeur, agreed to escort Qiu, Qiudi, and the herbalist about a hundred miles south to the mountains where this plant grew. The excursion was successful, but the second time Bao took the potion containing this drug he fell seriously ill, vomiting and being unable to keep any food down for three days. When Bao's wife reappeared in Qiu's practice on the fourth day, tears were running down her face. Qiu urged her to send her husband to the private hospital down the street for an intravenous glucose treatment.[24] She meant well, he said, implying that she had not followed his instructions carefully, and given her husband an overdose of a very Potent and Toxic Drug (*duyao*). When I saw Bao a week later he was thin and frail and by December he was so weak that he and his wife moved into a room of an empty, newly built private apartment house belonging to one of Qiu's friends. It was only ten minutes' walk away from the practice so that Qiu could deliver treatment there – on an old mattress laid onto the bare cement floor, in a draught coming from hollow window frames that time and again put out the flame of a candle. When I left Kunming at the end of December he had been admitted to the emergency station of the Red Cross Hospital after a fainting spell four days before. He survived the trip to Guizhou, Jade Blossom wrote me in a letter, and was able to bid farewell to his two daughters before dying in early January.

Bao's liver cancer, with the illness course briefly outlined above, was a case for which Qiu sought Qiudi's assistance in order to treat the

---

[24] Intravenous glucose treatments were considered to 'invigorate' (*bu*) the body; see White (1993:269) and Hsu (1992b:97).

patient with joint energies. After he had treated Bao for the first ten days, the question arose as to whether treatment should be continued. The decision was taken after attaining general agreement that the client's health had improved. This agreement was not based on biochemical evidence but on several opinions that coincided. Jade Blossom, Qiu, I, and long-term patients in Qiu's consultation room all noticed that Bao's look had become brighter; he had more Spirit (*shen*) in his eyes. Furthermore, Qiu declared that he could see (with his penetrating vision) and feel (with his trembling hand) that Bao's liver had 'softened' (*nen*) and was smaller than before, and most important, Bao had agreed that he felt less pain. Bao and his wife, both government-employed cadres, were naturally quite uncertain whether they should rely on *qigong*, and once when we happened to meet in the street outside Qiu's practice, they expressed their doubts to me. Yes, I told them, I had my doubts too, but Qiu was certainly one of the best healers I knew in Kunming. Yes, I had witnessed the recovery of one woman last year who had had a tumour in her uterus; x-rays had shown that it had almost disappeared after six months of regular *qigong* treatment.[25] I emphasised that I was not a doctor and that they should continue with biomedical care at the hospital. They replied that Bao had just given up his chemotherapy but they had been there for a check-up.

In view of his patient's commitment, Qiu suggested doubling the *qigong* sessions in the conviction that this would double the therapeutic effect. Qiudi delivered the first one. He sat on a stool in front of the bed where the patient lay, shut his eyes, murmured the incantations, made the opening gestures, and put his hand on the right side of the patient in the region of the liver. It was a long session, more than half an hour. The healer's shirt was soaked with sweat, and the patient had beads of sweat on his forehead. He felt completely exhausted and indicated that he felt pain in the region of his liver. Without addressing a word to Qiudi, Qiu instantly took his place and talked to the patient, asking him about his pain and calming him, saying that Qiudi was still inexperienced but he need not be anxious, that everything would be all right in a moment. After a rest of about a quarter of an hour, he suggested performing a second session, which proved half as long as the previous one. After this session the patient's exhaustion disappeared and he no longer felt pain. He then sat on the bench to rest and chat before leaving, guided by his wife, shortly before lunch.

---

[25] At the time I did not know that: 'One of the most frequent disorders of the uterus and the most frequent tumour of women (three of four women affected) is the uterine leiomyoma, or fibroid tumour. 75 per cent of women with leiomyoma are asymptomatic' (Harrison's 1987:1836). Apparently such tumours come and go for unknown reasons.

In this case Qiudi had made a serious mistake, and Qiu continued the treatment without addressing a word to him. Sometimes, he would shake his head, but I never saw him scold his disciple in public. Once, when Qiudi had spilled out some herbal drug powder, his sister cursed him, but Qiu did not get angry and, with a laugh, crouched down to help him to take up the powder from the ground.[26] This time, after Bao and his wife had left and I entered the backyard, I could hear from a distance how Jade Blossom told off her brother: 'How dull and stupid you are', she exclaimed; 'it's not the longer the better and the stronger the better!' Qiu was in the kitchen too: 'You've got to use "imagination" (*yinian*)', he said, for the first time with a strong note of reproach. When he noticed that I had entered the kitchen he became silent and urged us all out of the kitchen into the opposite room for lunch. He continued at the table in a friendlier and more instructive tone: 'You have to imagine how his Liver (*gan*) becomes smaller and smaller and at last, when it's really so small that it fits into your hand, you fold it away and take out the bad stuff.' Qiu made a gesture of drawing the outstretched fingers of his hand together into a fist. '*Qigong* is done by imagination (*yinian*), not by force, it's as simple as that.'[27]

The Light that changed the healer's gaze

'Experiencing the Light' (*jian guang*) marked a boundary in Qiudi's training[28] comparable to the boundaries that initiation rites make between laypersons and the initiated. This social differentiation was grounded in an important change of cognitive faculties: only those who were able to concentrate *qi* and control its flow would experience the Light that changed the healer's gaze and endowed him with healing powers.[29]

---

[26] Qiudi's apprenticeship differed in this respect from Cooper (1980:27) who found that 'Many workers seriously believe that the only way to get a boy to learn is to beat him.'

[27] Engelhardt (1987:17) makes the same point about *qigong* exercises in general and provides various examples; see also Despeux (1995:138). Sharma (1996:258) argues that 'Anthropologists have had little to say about imagination', pointing to the importance of imagination in many so-called alternative therapies which adopt a 'holistic' approach to the body and healing. She proposes to use a 'culturally active imagination' as a means to overcome the mind/body dualism inherent in academic anthropology, although she is 'not optimistic that it will be possible to overcome the dualisms embedded in western culture' (p. 262).

[28] Not every *qigong* healer spoke of a Light. For descriptions of the Light in other traditions of meditation, see Robinet (1989a). Qiu's meditation took place in absolute silence and differed in this respect from that described by Tambiah (1977:102) in which the master led his disciple-patients by verbalising visualisations, and McGuire (1983:231–2), in which verbalised problems were burnt in a visualised fire.

[29] Shamans are generally believed to possess cognitive capacities that distinguish them from others, see for instance Blacker (1975:168). The ascetic may be initiated by a dream, by 'possession' (*lamagakari*) and, less frequently, by mantic journey into the other

After Qiudi's mistake in treating Bao, the atmosphere in Qiu's household was tense. During the lunch, I asked Qiu how he had cured the 'kidney infection' (*shenyan*) of one of his current patients. Qiu's answer was short: 'With the Red Light.' Ideas about the Light's impact on cognitive and healing faculties diverged greatly among laypersons, and those who had experienced it themselves were reluctant to speak about it. Lao Yi, the neighbourhood herbalist who was having lunch with us, seized this opportunity to comment on Qiu's answer. 'A kidney infection' (he used the same biomedical term as I had), he said, 'is cured by the principle of the Earth overcoming Water (*tu ke shui*).' He was evidently reasoning in terms of the Five Phases (*wuxing*): Water is associated with the Kidneys and Earth with the Spleen. In order to cure the Kidneys one had to 'invigorate the Spleen' (*bu pi*). He declared that Qiu should 'emit Yellow Light' (*fa huangguang*) because that colour corresponded to the Earth and the Spleen. Qiu, however, emitted Red Light; Red Light corresponded to Fire, Fire gave birth to Earth (*huo sheng tu*), and Earth overcame Water (*tu ke shui*). Qiu remained silent; it was clear that the herbalist had overgeneralised maxims of treatment in terms of the Five Phases. These maxims can be used to determine the composition of ingredients of Chinese medical drug treatments, but they are inappropriate for explaining the workings of *qigong* healing.

That evening I dropped in on Qiu and his wife again, hoping to clarify the issue that Lao Yi had raised. Qiu laughed, still unwilling to speak: 'Have you ever heard anyone speak of the Yellow Light!?' Jade Blossom was more cooperative. She explained that the Red Light could shine through the red tissue of the body and that by 'emitting Blue-green Light' (*fa qingguang*) a *qigong* healer could find stolen or lost things in blue-green water. She fell silent, however, when she saw her husband frown. It was only in the context of my training later that evening that Qiu spoke of the Light. As usual, his explanation was brief and vague. He said that the Red Light was most powerful because one had penetrating vision and quickly added that, despite previous events that seemed to prove the contrary, only he (and not Qiudi) knew how to emit it. The Red Light that he saw, but not the White Light Qiudi saw, enabled one to see bones, Obstructions (*bi*), and 'accumulating *qi*' (*qiji*). Sometimes Obstructions and accumulating *qi* were symptoms which the patients themselves perceived, but usually they were a visualisation of the disorder which only the *qigong* healer could achieve by emitting Light.

world and thereafter endowed with the cognitive powers of clairvoyance, clairaudience, and insight into hidden things, apart from many others such as mastery of fire and flight to heaven. On the assessment of cognitive capacities by psychological tests among shamans in Zinacantan, see Shweder (1972:407–12).

Destiny and the legitimation of knowledge

'That territory is yours, but this is mine. First make this vow and then I will teach you all my knowledge.' One of the Chinese doctors who introduced me to Chinese medicine, had earlier expressed the thoughts that Qiu was now having about transmitting his secret knowledge. A disciple may become more powerful than his master, and therefore he must promise never to try to compete with him. Qiu sat on a stool in front of my desk and sighed. In autumn 1989, he had repeatedly expressed his aversion to teaching Qiudi: 'I don't like him', he said. 'This hasn't always been so', I replied. I remembered having seen the two walking hand in hand as good friends frequently do in China. 'He's so silent. I don't know what he's thinking', Qiu continued. 'Moreover, he is stupid. It is impossible to teach him the herbal drugs.' I asked whether Qiu was implying that knowledge of the herbal drugs was indispensable for becoming a successful *qigong* healer. No, he said, but it was crucial for running a practice. He was disturbed that during an outing to collect herbs on a hill in the suburbs Qiudi had had difficulty recognising the plants. But, I reminded him, Qiudi was being confronted with the world of plants for the first time, and it was unfair to compare him with me, a graduate in botany. Qiu insisted on his view. He said that he had hesitated to teach his brother-in-law from the very beginning. 'You can't imagine how bad the Chinese are', he confided in me, the foreigner. A year earlier he had expressed to me his fear that his wife wanted him to teach her brother in order to divorce him later and set up a medical practice with her brother in her home province. Apart from pointing to the marital tensions between these two individuals, these suspicions revealed more trust in consanguineous kinship than in affinal bonds. Qiu's affection and respect for his wife increased after she had become the mother of his son in summer 1989, but even then he showed little interest in teaching Qiudi. Although Qiudi continued to meditate, he rarely had visions any more. In September 1989 his sister scolded Qiu because it was obvious that her brother was making no progress. Qiu shrugged his shoulders and remained indifferent to the failure of his disciple.

Naturally, no disciple can force his master to teach him, and even if a master has accepted a disciple he is free to keep as much of his knowledge to himself as he wishes. Qiu's Buddhist friend once explained to me: 'That is why the older a book of secret knowledge, the more value there is to it. Imagine, for centuries each master has taken a bit of that secret knowledge to his grave – probably even the most important bit, the one which ensured him security against the rivalry of his disciple.

How watery the knowledge of these days is compared with that of the golden age!' Knowledge not only enhances one's power but, once transmitted, can be used against one. Limited as it is believed to be, it can be possessed like a commodity.

Qiu had come to my room at the TCM college to fetch his knowledge commodity – his notebook of Daoist incantations. 'Don't lose it; it is my source of life', he had said when handing it over to me two days earlier. I was to photocopy it, because he knew that I would keep him separated from it too long were I to copy verse after verse by hand. He forbade me to have it photocopied in one of the stalls in the streets, but the power supply at the college had been interrupted, and therefore I had not had the opportunity to return it to him earlier.

'To learn this knowledge you have to be destined for it', he explained. For every verse there was a prescribed gesture for magical healing. His *wushu* master had had him learn verse after verse by heart, writing each verse on a separate piece of paper and telling him to burn it, once he had memorised it. At the beginning of each weekly session, he would ask to hear the verse, and only if Qiu recited it correctly would he teach him the gesture for it. Qiu was a small boy at the time, and sometimes, when he stood before his master, he just could not remember the verse. When he failed, instead of giving him another chance at it, the master would teach him a new verse. He was convinced that some verses fitted his disciple and would therefore be easy for him to remember. For those verses the disciple had a predestined fate.[30]

I myself had, I reflected, met Qiu by chance. Qiu's older brother had wanted me to learn *qigong*, and, curious, I had agreed. I had learnt the 'ten precious movements' without much difficulty – I just remembered them – and when Qiu noticed this he had been eager to teach me more. He was convinced that it was fate that I had come, and that I should learn *qigong*. I believed this too. But I did not make as rapid progress as Qiudi. The day we chose for the beginning of my training in meditation in tranquillity was 3 June 1989. It was fate again that that was the night in which the students' movement in Beijing was drowned in blood. Nights of anxiety instead of calm and concentration followed.

---

[30] I was reminded of the phrase a Naxi *dtomba* had repeatedly murmured when I visited him in his hut and asked him what had motivated him to learn the knowledge of the *dtomba*. His father was a peasant like everyone else, he replied, and he was to become one too, but when he was small he used to go to an old and powerful *dtomba* in the neighbourhood. The many myths he was told, he 'just remembered'. It was not so much by vocation as by his fate of 'just remembering' these myths that he later became the *dtomba* of the area. The Naxi are a people of *c.* 250,000 persons who inhabit parts of northwestern Yunnan; the *dtomba* are ritual specialists of a literary tradition notated in a pictographic script (Oppitz and Hsu 1998).

A month later my stay in Kunming was disrupted by a sudden death back home. When I returned three weeks later, Qiu said that my life was too turbulent. He and his older brother had hoped that I would make *qigong* known to the world and, powerful and famous as I would be, would invite my master to come abroad. 'You have no trust in the powers of *qigong*, and there is no continuity in your life. How can I teach you when I constantly feel your critical mind?' He had once believed it was my destiny to learn *qigong*; now he believed it no longer.

Qiu said the above exactly a year after we met, in September, and now, in November 1989, he rejected his disciple Qiudi, too, though for a different reason. He began to concentrate on plans for his son. This child would become a great *qigong* master and, unlike himself, who had only minimal writing skills, go to the university. He would start to teach his boy as soon as he was three. Since the baby's birth, he had been exposing him every evening to tape-recorded *qigong* meetings by Yan Xin. Qiu's decision precipitated a crisis in his family. 'Qiu wants to send Qiudi away,' Jade Blossom exclaimed, 'but I would rather get divorced than have my "dear younger brother" (*qin didi*) sent away.'[31] 'He has learnt nothing during the past year. He has no job, no home – he can't return to his parents without any skills, without even a penny in his pocket.' She dreaded the idea of being alone in Qiu's family. As she started to talk in a lowered voice, she pulled me onto the other side of the street. From a distance I could see Qiudi in the backyard grinding herbs. Qiu was squatting in the sun in front of an empty practice. For the past ten days, no new patients had sought him out. Was it because of the new, more stringent regulations with regard to *qigong* practice, or was it perhaps because Qiu had let me photocopy his secret knowledge? Here Jade Blossom was voicing Qiu's unspoken fears.

When I returned several days later, things seemed to have returned to normal. Qiudi was said to have shown his gratitude to Qiu by hard work, and Jade Blossom had found a temporary job for him somewhere in town. I was about to leave China and, considering that Qiudi's training was taken more seriously when I, the anthropologist, started regularly to visit Qiu's family in the autumn of the previous year, I wondered about the incidence of Qiu's turning away from his disciple at the very moment I was turning away from them.

The secret mode of transmission

Competence in many different frameworks of knowledge and practice was required to become a *qigong* healer. Qiudi learnt how to administer

---

[31] *Qin* designates consanguinity in this context.

Western biomedical drugs and interpret x-rays according to Western biomedical anatomy, he became familiar with herbal drugs and Chinese medical drugs, he engaged in *qigong* healing performances and meditation, and he memorised how to write Daoist *fu* and recite incantations.[32] His master considered biomedical knowledge more accessible than Chinese medical knowledge and was most secretive about *qigong* and, in particular, the Daoist signs and incantations.

The disciple Qiudi learnt by imitation and was trained by repetition – daily meditation and daily exercise consisting of the repetition of the same sequence of movements, three, seven, nine, twenty-four, forty-nine, or sixty-six times. The process of learning was not didactically structured; the different stages through which a disciple had to pass were not outlined in the beginning. Perhaps the master was intentionally concealing his knowledge, or perhaps the course of learning could not be known in advance. The endless repetition of apparently mindless movements was intended to produce sensations, feelings, emotions, and visions to which the disciple was told to be attentive. In Qiudi's case, the direction of further training seemed to depend largely on his particular experiences.

Everyone agreed that an apprentice in *qigong* needed guidance. In the learning process, the disciple was bound to encounter many dangers and dazzling experiences (unusual sensations, visions of dangerous beings, or injuries that needed treatment). When Qiudi experienced the White Light, when he saw the eight trigrams and Taishang Laojun, and when he experienced the Red Light, the master offered guidance: he put the disciple's experiences into words, gave them form, and told him what to expect next.

The development of physical agility was a *sine qua non* for spiritual progress. Qiudi was told that he would not be taught the movements for entering into meditation in tranquillity until he was able to sit, soles upward, with crossed legs. Since bodily agility can be attained only by repeated exercise, it was also taken as a sign of the disciple's commitment. Qiu's trust in his disciple visibly increased as Qiudi became more agile. Bodily and spiritual subtlety were thus both being trained. The training was directed at a mindful being in the body.

The style of knowing that Qiudi acquired can be characterised by the automatism of bodily movements, on the one hand, and the unpredictability of spiritual experiences, on the other. Mindless repetition of the same sequence of movements, on the one hand, and sudden, mind-boggling experiences, on the other. This style of knowing

---

[32] By contrast, *qigong* in the West and among many adherents in China consists only of exercises for the mastery over one's mindful body (N. N. Chen 1995).

consisted in the ability to enter and leave such states of knowledge; the acquisition of secret knowledge was marked by uncertainty. Secret knowledge was not always accessible; it presented itself in different ways, and it sometimes bore the danger of overwhelming the person who had achieved access to it.

Qiu maintained that the recitation of Daoist incantations was even more powerful than the gestures and bodily movements. His gestures were fairly intelligible if one accepted the reality of qi – the healer moved it about with his hands – although he generally did not explain why he made one gesture and not another. The meaning of the incantations was not always clear to Qiu himself; one did not have to understand them to be knowledgeable and powerful. Moreover, one's efficacy did not depend on knowing many different ones.[33] They were limited, like a commodity, condensed in a booklet of incantations. Their message was 'densely compressed' in a 'highly abstract form', just like value in money, which makes transactions possible with an 'otherwise unobtainable secrecy' (Simmel 1950:335).

The Daoist incantations accompanied the gestures in a manner reminiscent of Tambiah's (1968:194) 'operational explanation': 'The rite of transfer portrays a metaphorical use of language (verbal substitution) whereby an attribute is transferred to the recipient via a material symbol which is used metonymically as a transformer . . . The technique gains its realism by clothing a metaphorical procedure in the operative and manipulative mode of practical action; it unites both word and deed.' Tambiah points out that the magic spells of the Trobriand Islanders recorded by Malinowski were uttered in alternation with the hands-on activity of, for instance, carving a ship out of a log. Evans-Pritchard (1937:475–7) made the same point: 'Magic is seldom asked to produce a result by itself, but is associated with empirical action that does in fact produce it.' The sower not only murmurs spells; he murmurs spells while sowing. Likewise, Qiu not only recited Daoist incantations but simultaneously performed gestures which manipulated the qi. These gestures can therefore be interpreted as 'operational activities'.[34]

As convincing as Tambiah's operational explanation is, it cannot entirely account for my observations: Qiu attributed magical power to the spoken word itself; he 'had a belief in the creative power of the magical words themselves, conceived of as active agencies' (Skorupski

---

[33] ter Haar (1992:18) points to the power of the repetition of a single word, the name Amitâbha. It gave a devout lay Buddhist without any education the hope of being reborn in the Western Paradise.

[34] Further 'operational activities', apart from Qiu's gestures, were treatment with massage, acumoxa, herbal drug potions, Chinese medical, and biomedical drugs.

1976:152). The spoken word was, like *qi*, an agent that effected change. Words were not 'one of the most realistic *representations* we have of the concept of force', as Tambiah (1968:184, italics added) puts it, but the so-called force in themselves. Tambiah (1977:109) himself makes this point forcefully elsewhere: 'We note as regards the *achan*'s [teacher's] technology that it is through the medium of words and substances that the *achan* transfers potency and efficacy. The power of words was in fact transferred as if it were a "physical entity", by hand gestures and blowing air.'[35]

Spoken words are emanations with power to induce change. They have tones and pitches, they depend on the voice of the speaker and its modulations, and they can be highly emotive. Words are alive, for some people, like powerful spiritual beings. They are something precious, essential to life, which has to be protected. Secrecy is a means of protection.

Only the correctly pronounced word has power. This conviction may prevail when the name and the thing to which it refers are considered to bear a necessary and internal relation to each other or when the word is not a representation of a thing, but a thing in itself. Whether a so-called correct pronunciation also includes the right tone, pitch, and modulation is unclear to me. *Qigong* masters like Qiu may not be quite sure themselves of all the criteria for correct pronunciation. From an outsider's point of view, the insiders' conviction that the transformative power is inherent only in the correctly pronounced word leads to the following features characteristic of the secret transmission of knowledge: firstly, it provides a legitimation of those in power; secondly, it allows for control over the distribution of knowledge; and thirdly, it excludes the possibility of a critical evaluation of the power of words.

The master usually knows the correct pronunciation from what he was taught by his master, but sometimes he may make decisions about pronunciation quite arbitrarily. This conviction that the master is always right may well ensure the continuity of the lineage in power, although a master need not perpetuate a given tradition but may well be innovative. Since the correct pronunciation can only be transmitted in a face-to-face relationship, the master has control over the authenticity of efficacious knowledge and its distribution.

[35] The Daoist *fu*, in their written form, were also considered powerful in themselves. They were said to be 'a kind of breath from the master' (Schipper 1982:82). The power of the written *fu* resided in this case in the same 'logic' as that of the correctly pronounced word. A *fu* was sometimes written on a paper that was burned and ingested. It would probably be going too far to speak of cannibalism in this case but clearly the master's powers were thus transferred into the client. The 'logic of transference', basic to Qiu's 'logic' of healing, applies also to the ingestion of written *fu*.

The *degrees* of communicating the very same secret can, however, be surprisingly negotiable. When Qiu first introduced me to the 'ten precious movements' he strictly forbade me to show them to anyone else, not even my closest relative or friend. On a subsequent occasion he suddenly began reciting incantations in the Kunming dialect speaking so rapidly that I could not understand them. At this point, he allowed me to teach the 'ten precious movements' and other meditation techniques of *qigong* but forbade me to reveal the recited incantations to anyone. A month later, when he was trying to build up Ma's confidence in his healing art, it turned out that these movements were already common knowledge – the 'friend' who had enticed him into teaching him the 'ten precious movements' had since published them. At Ma's request Qiu had performed them in front of all of us in his widely open practice. This did not prevent him, on a later occasion, from forbidding me to show the movements to anyone except – and this exception is crucial – if circumstances some time in the future were to force me to make my livelihood by giving classes on *qigong*. There were also various degrees of communicating the Daoist incantations. Qiu let me photocopy the verses and eventually even agreed to let me study and translate them; he explained to me that this form of 'giving away' (*wang wai zhuan*) the secrets of his master was not a betrayal (although he was a bit in doubt of this during the ten days when he had no clients). He maintained that only the orally transmitted verses were endowed with magical power; in their written form they had no power.

The conviction that words have power only if correctly pronounced prevents a critical evaluation of the content of the spells: 'Ritual didn't fail because you used the wrong invocation, but because you didn't use it properly' (Luhrmann 1989:253). Lewis (1980:22) points to the distinction between 'type' and 'token': 'Not every property that can be predicated of the performance must necessarily belong to the type.' The written verses in Qiu's booklet were a commodity that contained knowledge of the type; the verses recited during a healing session were tokens. The effect of a token could be evaluated in terms of whether the client was cured or not. If only the power of the token counts, how can one examine the power of the type? The authority of those who have knowledge is thus secured from any doubt.

The secret transmission of knowledge legitimates the right of those who have access to knowledge, secures their authority, and hinders uncontrolled distribution of knowledge. It strengthens group identity. Secretly transmitted knowledge is often orally transmitted, and this requires a face-to-face relationship, generally within a small group. In the case of Qiu and Qiudi, the secret knowledge was transmitted in a relation of kinship. The relation between master and disciple was primarily one between senior and junior kin. The incantations were viewed as a commodity that could be possessed and was finite. It was possible to appropriate this commodity by imitation and repetition (memorisation). Knowing did not mean understanding. Knowing how to recite incantations consisted in knowing how to pronounce them correctly and how to invoke the forces that effected change. It also consisted in awareness of the unpredictability of the results of one's actions. This style of knowing entailed risk of self-destruction for those who acquired it, but it was considered extremely powerful.

Excursus: secrets and social relations

Research on Qiu's family practice threw light on aspects of the sociology of secrecy that are not directly relevant for identifying the modalities of secret knowledge but are nevertheless worth mentioning. If we view the secret, as Simmel (1950:331) did, as 'a general sociological form', it is not the contents of the secret but the mere fact that one person has a secret and the other is excluded from it that is significant. Secrecy concerns a relationship between at least two people; a person who makes a secret and a person who is excluded.

An individual may guard a secret for life and take it to the grave, but more often secrets are revealed, albeit to different degrees. Bellman (1975, 1984), unlike Simmel (1950), does not emphasise so much the boundary between those initiated into a secret and those excluded. He points out how eminently important the communication of secrets is and calls this the 'paradox of secrecy'. He considers anything that is purposefully concealed and only partially communicated a form of secrecy. It may be socially approved, as in the case of discretion, politeness, and encouraging praise (instead of tactlessness), or socially disapproved, as in the case of deceit, pretence, and hypocrisy (instead of truthfulness). 'Parables, dilemma tales, pretalk in palavers, gnomic expressions, exaggerated descriptions, allegorical accounts' all communicate information that is 'not immediately observable by direct examination of the linguistic code'. These different styles of verbal communication represent, according to Bellman (1984:139), different *forms* of revealing the concealed.

Just as there are different forms of revealing the concealed in verbal communication, there are various forms of social relationships that are established when secrets are communicated to others. In the following, secrecy is not simply associated with the politics of power, its most conspicuous aspect. Creating and maintaining a secret can also be a weapon of the weak and a form of personal adornment.

Family secrets – secrecy as attribute of those in power

Qiu's case cannot be taken as typical of the handing down of medical knowledge in the agnatic line because he did not learn his secret knowledge from his father. He 'venerated' (*baifang*) many 'masters' (*shifu*) and was proud of it.[36] As we have seen, there were two masters to whom Qiu was deeply committed: one was a *wushu* master, an 'old friend' (*laopengyou*) of his grandfather and the other a neighbour, the senior doctor Luo, who became friends with his grandfather and was the father of one of his bond brothers. In typical families of Chinese doctors, I was told, medical knowledge was transmitted to boys, who would help their parents from early childhood onward; girls were excluded because they would later marry into other families. In Yunnan, people would illustrate the Socialist 'progressiveness' of southern China in comparison with northern China by pointing out that daughters-in-law there were more likely to have access to the family treasure of secret medical knowledge.[37] My observations did not corroborate this: Qiu made the diagnoses on which his *qigong* treatment was based, while Jade Blossom was busy with delivering acumoxa treatment to those who needed it. In another case, a senior doctor took the Pulse and wrote the formulary while his wife was kept busy preparing and weighing the various ingredients of such prescriptions, and in yet another case, a smart young woman would attract clients on the street with a strange machine for ear diagnostics while her husband, an itinerant doctor, treated them in a room on the first floor of a hostel, often after an additional Pulse and Tongue diagnosis. In all these cases, the doctors had married much younger women (nine, fifty, and twenty years younger respectively), who helped run their private practices but were too busy with their own activities to learn their husbands' secret knowledge.[38] The secret knowledge that enabled a doctor to provide effective treatment and become prestigious was confined to the males in the family.

---

[36] Naquin (1976:37) says that converts, particularly those 'who specialized in the fighting skills of the White Lotus tradition', had only one teacher at a time but several in sequence. I noticed this attitude among many healers in Kunming and find it characteristic of the personal rather than the secret mode of the transmission of knowledge, considering the strain on family loyalty which arises from venerating many masters.

[37] North–South differences are widely acknowledged (e.g. Goody 1990:105–10). Goody (1990:109, table 4) notes a higher divorce rate, more frequent remarriage, and weaker affinity in the South, possibly related to the absence there of strong competitive lineages.

[38] In their ethnography on rural Yunnan, Fei and Chang (1949:22, 36, 66) remark on the amount women worked, even in wealthy families, although the additional labour did not enhance their status significantly.

Secret societies – secrecy as a weapon of the weak

The secret knowledge that Qiu shared with his bond brothers was in a booklet of Daoist incantations. Their master had apparently been a member of a local Daoist group, but Qiu and his bond brothers had, to my knowledge, no ties to this Daoist tradition; a building on the site of the local temple had been transformed into a public toilet. Although their individual life histories had eroded the loyalties among them, their group had some features of a so-called 'secret society', a term that still enjoys great popularity in the Western literature but is best replaced by more specific, indigenous terms.[39] In Imperial times, *jiao* (sects) were congregations for religious purposes, often organised in ways which were not approved by Confucian orthodoxy (Naquin 1976:41–2).[40] *Hui*, as 'triads', formed an important alternative to kinship for poor peasants and for the marginal and mobile transients in town (Wakeman 1972), but they were not limited to criminals, rebels, and the poor and destitute of the floating population. As Ownby (1993) stresses, *hui*, as 'associations', were also fraternities that were fully embedded in law-abiding communities. Their ethics stressed mutual aid and lifelong solidarity, reinforced by blood oaths or tattoos.

Qiu and his bond brothers are likely to have constituted such a 'fraternity' (*hui*) on a very small scale. Qiu had a tattoo of a sword on his left arm and so did Luo. Though their personal relations were strained, some of Qiu's actions are intelligible only by assuming a very strong bond between them.[41] Their group certainly had a mutual-aid character, and although the three avoided each other in the late 1980s, it seemed that their solidarity was supposed to be lifelong. Notably, it

---

[39] 'Secret societies' tend to be conceived of as tightly organised groups outside the central control of the state (e.g. Dunstheimer 1972), but the term lacks a clear definition. It blurs, for instance, distinctions between *jiao* (sects) and *hui* (associations) (Naquin 1976:268). It also has discriminatory connotations; Qiu would vehemently deny that he and his bond brothers constituted a *mimi shehui* (secret society).

[40] The agenda of society members, as recorded by Naquin (1976:24–31), applied also to Qiu and his bond brothers: protective incantations, meditation practices, massage and other healing techniques, and boxing. However, the structure of such sects was fundamentally hierarchical: 'Fellow believers, even pupils of the same teacher, did not refer to one another as "brothers"' (p. 41). This was not the case among Qiu's master's bond brothers. F. L. K. Hsu (1983:23) suggests that what he earlier identified as public 'prayer meetings' were, in fact, '*jiao* meetings' which seems to imply that some *jiao* and their priests would, in times of crisis such as the cholera epidemic in West town, openly fulfil functions for the community at large.

[41] For example Qiu's inviting Luo's family to a separate wedding banquet after his wedding and his paying thousands of *yuan* to Long towards an enterprise he obviously did not want to get involved in.

was very difficult to find out anything about this brotherhood, and everything I was told bordered on the fantastic.

If one takes the *jiao* and the *hui* as groupings of the unorthodox and the weak, their secrecy is best viewed as a form of protection in a hostile environment. Secrecy here is upheld by those who fear destruction, a weapon of the weak.

Secrecy in self-cultivation – secrecy as adornment

To a certain extent, the secrecy in which *qigong* was veiled was also important to Qiu as an individual. Secrecy heightened the value of his knowledge and operated as a 'purely socially determined attraction', because 'for many individuals, property does not gain its significance with mere ownership, but only with the consciousness that others must do without it . . . what is denied to many must have special value' (Simmel 1950:332). By the mere claim that his knowledge was secret, Qiu drew a boundary between himself and others and thereby increased his importance. Qiu demonstrated with his healing performances that he had a secret. His gestures were strong and elegant, pregnant with a meaning that was not revealed. Simmel (1950:337) comments: 'The secret also operates as an adorning possession and value of the personality. This fact involves the contradiction that . . . one should appear as a particularly noteworthy person precisely through what one conceals.' Qiu's gestures clearly operated as an adorning possession. They increased the value of his personality. Observing simultaneously the client's upright posture and calm face, one was put at ease and felt respect for both Qiu and the client.

The idea that *qigong* healing performances are an adornment to the healer generally goes unmentioned in the literature, but these aesthetics are not to be underestimated. They attract the eye of even the casual passer-by and thereby ensure the necessary audience for the ritual performance (as which *qigong* healing is presented in this monograph). More important, as Simmel (1950:338) points out, 'Adornment has, in fact, a societal significance with a structure analogous to that of secrecy itself.' Like any secret, adornment 'singles out its wearer, whose self-feeling it embodies and increases at the cost of others', but unlike most secrets, it is not only egotistic but altruistic: 'Its pleasure is designed for others' (p. 339). The healer presents himself as outstanding 'not by means of power manifestations, not by anything that externally compels the other, but only through the pleasure which is engendered in him [the other] . . . One adorns oneself for oneself, but can do so only by adornment for others. It is one of the strangest sociological combinations that an act, which exclusively serves the emphasis and increased significance of the actor, nevertheless attains this goal just as exclusively in the pleasure, in the visual delight it offers to others, and in their gratitude.' Though directed at the other, adornment ultimately 'intensifies and enlarges the impression of the personality by operating as a sort of radiation emanating from it' (Simmel 1950:339). *Qigong* healing performances enlarge the impression of the personalities involved, both the healer and the client. In the case of self-cultivation, the aesthetic aspect is substantiated in the scents, for example, of jasmine blossoms, which in certain circumstances may emanate from the *qigong* master's body.[42] The production of such scents, more than a side effect of *qigong* meditation, may be a goal of *qigong* practice in itself.

Qiu's claim and his performative demonstration of possessing a secret that others did not have, enlarged the social distance between him and others. Social distance may lead to alienation, but Qiu was able to bridge this gap precisely because his healing performances were a form of adornment. Like any adornment, they were marked by their 'being-for-the-other'. They had affinity with 'the flash of the precious stone . . . directed at the other', which 'carries the social meaning of jewels, the being-for-the-other', and 'returns to the subject as an enlargement of his own sphere of significance'. Their brilliance and radiation increased the social distance between the healer and others, but healing performances were staged for the sake of others. They signified, like jewellery, 'in one and the same act, an increase in distance' and simultaneously 'a favour' (Simmel 1950:342). This aspect of adornment is probably intrinsic to many healing performances.

---

[42] Qiu did not claim to have this ability, but I was assured by clients of another *qigong* master that they had smelt orange blossoms in his presence.

2   *Qigong* and the concept of *qi*

Qiu's *qigong* healing performances left observers puzzled, wondering how Qiu's murmurs and movements could have a therapeutic effect. This chapter first accounts for *qigong* from the outsider's viewpoint by identifying five stages of social interaction in the therapeutic process. The insider's view, discussed thereafter, explores Qiu's 'logic' of healing. There is evidence that it was primarily grounded in the notion of 'life-for-life', although Qiu also spoke about restoring balance, as is characteristic of Chinese medicine or any other scholarly medical tradition. The concept of *qi* and how it relates to conceptions of the body in *qigong* and Chinese medicine is explored at the end of the chapter.

The outsider's observations

Qigong therapy was not passively consumed but characterised by interaction between healer and client. As an outsider I could observe five different stages: (1) the client's choice of therapy, (2) the healer's effort to recruit clients, (3) mutual commitment, and (4) reaching consensus about the termination of treatment. Yet, even if treatment was successful, the healer–client relation was often not dissolved. The last stage concerned (5) the conversion of client into 'friend' (*pengyou*).

(1)   Choice of therapy

Most of Qiu's clients had turned to *qigong* as a last resort after consulting all kinds of other therapists. Many had previously sought treatment in government hospitals. Depending on the ailment they suffered, they had consulted biomedical and/or TCM doctors and private practitioners of 'Chinese medicine' (*zhongyi*), 'herbal medicine' (*caoyi*), or traditional 'massage' (*anmo*). Only a few had been to another *qigong* healer. In general, they suffered from psychosomatic syndromes such as 'insomnia' (*shimian*), 'headaches' (*touteng*), and what Chinese biomedical doctors call 'neurasthenia' (*shenjing shuairuo*); chronic ailments such as 'rheumatism' (*fengshibing*), 'high blood pressure' (*gaoxueya*), 'hyperosteogeny' (*guzhi zengsheng*), 'hearing loss' (*erlong*), 'myopia' (*jinshi*), 'stomach ulcers' (*weikuiyang*), 'epilepsy' (*dianxian*), 'asthma' (*chuan*); or terminal diseases such as 'cancer' (*aizheng*). Apart from the clients coming from elsewhere in the city or, occasionally, from distant counties, seeking *qigong* treatment, Qiu's practice was also frequented by neighbours requesting primary health care. They would want Qiu to bandage a wound or would ask for an aspirin or for an injection of antibiotics. They often made up the audience of *qigong* performances and thereby enhanced Qiu's prestige, but they rarely asked for *qigong* treatment.

Qigong was a stigmatised therapy, repressed during the Cultural Revolution and in the late 1980s often met with ambivalence. Valid criteria for separating the upright practitioner from the swindler have not been and are unlikely ever to be found. Even those who declared a belief in the effects of *qigong* were aware of the risk of falling victim to quacks. Most followed the advice of a neighbour, relative, or friend who had been successfully treated. When asked why they had chosen *qigong*, several answered that they had been told that Qiu was a good doctor. Many clients had not known that *qigong* could be delivered in healing performances. Their choice of therapy depended more on their knowing the person and personality offering the therapy than on the rationale of the therapy itself.

(2) Forms of recruitment

Qiu cared about maintaining a reputation for respectability. First, his dress indicated status, he wore a white coat, and obviously not for hygenic reasons – it had hardly been washed more than twice that year. Then, his therapy commanded very prestigious prices (usually ten *yuan* per session), more than twice as much as 'acumoxa' (*zhenjiu*), 'massage' (*tuina*), and 'herbal drug' (*caoyao*) treatment combined. He also behaved like a person of authority, as is expected of the senior male in a household. Qiu and his wife divided their labour as Qiu's parents did rather than according to the Socialist model of emancipation. Cooking, washing, household finances, and child rearing were the wife's and mother's obligations and, despite occasional angry outbursts from his wife, Qiu consistently refrained from almost all household work.

Qiu was the social representative of the extended family. This came naturally, since most visitors were either his friends or clients. Jade Blossom, who was from a neighbouring province, had come to Kunming only after graduating from high school. She had no former schoolmates and only two elderly aunts in town. It is not insignificant that Qiu had chosen to marry a girl younger by almost ten years, a pretty accountant at the hospital where he had formerly been employed. Although she had received more formal education than he himself, he felt that he had made her a doctor by paying her fees as a self-funding student for a year, in 1987–8, at the Chengdu TCM College.[1]

Qiu's status was enhanced by his wife in indirect ways. He would smile while she scolded his clients. He remained silent while she informed them about petty technicalities. He received the money, while she was responsible for the accounts and therefore for any accounting mistakes. He was generous and 'cheerful' (*kailang*) while she was loud and sometimes quarrelsome. To fulfil the expectations of being a respectable healer, Qiu depended on his wife.[2]

As master of his practice, Qiu required his clients to adapt to its pace. No one's urgency could disturb him. Clients waited for quarter of an hour to an hour and a half. Admittedly, Chinese medicine requires that the patient rest before treatment, and everywhere in the PRC, whether in a department store or a hospital, clients have to wait. A shop attendant's slowness would annoy a client, but Qiu's was a matter of prestige. In cases of conflict he could not be disturbed by an irate client. His respectability allowed him also to ignore direct questions or answer them as briefly as possible.

Qiu showed no interest in his new clients while, at the same time, he subtly and indirectly persuaded his audience – the potential client included – of the powers of *qigong*. Once he had spotted a potential client, he would either give a very extensive and concentrated *qigong* performance or suddenly start talking about cases of successful *qigong* treatment. The following episode illustrates this point clearly:

Qiu had just come back from the market with a basket full of mushrooms and was now preparing them, squatting in the sun in front of the consulting room. A passer-by who had stopped to read the sign advertising the practice,[3] asked Qiu if he could really treat deafness. Hardly looking at the potential client, Qiu's reply was abrupt, and he went on working on the mushrooms. Then he disappeared into the backyard to wash them while the man remained squatting in the doorway. After a while Qiu came back, handed the mushrooms to his

---

[1] She enrolled as a self-funding student at the Yunnan TCM College from 1990 to 1992 without giving up her acumoxa patients and passed the exams for 'TCM regular practitioner' (*zhongyishi*) in 1993.

[2] On the dialectics between healers and their wives, see Roseman (1991:76–8).

[3] Newly painted in May 1989, it read: 'The therapeutic range of massage, *qigong*, and acumoxa combined with the therapy of acupressure is: 1. internal medicine, gynaecology, paediatrics, 2. five sense organs, external medicine, 3. pain in the shoulder, pain in the lower back and legs, 4. all the various complaints that are difficult to cure, 5. we provide injections, measurement of blood pressure. For the above, we guarantee a sure cure.'

wife, who was cooking behind the counter, removed the needles from a girl whom she was treating with acumoxa for epilepsy, and seated the girl on a stool in the middle of the practice. He now beckoned the man to take a seat on the bench next to me and proceeded to perform a long *qigong* healing session. The man followed his movements with curiosity and scepticism. Thereafter, another client was treated, just as extensively. Now it was the newcomer's turn. He was told to sit straight, put his hands in his lap, one on top of the other, palms upward and open. (notes, September 1988)

Like many others, this client was given time for critical observation and reflection and, at last, also a bit of encouragement, before he agreed to undergo treatment. After all, how can the efficacy of a treatment be ensured? Why trust treatment which is potentially powerful but simultaneously stigmatised? One may consider the client a consumer and set out to persuade him or her to accept treatment, but Qiu was obviously not a merchant. As a healer he knew that he was successful only if his client felt cured. In the end it was the client who decided whether he or she felt better or not. Clients were given time, in the very beginning, to decide what chances they themselves gave this unusual treatment. The outcome of the treatment was thus largely determined before treatment had begun.

Usually, a client had to commit himself to pay for a cycle of ten treatments before being treated at all (offered at a discount rate of 65 *yuan* in 1988 and 85 *yuan* by the end of 1989). One occasion that is in retrospect very telling occurred when I, the 'innocent anthropologist', intervened:

A possible client had been standing for a very long time in front of Qiu's practice, hesitating but tempted. 'Why don't you give it a try?' I asked when I passed him on the way to the backyard to wash some fresh vegetables. Returning quarter of an hour later, I continued: 'What, you're still here!' This client eventually picked one *yuan* note after another out of his purse. After I had done all this preparatory work of persuasion, Qiu exceptionally agreed to treat this person for one session only. He had the patient sit on the stool in the middle of the room and told him to relax and close his eyes. 'Relax', he said, hitting the client's shoulder very hard: 'Relax!' The man sat stiff as a tailor's dummy. After the session he exclaimed loudly: 'I don't feel a bit better!' At this, Qiu laughed, just as he had been laughing throughout the session. He had reciprocated the client's lack of commitment. The client became very angry and wanted his money back. Now it was the healer's wife's turn to act and she drove him away with curses. (notes, April 1989)

The principle of treating only committed clients is ancient wisdom. 'Never treat those who believe in shamans and not in doctors.' Qiu did not refer to Bian Que's sixth principle of ethics (*Shi ji* 105 (Sima 1959:2794) but clearly acted in accordance with it.

(3)   Mutual commitment

The above-mentioned client suffering from Deafness (*erlong*) and Ringing in the Ears (*erming*) reported that his ears had started ringing more than ten years ago while he was in military service, probably because of the shooting. Several years after retirement from service,[4] he went hunting and, after firing his gun, he suddenly lost the hearing in his right ear. He had sought treatment in several hospitals, but neither Western nor Chinese medicine had relieved his symptoms. He had always declined to be treated by acumoxa and continued to do so, but eventually he agreed to *qigong* treatment.

During this session, which began like all others, Qiu suddenly interrupted the flow of his movements, took a needle out of the drawer of the table behind him, and stuck it with an elegant movement and few words of warning into *tinggong*, an acu-point in a groove in front of the deaf ear. The man shivered; Qiu laughed and continued his performance. After the session, the client's hearing was obviously much better. 'My hearing improved the very moment you stuck the needle into my ear', he kept repeating. Qiu ignored him. Later, when other potential clients asked him whether he could cure deafness with *qigong*, he would tell the story of this case without, however, mentioning his having needled the ear.

Although the client had never allowed anyone to needle him, he had accepted it during a *qigong* session. He had certainly not expected it and Qiu had gained his compliance by a reinterpretation: his needling was part of a *qigong* healing session and not acumoxa therapy. I doubt that Qiu knew from the start that he was going to use a needle. It was the only time I ever saw him resort to needling during a healing performance. The intuition that this was the right thing to do in this case remains a puzzle but it was by no means unique to this episode.

Reinterpretation of his clients' ailments was among the main achievements of Qiu's therapy. The following case, which illustrates this nicely, shows how Chinese medical reasoning tied in with the everyday life experiences of Qiu's clientele:

I arrived to find Qiu massaging a young woman on the cot behind the curtain. When I entered the practice, he stopped. He refused to talk to me about what he was doing, but the client was quite willing to tell me about herself. She had

---

[4] The army recruited soldiers in their late teens and released most of them after eight years. It was the major institution in the PRC for peasants from 'townships and villages' (*xiangcun*) to acquire upon retirement a 'household register' (*hukou*) above the administrative level of the 'county' (*xian*), and thereby enabled them to migrate into less rural areas.

had an abortion four months before, and at the hospital she had been diagnosed as suffering from neurasthenia. 'This is wrong', she said. Qiu had given her the correct diagnosis: Blood Depletion giving rise to Wind (*xue xu sheng feng*), which induced 'dizziness' (*tou xuan*) and headaches. She had been in treatment for five days now, taking massage, herbal drugs, and *qigong*. She no longer had headaches except when she was unhappy or angry, but now she 'felt nauseous' (*xiang tu*).

Why did she have an abortion in the fifth month? She said she had had stomach problems and taken many drugs, macerated in alcohol. Her sister, a biomedical doctor, said that so much alcohol would make her child mentally retarded. So she aborted it, but after the abortion, she 'had not gone into confinement' (*zuo yuezi*).

'Disregarding confinement is a typical case for Blood Depletion giving rise to Wind', Jade Blossom commented. 'She went shopping and didn't even cover her head!' She had exposed herself to the wind in the streets and thereby attracted the Wind in her head.[5] This was a layperson's view, based on reasoning reminiscent of sympathetic magic. Chinese medical reasoning is more sophisticated: the client's complaint of a headache is often associated with Wind, a Disease Factor (*bingyin*). When there is Blood Depletion, which is a postulated process inside the body, Wind can arise and tends to ascend to the head, whether or not the patient has been exposed to an outside Wind. Needless to say, the loss of blood during the abortion had caused the Blood Depletion. (notes, August 1989)

Qiu later explained to me that the client had had a drinking problem after being divorced by her husband and subsequently had aborted the child. He showed much affection for this young woman, and his wife, who noticed this too, was eager to have him terminate treatment soon.

Qiu's reinterpretation in Chinese medical terms fitted very well into the client's worldview and reinforced her values. Confinement after birth (traditionally for forty days) is advocated and practised even by Chinese biomedical doctors. This client explained that she had never thought of confinement after an abortion, and I had not heard of it either. Qiu's reinterpretation of this particular case was in several respects quite accurate, however: her experience of the abortion was as a birth, albeit of a dead foetus, and going into confinement would have meant that someone would have had to cook and care for her. She had missed out on this; no allowance had been made for her pain and suffering.

The client could easily relate to Qiu's statement that she suffered from a Blood Depletion. As a technical term, of course, Blood Depletion (*xue xu*) was not directly intelligible to her. She probably understood that it referred to a loss of blood, the blood she herself had seen

---

[5] Wind (*feng*) is one of the most pervasive concepts in Chinese medicine. On the notion of Wind in the *Inner Canon*, see Unschuld (1982); on Wind in Chinese antiquity, see Kuriyama (1994).

flowing. Specialised medical terms were often the same words as those of everyday language, but their meaning was not quite the same. Blood (*xue*) in Chinese medicine did refer to the blood that the patient had seen flowing, but it was also a more encompassing term within a system of similarly encompassing terms. Blood Depletion referred to a state of the person that could be identified by particular diagnostic signs such as a Pale Complexion (*se cangbai*), a Thin Pulse (*mai xi*), and a Pale Tongue (*she danbai*). It may be diagnosed even if the patient has not suffered an obvious blood loss.[6]

The treatment of Blood Depletion also made sense to her: it was common knowledge that a diet of eggs, meat (particularly liver and fish), and 'red sugar' (*hongtang*)[7] would restore her Blood. She also drank the Blood-restoring drug potions, although she complained that they were 'too bitter' (*tai kuliao*). She was not only given massage and *qigong* but also learned some *qigong* movements to practise on her own. Qiu's cheerfulness and sympathy obviously lifted her spirits, and her evening meditation at home, she said, enabled her to fall asleep. In contrast, the Western neuroleptic drugs she had been taking had only increased her dizziness.

Reinterpretations of an ailment such as the above not only restructured the clients' illness experience but also helped Qiu to gain their compliance and engage them actively in their therapy. The above two cases show, moreover, that not only the client but also the healer was committed. Sometimes his commitment became manifest in his intuitions, as in the first case. In the second case, it was remarkable how often he complained about headaches and fatigue during the period of her treatment. Several months before, I had witnessed the same attitude towards another patient:

Qiu had been complaining of severe pain in his shoulder. His wife, familiar with the sort of compassion he could develop for his clients went through a mental list of them and guessed that it was an old man's 'periarthritis of the shoulder' (*jianzhouyan*) which had induced his pain. An hour later, I was amazed when this very client, within seconds of seating himself on the bench to await treatment began to complain of an unusual pain in his shoulder the night before. (notes, March 1989)

---

[6] A Distinguishing Pattern (*bianzheng*) such as Blood Depletion giving rise to Wind does not contain any information on the etiology of the condition (see also Farquhar 1994a:86–91). Rather, it contains a therapeutic maxim: if a doctor 'diagnoses' Blood Depletion, this means that the therapy should be directed at restoring the Blood.

[7] Brown sugar. Calling it 'red' (*hong*), links it with happiness and wealth and, in medical terms, with enlivening *yang* qualities. On food that is 'invigorating' or 'supplementing' (*bu*), see Anderson (1988:235–8).

It is unlikely that this episode was staged to impress. Whilst I did observe this capacity for empathy among other *qigong* masters, it was by no means evident in all of them, and Qiu certainly did not have it with every client.[8]

(4)   Reaching consensus

Many patients came for treatment for several months, others sporadically for years. One had been in fairly regular treatment for over a year. Chronic ailments and psychosomatic syndromes are naturally not cured overnight, nor do they necessarily disappear completely. At a certain point in time, however, the decision to cease treatment has to be taken. To make this decision, patient and healer have to reach agreement over the patient's condition.

When one feels absolutely cured or considers oneself cured despite lingering pain, the treatment has been successful and can be ended. When this is not the case, one may want to continue treatment if one considers it the appropriate one, cease treatment with one healer and seek it with another one, or give up seeking treatment altogether. This sounds simple, but it has implications not always easily assessed. If one feels cured, is one really cured? If one does not feel cured, is the problem the specific therapy or the choice of practitioner, or is it perhaps that no cure is possible?

Considering the cases reported so far, it is apparent that the 'therapeutic efficacy' of a treatment from a biomedical point of view need not necessarily coincide with 'therapeutic success'.[9] Ma, for instance, certainly felt better after several weeks of treatment, but she still had pain in the shoulder and could not lift her arm much higher (see pp. 34–40). From a biomedical point of view the *qigong* treatment was not efficacious. This would not, however, do justice to Ma's case. After the excitement over Qiudi's successful first healing session she stopped seeking treatment with anyone. Despite an improvement only in degree, her behaviour

---

[8] Some *qigong* healers exploited this capability of empathy systematically for diagnostic purposes. According to TCM, parts of the face, ears, or hands represent the Inner Organs (*neizang*). The five fingers, for instance, represent the Lungs (*fei*), the Heart (*xin*), the Spleen (*pi*), the Liver (*gan*), and the Kidneys (*shen*). By touching the client's finger with the index finger of one hand and observing the change of colour patterns in the fingertips of the other, a *qigong* healer may diagnose the state of balance in the corresponding Organ of the patient.

[9] For a proposal to distinguish the biomedically assessed 'therapeutic efficacy' and the social scientist's assessment of 'therapeutic success', see Hsu (1996b).

changed from that of an ill to that of a healthy person. In this respect, Qiu and Qiudi could claim that their therapy had been successful.[10]

This need not mean that the patient's subjective point of view alone can alter the course of an illness. In Bao's case, for instance (see pp. 42–4), general agreement among other clients, the encouraging talk of Jade Blossom, and Qiu's reconfirmation that the Liver had 'softened' (nen) and shrunk assured him that he had regained Spirit (shen). His wife certainly felt that he was better, and when I asked him if he was he nodded. At the time Qiu spoke of a successful treatment. However, in terms of a biomedical assessment it is doubtful that Bao could have been cured. In the case of the young woman suffering from chronic fatigue and headaches (see pp. 62–4), Qiu's wife eventually decided that the woman's condition had improved immensely, and refused to allow Qiu to continue treating her. In still another case, presented below, agreement that the treatment would last for one cycle of ten treatments at most was achieved at the very beginning.

These examples illustrate that the criteria for terminating treatment are manifold and complex. Biomedically efficacious treatments need not necessarily be therapeutically successful. Success is a matter for negotiation among the participants involved in a therapy (the client, the healer and his wife, fellow clients, and the client's relatives and friends). Well-being depends on reaching consensus about the client's condition among the client, the healer, and the other participants in the therapeutic process.

(5)   From patient to pengyou

As the treatment comes to an end, however, the relation between the healer and his clients is generally not interrupted. Qiu's former clients kept returning to his practice; some quite regularly, others once in six months, as did Ma and her husband. Some recommended him to their friends and relatives and sometimes introduced them personally to Qiu for a first assessment. Others entered into economic transactions with Qiu. One, for instance, enabled him to buy drugs wholesale from his work unit; another sold him cigarettes at a lower price, and still another, who owned a restaurant, was at his disposal when he had to treat a friend to a banquet.

Qiu's recruitment of clients was basically dependent on former clients' word of mouth. It came naturally for a client to praise the healer

---

[10] Many cases recorded in the anthropological literature point to the same phenomenon, see for instance Favret-Saada (1980: section 6.2).

who had provided successful treatment, and it would be wrong to speak of any unwritten rule that a cured client was expected to ensure the continuation of Qiu's practice by oral recommendation. Yet, natural as it may appear, such behaviour can be interpreted as a way in which clients paid their debts to the healer.

One may wonder why a client, after having terminated treatment, should still be indebted to the healer. The treatment had been extremely costly: why continue paying him tribute in the form of visits or good press? It is precisely this high cost of treatment that suggests that a *qigong* healer's therapeutic intervention is distinct from that of a medical doctor. A *qigong* healer's therapy cannot be paid for with money. The price of it, it seems, is the client's lifelong indebtedness. A *qigong* healer, like a shaman, is building community through his treatment. To understand this, let us explore the *qigong* healer's point of view.

The insider's view

Qiu's explanations for his actions were extremely sparse. Therefore I tried to make sense of his gestures. Some gestures indicated that treatment was directed at extracting bad 'stuff' (see Sivin 1987:47) from the body. Others indicated that good, enlivening powers were being transferred into the patient. Finally, there were gestures, circular movements with both arms around the client, that looked as if Qiu was harmonising vibrations within and about the client. These gestures and Qiu's comments on them led me to the conclusion that the 'logic' of his healing built on three different conceptions of the body and the universe (see table 2.1). The circular gestures seemed to build on a notion that the body and the universe are, as macrocosm and microcosm, in mutual resonance. Qiu himself did not comment on these gestures. The two concepts he spoke of were Bad *qi* (*xieqi*) and Primordial *qi* (*yuanqi*).[11] These concepts share the features of being by definition good or bad – Bad *qi* is never beneficial and Primordial *qi* cannot be excessive – and of occurring within a conceptual framework in which the inside and the outside world are viewed as opposites and not, like macrocosm and microcosm, as analogous.

Bad *qi* (*xieqi*) is associated with illness as affliction and an act of healing through extraction or, in *qigong*, diversion. The inside world needs to be protected from the bad stuff that comes from the dangerous outside world. Primordial *qi* (*yuanqi*), by contrast, is associated with

---

[11] Qiu never opposed the two terms but in his explanations they shared the feature of both having an absolute value: good or bad.

Table 2.1. *Notions of healing*

Notion of Illness	Treatment	Conception of the Universe
Affliction	Extraction of Bad *qi*	Inside seen in opposition to a dangerous Outside
Loss of Vitality	Transmission of Primordial *qi*	Inside seen in opposition to an enlivening Outside
Disharmony	Regulation of the Orchestra of *qi*	Microcosm–Macrocosm

illness arising from a loss of vitality, and healing consists of a transference of enlivening powers. The inside world of the body receives vitality from an outside world that is uncultivated and in this sense wild and full of life. In both cases healing is directed at effecting a transition of *qi* across the boundary between the inside and the outside world. Qiu's *qigong* healing is hence best viewed as a ritual activity that is primarily concerned with effecting the transition of *qi* across a boundary. This 'logic' of healing by crossing boundaries is inherent in many folk medicines (e.g. Lambert 1992). It can be found in Chinese medicine too, though Chinese medicine is primarily directed at regulating complex processes analogous to microcosm and macrocosm.[12]

Bad qi *and illness as affliction*

Xieqi is generally presented as the opposite of *zhengqi*; therefore Porkert (1974:54) and Sivin (1987:49) translate it as Heteropathic as opposed to Orthopathic *qi*.[13] This opposition of medical terms parallels that of moral ones: the Confucian values were 'orthodox' (*zheng*), those of other traditions 'heterodox' (*xie*). Qiu rarely used the term *zhengqi*, however,

---

[12] Both *qigong* and Chinese medicine include the entire range of notions of healing listed in table 2.1. The difference is emphasis. Although Chinese medical doctrine builds primarily on the analogy of microcosm and macrocosm – with the quality of *qi* depending on its location – it recognises also *xieqi* and *yuanqi*. In their discussion of Disease Factors, Sivin (1987:275–85) and Farquhar (1994a:86–7) present these two notions as predominant in Chinese medical reasoning, which reflects the contents of TCM textbooks emphasising the 'dialectics' between *zheng* and *xie* (see below). However, as far as I can tell, such 'dialectics' were not nearly as prominent in medical practice, and certainly not in Qiu's practice.

[13] See *TCM Fundamentals* (Yin 1984:102–3), section on 'Principles concerning the Disease Development' (*fa bing yuanli*). Notably, not discussed in the same section as *yuanqi*, which is discussed in the section on 'The Distribution and Kinds of *qi*' (*qide fenbu he fenlei*).

and it seemed to me that *xie* in his mind might have some moral connotation. Translating *xieqi* colloquially in this context as 'Bad *qi*' (morally not as definite as Evil *qi*) is consistent with his use of it. *Xieqi* is *qi* that invades the body from outside. It is best kept outside the body and, if it has penetrated it, best completely expelled. Illness is understood as affliction; something bad has penetrated the body, and curing the illness consists in its extraction. This principle of Qiu's *qigong* healing has many parallels in other cultures: the Kwakiutl shaman Quesalid performed tricks that consisted of spitting out a bloody worm in a small bundle of feathers, identified as the pathological substance that had induced sickness in his clients (Lévi-Strauss (1958)1963:175), and Azande medicine men learnt how to use ointments to rub out bad things – charcoal pieces, for instance – from their patients (Evans-Pritchard 1937:230–1). A simplistic knowledge of modern germ theory builds on this understanding of illness as affliction too: bad germs invade a weak body.[14]

Once the bad *qi* has been extracted from the body, it is not actually destroyed, but transformed or diverted. Several gestures in Qiu's *qigong* performances indicated an extraction and subsequent diversion of *qi*. At the beginning of a *qigong* session, Qiu always first asked the name of the client and then told him to keep his eyes shut throughout the session. Then he himself would close his eyes for a moment and lift his right arm above his head, palm up. He would murmur a spell and make a gesture of throwing something on the head of the client. From then on one gesture evolved out of another without interruption until he terminated the session. After the first throwing gesture, he always drew with outstretched index and middle fingers a circle that he called a *fu* (sign) in the air above the client's head. In the case of the woman suffering shoulder pain, he then drew a complicated figure, again a *fu*, at the centre of the pain and began pulling and pushing with his opened palms in the air around the afflicted area, towards and away from it. He repeated this gesture for several minutes while smiling at neighbours passing by, greeting other clients, or even chatting with one of his many visitors. In some sessions he used a repeated stroking motion with both opened palms down the length of the arm of the injured shoulder, still without touching it. Then he put his right hand on her shoulder, touching it for several minutes, with his left hand on his own back. Finally, to terminate the session, he folded away his right hand and simultaneously

---

[14] Ohnuki-Tierney (1984:26), in her chapter on 'Japanese germs', astutely remarks that Japanese wear masks to prevent the intrusion of the bad 'germs' from the outside world (by contrast to Western biomedical surgeons, who wear them to prevent the transmission of their own bad germs).

blew onto the client's shoulder, instructing her to blow into the air immediately afterward.[15]

When asked to explain, Qiu said that he held his palm up at the beginning of a session to gather the '*qi* of the universe' (*yuzhou zhi qi*) that he threw on the patient.[16] The *qi* of the universe had enlivening powers, like *yuanqi*. For the following gesture of drawing a circle above the patient's head Qiu had no explanation, but it was obvious that he was drawing the boundary between the inside and the outside world. What he did with a gesture of the hand, Azande medicine men do with sticks and kicks, keeping the crowd of spectators off their square ritual dance ground (Evans-Pritchard 1937:156); he was measuring out a space for ritual activity (see also Obeyesekere 1969:178–9).

Qiu explained that he had to 'emit *qi*' (*fa qi*) during a *qigong* session. This *qi*, his own precious Primordial *qi*, he directed from his index and middle fingers, as if it came out of a gun, onto certain parts of the body, often onto acu-points or onto the particular spot of pain, always without touching the patient. With this gun-formed gesture he also drew the *fu* into the air.

The gestures which were most transparent indicated that Qiu was extracting bad stuff from the body. He explained that gestures of stroking downwards along a limb indicated the intention to divert the Bad *qi*. It was usually led towards the ground, which was dark and *yin*. I suddenly understood why sometimes the *yinqi* from the ground, associated with rheumatism, for instance, had connotations of Bad *qi*. In acumoxa treatments too, Jade Blossom explained, Bad *qi* was drawn downwards and outwards from the deeper parts of the Circulation Tracts (*jing*) to their shallower parts.[17] Bad *qi* could also be extracted locally from the body, but, I was told, only when mingled with blood, usually by certain 'cupping' (*huoguan*) or acumoxa treatments.

I also saw a *qigong* healer who not only diverted the *xieqi* as Qiu did but took it up into his own body by leading it from the fingertips of one hand through his outstretched arm into the fingertips of the other hand and towards the ground behind him. Alternatively, he took it up into his arm and shook it off before it penetrated into the deeper parts of the system of Tracts and Links (*jingluo*), at the *he* acu-points around the elbow. The evidence from other healers indicated also that the diversion

[15] Compare with Creery's description of the *hoat-su*'s of the Dance of the Five Forts (1973:29).

[16] Qiu did not explain why he used the right hand. Creery (1973:129) comments on a similar opening gesture that the right side is the active one.

[17] Since patients in acumoxa clinics often lay on beds, *xieqi* was diverted not towards the ground but towards the extremities.

of *xieqi* was one of the central activities during a *qigong* healing session. Once it had been diverted, the inside world was cleansed and health was restored.

Primordial qi *and the transmission of well-being*

The ritual activities of a *qigong* healing session comprised more than a cleansing of the body. This becomes obvious from the gestures described above and the second central concept that figured in Qiu's explanations: *yuanqi*. He emitted Primordial *qi* to manipulate Bad *qi* and also to transmit it directly: for instance, by laying a hand on the painful part of the body.

In a non-medical text from the Han dynasty (206 BC – AD 220) Primordial *qi* is the *qi* of the origins before there was Heaven and Earth (*Han shu* 21 (Ban 1962:964)). In medicine, the *locus classicus* for its definition is the *Classic of Difficult Issues* (*Nan jing*): 'As to the Gate of Life (*mingmen*), it is the housing of the Essences and Spirits and the connection to *yuanqi*, in the man it is for storing the Essence, in the woman for connecting with the Uterus' (*Nan jing* 36 (Nanjing zhongyi xueyuan yijing jiaoyanzu 1961:90)). The concept of the Gate of Life was much elaborated in the late Ming dynasty (1368–1644) and attributed the vital importance indicated by its name.[18] Among TCM doctors, Zhang Jiebin's (1563–1640) definition was most likely to be cited: 'The Fire of the Gate of Life, is called *yuanqi*, the Water of the Gate of Life is called *jing* (Essence)' (Yin 1984:42). *Nan jing* 36 stated the opposition of *jing* and *yuanqi* as the one between 'man' (*nanzi*) and 'woman' (*nüzi*), Zhang Jiebin stressed it as one between Water (*shui*) and Fire (*huo*). In all these citations, *yuanqi* had to do with coming to life.

In a Jin dynasty (265–460) text, *yuanqi* is opposed to the *qi* that is acquired by ingesting the *qi* of the Grains (*guqi*).[19] This opposition between *yuanqi* and *guqi* was later elaborated into the opposition between *xiantian* (Primordial State) and *houtian* (Worldly State).[20] *Xiantian* is the state of the unborn, and *yuanqi* is acquired in this state of being. *Houtian* is the state after birth (Tao, p.c.) or after the ingestion of food other than mother's milk (Cao, p.c.) or, in other contexts, after first sexual intercourse (Zhang, p.c.). *Houtian* is a state of the intermingling

---

[18] Discussed in small print in an appendix to Kidneys (*shen*) in the *TCM Fundamentals* (Yin 1984:39–43), it was rarely mentioned in the classroom. It was more often referred to in medical practice.

[19] *Wu li lun* (*Treatise on the Patterns of Things*) by Yang Quan, cited in *Tai ping yu lan* 837 (Li (1963)1985:4.3740).

[20] Probably from the Song dynasty (960–1279) onwards, but still under investigation.

of *yin* and *yang* within one body, and some of my teachers explained that, by opposition, *xiantian* is a state of 'complete *yang*' (*chunyang*). Primordial *qi* is considered essential for living beings. It determines one's general disposition and health and, accordingly, length of life. In the modern understanding it is taken as equivalent to determining one's genetic constitution. Since it is *xiantian*, it is considered something extremely precious that is increasingly exhausted with age. It can be strengthened in later life by certain diets and drugs, and, indeed, I saw Qiu taking Invigorating Drugs frequently although he was in the best of health.

Interestingly, the strengthening of Primordial *qi* by accurate nourishment during the Worldly State is increasingly stressed in TCM textbooks (*TCM Fundamentals* (Yin 1984:57); *Organ Clusters* (Yunnan zhongyi xueyuan 1988:51–2)).[21] This reflects a this-worldly attitude to human life which is not only Marxist but also fundamental to current politics of development aid. It reflects an attitude to life that is typical of modernity.[22] The idea that Primordial *qi* is strengthened in the Worldly State can also be found in the medical archive: '*Zhenqi* (True *qi*), also called *yuanqi* or *jingqi* (Essential *qi*) produced by the primordial self, cannot grow without the Stomach's *qi* (*weiqi*).'[23] Considering the this-worldly attitude of TCM doctors, it is perhaps not surprising that many made frequent reference to Li Gao's *Discussion of the Spleen and Stomach* (*Pi wei lun*).

This understanding of Primordial *qi* is contrasted with that found in texts on self-cultivation. In the Zhangjiashan manuscripts (*Wenwu* 1989, 7:74, cited in Harper 1990b), for instance, self-cultivation is explicitly directed at emptying the Five Depositories (*wuzang*). In a similar vein, Yang Quan (third century) states that one should avoid the *qi* of the Grains which only fattens the body and decreases one's prospects for longevity (see also Engelhardt 1987:157ff.). Qiu was not very rigorous in avoiding the influences of the Worldly State, that is the *qi* of the Grains, but he made it clear that diet and drugs alone would not provide him with the necessary Primoridal *qi* for healing purposes. This he attained only through meditation. Qiu invariably spoke of Invigorating *qi* (*bu qi*), while it was clear that he differentiated between supplementing

---

[21] Primordial *qi* (*yuanqi*) is here also called Original *qi* (*yuanqi*) or True *qi* (*zhenqi*), and differentiated from Gathering *qi* (*zongqi*), Nourishing *qi* (*yingqi*), and Protective *qi* (*weiqi*).

[22] This attitude has a striking parallel in the interpretation of Pali chants in Buddhist rituals of northeastern Thailand: 'The intriguing paradox is that the conquests of Buddha which relate to the withdrawal of life are in the process of transference transmuted into an affirmation of life' (Tambiah 1968:180).

[23] In Li Gao's (1180–1251) *Discussion of the Spleen and Stomach* (Li 1976:296). I thank Ma Kanwen for drawing my attention to this text passage.

Primordial *qi* through drugs and diet (e.g. eggs and sticky rice) and regenerating it through meditation. In this respect his understanding of Primordial *qi* diverged from that in TCM textbooks.

Qiu's notion of Primordial *qi* pointed to a concept of healing that consisted of a crossing of boundaries: the transference of Primordial *qi*. This transference was effected in two complementary ritual acts: the openly shown healing performance and the hidden practice of meditation. During the public healing performance Primordial *qi* was transferred from healer to patient and during meditation Primordial *qi* was restored to the healer.

With regard to the practice of meditation a senior doctor maintained: 'The goal of meditation is to "nurture one's Nature" (*yangxing*). In order to nurture your Nature you have to attain the state of complete *yang*. You need to invert your state of being from the Worldly State into the Primordial State that is complete *yang*.' He spoke in terms of 'inner alchemy' (*neidan*) (discussed in Robinet 1989b). Self-cultivation consists of this inversion through meditation. Vitality is restored through daily regeneration, and repeated regeneration prolongs life. Whereas Christianity has dealt with the problem of immortality by dividing the person into a mortal body and an immortal soul, the Daoist approach 'refuses to search for the absolute in ideas' (Schipper 1982:16). Immortality is achieved through longevity by physical self-cultivation. According to the above idea, coming from inner alchemy, the prolongation of life is achieved not by turning into an enduring thing (like a jade stone), but by repeated inversion and thereby regeneration.

This understanding of the attainment of longevity is found in a text passage on self-cultivation in the *Writings of the King of Huainan* (*Huainan zi* (Anon. 1954:105), italics added): 'The changing returns to the Formless; the unchanging and Heaven and Earth, all give birth. The wood dies, green greening fades away. That which makes the wood give birth, how could it be the wood itself? Again, that which fills the Form has no Form. *Therefore that which gives birth to giving birth never dies.* Whatever it gives birth to then dies. That which changes the things never changes. Whatever it causes to change then changes.'[24]

Meditation is an act that is directed at an inversion, the crossing of the boundary between the Worldly and the Primordial State. This constant return to the Primordial State hinders one from reaching one's full development and allows one to attain longevity. In the case of a healer like Qiu, it was his regeneration during meditation which made his loss of vitality during healing performances reversible.

---

[24] I thank Donald Harper for drawing my attention to this text passage.

With regard to the healing performance, Qiu explained that a *qigong* healer had to emit Primordial *qi* for an effective cure.[25] All the *qigong* healers I met maintained that they endangered their health and prospects for longevity by their therapeutic activities. Novices who had not strengthened their Primordial *qi* long enough before conducting healing sessions were particularly at risk. Even experienced healers were advised not to treat too many patients a day (Qiu said five at most, but he usually treated more). Therefore, the charges for *qigong* treatment were very high.

Qigong healers gave away their vitality, in contrast to doctors who treated their patients by technical regulation of bodily dynamics. In his description of Daoist ritual, Schipper (1982) notes that 'the master uses his own vital force for nourishing the life of the lay people' by writing a *fu* on a yellow strip of paper with a brush dipped in red ink. 'The *fu* is a kind of breath from the master, a distilled and exquisite energy that, taken out of the master's body, compensates accordingly for the lack of energetic breath [*qi*] in the patient. In Daoist rituals, this act is called to "diffuse the Breaths" (*bu qi*) . . . This service costs nothing, since it is a banality, evident, and since payment would not be able anyway to compensate for a gift that is as spontaneous as this one' (pp. 82–3). A Daoist master may say so but an anthropologist may be bothered by the question of how a client can repay this 'gift of life'. I discussed this matter with Qiu. The high charges for treatment were not satisfactory compensation in themselves, Qiu and I agreed. Why, then, since he knew that he was killing himself during his healing performances would he undertake them? Qiu looked at me in surprise, then he shrugged his shoulders and said: 'I am serving the people' (*wei renmin fuwu*) – a Communist slogan that can be understood as reiterating the Daoist master's explanation given above.[26]

Someone else might have considered my question invalid because it overgeneralises the principle of the gift, *do ut des*, and that it cannot be applied to behaviour in non-Western societies. However, the anthropological literature which builds on this principle of reciprocity (Mauss 1950) informs us that clients do recompense their healers, even if only indirectly. Fabrega and Silver (1973), for instance, observed that shamans in Zinacantan were allowed to join the 'cargo' system at an earlier stage in life than laypersons. A successful healer, they explained, was

---

[25] Some healers admitted that they only did so to treat serious cases.
[26] Compare and contrast with a Thai cult of healing through meditation (Tambiah 1977): the *achan*'s powers are gained through meditation (p. 124), and he is a 'merit-laden figure acting on behalf of the world with kindness' (p. 128). The notion of being 'merit-laden' did not figure in Qiu's reasoning.

enabled to build up 'a network of debt relations' much earlier than a layperson (p. 62).

Debt relations are long-term credits; they imply mutual trust, the trust that allows individuals to form a community. The Daoist master giving away his vital energies may thus be seen as creating the debt relations that are community-building. A *qigong* healer like Qiu transferred his enlivening qualities to his clients as well, but he lived in a city of a Socialist state, and compensation in the form of a religious community around him partly fell away. The lifelong friendships in which his therapy often resulted may, however, be taken as evidence of the community-building relations that such healers can establish.

'Life for life':[27] the way Qiu put it made it seem that he was sacrificing himself for the benefit of his clients. The notion of self-sacrifice is not alien to Christians, but I hesitate to equate Qiu's transference of vitality with a sacrifice. Although anthropologists have, ever since Hubert and Mauss ((1898)1964:13),[28] viewed it as a universal scheme, our understanding of it is tinged by our Judaeo-Christian background. Nevertheless, the literature on sacrifice proves helpful for understanding Qiu's ritual action.

For one thing, this literature made me aware of the vital importance attributed to Primordial *qi* and *qi* in general. The notion of *qi* and, in particular, Primordial *qi* in Qiu's practice of *qigong* healing is comparable to that of blood in many other cultures.[29] Sacrifice can be seen as an act of destroying life in order to perpetuate life: a consecrated victim is put to death, and blood must flow.[30] In *qigong* healing not blood but *qi* must flow[31] – the Primordial *qi* which the healer transmits to the patient. *Qi* is vital.

In sacrifice, a consecrated victim is put to death – a death that we experience as absolute and irreversible. In *qigong*, this death is replaced

[27] The notion of 'life for life' applies to the notions of sacrifice, 'non-sacrificial ritual killing' (Ruel 1990), and many rituals of curing (e.g. Obeyesekere 1969:178).

[28] Hubert and Mauss 'universalised' sacrifice in that they applied this scheme not only to Semitic sacrifices but also to some Greek and Vedic ones.

[29] Blood figured also in *qigong*, but not as prominently as *qi*. It was usually taken as the *yin* aspect of *qi*.

[30] This point is also underlined in de Heusch's (1985) 'Sacrifice in Africa'. If blood must flow, only animals and human beings can be sacrificed. However, vegetables can substitute for animals, according to Evans-Pritchard (1956:146), 'by cutting in two a wild cucumber'. The wording describing this process is the same as that during an animal sacrifice: 'Badness goes into the earth with the blood and the chyme'. Hayley (1980:128) describes sacrificial vegetable offerings as grounded in the idea that sins are destroyed by digestion: 'The Brahman . . . is believed to digest the impurity without himself becoming impure.'

[31] When making offerings, by analogy, vapour (*qi*) must rise, the vapour that ascends from cooking pots of the consecrated animals and cereals.

by a reversible form of dying. The transition across the boundary between death and life is easily made, at least in some Chinese legends.[32] Moreover, it is possible to make the transition between the state of the unborn and the postnatal state; *qigong* masters achieve it daily. This points to interrelations between states of being before, during, and after life that differ immensely from the definitions of life and death in sacrificial rituals. Qiu's self-immolation cannot be viewed as a form of sacrifice.

Ruel's (1990) 'non-sacrificial ritual killing' offers insights for an interpretation of Qiu's *qigong* practice. His analysis is built on the assumption that sacrifice involves a personalised deity in whose eyes the sacrificer's condition is improved.[33] He describes ritual killing among the Kuria in East Africa, which is not seen as an offering to a deity but as 'concerned with impersonal qualities of life and well-being'. This ritual killing differs from sacrifice in that 'it is not the life *of* an animal that is at issue but rather the life *in* the animal'. Ruel therefore speaks of 'non-sacrificial ritual killing'. Applied to the Chinese context, this analysis suggests that the transference of Primordial *qi* in a healing performance is a 'non-sacrificial' form of transmitting well-being.

Certain parallels between the Kuria's non-sacrificial ritual killing and a *qigong* healing performance are striking. The core of both ritual activities concerns a transfer of enlivening powers within an impersonal cosmological framework: the Kuria suffocate a goat and smear the contents of its stomach, its chyme, all over the homestead. Similarly, Qiu impairs his Breath (*qi*) and performs gestures that envelop the client in Primordial *qi* during a *qigong* healing session. The comparison shows that Qiu, like the Kuria goat, serves not as 'a surrogate offering of a life' as in Evans-Pritchard's (1956:146) analysis of Nuer sacrifice but rather as a 'vehicle' for transmitting enlivening power.[34]

---

[32] See for instance the legend on Wei Boyang, translated by Giles (1948:67–8), cited in Hsu (1992a:80–1). See also Boehmer (1977:55): 'death can be reversed', and Kuhn (1990:98, 249, n. 14).

[33] Ruel's definition of sacrifice is in several respects problematic, and disagreement has been voiced on this point; see for instance Beattie (1980:32): 'What seems to underlie the institution of sacrifice . . . is a reference to a non-empirically grounded power or powers, whether individual . . . or not.'

[34] The goat's irreversible death by suffocation is, just like Qiu's reversible impairment of Breath, considered a non-sacrificial form of killing. The problem explored here is not whether death is reversible or not, but the difference between a 'surrogate offering of a life' and a 'vehicle for transmitting enlivening powers'. Ruel considers the former a sacrificial offering, the latter not. If I understand Ruel rightly, he builds on the assumption that sacrifice involves a personalised deity, which means that the offering would be non-sacrificial even if the goat were killed so as that blood would flow and be smeared all over. According to the analysis presented below, the crucial difference between a non-sacrificial and a sacrificial offering is that the goat is killed by suffocation and that chyme and not blood is central to the ritual.

One may wonder what difference is envisaged between the expressions 'the life *of* an animal' and 'the life *in* an animal'. In terms of grammar, the former expression is possessive, the latter locative. Within a cosmological framework devoid of personified deities, Primordial *qi*, and chyme probably likewise, is an impersonal substance and force that is not personally assimilated and possessed: Primordial *qi* is the *qi* of the Universe that is undifferentiated in the healer and has not yet become assimilated and specified by being located in, say, a particular Organ; similarly, chyme is nourishment that has become undifferentiated matter but is still in the digestive tract and has not yet been assimilated and absorbed into the goat's blood. Primordial *qi* and chyme can be taken for life that is in the animal but does not belong to it, and thus Qiu and the goat are vehicles for well-being.

In the conceptual framework that underlies the non-sacrificial ritual killing of the Kuria, the environment is conceived of as life-giving. *Obohoro* (well-being), which takes the form of chyme in the goat's stomach, comes from the outside world. The understanding of a life-giving natural world also underlies the notion of healing by the transference of Primordial *qi*, if we take into consideration how Primordial *qi* is restored during meditation. In the Primordial State, the *qigong* healer becomes one with the universe, and Primordial *qi* in his Cinnabar Field (*dantian*) is thereby restored.[35] If Primordial *qi* is the *qi* of the universe *in* the Cinnabar Field of the healer, the transference of Primordial *qi* from healer to patient during a healing session implies a transference to the patient of enlivening powers from the outside world.

It cannot be stressed enough how important the insight is that Primordial *qi*, as well as any other *qi*, cannot be possessed by a person. It explains, first, why Qiu was not engaging in self-sacrifice: he simply was not in possession of a self that he could sacrifice. The Primordial *qi* that he transmitted was not his Primordial *qi*. Rather, it was *qi* of the universe gathered in a primordial state in his Cinnabar Field. The insight that *qi* does not intrinsically belong to anyone or anything has, furthermore, far-reaching consequences for the conceptualisation of the body and the universe.

Qi and conceptions of the body

As we have seen, the concept of *qi* that is basic to *qigong* and Chinese medicine is grounded in an understanding of the universe that redefines

---

[35] It would be wrong to say that the *qi* of the universe is transferred to the Cinnabar Field, where it becomes Primordial *qi*, because there are no boundaries between the self and the universe in the Primordial State.

not only modern Western notions of the self, but also death, life, and the state of being unborn. The concept of qi also has implications for conceptions of the body in its usual and its disordered state. While the notions of qi that Qiu mentioned most often, Primordial qi and Bad qi, were grounded in an understanding of an inside world seen in opposition to an outside world, his gestures indicated that he simultaneously had a notion of a 'body ecologic' in which, as in Chinese medicine, microcosm and macrocosm are in mutual resonance.

The body ecologic

In their article 'The Mindful Body' Scheper-Hughes and Lock (1987) distinguish three bodies that are largely determined by one's choice of theoretical approach. A phenomenological approach, which attributes great importance to subjective experiences of the individual, leads to a description of the 'individual body' such as Ots (1990) provides for TCM. A structuralist approach accounts for the 'social body', recognising representations of the body in social institutions or representations of social institutions in the body, and is, for instance, invoked by Unschuld ((1980)1985:48ff.) in his assessment of the 'medicine of systematic correspondence'. The poststructuralist and the Foucauldian approaches are interested in power relations of the society at large, and the way in which they are embodied in the individual informs on the 'body politic'. Chinese medical scholarship has so far not made the 'body politic' a major theme of discussion, although various writers have addressed the issue, implicitly and explicitly.[36]

When applied to Qiu's practices and explanations and in particular those of Chinese medical doctors, the above approaches to the body have certain drawbacks. All three build on an analysis of synchronic processes in society, but current conceptions of the body in Chinese medicine and *qigong* are difficult to explain without a historical perspective. Therefore I suggest a fourth approach to the body that is grounded in an anthropological analysis tailored to describing the body in Chinese medicine and other scholarly medical traditions.[37] This approach

---

[36] Farquhar's general approach to TCM reflects much awareness of its body politic. Furth and Ch'en (1992:45), in their discussion of Taiwanese women's menstrual beliefs and practices, have, without any jargon or reference to Foucault, explicitly addressed the issue of power relations between male and female: 'All three frameworks for understanding menstrual meanings in Taiwan could be said to carry negative messages about female gender: religious taboos evoke images of female dirt; Chinese medicine draws attention to bodily weakness as the price of childbearing capability; and biomedicine supports a stereotype of female emotionality.'

[37] No doubt contemporary conceptions of the body in societies without written records have also developed historically, but their histories can, unfortunately, hardly be accounted for.

builds on the recognition that contemporary concepts and practices are the result of complex historical processes and that their shades of meaning can be identified through study of their history.

I am not the first to point this out. Morris (1990), without being a specialist in the field, decided that Chinese medicine and its complex 'symbolic classifications' were suitable for illustrating and reinforcing his plea that 'rather than attempting to wed anthropology with the cognitive sciences, both anthropology and psychology should link themselves to historical studies' (p. 30). He attacked the narrow hermeneutic approach to explaining symbolic classifications as well as the conviction of many cognitive scientists that symbolic systems can be traced to innate proclivities and underlying universal principles. He called for a 'historical sociology' by highlighting the problems posed by an anthropological analysis of the symbolic system of Chinese medicine. And Dissanayake (1993), concerned primarily with social theory in the West and its prospects for further development, pointed to the predominance of the 'question of historicity' in East Asian traditions of thought and practice. He suggested that, if taken seriously and integrated into endeavours of Western scholarship, this East Asian preoccupation might well provide a basis for innovation in Western social theory. He encouraged 'a historical perspective to the relationship between body and society that is conspicuously absent in phenomenologically oriented Western social theory' (p. 33).

Historical processes are often best understood as historical accident, and the contemporary conceptions of the body are thus best viewed as a result of such historical accident. Zimmermann ((1982)1987:1–95) demonstrates this convincingly in his study of the Ayurvedic notions *jangala* ('dry') and *anupa* ('wet'). The 'dry' (*jangala*) is in Ayurveda generally associated with higher values than the 'wet' (*anupa*). The dry correlates with the acacia and the black buck which was, apparently, the epitome of Hindu society. The meats of the *jangala* are warm and dry and have a pleasant, ethereal smell. They are 'light' (*ruksa*), which is highly valued, in contrast to the cold, wet, and unpleasant meats of the *anupa*, which are 'heavy' (*snigdha*). Instead of projecting all-embracing universal principles into this cultural classification of 'dry' and 'wet', Zimmermann's analysis highlights the interrelatedness of the high value attributed to *jangala* in Ayurveda to historical accident: the dry Deccan was the preferred site of habitation for the Aryan invaders who laid the foundations for contemporary Ayurveda.

Zimmermann's study is ground-breaking not only because of the historical dimension it brings to the analysis of contemporary body concepts but also because it takes account of ecological and geographic circumstances and their impact on cultural classifications. The above

framework of the three bodies, by contrast, focuses mostly on contemporary sociopolitical processes. It furthermore neglects to investigate the ways in which people perceive and interact with their natural
environment. Yet precisely such ecological considerations are central to
the analysis of contemporary 'humoral medicines', as Laderman (1981)
put it, and scholarly medical traditions such as Ayurveda and Chinese
medicine.[38]

The notion of the 'body ecologic' is thus meant to provide a framework for an analysis that includes the concerns of people in their interaction with the natural environment. However, rather than attempting
to order these people's 'ethnoscience' in neat tables and lists, the study
of the 'body ecologic' builds on the awareness that these concepts have
a history and have evolved by complex historical processes that are
often best comprehended as historical accident. An investigation of the
'body ecologic' therefore deals with aspects of contemporary concepts
and practices that are best explained by investigating the historical
processes which determined the conception of the natural environment
in the societies from which they evolved.[39] With regard to the body in
Chinese medicine, the concept of *qi* is, for instance, best explained in
terms of the 'body ecologic'.

In China, the idea that processes in the macrocosm and the micro-
cosm(s) are analogous became predominant among philosophers of the
three last centuries BC. The cosmos, the state, and the body 'were so
interdependent that they are best considered a single complex' (Sivin
1995e:5). The notion of 'stimulus and response' (*ganying*) explained
how they were aligned with each other (p. 24). Sivin (pp. 25ff.) points
to temporal cyclicity, hierarchic orders, morality, and emotions, all analogous in macrocosm and microcosms. Kuriyama (1993:55), in his
discussion of concepts of disease in the Han period, stresses that the
body was subject to seasonality.[40]

During that period, the concept of *qi* gained in importance as a
'shared substrate' which 'suggested not only that men and the physical
world followed common principles, but also that they acted upon one
another through the medium of *qi*' (Lewis 1990:213). *Qi* became the

---

[38] Hanson (forthcoming) shows in a similar vein that, depending on the climate and
'geographic ecology', different remedies are considered important for dealing with the
same disorders. She argues that the medical doctrine of the *Shang han lun* (*Treatise on
Cold Damage Disorders*), when transposed from the north to the south, was transformed
into a new doctrine, that of the *wenbing* (Warmth factor disorders).

[39] On ethno science, see Sturterant (1964) and D'Andrade (1995). On the 'body ecologic',
see Hsu (forthcoming).

[40] Ma (1994:526ff.) speaks of 'ecological conditions' (*shengtai zhuangkuang*), without
however elaborating on them as I do here.

'key term in the Chinese articulation of *the dialectic of nature and culture*' (italics added), when the universe began to be conceived of as subject to an 'all-embracing interdependence'. Lewis (1990:218) linked the emergence of this idea of 'all-embracing interdependence' to changes in patterns of sanctioned violence in the Warring States period (453–221 BC). During the last three centuries BC, 'the aristocratic pattern of sanctioned violence in the Zhou city-states [changed] to the *universal, authoritarian* pattern that characterized the territorial states' (p. 234; italics added). That cosmos, state, and body are all subject to an 'all-embracing interdependence' expresses lastly an ideal of a totalitarian and even despotic ruler.[41]

The all-pervasive *qi* that permeated macrocosm and microcosm(s) had, in Chinese medical doctrine, innumerable facets. Although unifying, the concept of *qi* lent itself to the expression of great diversity. In the medical classics one of the most salient features of *qi* was that its qualities varied with its location or its position in comparison with other *qi*.[42]

The interpretation of Qiu's ritual action indicates that *qi* is not intrinsic to anyone or anything and cannot be possessed. *Yuanqi* is not *of* the healer, but *in* the healer. The Primordial *qi* in the Cinnabar Field may well be the *qi* of the universe acquired in the Primordial State. The healer transfers this Primordial *qi* to the patient. Although he transfers vitality, we have seen that one cannot say that he sacrifices himself: it is not *his* vitality that he transfers, but vitality *in* him. Qiu himself did not explicitly say this but, if the above analysis is correct, acted accordingly.

Chinese medical doctors were more articulate. *Qi* that comes from the rubric of the Direction-Season[43] of the Cold (*han*) is *hanqi*; *qi* from the Dry (*zao*) is *zaoqi*; *qi* from the Damp (*shi*) is *shiqi*, and *qi* from Wind (*feng*) is *fengqi*.[44] The notion of Direction-Season indicates that seasonality in Chinese medical reasoning is associated not only with temporal

[41] This contrasts with the romantic view of those who tend to liken Chinese medicine to an art of natural healing that evolved in a golden past in which man and nature were one.

[42] These 'qualities' of *qi* are not 'intrinsic' to *qi*, nor are they loosely connected 'attributes'. They reflect aspects of *qi*, relative to the speaker's perspective: the Heart is *yin* when compared with the Small Intestine (*xiaochang*) because of its inner location, and *yang* when compared to the Kidneys because of its upper position (Porkert 1974:32).

[43] Season (*shi*) and Direction (*fang*) are not variables of two separate dimensions, time and space, but different aspects of one and the same 'rubric' (see pp. 109–11).

[44] In the text in which this word sequence is mentioned (see pp. 109–11), the rubric Summer-heat (*shu*) is also mentioned, but the compound word *shuqi* strikes me as unusual, and I have not listed it above. Correlations in Chinese medicine are often not systematic but systemic.

regularity, as it is in Western thinking,[45] but clearly has spatial aspects. This I learnt from mentor Zhang. The 'shared substrate', *qi*, changes its qualities according to the time–space rubric in which it is positioned.

According to my teachers at the TCM college, *qi* dwelling in the Heart (*xin*) is *xinqi*, *qi* in the Lungs (*fei*) is *feiqi*, *qi* in the Liver (*gan*) is *ganqi*, *qi* in the Kidneys (*shen*) is *shenqi*, and *qi* in the Spleen (*pi*) is *piqi*. The notion of space in TCM, which implicitly shared features of Zhang's rubrics, was, however, increasingly modelled on the three-dimensional notion of space known from Western biomedical anatomy. But whatever the notions of space and time, *qi* varied in its qualities according to its location.

There was not simply one *qi* but a whole chorus of them. In Chinese medicine and, as some of Qiu's gestures indicated, also in *qigong*, the interrelations of *qi* in different locations were important. Disharmonic dynamics of *qi* were held responsible for disorders in the body.[46] It was not the *qi* in a single location, for instance the Liver *qi*, which was relevant to a person's well-being but the way in which *qi* in different locations resonated with each other. Just as in music, where not the tone in itself, but only a chord or a sequence of several tones gives one a sense of harmony or disharmony, the well-being of a person depended on the harmony of the chorus of *qi* in different locations, inside and outside the body.

The notion of the 'body ecologic' highlights the idea of mutual resonance between macrocosm and microcosm and the continuities between the inside and the outside of the physical body. The 'shared substrate', *qi*, that permeates the universe constantly transforms itself: *qi* is not only in constant flow, but also in constant flux (in the sense that it is subject to constant transformation). This conception of the body as part of its environment is characteristic of Chinese medicine. Sometimes the boundaries between the body and the environment are blurred to the extent that when the *qi* of the environment becomes dense life emerges and when it disperses death occurs.

Notably, the 'body ecologic' is, like the body politic, intricately interwined with its environment, so body and environment cannot be dealt with as separate entities. This contrasts with the notion of the individual and the social body, which refer to a clearly bounded, 'classical' body (Connerton 1992:352). The subject of the 'body ecologic'

---

[45] Western scholars who emphasise the notion of temporality in Chinese medical reasoning may do so in recognition of the importance of seasonality, reducing the Chinese notion of seasonality to one of temporality and overlooking these spatial aspects.

[46] TCM textbooks speak of 'equilibrium' (*pingheng*) rather than 'harmony' (*tiaohe*). Because 'balance' is easily misrepresented as equilibrium, I prefer to speak of harmony.

changes permanently within a field of changing flows and fluxes, just as that of the body politic constantly negotiates its position within a field of power relations that are present everywhere, above and below, and cannot be reduced to those between rulers and the ruled (Foucault (1976)1990:94). The subjects of the body ecologic and the body politic are not clearly defined entities, so I use 'body ecologic' (rather than 'ecological body'), paralleling the 'body politic'. The notion of self is less clearly bounded for the body politic and the 'body ecologic' than for the individual and the social body.

Accumulating qi

In Chinese medicine disorders were often explained by reference to disharmonic dynamics: '*yinyang* have no intercourse' (*yinyang bujiao*), '*qi* and Blood are not in harmony' (*qixue butiao*), 'the Five Organs are not united' (*wuzang buhe*). Qiu, however, reasoned only occasionally in terms of the Five Phases and *yinyang*. His talk mostly made reference to *qi*. *Qi* had to be in constant flow and flux (in the sense of transformation); illness arose if this flow and flux was disturbed. *Qi* in the process of accumulating was his predominant explanation for such disturbances.

Qiu spoke of 'accumulating *qi*'(*qi ji*); he could see the *qi* accumulating in the Red Light. Signs and symptoms of accumulating *qi* were palpable or visible to him and were often experienced realities to his clients: when Qiu palpated Bao's liver (see p. 43), he said he felt the Tumour (*liu*) of Bao's liver cancer. After two weeks of treatment he maintained that the Tumour in the Liver had become 'soft' (*nen*) and 'small' (*xiao*). This palpable sign (which I could not detect) indicated the improved condition of Bao's liver.

In both *qigong* and TCM, *liu* designated a bump or hill, which was usually palpable; in Chinese biomedical terminology it referred to a biomedically diagnosed tumour. The term *liu* is more or less the equivalent of the English 'tumour', which originally designated an unspecific swelling and later acquired a more restricted sense in biomedicine (*OED* 1978). *Liu* was also used in everyday language in a more general way, along with other originally technical terms such as neurasthenia, rheumatism, periarthritis of the shoulder, and sciatic pain. The following episode illustrates this:

A client once came to Qiu's practice complaining of a Tumour (*liu*) in his hips. While Qiu took his Pulse, he said that he had suffered from other Tumours earlier. One had grown at the base of his neck, the other in his armpit. Both had been cut out at a Western medical hospital. But 'operations were dreadful' (*kaidao kepa*), and therefore he had decided to try *qigong* therapy. Qiu had him lie on the bed, palpated his back and hips, and said: 'You seem to have severe hip pain.' The patient, delighted at the skill of his doctor in detecting his ailment, began complaining at length about the constant pain that made it difficult for him to walk. A *qigong* and acumoxa treatment of ten days would probably cure him, Qiu said after a while, adding (as usual after such a favourable prognosis) that he could not give any guarantee. While Jade Blossom treated the patient by needling acu-points associated with the suppression of pain (*dachangshu*, *huantiao*, *weizhong*, etc.), a client awaiting her treatment on the bench next to me turned and said: 'Operations are dreadful!' She started to talk about 'ear acupuncture' (*erzhen*), which made gallstone operations unnecessary,[47] and she praised Qiu's therapy, which would allow this patient to avoid a third operation. Qiu nodded: Tumours and 'gallstones' (*danjieshi*) were 'lumps' (*kuai*) which 'gradually grew' (*zhang*) bigger and bigger. Such lumps could sometimes grow just because one was constantly thinking of them. He himself had once had a lump in his hip and he had eliminated it by practising *qigong*. (notes, August 1989)

The lumps that Qiu was referring to belonged to very different bio-medical disease categories. He explained to me later that the lump he had treated in the client's hip was a 'thickening' of some muscles, but Tumours on the neck and in the armpits were different. Their location coincided with the 'lymphatic nodes' (*linbajie*). He agreed with the bio-medical treatment and considered it unlikely that an operation could have been avoided in those two cases. He used the same term, *liu*, as his patient but clearly differentiated between different kinds of *liu*. He reasoned according to a principle that is basic to Chinese medicine, namely, that the same phenomenon at different locations indicated different disease processes.[48]

Qiu was not unaware of the varied biomedical etiology of the lumps, but it did not disturb him to mention in one breath gallstones, tumours, muscle thickening, and lumps originating in the imagination and call them all Tumours. It would be wrong to conclude from this that he had an entirely phenomenological approach to disease. All these lumps had an underlying process in common: their gradual growth. This gradual growth was at the centre of attention in the *qigong* healer's 'imagination' (*yinian*). In the process of healing he inverted the directionality of the growth, from expanding to shrinking. Crucial to *qigong*

---

[47] For the history and rationale of ear acupuncture, see Lu and Needham (1980:164–8) and Hsu (1995, 1996a).
[48] According to Kaptchuk (1983:xix), 'an eruption on the face indicated a different disease process than did an eruption on the trunk'. Kaptchuk emphasised the 'holistic view' and 'the relationship of the symptom to the whole body', but this example could also be interpreted to indicate that disease processes are differentiated in terms of the locations in which the symptom occurs.

treatment was a process. The focus on processes rather than static entities is common to both *qigong* healing and Chinese medicine. The flow and flux of *qi* can be disrupted in many different ways. Counterflowing *qi* (*qi ni*) was, for instance, one of the frequently mentioned concepts in acumoxa and sometimes occurred also in Qiu's talk.[49] Accumulating *qi* remained, however, central to Qiu's conceptualisation of adverse processes in the body. His stress on illness arising due to accumulation appeared to me an interesting thought, and in investigating Chinese medical disease concepts I found a great wealth of technical terms pointing to a process of accumulation that would cause stagnation.[50] In many early medical texts accumulations were considered to disrupt the fluxes and flows in and about the body.[51]

It is worth noting that in early medical accounts the character *zheng*, which is homophonous with the Chinese characters that Farquhar (1994a) refers to as 'sign', 'symptom', and 'syndrome', has the meaning of a Concretion with connotations of an accumulation. In fact, none of the three currently used *zheng* but only *zheng*4 (Concretion) appears in early Chinese medical texts. In the *Historical Records* (*Shi ji* 105 (Sima 1959:2785)), the mythical figure Bian Que received drugs and instructions from a stranger, and when 'he used those for inspecting the illnesses, he saw right through to the Concretions and Knots in the Five Depositories (*wuzang zhengjie*)'. The processes in the body considered responsible for illness were Knots[52] and Concretions.[53]

Technical terms that convey the idea that a pathological condition arises from an accumulation are, for instance, found in the wide range

---

[49] Motion or Impulsion (*dong*) was also conceived of as disturbance, see 'Yinyang shiyimai jiujing' (MWD 1985b:7–13): 'If this vessel *comes into motion* then the [following] disorders arise' (*shi dong ze bing*) is a standard phrase which introduces a number of disorders for every vessel. See also: Zhangjiashan manuscripts (*Wenwu* 1989, 7:74): 'If *qi* comes into motion, then there is anxiety' (*qi dong ze yu*). According to the *Bei ji qian jing yao fang* (Sun 1955:3), diagnosis is best made when 'The *yin*-aspect of *qi* has not yet come into motion and the *yang*-aspect of *qi* has not yet dispersed' (*yin qi wei dong, yang qi wei san*).

[50] Western scholars emphasise stasis (e.g. Sivin 1995a:6); my point is that many stagnations arise due to an accumulation.

[51] It would be wrong to surmise that I consider *qigong* healing more archaic than TCM, but the above-mentioned emphasis that accumulations bar the flow of *qi* is reminiscent of conceptions known from early China. Qiu's conception of *bi* (Blockage) was much the same as that of TCM doctors insofar as it built on the biomedical model of channels narrowing as in arteriosclerosis rather than on the idea of an Obstruction (Hsu 1992a:124). *Qigong* is, like TCM, a recent Chinese therapeutic practice, a phenomenon of modern life in Socialist China.

[52] On the ritual significance of Knots (*jie*), see Harper (1985:475ff.): *jie* is glossed as *di*, 'a Knot which cannot be untied', as opposed to *niu*, 'a Knot which can be untied'.

[53] The commentator Zhang Shoujie (fl. 737) interprets *jie* and *zheng* as Pulse Images, but my translation is based on their interpretation in the *Zhongwen dacidian* (1973–6: no. 23121).

of different terms for Boils on the body surface (e.g. *yong*), Abscesses (*ju*), or accumulations in the body such as Obstructions (*bi*),[54] Conglomerations (*jia*),[55] Accumulations and Gatherings (*jiju*),[56] Amassments (*shan*),[57] and Piles (*zhi*).[58] Extensive classifications of, for instance, Piles (Schall 1965:30) and numerological categories such as the Five and Seven Amassments (*wushan, qishan*)[59] or the Five Accumulations (*wuji*)[60] underline the preponderance of such disorders.

In the acumoxa clinic I also encountered disorders which, without being referred to as the visibly perceived Accumulating *qi*, were attributed to an accumulation of *qi*. Some were subjectively felt by the patient, for instance, in the form of choking as if one had swallowed a Plum Pit (*meihe*).[61] Others, such as manifestations of a *qi* Amassment (*shanqi*), were palpable.[62] Others could not be detected by the senses, among them a Concretion and Accumulation (*zhengji*) or a Conglomeration and Gathering (*jiaju*),[63] often just rendered as Concretions and Conglomerations (*zhengjia*). Clearly, there were other processes, such as Counterflowing *qi*, stagnations, or unspecific blockages, that were also postulated to take place inside the body, but accumulations continued to be important for explaining pathological conditions.

Qiu saw *qi* accumulating. Texts of the past mention accumulations, but they are not very specific about what it is that accumulates. In these texts, clearly, the process of accumulation is of greater concern than the material aspects of the accumulated stuff. In order to find out what

---

[54] Obstructions are in TCM conceived of as blockages of the flow of *qi* in Tracts and Links or in the Joints (*guanjie*) (*Acumoxa Therapy* (Yang 1985:87)). In *Su wen* 43 Obstructions are not in Tracts, but conceived of as accumulations and according to *Ling shu* 6 they have Form (*you xing*) (Hsu 1992a:123–8; appendix 7). Hence *bi* is translated as Obstruction; its rendering as Blockage invokes the TCM doctors' idea of a blocked pipe. On blocked *qi* as threatening, see Bray (1995).

[55] E.g. *jia* in Zhangjiashan manuscripts (*Wenwu* 1989, 7:72). See also *jia* in *Shi ji* (Sima 1959:2785, 2809).

[56] E.g. *Nan jing* 55 (Nanjing zhongyi xueyuan yijing jiaoyanzu 1961:120).

[57] E.g. *Shi ji* (Sima 1959:2799, 2804, 2812, 2813).

[58] E.g. Zhangjiashan manuscripts (*Wenwu* 1989, 7:72).

[59] There are many different renderings of *wushan* and the *qishan* (see *Zhongyi dacidian* 1987:2–3, 29).

[60] For *wuji*, see e.g. *Nan jing* 56 (Nanjing zhongyi xueyuan yijing jiaoyanzu 1961:121), see also *Zhongyi dacidian* (1987:130).

[61] Globus hystericus (Ou 1988:28).

[62] See Ou (1988:310): (1) hernia, (2) diseases of the external genitalia, testes and scrotum, (3) severe abdominal pain.

[63] Most TCM doctors were uncertain about their exact denotation, while teacher Tao maintained that *zhengji* were associated with an Outer Disease Factor, Malignant Dampness (*xieshi*), and *jiaju* with an Inner Disease Factor, when *qi* stagnates (*qi zhi*). He maintained that a *jiaju* was more likely to have Form than a *zhengji* (clinic notes, May 1989).

exactly Qiu meant by *qi*, I talked with him about accumulations. According to him, accumulations had substance – they were not merely imaginary lumps – and Accumulating *qi* was a process – it involved an agency or transformative force. *Qi* was a 'matter-agency' or a 'substance-force'. Porkert (1961; 1965; 1974:167) approximates *qi* as 'energy' or, more precisely, as 'configurative energy' and 'energetic configuration'; Unschuld ((1980)1985:72) as 'finest matter influence'; Sivin (1987:46–7) as 'basic stuff', namely 'stuff that makes things happen' or 'stuff in which things happen'. 'Vapour', the translation adopted by Harper (1998) for early medical texts, captures the aspects of *qi* insofar as vapour is matter that is in motion and has force – a transformative force (for steaming, for instance) – or is a force that effects motion. Regardless of how one best approximates *qi* in English, pathological conditions that arose in the body ecologic were often ascribed to a process of accumulation that disrupted its constant flow and flux (in the sense of transformation). It was the *process* which brought about disharmony, not the material aspects of the accumulation, that was important. This conception of the body in its disordered state was common to *qigong* and Chinese medicine.

3   The personal transmission of knowledge

Zhang was a learned doctor who had scarcely participated in the reforging of Chinese medicine at government institutions. In the beginning of the 1980s, he founded a collective enterprise for health care and had, by the end of the decade, gathered a group of unemployed youth around him whom he trained in 'acumoxa' (*zhenjiu*) and 'massage' (*tuina*). He was an outsider of the Traditional Chinese Medical profession in the Socialist state, and precisely for this reason he appeared to me worth investigation. He seemed to have retained values and habits of Chinese medical learning that elsewhere had been abolished.

Zhang's biography was most unusual, his medical practice idiosyncratic, and the forum of our encounters, seminars on classical Chinese texts, had been instigated on my initiative. Nevertheless, his teaching and, especially, his mode of interpreting classical texts had certain features in common with others who called themselves 'senior Chinese doctors' (*laozhongyi*). Since he emphasised, like other senior doctors, the personal component in the relationship between the mentor and his followers, I propose to speak of the 'personal transmission of knowledge'.[1]

The setting and reminders of French colonialism

Zhang's practice was situated on the borders of Green Lake which surrounded a park of sweeping bridges and dainty pavilions, rowing boats and weeping willows, mirrored in still water. Old men with waterpipes and birdcages,[2] sipping tea over a game of *majiang*,[3] and the

---

[1] 'Personal knowledge' is also used by Tu (1993:29–44) to characterise Confucian ways of learning.
[2] Tame starlings. In urban China, pets were forbidden but potted plants, goldfish, and birds became increasingly popular in the 1980s.
[3] Mah-jongg, a game which is almost always combined with gambling, had as a sign of decadence been strictly forbidden ever since the Communist revolution in 1949. In the 1980s it became popular mostly among women and young people and was usually played in the backyards of private dwellings. Old men in the streets were usually seen playing 'chess' (*xiangqi*) and 'go' (*weiqi*) or 'playing cards' (*da paizi*).

local singers[4] who joined them in the late afternoon, made for an idyllic
scene, but the water was smelly, the boats out of order, and the ground
spotted with spittle. Nevertheless, the space and silence in and around
the park conveyed something of forgotten nobility. Old villas in over-
grown gardens indicated that the French used to reside in this part of
Kunming, in those days known as Yunnanfu.

On the hill to the north of the lake, the French had built Yunnan
University in a neoclassical style, overwhelming anyone who stood
under the subtropical foliage and looked up the fleet of stairs, flanked by
palms and fountains. A private school with thirteen lecturers had been
opened in 1922 under the name Dongji University. It was inaugurated
by the province in 1930, was given its present name in 1934, and it
added as a fifth faculty that of Western medicine in 1937. South of the
park was the first Western medical hospital.[5] It had been inaugurated
by the French consul in 1901, mainly to provide care for the builders of
the railway which was to link Yunnanfu to Hanoi, the capital of the
French protectorate Tongking, in 1910 (Tian 1987:104). In the nine-
teenth century, French and British colonialists had competed over
Yunnan not only for geopolitical reasons but also for its rich mineral
resources (Fairbank and Liu 1980:99). French influence became prevalent at the beginning of the twentieth century, and elementary schools,
hospitals, and mail services were set up at the few points of administrative presence in Yunnanfu, Simao, and Mengzi with the explicit goal of
reinforcing it (Doumer 1902:123). France also increasingly provided
opportunities for higher education. Whereas the majority of the students
sent abroad during the first two decades of the twentieth century had
studied in Japan (Cordier 1925:410), the liaison with France, Lyons in
particular, became important for medical training during the following
decades (Tian 1987:111).

The French influence is still noticeable in the architecture around
Green Lake, but dominant nowadays are the provincial People's Palace,
a grand exhibition hall, and the Green Lake Hotel, south of the park,

[4] Local operas, also branded for their decadence, were revived in the taverns of little back
streets all over Kunming. In this park, retired women and some young female workers
used to sing in their work clothes.
[5] The first hospitals in this city were built for professional groups: the first was for the
railway builders, the second, installed in 1908 by the Qing court, was for the army and
the third, in 1914, for the police force. In 1919 a leprosy asylum was opened by the
Chinese administration. In 1920 English Methodists and in 1928 American missionaries established hospitals. In 1928 a Chinese biomedical doctor succeeded in raising
private funds to establish a Red Cross hospital. The provincial government opened a
Western medical hospital for the public as late as in 1939. The university hospital was
established in 1941 (Tian, p.c., April 1989). For the prevalent diseases in Yunnan, see
Tian (1987:141–80); on the plagues of the last century, see Benedict (1996:17–48).

built in the revolutionary Socialist style of the 1950s. These buildings have partly replaced the crowded private households in which meals were prepared on charcoal stoves; the air around the lake was relatively fresh. The area was indeed sometimes a peaceful and unworldly place. During the outbursts of the people's movement in May and June 1989, when demonstrators filled the avenues of the city centre, paralysing the traffic, and the crowd of spectators was so dense that pedestrians could not elbow their way through it, old men and women played French boules at leisure in the shade of the trees along the lake.

Zhang had installed his practice on the ground floor of a provincial government hostel, hidden in the backyards of a work unit where no one would expect to find it. The room was spacious (30–40 square metres) and never crowded. Zhang treated provincial government officials, university lecturers, and high school teachers almost exclusively. He often sat behind a massive wooden desk, and diagnosis took place there once a family member or friend had arranged it. Treatment began on one of the following days; a minimal period of therapy was six sessions. The patients were always treated with much discretion, behind a screen on one of the three plank-beds. Zhang's main interests, however, lay in scholarly research, as the apparatus and pictures on the walls of his clinic revealed.

Biographical notes and trends in medical politics

Zhang was known as a 'senior Chinese doctor' (*laozhongyi*). Some even called him a 'famous senior Chinese doctor' (*ming laozhongyi*), but he was not one of Kunming's famous four.[6] In fact, he was disliked by most doctors who knew him, possibly because of his background. He was brought up in a French missionary school, and in the jargon of former Communist Party pronouncements Chinese who had had contacts with foreigners were 'running-dogs of imperialism' (*diguozhuyi de zougou*). After the Revolution which came to Yunnan in 1950, Zhang's father, who was a Chinese doctor, had had him study Western medicine and in 1955, when the government began promoting TCM in Kunming on a larger scale, he had managed to arrange for his son to participate. After a one-year 'improvement course in acumoxa' (*zhenjiu jinxiuban*) he had been hired, despite his youth, as an acumoxa teacher, first at the institution which preceded the Yunnan TCM College and later at the City TCM Hospital. In the early 1960s quarrels with his superiors and colleagues had become so intense that he had resigned

---

[6] According to TCM officials, these were Dai Lisan (1901–68), Tao Zhenbai (1910–79), Kang Chengzhi (1899–1970), and Wu Peiheng (1888–1971).

from his post. In the early 1980s, when college curricula were to be improved, able doctors from all over the province were rehabilitated as college lecturers, but Zhang declined the offer to return to the Yunnan TCM College. Instead, he set up a medical practice.

A board leaning on the wall next to the door of the practice indicated that it was not a private enterprise but the clinical research centre of an association. 'Associations' (*xiehui*) and 'collective enterprises' (*jitihu*) were, in contrast to 'work units' (*danwei*), not funded by the state. In many respects they resembled the 'private enterprises' (*getihu*) of Chinese urban society: they were responsible for their own profits and losses. Since they were not as closely regulated as state-run firms, they had more flexibility to adjust to fluctuations in market demand. Moreover, they were open to a labour force with limited educational skills, particularly women and unemployed youth. In principle they operated on a smaller financial scale than the government work units, but sometimes they were closely linked to a work unit through shared personnel and buildings and even had budgets of similar size.

In terms of the labour employed and the capital involved, the collective and private work enterprises were reminiscent of the informal sector in Third World countries. According to the investigations of Whyte and Parish (1984:30ff.), the gap between the formal and the informal sector of the labour market was smaller in China in the late 1970s than in Third World countries. About three-quarters of their sample of the labour force were employed by the state in work units; only 4 per cent were in independent enterprises and 23 per cent in collectives. The statistics of the late 1980s show that the importance of the informal sector had increased significantly (Gold 1989:177).

In addition to this small clinic next to Green Lake Zhang directed a small hospital in the suburbs of Kunming. He emphasised that he was employed by an 'organisation of the masses' (*qunzhong jiguan*) and not the government. He had three employees, recruited on grounds of mutual choice. In 1989 he was planning to establish, with the support of the same association, a new hospital and outpatient clinic which would also function as a TCM training centre for foreign doctors. He spoke of taking on two more employees and, in anticipation of increasing his contacts with French acupuncturists, having them trained as French interpreters. These grandiose plans could not have been nourished without certain advantageous 'connections' (*guanxi*) with representatives of the provincial government, but, in spite of them, Zhang encountered many difficulties.[7]

---

[7] Zhang's plans were never realised. In January 1992 I learnt from one of his followers that he had moved to a province of southern China.

In the part of the consulting room that was light and open the apparatus for clinical research was on display. Most impressive was the expensive Western biomedical equipment which, covered with cloths, was neatly set out on a table under a long window front. Photographs on the wall gave the impression of a modern Western biomedical laboratory by indicating that these machines had once been used. Zhang explained that he had done biomedical research earlier on Chinese medical concepts by measuring the velocity of the flow of blood in the arteries and registering the amplitude of the corresponding pulse. He often spoke about his plans to describe the rhythm of electro-cardiogram curves in terms of certain Chinese medical principles and the 'hexagrams' (*gua*) of the *Book of Changes* – in other words, to conduct Chinese medical research on Western biomedical concepts.

Other photographs showed Zhang with doctors from abroad, mostly French. In the 1980s the prestige of a Chinese doctor was enhanced not only by integrating knowledge of Western medicine into his practice but also by contacts with Western doctors. The French, no longer called 'imperialists', were now 'friends' – 'friends from foreign countries' (*waiguo pengyou*).

Two brightly coloured posters of the 'eight trigrams' (*bagua*) hung on the same wall (see fig. 4.2). Instructive indices showed how each trigram corresponded to one of the Organs and Bowels (*zangfu*), Tracts and Links (*jingluo*), Seasons (*jijie*), and a timespan of two hours within a day (*shi*). Zhang explained that these two posters simplified the 'profound' (*shen'ao*) knowledge of 'phase energetics' (*wuyun liuqi xueshuo*),[8] which was for him the most refined aspect of Chinese medicine. He considered phase energetics to be grounded in the principles expounded in the 'Commentary on the Appended Aphorisms' (*Xi ci zhuan*) of the *Book of Changes* (*Yi jing*).

A French acupuncturist who had been friends with Zhang for several years and a French research student who had consulted him in 1988 had shown great interest in the *Book of Changes*, and it seemed to me that these encounters had revived his interest in this ancient and profound knowledge. Recent contacts with the West had not only stimulated modern Western biomedical research but had also promoted a nationalist interest in China's ancient knowledge. The motivation for turning to the *Book of Changes* in some circles of the West and in China undoubtedly arose from very different problems specific to each society. The French acupuncturist was turning away from biomedicine to an

---

[8] For an outline of the doctrine, see Porkert (1974:55–106) and Despeux (forthcoming). See also ch. 4, n. 1.

'alternative medicine', whereas Zhang was full of praise for Western bio-medicine, but his admiration did not prevent him from the nationalist sentiment of finding Chinese medicine and philosophy more profound. At the TCM college, both the middle-aged college teachers who occasionally consulted the medical classics and the young teachers who showed little interest in them met my interest in the *Book of Changes* with an indulgent smile: 'The *Book of Changes* is too mysterious and profound to be understood' (*Yi jing tai shen'ao le*). It had earlier been branded as 'superstitious' (*mixin*) in content and the implication was that a TCM professional need not study it. By contrast, Chinese intel-lectuals outside the college would say: 'If you really want to understand Chinese medicine, you have to be able to read classical Chinese.' Many added: 'And, of course, the *Book of Changes*.' This gap between the beliefs of laypersons and TCM professionals narrowed as I got to know my colleagues at the college better.

Towards the end of my fieldwork, I spoke with several TCM profes-sionals who showed an interest in the *Book of Changes*. One graduate student, for instance, expressed the wish, which he considered unrealis-able, to get a stipend as a 'research student' (*yanjiusheng*) on the *Book of Changes*. He was one of the only students I interviewed who had chosen to study TCM because of his interest in ancient Chinese philosophy, and he was among those who came to dislike TCM during their first and second years of study. I also found textbooks for correspondence courses on this topic in young teachers' college dormitories, and during work at a TCM hospital I once saw a young TCM doctor editing an essay that a middle-aged colleague had written on the relevance of the *Book of Changes* for acumoxa. When I visited the latter in his apartment, he showed me the manuscript of a planned textbook on the *Book of Changes*. One such textbook (Zhang Zhongjing guoyi daxue shiyong jiaocai 1985) was already available.

Zhang, with his interest in the field called the '*Book of Changes* and medicine' (*Yi jing yu yixue*), was by no means alone in the PRC of the late 1980s.[9] In November 1989 an evening course was delivered at the TCM college on two methods of acumoxa – phase energetics and the 'eight methods of the Divine Turtle' (*linggui bafa*) – said to be based

[9] There are groups of scientists in the PRC studying so-called principles of the *Book of Changes* (by which they mean mainly negative–positive polarities and the exponen-tial progression (2-4-8-16-32-64)) in discoveries of the natural sciences (Needham Research Institute Newsletter, January 1991). A representative of these scientists gave the nationalist 'China has a science of its own' as justification for engaging in this kind of research. For an account of a village diviner whose practice is grounded in the *Book of Changes*, see Farquhar (1996).

on the principles of the *Book of Changes*. Various invitations to con-
ferences on the '*Book of Changes* and medicine' circulated in Kunming's
TCM hospital wards. TCM doctors were denied leave or finances for
participation, but Zhang travelled by his own means to Guiyang, where
an international conference was held in October 1989. The titles of the
subjects to be dealt with sounded ambitious, but Zhang was disappointed
when he returned. The discipline was still in its infancy, he said.

Although the idea that the *Book of Changes* is fundamental for Chinese medicine has attracted increasing attention in recent years, it is
by no means new. Zhang Jiebin (1563–1640) remarked in the chapter
'Meaning of the Changes for Medicine' (*Yi yi yi*) of the *Appendix of the
Categories* (*Lei jing fu yi*) (Zhang (1624)1799:20b–21a):

I therefore say: the *Changes* provide the principles of medicine, and medicine
realises the functions of the *Changes*. Those who learn medicine without knowing the *Changes* must consider medicine simple and know no more . . . Those
who know the *Changes* but not medicine, must consider the principles of the
Changes profound and mysterious. In such vagueness and uncertainty they
will have difficulty using them. Moreover, they will be like one who suffers cold
and has a fur coat but will not wear it or one who suffers hunger and has gruel
but will not eat it. What a pity, they have missed their life! Therefore medicine cannot exist without the *Changes* and the *Changes* cannot exist without
medicine. If one can combine and understand them both, then the alterations
of the *Changes* come from Heaven and the application of medicine comes from
oneself.[10]

Zhang Jiebin referred to earlier masters such as Sun Simiao (*c.* 581–
682) who was said to have emphasised the importance of the *Book
of Changes* for understanding the basic principles of medicine ((1624)
1799:1a; Zou 1986:9). No doubt, for Zhang the 'Commentary on the
Appended Aphorisms' in the *Book of Changes* was most important
because it laid the basis for the chapters of the *Yellow Emperor's Inner
Canon* (*Huang di nei jing*) that he considered most profound: those on
phase energetics.

The person and his personae

Zhang was an exponent of many strands of learning, embodying the
personae of scholar doctor and aspiring Confucian gentleman (Hall and
Ames 1987), senior Chinese doctor (Farquhar 1994a), and modern intellectual (Schwarcz 1986).

---

[10] For a preliminary translation of the entire chapter into French, see de la Robertie
(1986).

The scholar doctor

Zhang was, as already said, called a senior Chinese doctor, but he considered himself a 'man of culture' (*you xuewen*). He identified himself with the scholars of traditional China, particularly with those who had fallen into disfavour with the Imperial Court. He had an impressive private library and claimed to have devoted his life to the study of profound knowledge in the canons. To be a scholar was one of the foremost virtues of a Confucian 'gentleman' (*junzi*). Neo-Confucian scholarship consisted largely of a thorough knowledge of the 'thirteen classics' (*shisanjing*). Zhang had not studied the *Mencius* (*Meng zi*), nor had he memorised the *Analects* (*Lun yu*) of Confucius, but he legitimated his interest in the *Book of Changes* with its 'Commentary of the Appended Aphorisms' by attributing its authorship to Confucius.[11]

Zhang highly valued comparative research into classical texts. He repeatedly stated how important it was to buy different editions of the same text and make lists of different interpretations of certain key terms. His attitude sometimes reminded me of that of 'evidential scholarship' (*kaozhengxue*) (Elman 1984), although he did not appear to me as rigorous in his scholarly standards as an evidential scholar. He collected many texts, compiled annotations, and sometimes compared them, but he hardly ever evaluated them critically.

Like an evidential scholar dedicated to textual analysis (Elman 1984:13ff.), he maintained that he strictly avoided all political talk. However, after the Tiananmen incident on June 4, it was only in Zhang's ménage that I found the television always on. Intellectuals generally claimed to be absolutely disinterested in politics and the legacy of the May 4 movement has called indifference on their part an expression of the 'traditional spirit of subservience' (Schwarcz 1986:31), but I observed that many were well informed. Politics have always been crucial to Chinese intellectual life. Even the evidential scholarship under the Manchu rulers did not lack political overtones (Elman 1984:17).

Zhang valued etiquette and politeness. He exerted patriarchal authority rather than impersonal control. His followers all spoke of him with the same standard expression: 'He is a very kind person' (*ta ren hen hao*). They seemed to allude to the notion of *ren*, 'a sensitive concern for others' (Elvin 1985:165), which designates the quality of a gentleman

---

[11] 'The significance of this commentary reached its highest point in the metaphysical thought of the Sung Neo-Confucians' (Shaughnessy 1993:220). The authorship of Confucius is, however, questionable; see Peterson (1982:72–9) and Shaughnessy (1994: 57–66).

in Confucian writings but is not used in spoken language.[12] Zhang cultivated several other virtues of the Confucian gentleman. In response to my request to learn Chinese medicine from the classics, he proposed to form a group of 'friends of learning'. The seminars we held can be viewed as one form of the intellectual exchange that is called *you* (friendship) (see Wu 1993–4:44).

The senior doctor

In sharp contrast to his Confucian ethics, Zhang was given to boasting. Self-promotion was common among the Chinese doctors I met, especially those who were called senior doctors, and was probably a habit rather than a feature of personal character. Most senior Chinese doctors were in private practice, and praise of their own skills advertised side-by-side with bone setters, herbalists, and masseurs was perhaps necessary in an environment of petty enterprise.[13] Possibly this self-advertisement influenced not only the clients' choice of therapy but also reinforced their own belief in themselves.[14] In the streets of small-scale business this self-advertisement did not strike one as boasting, but in Zhang's surroundings it was incongruous with his Confucian ethics.

As a gentleman comparable to the scholar doctors of Imperial times, Zhang distanced himself from the artisans and the petty merchants who addressed the uneducated masses and advertised their skills or goods. Such purpose-oriented use of knowledge and skill was considered 'shallow' (*qian*) and such people 'petty' (*xiaoren*). Confucian ethics advocated consciousness of status and may have encouraged the segregation of social groups in Socialist China which resulted in a gap between the realm of government work units and that outside it. The intellectuals of a work unit readily mixed with people from other work units but they showed reserve towards those who made their lives outside the realm of work units, 'among the people' (*minjian*). 'In the streets it's not safe' (*jieshang bu anquan*), they would say. 'He or she mixes freely' (*ta daochu pao*), was an expression of slight disapproval. Notably, one of Zhang's

---

[12] Chao (1995:215–23) underlines the importance of *ren* among elite physicians in Late Imperial China.

[13] Compare with Landy (1977:469): 'In addition to ameliorating the effects of illness and disease, the curer's activities were oriented toward enhancing and/or reinforcing his social position.' Or Janzen (1978:225): 'The *Banganga* spend considerable efforts lauding their own skills.'

[14] Alfred Leder (p.c.) points out that boasting is, from a psychological point of view, a form of self-persuasion. Particularly for treating difficult patients, therapists need to strengthen their belief in themselves.

mottoes was from the *Analects* (Lau 1979:60; verse I.8): 'Do not accept as friend anyone who is not as good as you.'

The *qigong* masters I knew who worked as private enterpreneurs were skilled at praising their art too, but rather than referring to themselves, they often cited other *qigong* healers for their skills. This did not necessarily reflect any ethic of mutual support among them, but was probably a response to the lack of general acceptance of *qigong* as a respectable therapy. *Qigong* healers had to assure their clients of the powers of their therapeutic methods before they could praise themselves.

In government institutions certain doctors and teachers boasted too, but most of them considered it a bad habit. TCM doctors tended to acknowledge their specialised skills or their sense of responsibility. 'The "skills for handling the needle" (*shoufa*) of my father seem to be so exceptional that many patients come to me for treatment', said the son of a famous senior doctor in charge of the acumoxa clinic at the City TCM Hospital. Of the acupuncturists working in the government institutions of Kunming city, he definitely had the largest clientele (fifty to eighty patients a day). A female acupuncturist at the Yunnan TCM College, known as 'conscientious' (*renzhen*) and 'warmhearted' (*reqing*), said: 'I'm always the last to leave our clinic at noon, I've got so many patients.' An acupuncturist at the Red Cross Hospital, specialised in treating eye disorders, said: 'See from how far away people come for my specialised eye acumoxa technique'[15] – this in the presence of a myopic boy from a county town who was staying with his aunt for treatment in the provincial capital during his summer vacation. Successful Chinese doctors measured their achievements by counting the number, the distance travelled, or the status of their clients. Zhang, for instance, treated few patients, but they were high-ranking ones.

In contrast to TCM doctors, who emphasised their technical skill and humanitarian concern, a senior Chinese doctor would almost exclusively boast of his 'experience' (*jingyan*). *Jingyan* was the attribute of a successful senior Chinese doctor. It explained why a doctor was very popular. Nobody would say: 'He has got much experience, but no clients.' If a Chinese medical doctor was not so popular, he would be praised for his 'understanding of theory' (*ta hen dong lilun*) or for 'being a highly cultivated person' (*ta you xuewen*). If a doctor was successful, he was said to have *jingyan*. This points to a conversational implicature (Levinson 1983:97ff.) linking *jingyan* with success in medical practice.

---

[15] This particular TCM doctor's boasting was as straightforward as that of a senior doctor, but like other TCM professionals he explained his popularity by pointing to a technical skill rather than his art of healing.

Farquhar (1994a:171–4) has earlier presented *jingyan* as the quality 'at the center of Chinese medical decision making', which is how Chinese doctors themselves put it. *Jingyan* comprises both the ' "experience of the Chinese labouring masses in their two-thousand-year struggle against disease" ' and the experience of 'the individual doctor and his life in medicine'. Farquhar underlines that '*jingyan* is a good deal more historical, collective, and discursive than the individualistic life narratives that the [English] word experience denotes' (p. 2). But it is important to see that *jingyan* is not only a descriptive term referring to a cognitive quality to which Chinese senior doctors and TCM professionals greatly aspired. *Jingyan* also meant efficaciousness, for it was an attribute of a doctor when he was popular and successful in medical practice, regardless of his skills, knowledge, and experience. This efficaciousness, *jingyan*, was attributed to Chinese medical doctors. *Qigong* masters like Qiu, who possessed secret knowledge, by contrast, had acquired 'techniques of being efficacious' (*you gongfa*). But for healing grounded in *jingyan*, it was not sufficient to acquire techniques. *Jingyan* was personal knowledge which was partly, but not completely, transmissible. It could not be learnt in the classroom or by mechanical imitation. Both the senior Chinese doctor and the TCM professional emphasised that the abilities of perception for a correct diagnosis in Chinese medicine – Palpating the Pulse (*qie mai*) in particular – could only be learned by *jingyan*. This efficaciousness and personal knowledge was acquired through medical practice.

Similar to the English word 'experience', *jingyan* included not only professional knowledge and experience but also life experience and maturity. Although a TCM doctor in his late twenties had more professional experience than his fifty-year-old colleague newly trained in TCM, the patients tended to place more trust in the one with the grey hair. There was still another aspect to *jingyan*. The daughter of the head of an acumoxa department at a Western biomedical hospital was believed to have acquired much of her father's *jingyan*; TCM doctors said that her father would not let anyone else acquire it. She was younger and professionally less experienced than her colleagues, who had graduated from a TCM college, but she enjoyed more popularity among the patients. In this case, *jingyan* explained her popularity and simultaneously referred to the knowledge her father had gathered in his family's tradition, enriched by his personal experience of a lifetime. Her *jingyan* was seen as in opposition to the textbook knowledge of university graduates.

This example highlights, furthermore, aspects of the relation between the concepts of *jingyan* and *laozhongyi*. The above-mentioned doctor had authority based on his *jingyan*, but was generally not called a senior

Chinese doctor. He emphasised that *jingyan* was crucial for correct diagnosis but did not boast of his own. To my knowledge, retired college professors who worked regularly in consulting rooms open to the public were not spoken of as *laozhongyi*. The signs advertising their practice referred to them as 'famous doctors' (*mingyi*), although they were generally unknown 'among the people'. This finding suggests that respected old Chinese doctors in work units avoided being called *laozhongyi*; they were either called *mingyi* or *ming laozhongyi*.[16]

A Confucian scholar is supposed to have the modesty to know that he does not know, but Zhang also had traits of the senior doctor who claims, on grounds of his experience, 'to be in the know'. He did not only boast about his 'own experience' (*wode jingyan*), but also about his knowledge of the classics, and the 'experience of the ancients' (*guren de jingyan*).

The modern intellectual

Liang Qichao (1873–1929) is quoted as saying: 'I love master Kong, but I love the truth even more.' The following generation of intellectuals, advocating the Chinese Enlightenment, made 'science' (*kexue*) along with 'democracy' (*minzhu*) an all-embracing alternative to Confucianism (Schwarcz 1986:33). These political overtones of the term *kexue* (science) cannot be overlooked.

I had several discussions on this term with TCM teachers and students. Teacher Tao once declared during a private lesson that 'making scientific' (*kexuehua*) meant 'splitting up': 'Science is characteristically divided into many subdisciplines.' Others said that being scientific meant proceeding 'step by step' (*yibu yibude*), a statement which pointed to the belief that by building on basic structures one could proceed to learning more complicated ones. To clarify their point, I offered them the example of the process of digestion. Starch, for instance, is considered in biomedical physiology to be gradually decomposed into its basic elements, glucose molecules. A step-by-step view of this process stresses unidirectionality of the flow of time. However, the same process can be viewed as oscillating between two polarities – the neutral milieu in the mouth, the acid milieu in the stomach and the more neutral and base one in the intestines. The step-by-step view was considered scientific; an emphasis on polarity and complementarity was characteristic of Chinese medical thinking. TCM teachers to whom I presented this example

---

[16] In the section called 'Senior Doctors' Farquhar (1994a:14–17) speaks of *laozhongyi* while the sources she cites all refer to *ming laozhongyi*.

immediately understood its message: that Chinese and Western medicine looked at different parameters to describe the same process.

TCM students often shrugged their shoulders when I asked them what *kexue* meant to them. Once, when I heard them speaking of *kexue qigong*, and asked what that was, they answered: 'With "scientific *qigong*" you can achieve rapid effects.' 'Rapid effects' are generally attributed to 'scientific' Western biomedicine, and this 'modern medicine' (*xiandaihuade yixue*) has characteristics generally attributed to the modern pace of life (Hsu 1992b). Another response was: 'You need not learn any mumbo-jumbo, it's quite straightforward, "directly perceived through the senses" (*zhiguan*).' Then I asked if anything directly perceived through the senses is scientific. 'It's just a label that makes people trust you', the student answered, aware of the political overtones of the scientific and the modern. *Qigong* was generally considered superstition and therefore, to forestall any doubt, it was called scientific. His colleague corroborated this: 'It's just a name.'

In everyday language, *kexue* had connotations of something refined and worthwhile. Once, for instance, I was told in a tone of admiration: 'The people in Western countries eat very scientifically' (*xifangren chifan chi de hen kexue*). People would scold others by saying: 'That's not scientific' (*bu kexue*), being scientific in this case being a moral virtue.

As a modern intellectual in the PRC, Zhang believed in science and, as did many Chinese intellectuals, he tried to reconcile scientific discoveries with the observations of the ancients. 'Science and the ancients use different languages for describing the same processes', he used to say. This juxtaposition of 'science and the ancients' (*kexue he guren*) implied that both were valid and authoritative sources of knowledge; he maintained that both described 'objective' (*keguande*) facts. He valued the results of scientific experimentation (which claims to be a means for questioning authority) alongside the authority attributed to experience.

In summary, one may say that Zhang was like every other senior Chinese doctor 'in the know'. His personal knowledge was grounded in experience, thus valid and authoritative. Like all traditional scholars, he understood that his authority lay in a thorough knowledge of the classical canons in which the experience of the ancients was recorded. As a modern intellectual, he valued science highly and compared the authority of personal experience to that of scientific experimentation.

The mentor and his followers

'The training of a disciple takes nine years', Zhang explained to me once: 'Three years for the master to evaluate his disciple, three years for the disciple to reconsider his choice of master and the last three years for the master to transmit the essential knowledge.' Zhang emphasised the importance of personal choice for transmitting the personal knowledge of Chinese medicine. A disciple, unlike a student, was expected to know and accept all aspects of his master's personality. This included the respect a son has for his father (*xiao*) and absolute loyalty.

Unlike Zhang's son, who often contradicted his father, his favourite follower, Zhangdi, was deferential and quiet and hardly ever criticised anything his mentor said. If Zhang made a mistake, the other followers would point to it in such a low voice that Zhang would not hear it; in contrast, Zhangdi either was silent or asked his mentor loudly for clarification. In general, he glanced at his mentor before engaging in any activity. Always attentive to his mentor's needs, he would act as his companion and help him where he could. Zhang treated Zhangdi differently from his other employees. He gave him tasks of greater responsibility, turned to Zhangdi for assistance, and felt familiar enough to scold and accuse him freely. Eventually, the disciple and his mentor would come to share certain gestures and attitudes as, for example, the way in which they lit a cigarette, answered questions, or greeted their patients.

The retired physics teacher in our reading seminar, who was senior to Zhang, claimed to have been friends with him for many years. He made a point of having an interest in the *Book of Changes* as a physicist and had attended the occasional evening courses that Zhang gave at the university. When Zhang planned to go to a conference in Guizhou, he accompanied him. He mentioned to me that Zhang was aged, which sounded as if he considered it his duty to keep him company. Their relationship was not intimate but one of mutual respect and friendship with regard to common scholarly interests. It was reminiscent of the relation of 'being good friends' (*yu zhi shan*) (Wu 1993–4:44) and evidently was one way of making possible the transmission of personal knowledge.

The wife of the physics teacher attended the seminars for no other reason than to spend her time with her husband. Although she claimed an interest in the texts, she did not seem to follow the lectures closely. As time went on, she was often absent. Similarly, one of Zhang's female employees, who was apparently the fiancée of his son, showed little interest in these seminars. It was her employer who had wanted her to join, she explained when I ran into her in a disco (where she looked much more in her element). The other female employee, a graduate student in French literature 'waiting for employment' (*daiye*) whom Zhang expected to become a translator for Chinese medicine, was, by

contrast, very eager to read the texts and prepared the seminars conscientiously. A female *qigong* teacher who was employed in the adjacent
work unit at first attended enthusiastically but soon gave up. Participation in the reading seminar was largely based on personal inclination.
The relationship between mentor and follower might last for a few
months or for years and could develop into one of rather close and
mutual dependency or remain fairly loose throughout.

The personal mode of transmission

One may wonder why the personal mode of transmitting knowledge
deserves to be identified as such. The anthropological literature generally recognises the distinctiveness of secret knowledge, and Chinese
doctors spoke of secret medical knowledge, on the one hand, and the
need to 'standardise' it (*guifanhua*), on the other. Yet for the purposes
of this study, the personal transmission of knowledge and practice needs
to be treated separately from knowledge and practice that is transmitted
in either a secret or a standardised way. The reasons for doing so have
to do with the social aspects of the relationship between mentor and
follower, aspects pertaining to cognition and style of knowing, and
historical considerations.

Firstly, the relationship between mentor and follower was based on
personal choice. Its history was different in each case and very personal.
To what degree and what kind of knowledge was transmitted depended
very much on the personalities involved. Whereas master and disciple
were often kin and were structurally expected to come to terms with
each other even if their personalities clashed, it was perfectly acceptable
for mentor and follower to accept and reject each other on grounds of
character and personality. Apprenticeship could be sought with many
different masters. Crucial was whether mentor and follower had faith in
each other and could build a relationship of mutual trust.

Secondly, the styles of knowing characteristic of personal transmission differed from those that were secretly transmitted. Admittedly,
Zhang did have much in common with Qiu: awe of the ancients; preoccupation with therapeutic practice (also when reading); belief in the
word (Qiu's in its power and Zhang's in its authority); time in vast
amounts devoted to getting to know a single disciple or follower; and a
relationship with disciple or follower which often ended in mutual dependency. The modes of learning were also strikingly similar. The main
path to the profound knowledge of a senior doctor was rote learning.
Zhangdi had memorised long text passages and assisted his master
in medical practice, learning mostly by imitation; a follower lacked

status to ask for explanations (Goody 1978). Repetition and imitation resulted in Qiudi's case in particular sensations and in visions. Likewise, the follower Zhangdi had been told that if he persisted in memorising texts and applying them to medical practice there might be 'revelations' (wu). Without the need for explanation, he would 'just know'.

There was, however, a crucial difference. Qiu's knowing was grounded in knowledge that was limited and transferable. The incantations and gestures could be appropriated by imitation and repetition, which were the same for every disciple. By contrast, profound knowledge was acquired through experience, which was personal and not easily transmitted. Access to profound knowledge depended on a personal style of knowing which was bound to vary from person to person. It was grounded in very personal ways of learning.

Thirdly, the aspects of the personal transmission of knowledge that I observed in Zhang's reading seminars may throw light on a social practice of transmitting knowledge and practice that has only recently been marginalised in China. This social practice may well have been predominant among the traditional elite of the Chinese empire. The Imperial institutions recruited their members by means of an examination system that allowed for a certain amount of social mobility. Rather than advocating the ideology of kinship alone, Chinese officialdom built up a system of personal trustworthiness.[17] Discipleship within it may well have been grounded in personal transmission of knowledge and practice.

The relationship between mentor and followers inevitably brings to mind that between patron and clients. However, there is consensus that patronage, at least in the Mediterranean setting, 'knows that it is itself not the official morality' (Gellner 1977:3). Seed-beds for patronage are found in incompletely centralised states, defective markets, and defective bureaucracies.[18] By contrast, the relationship between mentor and

---

[17] The term 'Chinese officialdom' is here meant to embrace both 'officials of, or close to, the central bureaucracy' (often approximated as 'the state') and 'local elites' who dominated much of social life in local societies in Late Imperial China. On the basis of a statistical evaluation of the record of physicians in local gazetteers, dynastic histories, and medical treatises and biographies, Chao (1995:160–2) concludes that in the Jiangnan area 'The elite physicians in the Qing did not come from families of physicians, as was commonly perceived, but . . . entered into the profession through a career choice'.

[18] Though other views on patronage exist, Gellner's analysis is advocated here in order to underline that patron–client relations are highly valued in an environment in which the personal transmission of knowledge and practice is fostered but not in one that favours the standardised transmission of knowledge and practice. The difference between Imperial China and the Mediterranean setting seems to be that it is the official morale in the former case and not the official one in the latter.

follower is a legitimate and highly valued mode of social interaction in the Chinese setting. A glance at the literature discussing such relations shows that during the Tang to Song periods (618–1279) 'when the idea of the Confucian physician probably originated' (Chao 1995:210),[19] scholars did indeed have a 'sense of discipleship' (McMullen 1988:48). The later periods of the Tang even witnessed 'the development of an *ideal* of independent teaching' (p. 61, italics added). There was evidently an official morality of discipleship among Confucian scholars; emphasis on personal relationships need not indicate a defect.[20]

---

[19] Chao (1995) translates *ruyi* as 'Confucian physicians', a term that is currently subject to controversy and elsewhere approximated as 'scholar-physicians'.

[20] According to McMullen (1988:62), this emphasis on personal relationships could easily be (mis-)used to sanction factionalism: 'Sometimes little more than scholarly or literary friendship linked with the vital element of political help was involved. But in the factionally divided and harshly competitive mid-Tang bureaucracy, Confucian scholars dignified such recognition and support as acts of profound insight.' This comment implies that during a period of a weak bureaucracy, patronage became important not only in the Mediterranean setting but also in Tang China. A difference is noteworthy, however: the officials in Tang China could justify themselves by speaking of a 'profound insight', which, as argued here, is possible only if one accepts the personal transmission of knowledge as an ideal.

4   Interpreting a classical Chinese medical text

Zhang's style of knowing was marked by the way in which he related to the 'experience of the ancients' (*gurende jingyan*), which became obvious already from the first two lessons in our round of seminars (20 and 21 April 1989). These lessons concerned the first paragraph of chapter 66 of the *Basic Questions* (*Su wen*) in the *Yellow Emperor's Inner Canon* (*Huang di nei jing*). This paragraph, which outlines the basic principles of the 'phase energetics' (*wuyun liuqi*), includes a number of concepts that are central to Chinese medicine: various notions of change, the concept of *shen* (Spirit, Spirits, Spirituality), numerological considerations, *qi* (Breath) and *xing* (Form), and *yinyang*. Zhang's mode of interpreting these concepts appeared to be incoherent and subjective. His reading of the text was sometimes non-linear, and I often failed to see the relevance of what he said. Only later did it dawn on me that his learning was directed at making sense of 'experience' (*jingyan*) – the experience of the ancients as recorded in the text – and its application to modern practice. Clearly, the relation to everyday practice of a canonical text was not like that of a modern Western scientific theory. The text was relevant to medical practice, but it was used and interpreted in unusual ways. A pattern or, rather, a variety of patterns can be detected which may be considered characteristic of these Chinese medical ways of relating text to practice. I propose to distinguish the following ones: the indirect mode of interpretation, the authoritative mode, the justificatory mode, the mode achieved by recourse to everyday life, and the creative mode.[1]

The personal adoption of the text

I had explained to Zhang that my aim was to learn 'real' Chinese medicine as opposed to the TCM knowledge taught at government

[1] In what follows, each section presents one of the above-mentioned concepts of Chinese medicine and one of Zhang's modes of interpreting the text; they are presented within one section for no other reason than that this was the way in which Zhang proceeded.

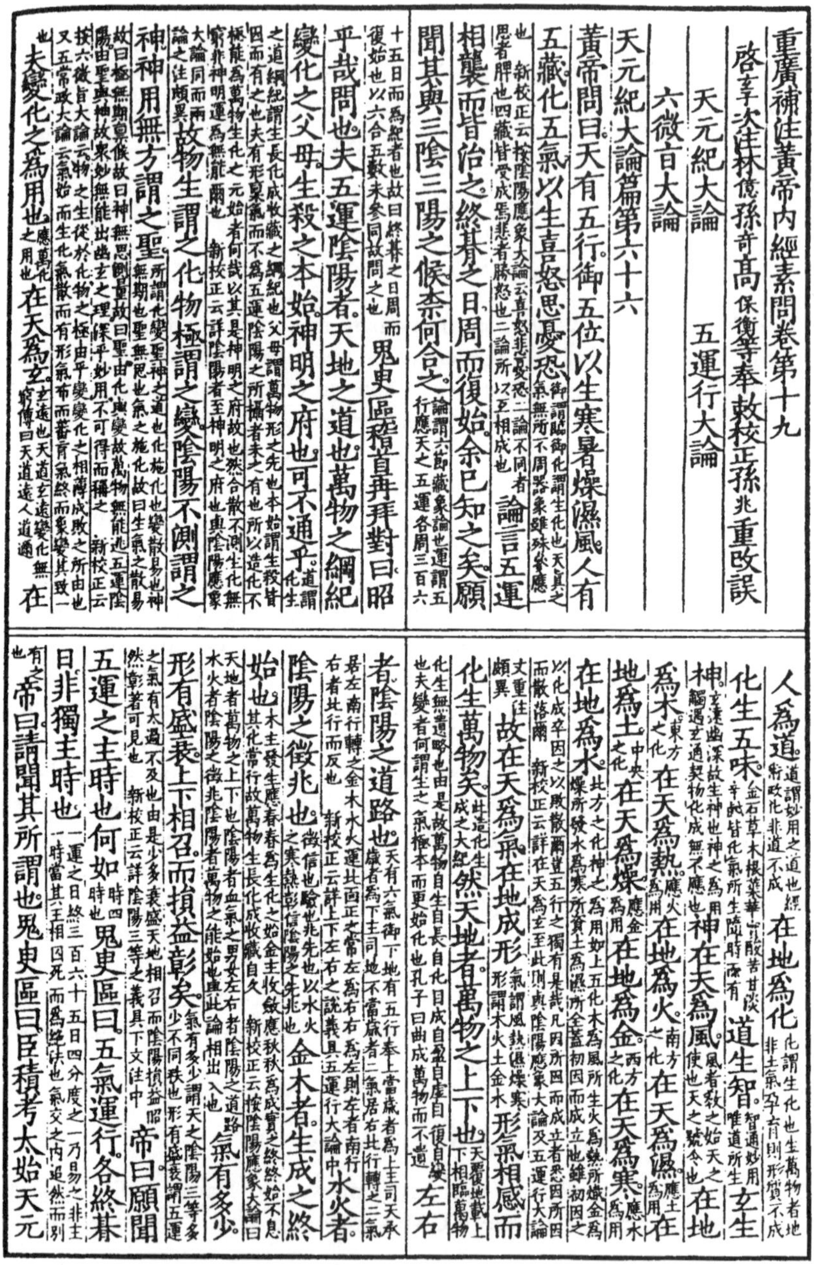

重廣補註黃帝內經素問卷第十九

啓玄子次註林億孫奇高保衡等奉敕校正孫兆重改誤

天元紀大論　　　五運行大論

六微旨大論

天元紀大論篇第六十六

黃帝問曰天有五行御五位以生寒暑燥濕風人有五藏化五氣以生喜怒思憂恐

論言五運相襲而皆治之日周而復始余已知之矣願聞其與三陰三陽之候奈何合之

鬼臾區稽首再拜對曰昭乎哉問也夫五運陰陽者天地之道也萬物之綱紀變化之父母生殺之本始神明之府也可不通乎

故物生謂之化物極謂之變陰陽不測謂之神神用無方謂之聖

夫變化之為用也在天為玄在人為道在地為化化生五味道生智玄生神

神在天為風在地為木在天為熱在地為火在天為濕在地為土在天為燥在地為金在天為寒在地為水故在天為氣在地成形形氣相感而化生萬物矣

然天地者萬物之上下也左右者陰陽之道路也水火者陰陽之徵兆也金木者生成之終始也氣有多少形有盛衰上下相召而損益彰矣

帝曰願聞五運之主時也何如

鬼臾區曰五氣運行各終朞日非獨主時也

帝曰請聞其所謂也鬼臾區曰臣積考太始天元

Figure 4.1   Extract from chapter 66 of the *Basic Questions*

colleges, and he had instantly understood what I meant. He had suggested reading the nine chapters on phase energetics in the *Basic Questions*,[2] which in TCM textbooks were confined to the appendices if discussed at all. Zhang considered the doctrine of the phase energetics 'profound' (*shen'ao*) knowledge that is 'understood only with difficulty' (*nandong*).

Chapter 66 of the *Basic Questions* is said to summarise the principles of the phase energetics. Some of the phrases in the first paragraph were often cited by Chinese doctors; some of these occurred also in *Basic Questions*, chapter 5. My translation is partly based on Zhang's exegesis and reflects a modern understanding of the text; it is, in Waley's (1934:13) sense, 'scriptural' and cannot aspire to be 'historical', which would reflect the understanding of the text at the time it was composed (phrases indicated by bracketed numbers are subsequently discussed).

[1] The Rules of the Origins of Heaven
The Yellow Emperor asked: [2] Heaven has Five Phases, and they couple with the Five Directions, thus giving birth to the Cold, the Hot, the Dry, the Damp, and the Windy. [3] Man has Five Organs, and they change the Five *qi*, thus giving birth to Joy, Anger, Worry, Sorrow and Fear.[3] [4] The 'Discussion' says that the Five Cycles mutually ride each other and that they all govern each other and that on the day when one arrives at the end of the year the circle is complete and starts all over again. I know this now, but what I would like to hear is how they can be reconciled with the stages of the three *yin* and the three *yang*.

Gui Yuqu kowtowed and bowed repeatedly and replied: What a splendid question! As to the Five Cycles and *yinyang*, they are the way (*dao*) of Heaven and Earth, the organising principles of the ten thousand things, the parents of change, the origin of life and death, 'the abode of the spiritual and bright' (*shenming zhi fu*), how can one not master them! Therefore, [5] when things are born, one calls it 'transformation' (*hua*) and [6] when things reach their extremes, one calls it 'transition' (*bian*); [7] when *yinyang* is not fathomed, one calls it Spirituality (*shen*) and [8] when the applications of the Spiritual are not discerned, one calls it 'sagacity' (*sheng*).

---

[2] The seven chapters 66–71 and 74, and parts of chapter 9 were, according to Ren (1982:13), added by Wang Bing (8th century). These chapters on the phase energetics, among which Zhang included parts of chapter 5, constitute one-third of the Song edition of the *Basic Questions*. The doctrine, which abounds in numerological considerations, became important in the Song and Yuan (Despeux forthcoming) and was well established by the Ming (Lu and Needham 1980:140). According to Porkert (1974:58–9), it was much elaborated by Zhang Jiebin (1563–1640) and Wang Ji (1463–1539). According to Lu and Needham (1980:149), Zhang Jiebin and a certain Wang Ji (1522–67) (whom I could not identify) 'criticised it severely'. For a formalistic account of the doctrine, see Porkert (1974:55–106).

[3] Five instead of Seven Emotions are mentioned in this text. The Seven Emotions are standard in TCM (*Fundamentals* (Yin 1984:98); Ots 1990).

[9] The applications of change are the profound in Heaven, the Way in Man and change on Earth. Change gives birth to the Five Flavours, the Way to wisdom, and the profound to the Spiritual. [10] When the Spiritual is in the Sky, it is Wind, and when it is on Earth, it is Wood; when it is in the Sky, it is Heat, and when it is on Earth, it is Fire; when it is in the Sky, it is Dampness, and when it is on Earth, it is Soil; when it is in the Sky, it is Dryness, and when it is on Earth, it is Metal; when it is in the Sky, it is Coldness, and when it is on Earth, it is Water. Therefore, when it is in the Sky, it is Breath (*qi*), and when it is on Earth, it takes Form (*xing*). [11] Form (*xing*) and Breath (*qi*) stimulate each other, and through their change give birth to the ten thousand things. (*Huang di nei jing su wen* (Anon. 1956:130))

Zhang presented this passage on a piece of paper in beautiful hand-writing and asked us first to copy it into our notebooks.[4] The handwrit-ten text in our notebooks took on a personalised form. It stood and was to be understood for itself. Zhang generally did not indicate the source of a citation or the context of a phrase.

Notions of change and the indirect mode of interpretation

Zhang's comments on the title and the first six phrases of this chapter touched on various notions of change. When he explained the title, it became apparent that change was an important aspect of the Spiritual (*shen*) in the universe.[5] From his comments on the following phrases it became clear that the text built on various notions of change. In order to grasp these notions, one had to employ different frames of reference: change was sometimes assessed with regard to the position at which it took place in a rubric of a Direction-Season, sometimes described in terms of different conceptions of time (cyclic or oscillatory, irreversible or reversible), sometimes conceptualised in terms of the observer's view-point and position in space.

Zhang first explained the chapter's title, *Tian yuan ji*, by paraphrasing each word with a modern Chinese word:

---

[4] Compare with Farquhar (1994a:207, n. 10): 'One elderly doctor whose practice I was observing instructed me to make two copies of his recent journal articles by hand. He had cast our relationship in a pedagogical frame and felt this exercise would be good for me. Naturally, he saw no value in the photocopying services I offered him by way of alternative.'

[5] In this text passage *shen* had the attributes of a 'matter-agency' or 'shared substrate' generally attributed to *qi*. See pp. 80–3.

[1] *tian*[6] 'nature'
    yuan[7] 'origin, basis, root'
    ji[8] 'rules'

His translation was 'the rules of the origin and the change that is the becoming of the phenomena of nature' (*ziranjiede xianxiang fashengde genyuan yu bianhuade guilü*). He insisted on this long and clumsy phrasing. 'The rules of the origins of Heaven', suggested as a literal translation, was wrong; the phrase 'the change that is the becoming of the phenomena' was, according to him, crucial for understanding the text. Later I discovered that he used this phrase to circumscribe the concept of the Spiritual.

The notion of the Spiritual was in fact central to this text, since the worldview underlying it was that the Spiritual constituted and simultaneously impregnated the universe. From the very start, our scholarly endeavours directed at gaining an understanding of this universe that is impregnated by the Spiritual were bound to be futile. Analytic thinking and a scholarly apparatus of commentaries cannot adequately account for the experience of the Spiritual (Andrès 1980:7–29). Perhaps the text was designed for meditation rather than interpretation, but Zhang was not a mystic; he considered himself a scholar and attempted an interpretation of the text.

[2] Heaven has Five Phases [Water, Fire, Metal, Earth, Wind], and they couple with the Five Directions (*wuwei*) [North, South, West, Center, East], thus giving birth to the Cold, the Hot, the Dry, the Damp, and the Windy.
[3] Man has Five Organs [Heart, Liver, Spleen, Lungs, Kidneys] and they change (*hua*) the Five *qi* (*wuqi*) thus giving birth to Joy, Anger, Worry, Sorrow, and Fear.

---

[6] For comparison see Fung (1953:19) who discusses *tian* as used by Dong Zhongshu (179?–104? BC): '"Heaven" . . . seems at times to be . . . used to denote the physical universe. At other times, however, he seems to mean by it something somewhat akin to the Western concept of "Nature", yet at the same time something that possesses cognition and consciousness.'
[7] For comparison see Fung's (1953:19) citation of Dong Zhongshu: 'What is called the single *yuan* is called the great beginning . . . Therefore *yuan* is the root of all things, and in it lies man's own origin. How does it exist? It exists before Heaven and Earth.'
[8] *Ji* in this sense often occurs together with *gang*, sometimes in the compound word *ji gang*, 'web without a weaver' (Needham 1956:407ff.) or *gang ji*, 'principle', sometimes in parallel phrases: 'For instance, silk fabrics have *ji* (warps) and nets have *gang* (large ropes with which they are drawn together)' (*Mo zi, Shang tong, shang* (Sun (1934)1939:49)). According to the *Shuo wen jie zi* (Duan 1981:645, 655), *ji* means 'easily distinguished [important] silk threads' (*bie si ye*) and *gang* refers to the 'large ropes of a net' with which the nets are drawn together (*wang hong ye*).

Parallel phrases of a similar kind are frequent in classical Chinese. 'For those who have insight into the changes of the seasons, the changes in the body are intelligible too', Zhang commented. He associated the Cold, the Hot, the Dry, the Damp, and the Windy with the excessive *qi* in the environment coming from the Five Directions (*wuwei*). Joy, Anger, Worry, Sorrow, and Fear, the Five Impulses (*wuzhi*), were understood to refer to excessive *qi* within the body. The above two phrases described analogous processes in Heaven (*tian*) and Man (*ren*), the macrocosm and microcosm, the body ecologic.[9]

Zhang dwelt on the notion of the Five Directions. This spatial dimension was of primary importance. It was a space that had dynamic propensities: '*Kan, li, zhen, dui*, and *kun* are hexagrams from the *Yijing* ... Water, Fire, Wood, Metal, and Earth are ... the Five Agents [Five Phases]. All of these express *directions* of transformation; all of these remind us ... that positions in space are not just abstract points in an isotopic coordinate system but rather gradients of change' (Kuriyama 1987:56, italics added). Zhang did not say so, but I got the impression that he thought along such lines. When I asked for clarification he seemed not to understand me.

The following does not record Zhang's lesson but may highlight what the notion of the Five Directions implied. Phrase [2] stressed the close correlation of the Five Phases, Directions, and Seasons: a Phase coupling with a Direction gave rise to a Season. Granet (1934:113) commented on this: 'Les Chinois ont évité de voir dans l'Espace et le Temps deux concepts indépendants ou deux entités autonomes ... Ils les [l'Espace et le Temps] ont decomposés conjointement en cinq grandes rubriques, dont ils se servent pour repartir les emblèmes signalant la diversité des occasions et des sites.' Emphasis on a differentiation *within* the rubric of a Phase-Direction-Season might have resulted in a clear differentiation between Directions and Seasons – that is, between the spatial and the temporal dimension with which we are familiar in modern Western thought. In phrase [2], however, the opposite was the case: the correlation between Phase, Direction, and Season was stressed,[10] thereby emphasising the differences between rather than within five 'rubrics'.

A reading of this text in modern times is the more difficult because the Phase-Direction-Seasons cannot be reconciled with the modern

---

[9] Joy correlates with Fire, Anger with Wind, Worry with Earth, Sorrow with Metal, and Fear with Water. Zhang did not comment on the different sequencing of the Phase-Direction-Seasons in phrase [2] and the 'Organ-Breath-Impulses' in phrase [3].

[10] Water–North–Coldness (i.e. winter), Fire–South–Heat (i.e. summer), Metal–West–Dryness (i.e. autumn), Earth–Centre–Dampness (i.e. late summer), Wood–East–Windiness (i.e. spring).

conception of space and time as homogeneous dimensions. 'Les Chinois ne se sont point souciés de concevoir le Temps et l'Espace comme deux milieux homogènes, aptes à loger des concepts abstraits' (Granet 1934:113). Space was not imagined as an empty container or time as a homogeneous flow. 'Just as space appears to the concrete mind not merely as a schema of extension, but as something filled with hills, lakes, and plains – in each of its parts open to different possibilities – so time is here taken as something filled, pregnant with possibilities . . .' (H. Wilhelm (1951)1977:17). H. Wilhelm, referring to the notion of time in the *Book of Changes*, makes the same point as Granet: extension, which is common to both space and time, is conceived of as filled with particularities. Changes in space and time are inherent in a certain position in space and time; change does not result from a cause that produces an effect and, in this sense, involves no causal relation.

This does not mean that the five rubrics of Direction-Seasons were the only concepts that accounted for temporal variation and change. The passage refers in phrase [4] to a cyclic conception of time:

[4] The 'Discussion' says that the Five Cycles mutually ride each other and that they all govern each other and that on the day when one arrives at the end of the year the circle is complete and starts all over again.

Zhang drew a circle on a piece of paper and said: 'To end means to begin, every end is a beginning; every winter is followed by a spring.' The changes observed in the world of plants indicated that every process in nature occurred in cycles. Within such a paradigm, based on the cyclic aspect of time, even death, which we experience as irreversible and absolute, may be understood to give way to rebirth. Even matter that we consider inanimate, such as rocks and minerals, may be understood to mature, fade away, and begin to grow again. Becoming and perishing and becoming again may be the same for all processes in nature, the main difference being the duration of a cycle (Sivin 1987:53ff.).

The notion of cyclic processes is important for understanding many processes in Chinese medicine, but not for all. Here we need to bear in mind that the *Basic Questions* were edited during the Tang dynasty (618–906) (Sivin 1993:202). While words, idioms, phrases, and sentences are apparently grounded in Han-dynasty grammar (206 BC – AD 220) (Keegan 1988:18), the overall text of the classic of Chinese medicine needs to be seen in the context of the *Zeitgeist* during the Tang, when Buddhism was being widely promoted by the Imperial Court. Buddhist teachings of rebirth and Indian theories of recurring world-resorption stressed the cyclic aspect of time with regard to 'all that concerned processes of biological change' (Needham 1956:420).

Without any doubt the paradigm of cycles was used in China long before the ideas that Buddhism brought became known, but it may not be appropriate to project a cycle onto every process. In the following two phrases, for instance, the cyclic aspect of time was not central for understanding change.[11]

[5]   When things are born, one calls it *hua* (transformation).
[6]   When things reach their extremes, one calls it *bian* (transition).

Zhang pointed out that *hua* and *bian* referred to different notions of change. *Hua* described the process of a movement or a development. It also described a change from Formless (*wu xing*) to Form (*you xing*). To illustrate this, he breathed on his glasses and we observed condensation on them. Similarly, *hua* could describe a change from Form to Formless.[12] Zhang raised the example of boiling 'water that changed into *qi*' (*shui hua wei qi*). *Hua* also described a pathological change in the body, a process of development from one stage to another: a common cold could *hua*-develop into diarrhoea. *Bian* denoted an alternation or a transition from one state to another. Zhang illustrated this by burning a piece of paper to ashes. He went on to say that Wind and Coldness from the outside world (*fenghan*), having trespassed into the inner world of the body, changed into a 'common cold of the Wind Cold type' (*fenghan ganmao*).

Zhang's comments were sparse. He explained these two terms of a philosophical text with simple demonstrations: the condensation of water and the combustion of paper. In other words, his mode of interpretation was indirect and non-verbal. This was significant: he left it to us to find words and offer a line of interpretation for what he had demonstrated without verbally clarifying what it meant. Was *hua* a physical change of state of the same compound and *bian* a change due to a chemical reaction such as a combustion? Was Zhang really extending the meaning of classical Chinese concepts to processes in modern physics and chemistry?

---

[11]   The Tang editor Wang Bing wrote a lengthy comment on *bian* and *hua* which ends in a quotation that evokes an understanding of cyclic change: '*Qi* begins and thereby gives rise to transformation (*hua*), *qi* disperses and thereby takes Form, *qi* spreads and thereby induces luxuriant growth, *qi* ends and thereby the phenomena are altered (*bian*); that which it brings about is one.' These comments evidently reflect the *Zeitgeist* of the Tang.

[12]   The distinction Chinese medical doctors make between things that have Form (*you xing*) and are Formless (*wu xing*) has scarcely been discussed in the Western literature. Kuriyama (1995:219) comments: 'The attention to dichotomies alien to Chinese thought [i.e. body–soul/mind dualism] has often led to neglect of distinctions that the Chinese did make.'

Seeking to understand the meaning of *bian* and *hua* in classical texts, we could conceive of change taking place within different paradigms of time. Leach (1961) speaks of 'two basic experiences of time' (p. 125): certain changes such as ageing are irreversible, others such as day and night repeat themselves like the 'oscillations of the weaver's shuttle' (p. 126). *Bian*-change and *hua*-change would then refer to these basic experiences of time. *Hua* would emphasise the experience of (temporarily) irreversible change grounded in a conception of time as a uni-directional flow and *bian* would delimit change by alluding to the repetitive and oscillatory aspects of time. The difference between *bian* and *hua* does not, however, seem to depend on such notions of time. Rather, the spatial location of an entity and the position of the onlooker observing that entity seem to play a role. In this context *Xun zi*'s (Zhang 1974:248) notion of 'entity' (*shi*) provides a key to understanding the difference between *bian* and *hua* in terms of the subjectivity of the observer and his position in space. One can read *Xun zi* as saying that *bian* designates change that can be observed from outside an entity, while *hua* refers to transformations within it (Hsu 1994).

It is also possible that, contrary to the suggestion evoked by the parallel presentation in phrases [5] and [6], *bian* and *hua* may designate notions of change that are not opposites.[13] Sivin (1990), who studied *bian* and *hua* in the 'Great Commentary' (*Da zhuan*)[14] of the *Book of Changes*, found, for instance, that *bian* occurred much more frequently than *hua*. In the three instances in which *hua* occurred as a separate word it was understood to designate 'natural change in general, process seen whole' (p. 34). *Hua* was not the opposite of *bian*; rather, the collocation of *bian* and *tong* was frequent. Sivin translated *bian* as an 'alternation or transformation' and contrasted it with *tong*, paraphrased as 'continuity'.

If one paraphrases *hua* as a 'natural change in general', as Sivin (1990:34) did, it is important to be clear about what 'natural' meant in ancient China.[15] In modern Western science, metamorphoses such as the change of a frog into a quail are not 'natural' processes.[16] The term

---

[13] 'Opposites typically differ only along one dimension of meaning: in respect of all other features they are identical, hence their semantic closeness; along the dimension of difference they occupy opposing poles, hence the feeling of difference' (Cruse 1986:197).

[14] What Zhang called 'The Commentary on the Appended Aphorisms' (*Xi ci zhuan*) is in the sinological literature often rendered as the 'Great Commentary' (*Da zhuan*).

[15] 'Nature' is conceived differently in every culture; see Lloyd (1991b) on the 'Invention of Nature' in classical Greece.

[16] The definition of *hua* in the 'Canons' (*Jing*) of the Later Mohists (*hua, zheng yi ye*) is followed by an example in the 'Explanations' (*Jing shuo*): 'A frog becoming a quail' (Graham 1978:295; A45).

hua, however, refers to conceptions of the universe in which such metamorphoses were considered 'natural'.[17] The paraphrase 'natural change' is for yet another reason somewhat infelicitous, since in modern Western scientific thought 'natural change' is limited by 'natural laws'. This modern Western view of nature subject to laws has evolved, according to Joseph Needham (1956:518–83), from earlier conceptions of lawgivers and laws. It is intrinsic to a modern reader's notion of 'natural' but not to that of the ancient Chinese.[18]

In the 'Commentary', *bian* often described the change of a 'line' (*yao*) in the 'trigrams' or 'hexagrams' (*gua*) from hard to soft or vice versa. The opposition of hard and soft was often paralleled by the opposites day and night, which highlighted the experience of oscillation in time. At the extremes of day and night, at dusk and at dawn, day changed into night or, vice versa, night into day. If the notion of *bian* in the 'Commentary' were to apply to *bian* in chapter 66 of the *Basic Questions*, *bian* might refer to processes conceived of as a change in polarity between two extremes. In terms of Zhang's example, the crossing of the boundary from Wind and Coldness to a common cold would be viewed as a change in polarity: reaching the extreme and shifting from the outside to the inside world. Possibly this change in polarity was not only a process of transition but also a 'trigger', with the Outer Disease Factors (*waiyin*) Wind and Coldness triggering the Distinguishing Pattern (*bianzheng*) of the common cold of the Wind Cold type.

This notion of change as a 'trigger' is also found in other passages of the *Inner Canon*. A phrase in *Basic Questions*, chapter 5, comes to mind: '*Yang* engenders and *yin* grows (*yang sheng yin zhang*).' The term *sheng* (engendering) implies aspects of triggering. Zhang explained the difference between *sheng* (engendering) and *zhang* (growing) during a later lesson by saying that without lightning and thunder the plants would be unable to sprout in the spring. Exploring the implications of the Primordial (*xiantian*) cycle and the Worldly (*houtian*) cycle of the 'eight trigrams' (*bagua*), he said that the Primordial cycle was best understood in terms of oscillation between opposite trigrams, the Worldly cycle as a description of the cycle of the seasons (see fig. 4.2). In the Worldly cycle, Thunder (*zhen*) was followed by a Mild Wind (*xun*), the former

---

[17] Further examples are given in Granet (1934:131) and Needham (1956:431).

[18] Consider also pp. 574–5: 'In 1474 a cock was sentenced to be burnt alive for the "heinous and unnatural crime" of laying an egg, at Basel; and there was another Swiss prosecution of the same kind as late as 1730 . . . The interest of the story lies in the fact that such trials would have been absolutely impossible in China.' For objections to Needham's view, see Bodde (1957, 1979). Bodde admits, in the end, that his is a 'minority viewpoint' (1979:154).

Figure 4.2   The Wordly Cycle (above) and the Primordial Cycle (below) of the Eight Trigrams

initiated the sprouting of the seedlings,[19] the latter enhanced their growth by gently soothing them. Possibly Thunder effected *bian*-change and the Mild Wind *hua*-change; the *bian*-transition may have had connotations of triggering and the *hua*-transformation of evolution within a single entity.

Zhang's indirect mode of interpretation inevitably led to deliberations in the subjunctive such as these. Instead of providing clear definitions of the words in the canonical text by means of explicit paraphrases in modern Chinese, he offered simple demonstrations – breathing onto his glasses and burning a piece of paper – and left it to us to decide which aspects of them were relevant. This shows how much room he left for a personal assessment of his indirect interpretation.

The concept of *shen* and the authoritative mode of interpretation

Shen is a fundamental concept in Chinese medicine,[20] but notoriously vague and polysemous. In early Chinese writings, *shen* were hybrid beings, simultaneously dangerous and sacred. In the concordance of the *Classic of Mountains and Lakes* (*Shan hai jing* (Yu 1980:59)), for instance, one finds a long list of Spirits (*shen*) that are hybrid beings inhabiting different mountains. However, in other traditions, for instance in the *Writings of the King of Huainan* (*Huai nan zi*), *shen* refers, as in medical writings, to an impersonal matter-agency (Roth 1990).

In the first paragraph of chapter 66 of the *Basic Questions*, *shen* occurs four times. Zhang gave a separate interpretation for each occurrence and made no attempt to find an underlying meaning applicable to all of them. During Zhang's lesson, phrases [7] and [8] were explained first and phrase [10] much later; phrase [9] was discussed in another lesson. This sequencing highlights Zhang's emphasis on the particularity of meaning and its implications for the authoritative mode of interpretation.

[7]   When *yinyang* is not fathomed, one calls it *shen* (Spirituality).

Zhang's comment, in standard modern Chinese: 'The normal phenomena of nature, the normal metabolisms in the human body; they cannot

---

[19] The role of Thunder is parallel to the role of percussion at the opening of certain rituals, for example, wedding or New Year festivities (Freedman 1967:17–18) or at the beginning of a scene in Chinese opera.

[20] On *shen* in Chinese medicine, see Porkert (1961; 1965; 1974:193–6), Davis (1996) Hsu (in press); on *shen* in the 'Commentary', see Peterson (1982:103–10); on *shen* in the *Guan zi* and *Huai nan zi*, see Roth (1990).

be researched or exhaustively described; what *yinyang* cannot explain is called *shen*.'[21]

[8]   When the applications of *shen* are not discerned, one calls it sagacity.

Zhang's comment: 'The changes of things.'[22]

[10]   When *shen* is in the Sky, it is Wind, and when it is on Earth, it is Wood; when it is in the Sky, it is Heat, and when it is on Earth, it is Fire; when it is in the Sky, it is Dampness, and when it is on Earth, it is Soil; when it is in the Sky, it is Dryness, and when it is on Earth, it is Metal; when it is in the Sky, it is Coldness, and when it is on Earth, it is Water. Therefore, when it is in the Sky, it is Breath (*qi*), and when it is on Earth, it takes Form (*xing*).

Zhang's comment: '*Shen* implies seasonal changes of nature and refers to different kinds of materials. Seasonal changes produce corresponding material changes; such are the normal changes of nature, and these are called *shen*.'

[9]   The applications of change are the profound in Heaven . . . the profound [gives birth] to *shen*.

Zhang's comment: 'Although the Heaven is profound and mysterious, its application becomes evident in the "changes of things" (*shen*). One can therefore search for the rules of all forms of change in nature by observing every form of change in things.'

These long and convoluted sentences convey much of Zhang's style of commenting on a text. The list allows us to identify a sense common to all four occurrences of *shen*, namely, 'the change of natural phenomena' which is reminiscent of 'the change that is the becoming of the phenomena of nature' (see p. 109). During Zhang's lesson, however, we were far from arriving at such a synthesis of meaning. On the contrary, *shen* was taught as having particular meanings in different contexts.

Once, Zhangdi pointed to an interpretation of a concept which contradicted earlier interpretations by Zhang. In general, although he made an effort, Zhang failed to understand any question. In responding he would either promise to talk about the issue later and never do so or elaborate on a sermon in which he would simply ignore the problem raised. On this occasion, Zhang eventually understood Zhangdi's problem. He responded by scolding Zhangdi, saying that he ought to know the basic rule for reading classical Chinese texts – that what was valid in

---

[21] When we read exactly the same phrase in chapter 5 of the 'Commentary' a month later, Zhang contradicted himself and, citing Sun Zhensheng's (1981:491) comment, said that *shen* meant 'to make use of the principle of *yinyang*'.

[22] Phrases [7] and [8] probably describe a hierarchy of qualities ascending from *yinyang* to *shen* to *sheng*, but Zhang did not comment on this.

one context was not in another. After this incident, I never saw Zhangdi point out contradictory interpretations of a text. In our group Zhang decided what was valid; he alone had the authority to do so.

The odd number three and the justificatory mode of interpretation

Confronted with text passages full of numerical statements such as those in *Basic Questions*, chapter 66, Zhang insisted that the various numbers were not an instance of numerology. 'They have a basis' (*you genju*), he said; they were grounded in the long-term observation and experience of the ancients.

In phrase [9], there was clearly a trilogy of Heaven (*tian*), Earth (*di*), and Man (*ren*). The odd number three occurs frequently as a modifier of entities in texts of Chinese medicine. There are, for instance, Three Lights (*sanguang*) in the sky: the sun, the moon, and the stars. In the human body there are Three Treasures (*sanbao*): the Spirits (*shen*), the Blood (*xue*), and the Essences (*jing*). According to Zhang, this prevalence of the odd number three was inherent in things in the world, rather than reflecting numerological considerations.

[9]   The applications of change (*bianhua*) are the profound in Heaven, the Way in Man, and change on Earth. Change gives birth to the Five Flavours, the Way to wisdom, and the profound to the Spiritual.

Since metonymical analogues came to mind, I understood the text to describe parallel processes of the Three Geniuses (*sancai*) or the Three Poles (*sanji*): Heaven, Earth, and Man.

Heaven	:	the profound	:	the Spiritual
Earth	:	change	:	the Five Flavours
Man	:	the Way	:	wisdom

Heaven is above, Earth is below, and Man is in between. This trilogy is one of the most pervasive elements of Chinese thought. The eight trigrams may be viewed analogically: *qian*, pure *yang*, is heavenly; *kun*, pure *yin*, is earthly; and the six trigrams of intermingling soft and hard lines are human. In the human body these six trigrams of intermingling *yinyang* correspond to the six qualifications of the Circulation Tracts (*jing*), namely the three *yin* (*taiyin, shaoyin, jueyin*) and the three *yang* (*yangming, taiyang, shaoyang*), as referred to in the above text passage. With this trilogy in mind, one could rephrase the text by saying that the profound was heavenly, change earthly, and the Way an attribute of humankind.

I am quite certain that Zhang would not deny that this line of thought was contained in the text. He might well have mentioned it himself on another occasion. During this lesson, however, he interpreted the text as follows: 'The applications of change are the profound in Heaven and [they are] change on Earth; change gives birth to the Five Flavours.' Then the seminar was over. At the beginning of the next seminar we continued with the second series of phrases without recalling the former ones: '[It is] the Way in Man, the Way [gives birth] to wisdom, and the profound to the Spiritual.' This non-linear reading altered the sense of the sentence. It divided the sentence into two instead of three parts. The first part, discussed at the end of the first seminar, emphasised the changes in Heaven and on Earth; the second part, discussed at the beginning of the second seminar, concerned the Way and Man.

'You see', Zhang commented with regard to the first part of the sentence, 'all living beings are born on Earth and die on Earth, "therefore" (*yinci*) we say that "the Spleen is the Basis of the Worldly State" (*pi houtian zhi ben*).' This well-known maxim of Chinese medicine seemed irrelevant for interpreting the text but Zhang pronounced it as if it were a direct consequence of the content of the text, using the conjunction 'therefore'. Admittedly, one may recognise a macrocosm–microcosm link between the Earth and the Spleen: the Earth, situated in the middle of the world, is the mother of life just as the Spleen, situated at the centre of the Five Organs (*wuzang*), is the source of well-being in the Worldly State. Additionally, there was an associative link between the text, Zhang's comment 'living beings are born on Earth and die on Earth', and the Worldly State: the Worldly State usually refers to the events of life on Earth (after birth and before death). The macrocosm–microcosm relation seems, however, insufficient to explain Zhang's use of 'therefore'.

One need of course not go to China to find people using conjunctions like 'therefore', 'so', and 'then' in inconsequential ways, but I became convinced that Zhang's use of 'therefore' reflected a certain habit of interpretation and that it would be unfair to put it down to carelessness or illogical reasoning – particularly when I found that other senior Chinese doctors reasoned in similar ways. Moreover, Zhang's use of *yinci* (therefore) in modern Chinese, struck me as reminiscent of the way in which *gu* or *shi gu* (therefore) is used in classical Chinese. One may object that classical and modern Chinese are two different languages and that it makes little sense to use the meaning of a word in classical texts to explain its usage in modern Chinese. Here it is important to recall that we are exploring not so much the semantics of words in different languages as the use and so-called 'performative significance' of words in social interaction. Zhang was engaging in an activity very similar to that of his forebears when he provided exegeses of classical texts. The word 'therefore' was, and still seems to be, used as an aspect of this social practice – a mode of interpreting texts that I propose to call justificatory.

In classical texts, Chinese writers and commentators often used 'therefore' in unusual ways. In the *Tao Te Ching* (Lau 1963), for instance, the phrases at the end of a verse are often introduced by 'therefore'. This conjunction does not seem to indicate a consequence or a causal relation between the two clauses that it links. Rather, it appears to introduce a phrase that rounds off the verse with a generally valid statement. A. C. Graham, whom I approached with this problem, was well aware of it and proposed as translation of *gu* 'for this reason we say' (p.c., December 1990). His translation could be understood to mean that *gu* linked a cause (namely, 'the reason we say') to an effect. It could, however, equally well point out that a rather lengthy description (an entire verse) is being placed in correlation with a shorter, summarising statement (the short phrase at the end of the verse). In Zhang's case, 'the Spleen is the Basis of the Wordly State' would accordingly be taken as the generally valid end-statement that summarised the contents of and the comments on the first part of the above sentence [9].

Lloyd (1996:111–12) has devoted some thought to this issue and presented four cases of the use of *gu*. In three of these, it introduced a phrase that repeated a previously mentioned statement.[23] In the light of this I suggest that *gu* need not always introduce a generally valid statement but may sometimes introduce a clause that refers to a previous statement. In the fourth example, however, the clause introduced by *gu* functioned as a conjunction that introduced a clause referring not to a previous statement but, arguably, to a previous assumption.[24] In all four cases, the clause beginning with *gu* rounded off a line of thought and

---

[23] The four cases are all taken from *Historical Records* (*Shi ji*), chapter 105, the latter part of which comprises 25 case histories. In case 1, the patient himself states that he has a headache (Sima 1959:2797). The doctor provides an explanation in terms of postulated processes which he ends with the statement: 'Therefore he had a headache.' In cases 6 and 18 (p. 2801 and p. 2808–9), *gu* is collocated with *yue*: 'Therefore I said'.

[24] In case 15, the previously mentioned statement is that the patient will die in summer, while the sentence introduced by *gu* is: 'Therefore death occurs when spring comes' (Sima 1959:2806–7). The previous assumption is given in the phrase that introduces the entire paragraph: 'As for that whereby [I knew] that, when spring comes, there would be a deadly illness [or: death and illness].' In his concluding clause to this paragraph, introduced by *gu*, the doctor says: 'Therefore death occurs, when spring comes' (Sima 1959:2807). A 'deadly illness' is not death, but one can assume that death is involved.

seemed to be a summary. Although this summary was not necessarily generally valid, it referred in these four cases to the previously known. Peterson (1982:87–8), considering *shi gu* ('therefore') in the first paragraph of the 'Commentary', suggested that the first five phrases referred to the realm of Heaven and Earth and that the conjunction 'therefore' introduced phrases concerning the processes at work in the *Book of Changes*.[25] He proposed to view the relation between these two groups of phrases as one of 'duplication': *shi gu* figured as a conjunction between different levels of reasoning, reasoning referring to the realm of Heaven and Earth being 'duplicated' by reasoning as recorded in the *Changes*.

Peterson's interpretation that 'therefore' was used to duplicate one level of reasoning by another can be applied to Lloyd's four examples: reasoning that describes the conditions of the patient's illness is 'duplicated' in the clause introduced by *gu* by reasoning with regard to prognosis or diagnosis:[26] *gu* links two different realms of reasoning, the former medical speculation about postulated processes in the body, the latter about prognostic and diagnostic data (that are relevant to the medical practitioner and directly linked to therapeutic intervention).

This interpretation is consistent with our observation that 'therefore' introduces a summary related to a previous statement or a previous assumption. In Peterson's example 'therefore' introduces a clause referring to previously mentioned statements in a book, the *Book of Changes*. Thus not only is the reasoning in one realm 'duplicated' in the clause introduced by *shi gu* but the reasoning in its duplicated form relates to the generally valid or previously recorded.

Graham (1986) discussed the beginning of chapter 3 in the *Writings of the King of Huainan* with particular attention to phrases introduced by 'therefore' (*gu, shi gu, shi yi*). He stated that it was obvious that 'therefore' did not provide a 'causal explanation' or an 'unimpeachable deduction'; rather, 'each correlative explanation presents what is seen as the *crucial factor* among the indefinite number of factors bearing on

---

[25] According to Peterson, *shi gu* links the first five phrases to the following five phrases. However, according to Sun Zhensheng (1981:482–3), *shi gu* links the first five phrases to only three of the following phrases. If one accepts that *shi gu* tends to link a rather lengthier account to a short clause at the end of a paragraph, there is reason to follow Sun's interpretation.

[26] In case 1, postulated processes inside the body are brought into correlation with a previously mentioned complaint of the patient. In case 6, signs of illness on the surface of the body are correlated with the doctor's previously mentioned prognosis. In case 15, signs of illness on the surface of the body are correlated with a prognosis that is implicit in an earlier statement. In case 18, signs of illness on the surface of the body are correlated with the doctor's previously mentioned diagnosis (Sima 1959:2797, 2801, 2806–7, 2808–9).

the case, very much as we pick out the crucial factor in offering a causal explanation' (p. 35, italics added). Whereas, as Graham points out, in Western reasoning the 'crucial factor' tends to be a causal explanation, in the above examples of Chinese reasoning, it seems to be a previous assumption. The conjunction 'therefore' links different realms of human experience, and the clause it introduces refers to a previously (sometimes implicitly) known experience.

What motivated Zhang to link the above statements from different realms of human experience with 'therefore'? Having read: 'The applications of change are the profound in Heaven, and [they are] change on Earth; change gives birth to the Five Flavours', he commented: 'All living beings are born on Earth and die on Earth' and summarised by saying: 'Therefore, the Spleen is the Basis of the Worldly State.' Zhang 'duplicated' the text from the *Inner Canon* with a generally known maxim of Chinese medicine. The maxim 'the Spleen is the Basis of the Worldly State' may have sprung to mind while he was reading the text, which is not unlikely to happen to a practitioner. This previously known, generally valid statement of medical practice became for him the 'crucial factor'. Rather than being interested in the cause as 'crucial factor', Zhang considered a practice-oriented maxim the 'crucial factor'.

It may have looked as if Zhang took the text as an authority giving guidance to his practice. The above analysis has however shown that Zhang's mode of interpretation consisted of using the text as a means of justification, it justified a maxim of Chinese medical practice which had intuitively come to his mind. In referring to an ancient text as an authority for justifying a generally valid maxim of medical practice, he subordinated the text to his interests in medical practice. While it is a commonplace in the West that Chinese medical doctors tend to use the past as justification of the present (the *classical* text is used as justification of the *modern* practice), the above analysis suggests that Zhang himself was concerned more with the interrelation between text and practice than with the interrelation of past and present (using the classical *text* as justification for the modern *practice*).

Xing and qi and Zhang's interpretation by recourse to everyday life

In text passage [10], *qi* (Breath) and *xing* (Form) occur as manifestations of the Spiritual. The Spiritual in the Sky becomes *qi* and the Spiritual on Earth becomes *xing*. Zhang did not comment on the relations between the Spiritual, *qi*, and *xing* in this text, but those familiar with the notion of *qi* may be perplexed to find that in this text it is contrasted with *xing*. The Breath (*qi*) of Wind, Heat, Dampness, Dryness, and Coldness is contrasted to the Form (*xing*) of Wood, Fire, Soil, Metal, and Water. The manifestation of the Spiritual in the Sky is Breath and refers to the Five Seasonal Influences (*wuqi*). The manifestation of the Spiritual on Earth is Form, possibly referring to the Five Materials (*wuxing*).[27]

Zhang here repeated the demonstration described above: he breathed onto his glasses. His comment this time was: 'Water changes into *qi*, and *qi* changes into Form.' This time instead of opposing the Formless to Form he opposed Breath (*qi*) to Form (*xing*).

Turning to the second part of phrase [9]: '[It is] the Way in Man, the Way [gives birth] to wisdom, and the profound to the Spiritual', Zhang explained: 'Although the Heaven is profound and mysterious, its application becomes evident in the "changes of things" (*shen*). One can therefore search for the rules of all the forms of change in nature by observing every form of change in things.' This interpretation, which seemed to invoke a synopsis of modern empirical and deductive theory, was too obscure for me, and I asked for an example. Zhang answered without hesitation: 'Look at the trees', he said, 'They start greening in spring, are abundant in summer, lose their leaves in autumn, and are dormant in winter.' He referred to a very familiar observation of seasonal variation, identified these changes of things as *shen*, and called them the profound in Heaven. He understood phrases of high abstraction in terms of experiences of everyday life. 'Why does a cow eat grass and produce milk?' he asked, and answered:

[11]   *Xing* and *qi* stimulate each other and through their change give birth to the ten thousand things.

Such jumps from questions of everyday life to highly abstract explanations were not unique to Zhang's reasoning but commonplace among all the senior Chinese doctors I met. The questions they addressed concerned observations of everyday life or their experiences with TCM principles (which to them were just as 'real' as observations). The answers they gave employed very general concepts made comprehensible by reference to observations of everyday life.

---

[27] *Wuxing* is in this context rendered as the Five Materials in consideration of Graham (1986:77): 'Down to 300 BC . . . water, fire and the rest of them are resources provided by Earth for human labour, explicitly called *cai* "materials" and included with grain among the *fu* "storehouses". They are not *qi* at all (it is sunshine, shade, wind, rain, dark and light, influences from Heaven, which are *qi*).' Chapter 66 was composed in or even after the Tang, many centuries after 300 BC, but the phrases themselves predate its composition (Keegan 1988:18).

This mode of interpretation is easily dismissed as 'unscientific', which it certainly is. It reflects preoccupations of another kind, highlighting a principle of the interrelation between Chinese medical writings and Chinese medical practice which is not the same as that between 'theory' and 'practice'. The generalities expressed in the above passage outline a 'doctrine', not a 'theory'.[28] Notions like *shen*, *qi*, and *xing* are 'empty' in that the adept fills them with meaning in the course of learning the practice of medicine (Boyer 1986; 1990:24–45). They may seem vague to the newcomer who has no experience in medical practice but their meanings can be very specific and precise, depending on the particular encounter with an individual client. With growing experience, the words may become increasingly polysemous. Since such 'empty concepts' are rarely defined by denotation in the text, they acquire their denotational meaning in medical practice.[29]

According to Zhang, the meaning of the writings could not be understood without experience in medical practice. The writings were memorised, often without being understood. They became meaningful in specific instances of medical practice. A follower had to learn when to remember which phrase of the medical literature was relevant to medical practice. The goal was to gain what Farquhar (1994a) has called 'virtuosity' in combining the two.[30] Zhang's mode of interpretation by recourse to everyday life pointed to a style of knowing that consisted of the 'virtuosity' of combining text and practice.[31] What appears to the outsider as 'jumps from questions of everyday life to highly abstract explanations' is a highly valued skill of combining medical practice with phrases from the medical doctrine. Although this style of knowing seems 'unscientific', its strength for providing therapeutic treatment cannot be overemphasised, particularly for medical doctors confronted with 'realities' of clinical practice that rarely fit a 'theory'.

[28] Sivin (1995d:197) makes the same point: 'The canons were not meant to be, nor were they, used as bodies of theory to be studied apart from therapeutic work. A better word for them is "doctrine". They were not learned as preparation and set aside. To the contrary, we can see from the beginnings to the present day that clinical work gradually reveals to the physician the meaning of canons before his career begins. But this is a reciprocal process. The understanding of the canons, as it deepens, organizes and gives meaning to diagnostic and therapeutic acts.'

[29] 'Denotation' is here used in the same sense as 'reference' (Lyons 1977:174–229): it defines the meaning of a word by pointing to the world outside the linguistic system.

[30] Farquhar (1994a:2) defines 'virtuosity' as 'a form of experience that links practice to history and practitioners to knowledge'.

[31] Lloyd (1995:30) points to case 22 in *Shi ji*, chapter 105 (Sima 1959:2810–11), which emphasises that the interrelation between doctrine and practice is not straightforward. This doctor treated his own illness by following the instructions of a text but, in light of the above analysis, he did so without applying the necessary virtuosity to it. As a result, he worsened his condition to the extent that he was expected to die.

The first paragraph of chapter 66 of the *Basic Questions* ended here. The second lesson continued in a similar manner but soon became very opaque because of numerological formalism. When I showed little interest in it, Zhang did not hesitate to abandon the chapter we had just begun to read[32] and proposed to turn to another text, the 'Commentary' of the *Book of Changes*.

Yinyang and the creative mode of interpretation

Zhang considered the 'Commentary' one of the oldest texts of Chinese scholarship and praised it for its profundity.[33] It is known for 'its fundamental ideas on the value of the Book [of Changes] and the use that can be made of it . . . the discussions about development of civilisation . . . and the maxims of behavior and character formation derived from the Book', and has been characterised as a 'catchall for all sorts of pronouncements about the *Book of Changes* emanating from the Confucian school' (H. Wilhelm (1943)1960:67–8). One of these lessons (11 May 1989) is worth mentioning because it throws light on still another aspect of Zhang's interpretation of texts. It concerns his exegesis of *yinyang*, which is mentioned for the first time in chapter 5 of the 'Commentary':

[12]   One *yin*, one *yang*, it is called the Way.

R. Wilhelm ((1923)1981), here taken as an example of Western scholarship, makes it his first concern to date the source material. He remarks that in the four preceding chapters hard and soft or day and night are generally taken as opposites and points out that the occurrence of *yinyang* may indicate that chapter 5 and the following chapters of the 'Commentary' were produced later. He then cites an explanation from the *Analytical Dictionary of Characters* (*Shuo wen jie zi* (Duan 1981:731)): *yin* and *yang* are explained as describing the shady and the sunny side of a mountain or a river bank. The *yang* side of a mountain or a river bank is exposed to the south and the *yin* side to the north. In conclusion Wilhelm mentions that the meaning of *yinyang* is later expanded to refer to polar forces of the universe and points to the

---

[32] Henderson's (1991:179) 'commentarial strategy', based on the 'commentarial assumption' that the canons were profound, implied that 'those parts of the classics which were not especially profound or philosophical were all but ignored, and attention was focused on a few particular books, passages, and ideas in the classics which were'. This may explain why Zhang had no problem with abandoning the study of a chapter we had just begun.

[33] On the *Yi jing* see Shaughnessy (1993); on the 'Commentary' of the received tradition see Peterson (1982); on the 'Commentary' and others excavated in Mawangdui see Shaughnessy (1994).

tendency, particularly of later Chinese scholarship, to accentuate with *yinyang* the circularity of processes (1981:275–6).[34]

Zhang, in contrast, showed no interest in dating the text or tracing the history of the meaning of *yinyang*. He read us the comments of a modern Taiwanese scholar:

Among all the changes of phenomena in the universe, there is none which is not a function of mutually resonating *yin* and *yang*. For instance: Heaven and Earth, light and dark, hard and soft, strong and weak, male and female, and so on. If there is *yin* there has to be *yang*; if there is *yang* there has to be *yin*. Their boundaries are clear, but they have to combine with each other and only then can they establish themselves. In the process of the intercourse of *yin* and *yang*, *yin* retreats if *yang* advances and *yang* becomes latent if *yin* becomes evident; although their quantities are not consistent, they have the alternating functions of mutual opposition and mutual support in an everlasting circuit. These alternating functions of one *yin* and one *yang* are exactly the rule of Heaven, and they are also the principle of the *Book of Changes*. (Sun Zhensheng 1981:490)

Zhang praised Sun for the accuracy and richness of his interpretation. A good commentator did not merely translate classical Chinese into a more intelligible language but enlivened the text with his personal interpretation. Someone who aimed at an exact translation was considered to have shallow knowledge. Like adding salt to a dish, the commentator was expected to make the text tasty by spicing it with his personal commentary. Thus, although Zhang appreciated the abundance of the cited opposites, he felt that it was necessary to add 'to prosper and to decline' (*sheng-shuai*) and 'to be preserved and to be destroyed' (*cun-wang*). These two opposites may seem merely two additional examples of the same principle, but to Zhang they were crucial. With them he had given the text a personal interpretation.

That commentators are encouraged to be creative has far-reaching effects. Great thinkers of the past presented their thoughts not so much in the form of monographs as in the form of commentaries (Henderson 1991:3). Commentators elaborated completely new styles and systems of thinking. Galen is a prime example: he considered himself a commentator on the Hippocratic writings while setting up a new medical doctrine. 'There was always more to faithful interpretation than mere repetition, and sometimes there was sophisticated, original thought stimulated by contemporary debate' (Lloyd 1991a:399).

The senior doctor's modes of reasoning

Zhang's seminars were not built on the idea that there are fundamentals and that initial simplification facilitates access to more complex

---

[34] This tendency is also visible in Wang Bing's comments on *bian* and *hua* (n. 11).

issues. With Zhang we read texts of the *Inner Canon* phrase by phrase, and the more we read and compared what we had learnt, the more confused we became – the wider the horizon, the tinier ourselves swimming in a sea of knowledge. There was no certainty on which we could build, no rigor which provoked contradiction; there was only the faint hope that gradually we would get the feel of the rhythm in language and learn to float with the waves of ideas that it conveyed.

Zhang valued highly the experience of the ancients in the classics, but he did not aim at their historical interpretation. He did not speak of identifiable hidden meanings. The profound knowledge he aimed at was practice-oriented – it could not be explained either in writing or in speech. This knowledge was particular and personal, just like experience. A mentor cannot teach experience, but he can use the text to convey his personal insights.

We have seen (chs. 1–2) that the *qigong* master made no attempt whatsoever to try to explain anything to his disciple that went beyond hands-on instructions. The one time I heard Qiu instruct his disciple verbally he was angry. Memorising incantations, imitating gestures, learning how to identify the plants in the mountains and grind them into powder – all these special skills could be learnt without much exegesis. In contrast to Qiu's secret knowledge, which was transmitted by imitation and repetition, Zhang's learning was transmitted by means of interpretation. TCM teachers, in contrast to both, believed in explanation. For them it was not only those who were 'predestined' (*you yuanfen*) to learn who were considered able to acquire knowledge. Knowledge, if didactically presented, was accessible to everyone. Zhang shared their open attitude, but he did not believe that knowledge could be explained. Rather, he provided idiosyncratic exegeses in the context of a personal relationship. For him there was no generally valid standard of medical knowledge; each doctor had his own, very personal virtuosity.

5   The standardised transmission of knowledge

With the legitimation of Chinese medicine in the mid-1950s, the Communist Party had instigated a programme for systematising its many strands and currents. This undertaking is reminiscent of earlier attempts at compiling and condensing medical knowledge, repeatedly carried out under government sponsorship throughout the last two millennia, such as the editing of the *Basic Questions* (*Su wen*) in the Tang (618–906) and again in the Song (960–1279). In recognition of the continuity that the current efforts have with those in Imperial (Unschuld (1980)1985; Ma 1994:499–516) and Republican times (Andrews 1996, Lucas 1982 with regard to health-care policies), I propose to conceive of them all, past and present, as being directed at a standardisation of knowledge and practice.

The current standardisation of Chinese medicine, elsewhere referred to as 'institutionalisation' or 'professionalisation', goes hand in hand with its Westernisation and modernisation. The term 'institutionalisation' makes it seem that there had been no institutions of Chinese medicine prior to the current efforts, and 'professionalisation' is a notion coined with regard to Western biomedicine in North America (Freidson 1970), which implicitly emphasises the hegemony of Western biomedicine and its model role for China. By speaking of a 'standardisation' rather than a 'Westernisation' or 'modernisation' one avoids polarising Western and Chinese cultures or so-called traditional and modern values. The term 'standardisation' is meant to emphasise the continuity of the ongoing processes with those in the past.

Some of the aspects of standardising the transmission of knowledge at the Yunnan TCM College were quite particular to Socialist China, some to Chinese culture in general, others to historical circumstances in Yunnan province; still others are common to all efforts at standardisation of the transmission of medical knowledge and practice. They will be summarised in the last section of the chapter.

The setting: a work unit

The Yunnan TCM College, founded in 1960, had 530 employees including 236 teachers, 91 administrators, 81 members of the school-intern printing press brigade, 76 workers, 46 laboratory technicians, and 1000 permanent students in 1988–9. As a work unit, which is an institution peculiar to Socialist China (see Lu 1989 and Bian 1994 in contrast to Li 1991), it continued to imply a 'specific way of life' in urban China despite recent economic changes (Hebel and Schucher 1991). Work units, with their facilities for work and administration, dormitories and apartments, canteens, shops, sports grounds, libraries, kindergartens, medical stations, sometimes fish ponds or even cinemas, have been characterised as cells of urban society marked by boundedness, self-sufficiency, and a certain degree of autonomy. They have traits of the total institution in Goffman's ((1941)1975:17) sense in that 'the central feature of a total institution can be described as a breakdown of the barriers ordinarily separating these three spheres of life [work, leisure, and sleep]'. But Henderson and Cohen (1984:8) rightly point out that 'Goffman's model is based on a Western conception of the individual' and that it may 'blind us to the reality of the experience from the Chinese point of view'. In an attempt to approximate to the latter, in what follows particular attention is given to administrative–functional units or 'compartments' and their spatial arrangement on the work unit compound.

The school was situated in the centre of the modern city, near the main square where the east–west and north–south axes of the city's major traffic routes met. The East Wind Avenue was flanked by the administrative buildings of the Provincial Parliament, the City Government, the City TCM Hospital, and the solid concrete of a Japanese joint venture, a luxury hotel in the process of construction. The apartment blocks of the governmental units were built in the former back-yards of the TCM college where fields had been cultivated during the Cultural Revolution (1966–76).

Like most work unit compounds, the school compound was secluded from the outside world, surrounded by a brick wall and designed to be as self-sufficient as possible. The school gate opened towards White Pagoda Street, where private commerce had been effervescent since the early 1980s. At the gate there were guards, one in uniform and others – employees, junior teachers, and students – taking over the responsibility by turns. The tiny brick cabin of the guards was divided into two even tinier spaces, one accommodating the night custodian on an iron cot and the other a bench, a chair, and a telephone (the only one available to the thousand students).

Connections with the outside world by foot, phone, and mail were all made through the gate. Opposite the guardhouse were the mailboxes. The newspaper wall with news from the outside world was also within sight of the guardhouse. Directives from the inner world were likewise made public at the gate: it was flanked by a blackboard bearing information for Party members and a wall on which administrative announcements were displayed. Most of the staff was housed outside the main compound and glanced at these walls daily before leaving it.

The gate ensured effective control over the traffic of people and information. During the demonstrations from April until June 1989, for instance, one of the college's five vice directors was stationed at the gate for several days. The school authorities' control could be tightened, and on certain occasions, as on the evening of 4 May,[1] the school gates were closed. After the events of 4 June,[2] every visitor to anyone on the school grounds was asked to write his name and unit in the guard's book.[3]

The concrete sports ground was the largest space within the school. Open to everyone, it was never deserted. Before dawn, often in complete darkness, *qigong* and *wushu* trainees, joggers, and other gymnasts enlivened it. After breakfast, murmuring students with green books in their hands started to populate it, learning by heart one textbook passage after another. Athletics, ball games, and martial arts were taught here during class time and often continued by groups of players before and after meals. Sports were the legitimate and favourite activity of most male and some female students as well as many unmarried male teachers. And at night, lovers would sit close to each other on the edge of the field behind oleander bushes in the shadow cast by the moon.

A compartment which stood in stark contrast to the open and often crowded sports ground was on the other side of the central building. It was reserved for the brigade which was responsible for housing equipment such as furniture and electric installations. A few single-storey houses, a workshop, and some offices surrounded a space which was open and very quiet, especially at noon when the sun was flickering on the white ground and the workers were dozing in the shade of a brick wall.

---

[1] On the 4 May movement, see Schwarcz (1986).
[2] On 4 June the people's movement in Beijing was crushed by military intervention (see for instance Pieke 1996:183).
[3] This practice was implemented in the colleges of Kunming only during the first month after the 4 June incident. In other cities such control over visitors was routine.

The brigade responsible for cars occupied a lofty corner of the compound. Several lorries, school buses, and cars were sheltered in well-maintained garages. At the end of 1988 the car brigade had expanded and the adjacent bicycle lot had been moved to a much smaller area. The compartment of the bicycle lot, like that of the school garden (which consisted mainly of a greenhouse), was framed by an iron fence. When it was reinstalled in an area with several rows of cypresses, trees were felled or branches cut only where necessary to accommodate the iron-sheet of the shed. Finally, a tiny brick house with a door and an iron-barred window was built, big enough to hold a stool and a small stove for the custodian. The requirements for an independent compartment seemed fulfilled.

Less visible but just as distinct were the quarters of the school administration which occupied the first and second floors of two buildings built in the Socialist style of the late 1950s. The architectural style and the building material of these constructions were qualitatively superior to the concrete of the classroom building or the soft red brick of the library. The rooms had the luxury of wooden floors, a matter of major significance in the continental climate of Yunnan, where temperatures fluctuated between burning heat and freezing cold.

On the ground floors of the administrative buildings were the workshops and offices of the printing brigade. The printing press was located on the ground floor of the central building and announced with rhythmic noises the college's printing productivity, scholarly and administrative, the latter being considerably intensified in autumn 1989.

At the far end of the compound were huge vessels for boiling thousands of litres of hot water daily. The kitchen of the two school canteens, one for Han Chinese and one for Muslims, was installed in their proximity. This corner of the compound was at intervals extremely crowded. At mealtimes, hordes of students jostled to get at the tubs from which, with large spoons, the food was dumped into their enamel bowls. The canteen was large and airy, but it lacked tables. The students took their meals in their dormitories, sitting with bowls in hand on the edges of their beds. After lunches and suppers the jostling continued, this time in front of the hot water taps to fill the two thermos flasks for each dormitory. Thereafter crowds of students streamed to the corner behind the steaming vessels to take showers.

A woman, in charge of accepting the tickets (0.2 *yuan* each), sat on a chair in front of the showers, well-sheltered under the wide and large bamboo hat which she wore in sunshine and in rain. Twenty showers, two to three of which were constantly out of order, were available three times a week for women and men on alternate days. They had to meet the needs of the thousand residential students, the hundred to two hundred short-term students, and three hundred or so employees and their family members who had no sanitary facilities in their apartments; everyone I knew took a shower at least once a week. Waiting times varied between one-quarter to three-quarters of an hour and once under the jet of hot water each person would take at least half an hour. Usually two people would use one shower and soap and rub each other with much vigour. In this dim light, in warm dampness and in steam, colleagues would meet each other and, with few exceptions, not be shy to be seen totally naked washing and walking around.

A large new toilet block was situated behind a slogan wall directly opposite the school gate.[4] In urban areas, toilets are usually contained in ten to twenty small and open compartments. Toilet compartments were often occupied, one person after another squatting in silence on her own, sometimes reading in the dim light, usually just staring into nowhere. In spite of its smell, this area seemed to be sought out as a place of privacy and retreat.

At the end of 1988 the walls along White Pagoda Street were torn down and a row of shop units built to be rented to private merchants for 1,000 yuan per month. With shops as walls the boundaries of the unit became blurred. Opening towards the outside had in fact begun two years earlier. First the Department of Traditional Chinese Pharmaceutics (zhongyaoxi) had opened a store to sell drugs, with the profits going partly to the department and partly to the individuals involved. Then the Department of Traditional Chinese Medicine (zhongyixi) had installed cabinets for consultation in which the school's most able doctors were allowed to give consultations three half-days a week, with the profits again being shared by the private person and the department. Finally, in summer 1989, the college dispensary rented a small room from the college authorities which was open to the street. The main staff members were biomedical doctors, and with the consultations they provided to outpatients they could make modest personal profits.

Formal inquiries

Assistant teachers: semidirected interviews

Some of the assistant teachers and I became good friends. We met to talk in the late evenings, went to the cinema together, and had lunch

---

[4] On the 40th National Day, 1 October 1989, the former slogan was white-washed. It was not replaced by a new one.

together at least once a week. In May and June 1989 we used to meet regularly in front of the research students' television to watch the 7 p.m. news. In November 1989, the month before I left, I performed semidirected interviews with all the assistant teachers of the acumoxa and massage staff.

In retrospect, it is apparent that semidirected interviews are the method best suited to anthropological inquiry in a Chinese work unit. The mode of interaction was a conversation which could only continue if both parties understood each other, which meant that short and general responses could be clarified. The interviews usually took place in the teacher's dormitory after lunch or supper. Most college teachers knew that I was studying 'medical anthropology' (*yiliao renleixue*), and many were curious to know more about this field of study. Since most of them had experience in answering questionnaires, they expected a similar mode of inquiry. I met their expectations with a series of questions on age, sex, profession of parents, place of birth, and educational background at the beginning of each interview. This drew a clear line between our daily interaction and the more formal talk. I signalled that what they would tell me thereafter would be data I would write about.

I hoped, nevertheless, to create a more informal atmosphere, and, indeed, by the time we started to talk about their educational background the interview had usually taken an individual course and sometimes become much more personal than expected. Topics of discussion were, apart from their life histories, their motives for studying TCM, their attitude towards their profession, their favourite subject, their view of acumoxa and *qigong* and of the future of these disciplines, their evaluation of students' opinions on TCM and Western biomedicine, their goals in teaching, and whether learning from classical texts was as important as Western medical training. I interspersed these standard questions during our discussions hoping to digress into topics about which they wanted to talk. We often talked for an hour and a half or even more. Some encounters were very moving; others ended with remarks like: 'Your questions make me think' or 'You look at things differently, but that's exactly what I found interesting.'

Students: questionnaires

The information gathered on the students is based mostly on our joint classes and clinical training in the mornings between September 1988 and December 1989, which I spent mostly with 'specialists of acumoxa and massage' (*zhenjiu tuina zhuankesheng*), but also with 'regular TCM undergraduates' (*zhongyi benkesheng*). Additionally, throughout my stay I had lunch with them about twice a week, as well as making irregular visits in the afternoons. In December 1988 I carried out an inquiry by questionnaire during our lunch breaks and interviewed about five male and five female students from each year in their dormitory rooms, repeating eight times the same procedure: I read out standard questions and they replied on paper. They were in general eager to be questioned and cooperative and usually concentrated as if they were taking an examination. Later I hired assistants to set up tables for statistical purposes.

The evaluation of the students' answers turned out to be extremely difficult because the answers I obtained in the questionnaires diverged at times significantly from my own observations and informally gathered information. There was a discrepancy between what I thought the students felt and their written responses to the questionnaire. This has partly to do with the nature of my questions, which sometimes touched on topics that concerned personal inclinations, and partly with their register (style of expression) and language use. Their formally phrased answers seemed partly to accommodate to social expectations and partly to result from a reluctance to think in a way that I call detached-from-the-environment. I have no doubt that they were honest.

Graduates: letter questionnaires

Most graduates were sent to work in the 'county town' (*xiancheng*) they had come from. Since the majority had come from an area which is remote and 'closed' to foreigners (*bu kaifang*), it was difficult to get in contact with them. Therefore, I asked for permission to send them letter questionnaires, and the college authorities were extraordinarily cooperative. One hundred questionnaires (but no more) were printed by the college's printing press and in November 1989, together with a cover letter from the administration, sent to the addresses I had obtained from teachers and colleagues.

The official sanctioning of the questionnaires was made possible only by my agreeing not to ask about the graduates' 'personal interests and activities of everyday life' (*sixiang he shenghuo wenti*). This did not much affect the proposed content of the questionnaire, because I was interested in their training and professional life, namely, the use graduates made of TCM textbooks, journals, and books at their workplace; a description of the work they performed daily; and their view on TCM curricula. Graduates tended in any case to answer any question that touched even slightly on personal issues in vague terms – even a question so easily answered as the difference in livelihood between a doctor and a student. Those questions were in passing addressed in semidirected interviews conducted with fourteen graduates in hospitals and clinics in and around Kunming who, in the course of completing the letter questionnaires, had also made comments useful for interpreting the other answers sent to me by mail.

More than three-quarters of the acumoxa and massage graduates and about half of the TCM graduates sent replies in which most questions were conscientiously dealt with. I acknowledged their cooperation by sending the preliminary results of the questionnaires to the college authorities and to all sixty respondents in March 1990. The responses to the letter questionnaires were much more uniform than those of the students. This has partly to do with my mode of inquiry (mostly multiple-choice questions), but one can also view this uniformity as a result of standardised instruction. Graduates had evidently learnt how to reply to standard questions with standard phrases.

Interviews with the administration

From May to July 1989, I interviewed an official in the college's foreign affairs office fortnightly. He welcomed it, and it kept us on good terms during this exciting but tense period of Chinese politics. He explained to me with great patience the structure of administration and introduced me to other members of the administrative staff. In December 1989 he arranged two short meetings with the City Health Bureau and the Provincial Health Department and one with cadres in leading positions of the college administration.

The teachers

Many of the details on TCM teachers' life histories, livelihood, motivation, and future prospects are characteristic of the staff of government work units throughout the PRC. The problems addressed here – underemployment of young staff, the struggle for a livelihood of the married staff, and the enormous workload for the senior staff – have arisen mainly from historical circumstance. Some aspects of the teachers' condition are, however, characteristic of any standardisation of the transmission of knowledge.

Firstly, teachers were hierarchically organised into ranks – assistant teachers, lecturers, associate professors, and professors (see table 5.1). Rank determined duty and salary, special rights, and the general respect with which a cadre was treated by superiors and colleagues. This hierarchical organisation was, however, strict only on paper. In practice,

Table 5.1. *Ranks and salaries of TCM teachers*

Rank	Monthly salary[5] (*yuan*)
assistant teacher (*zhujiao*)	76
lecturer (*jiangshi*)	108
associate professor (*fujiaoshou*)	135
professor (*jiaoshou*)	150 / 200 / 400 and sometimes more

administrative standards were not implemented systematically but manipulated with flexibility and much attention to the particular. As a result, the staff tended to form clusters in terms of kinship relations, a common native place,[6] comradeship during school and university studies, or a shared revolutionary background. This did not hinder anyone from continuing to profess the hierarchical order of the bureaucracy, but everyone who dealt with it took the clusters into consideration.

Secondly, the teachers' lives were often marked by a lack of direct correspondence between their efforts and their rewards. Often, major decisions in the teachers' lives had been made on grounds of particular circumstance and historical accident. Personal initiative was generally met with suspicion; life in a work unit meant being subject to institutional constraints which actively fostered indifference towards work and working relations – an inevitable consequence of standardisation.

The xiaxiang *year: alienation from the profession*

The career of young staff members usually began with a compulsory year of teaching English at a 'high school' (*gaozhong*) in a county town. Although 'going down to the countryside' (*xiaxiang*) lasted only a year, all the assistant teachers I interviewed considered it 'a waste of time', 'boring', 'a very bad time', 'a much disliked experience', 'with financial

---

[5] The monthly income consisted of 'salary' (*gongzi*), 'bonus supplement' (*jiangjin*), supplements for 'medical treatment' (*yiyao*), 'gas' (*meiqi*), 'water and electric' (*shuidian*), 'cereal supplements' (*liangtie*), and many more. The bonus supplement modified the monthly income most significantly. In certain collectives but not in educational work units such as the college it constituted 150–200 per cent of the salary. This additive composition of the monthly income allowed for much flexibility; during my stay teachers' monthly income was often modified.

[6] National identity was generally of minor importance in comparison to identification with one's native place (Wodiunig 1992:41, 137), possibly with the exception of the 'Muslim' (*huizu*). The Yunnan Muslims, who trace their origins to Khubilai Khan's army, have ever since 1253 constituted an important minority.

and intellectual drawbacks for the profession'. Only one, the youngest, eventually agreed that 'there were advantages' (*you haochu*) for urban youth in being sent to rural areas.

The three cleavages of Chinese society – between classes, between centre and periphery, and between rural and urban – were a common concern among urban residents. Mao's policies for overcoming them had been abandoned, and recent developments such as key schools (Bastid 1984:194) had widened the rural–urban cleavage to a gap that Potter and Potter (1990:296) have characterised as castelike. Aware of this gap, the youngest teacher I interviewed agreed that going to the countryside was positive for her personal experience, but she insisted that this benefit was minimal in comparison with the professional drawbacks of that year.

Another teacher, Hu, would have found it reasonable to be sent to a village medical station or a county hospital. He emphasised how devastating the alienation from his profession was due to this first year of employment as an English teacher, very much aware of his poor English. However, he said that having been sent from the cultural metropolis Shanghai into a rural nowhere he had matured markedly during this year. He struck me as someone well adapted to the social demands of a work unit. This became obvious, first of all, from the course of our interview that consisted of a series of question–answer exchanges lasting less than an hour. Hu gave clear answers to every question and sat silent while I took notes, awaiting the next question. Not once did he offer an additional thought, memory, or topic for discussion. This did not mean that he was uncooperative; when I asked him, for instance, to substantiate his argument with another example, he made the effort to think of one. He was not unwilling to express personal viewpoints, but he would not reveal anything about himself without seeing a definite reason for doing so.

When I asked him whether he enjoyed the work of his profession, he answered: 'It's all the same to me' (*wusuowei*).[7] Chinese medicine meant to him as little today as in the past. His plans for the future? None. Any interests in research, hope of going abroad, desire to work in the clinic only? No. He neither particularly liked nor disliked his profession, Hu explained, and there was no sense in cultivating any hidden wishes for the future. This *wusuowei* attitude was not only widespread among his colleagues but generally encountered among many cadres in work units.

[7] Considering that this interview took place in November 1989, *wusuowei* may have had political overtones, since it was one of the last things Zhao Ziyang had said to the crowd on Tiananmen square before he resigned on the eve of 4 June (Wang Jun, p.c.). The attitude I refer to was, however, widespread in work units well before 1989.

In response to my question of what he usually did in his spare time, the answer was 'Watch TV'. And on Sundays? 'Sleep, read novels, or see friends'. His answers were in content similar to those of his colleagues. What about hobbies? He sometimes played tennis with his father, whose work unit had courts. Moreover, he liked Western classical music and played the guitar quite well. I wondered whether he maintained a richer inner life than it seemed.

Hu was certainly one of the best-adapted cadres at the college. Adaptation to life in a work unit consisted of maintaining a minimum of interest in his profession without losing a certain sense of responsibility towards his patients, keeping discreetly informed about current events while maintaining a low profile, and avoiding gossip in the unit while cultivating an inner life. The experience in the countryside had furnished him with an indifference that would last a lifetime.

Assistant teachers: underemployment

'Assistant teachers' (*zhujiao*) lived, like students, in dormitories. The differences were that a teacher shared a room with one to three colleagues while a student shared it with six to eight and that the electricity was not cut off after 10.30 p.m. in the teachers' house.[8] I rarely heard assistant teachers complain spontaneously about housing, food, and sanitary conditions, even jokingly, although when I raised the subject they had many complaints. This absence of actively voiced complaint may be explained by their perception of their status as temporary and comparatively prestigious.

The work morale among the acumoxa and massage assistant teachers was relatively high.[9] This does not mean that their lectures were didactically well structured, let alone lively or inspiring. On the contrary, teachers often repeated more or less verbatim passages from the textbooks, which some had memorised word for word, often in a monotonous voice. A senior teacher corrected most of their lecture notes and sometimes supervised their lectures, which they generally prepared conscientiously. Officials explained that they recruited only graduates who

---

[8] Several unmarried teachers lived in their parents' homes but still claimed beds in the teachers' dormitory; this was the only way they could secure their right to claim an apartment from the college once they were married.

[9] Acumoxa and massage courses were offered at the college from 1986 onwards. The young acumoxa and massage staff had been sent to the Shanghai TCM College as 'regular students in acumoxa and massage' (*zhenjiu tuina benkesheng*) in 1981 and 1982 (Hsu 1996c).

had been excellent students and were politically sound (not necessarily Party members). To be employed at a college was considered more prestigious than to work at a hospital.

All assistant teachers felt underemployed, and many wanted to work more: 'It's mid-term now, and next week I will be allowed to give my first lecture.' 'This college doesn't care about its young staff and least about the acupuncturists.' 'Here young people can't bring their enthusiasm to bear fruit.' 'Young people don't like to do nothing.'[10] In contrast to the majority of students (see below), the assistant teachers were interested in their subjects. I found much individual initiative among them: one teacher arranged part-time work in a private practice for several weeks during the summer vacations for herself and two colleagues, another made use of his 'connection' (*guanxi*) with a doctor at a hospital and worked three mornings per week (without pay) as one of the doctors in the hospital ward. Yet another spoke of contacting a friend of a friend to pursue her interest in children's massage.[11] This teacher was in addition taking three different evening courses in English.

These three teachers tried to keep their undertakings as inconspicuous as possible. Their motivation may have been suspect because all of them fostered the private hope of going abroad,[12] but teachers who had no wish to go abroad kept their personal interests secret too. During an interview I watched with bewilderment how one teacher climbed onto her cupboard, opened her suitcase, and pulled out a stack of books on *qigong* that she had bought with savings from her salary. With these books in her hands she revealed fantastic dreams of going with her brother, who was a truck driver, to Sichuan province to venerate the famous *qigong* master Yan Xin. It was obvious that individual initiative was not encouraged by the work unit members or superiors. Private initiative was no longer decried as bourgeois and capitalist, but ambition was met with suspicion and outstanding talent with envy: 'Never make a work unit member your friend.' Social control in work units was to a large extent effected through gossip which sometimes entered the more formal forum of political education on Friday afternoons.

[10] Cf. Bastid (1984:198): 'With four students to one teacher, China's higher education probably boasts the lowest rates in the world. Such low ratios, however, reflect low teaching loads rather than small classes.'

[11] Children's massage, hardly known in the West, is said to be most effective against digestive disorders and emotional imbalance.

[12] In 1996 one of them had left China on his own initiative, and Hu had temporarily been sent to Spain as a lecturer on a newly established acumoxa course organised by the college and an acupuncturists' society near Barcelona.

Table 5.2. *Recruitment of the junior acumoxa and massage staff*

Group*	Period of TCM Studies	TCM College	High School Education	CCP Membership	Father's Occupation	Mother's Occupation	Influence on Choice of TCM Studies
A	73–76	Yunnan	Kunming	1975	Cadre	Cadre	CCP propapanda group
	74–77	Chongqing	Chongqing		WBM doctor	WBM doctor	CCP slogans and parents
B	77–82	Yunnan	Zhaotong	1981	Cadre	Cadre	Good in classical Chinese
	79–84	Yunnan	Kunming	1984	Cadre	Cadre	Own wish
C	81–86	Shanghai	Kunming		Cadre	Cadre	Family
	81–86	Shanghai	Jinghong	1985	School director	Worker	Family
	81–86	Shanghai	Wenshan		Cadre	Employee	Family
	81–86	Yunnan	Zhaotong		TCM doctor	Worker	Family
	81–86	Shanghai	Henan Province	1986	Army general	School teacher	Own wish
D	82–87	Shanghai	Qujing	1984	University lecturer	WBM doctor	Family
	82–87	Shanghai	Kunming	1987	Cadre	Cadre	Own wish
	82–87	Shanghai	Lincang		Cadre	Cadre	Mother's and own wish

* group A: lecturers who had been educated as worker-soldier-peasant students
group B: lecturers who had passed the first nationwide university exams, for which they had prepared at home on their own initiative
group C: the first group of assistant teachers recruited and trained at Shanghai to teach the acumoxa and massage course at the Yunnan TCM College (with one exception)
group D: the second group of assistant teachers trained in Shanghai

Lecturers: struggle for a livelihood

The responsibilities of a 'lecturer' (*jiangshi*) were little different from those of an assistant teacher, but because most lecturers were married their living conditions were different. To marry was 'to have one's life problem solved' (*wenti jiejuele*), to step into adulthood. Female assistant teachers in their late twenties were under considerable pressure to marry. Their superiors were not embarrassed to talk with them about this issue in a casual way, and close colleagues arranged meetings with young men they considered suitable. Between 1988 and 1990 four assistant teachers married, one of whom had been 'introduced' (*jieshao*) to her partner in this way. A married couple had the right to claim an apartment, but only one of the five married assistant teachers had been given one (he was divorced a year later, but could keep it).

Complaints by married couples were considered legitimate and were frequent and often substantial. Family life was known to increase 'daily problems' (*shenghuo wenti*). One couple had been waiting for years to be assigned an apartment, another lived apart in different provinces, families had difficulties in making ends meet, children needed schooling and grandparents medical care, housing conditions were cramped, and inflation was soaring. The college administration was apologetic: 'China is a poor country, and this work unit is the poorest college in Kunming city.' Teachers were cynical: 'What do you expect after the politics of the past forty years?' Or indifferent: 'The college administration is bad, but which one isn't?'

Lecturers, in particular, had experience in dealing with the college administration as an aggregate of clusters rather than a hierarchy. They all had a rather peculiar biography (groups A and B in table 5.2). The Cultural Revolution had had a great impact on their education, and they had had a difficult time reaching their position.[13] Their experiences had demonstrated to them that norms were negotiable. Independent of previous initiative and personal history, they were simply disillusioned, probably precisely because of their endless struggle. For instance, two teachers of this 'lost generation' answered my question about the future of Chinese medicine in exactly the same way, by drawing a circle on a piece of paper. The first commented in the Party's terminology: 'Difficulties with development', the latter sighed: 'eighty million illiterates, a two-thousand-year-long history, impossible to get out of this.' Despite their contrasting careers – one had been a 'worker-peasant-soldier'

---

[13] Gold (1991) differentiates between the 1970s, 1960s, and 1950s cohorts, which roughly correspond to the age-groups discussed here. He characterises the 1950s cohort as showing the most initiative; I found that it showed most disillusionment.

(*gongnongbing*) student recruited in recognition of his 'revolutionary' background, the other was the offspring of the 'stinking old number nine' (*chou laojiu*), as the 'intellectuals' (*zhishi fenzi*) were called at the time – their view of China was similar. They could not rid themselves of the feeling of going in circles.

Motives for the choice of the profession

The lecturers had graduated from high school in the early 1970s, the assistant teachers in the early 1980s, and their reported motives for deciding to study TCM had been different. The lecturers had followed the Party line and done it for 'society' (*shehui*). The majority of the assistant teachers, by contrast, had followed the advice of their parents or elder siblings and done it for the 'family' (*jia*). The lecturers assured me that their choice had not been imposed on them – that they had sincerely believed the Party and willingly followed its directions. The assistant teachers maintained, likewise, that their parents had not forced them in any dictatorial way; their parents' advice had simply had most weight, certainly more than any individual's desire. 'At that time, we did not know anyway.' The lecturers expressed their motives for studying medicine as follows: 'With medicine you can serve the people'; 'Chinese medicine is our cultural heritage'; 'Society needs and selects you, follow the needs of society'; 'It sounds hollow to say this these days, after the reforms of the eighties, but we firmly believed in serving the people, only ten years ago.' Assistant teachers said: 'It's best to have a doctor in every family'; 'Your elder sister studied Western medicine, you ought to complement her studies with Chinese medicine'; 'Your grandfather was a "herbalist" (*caoyi*), we have to keep the tradition in the family.' In both cases, the question was not: 'What do I want?' but: 'How do I fit best into the whole?' Relationships were important. Just as in Chinese paintings in which a human being is a dot in a vast landscape, the individual's importance lies in its location in the landscape rather than its size and shape.

Regardless of their motivation, lecturers and assistant teachers had one significant feature in common: they were all the offspring of cadres (see table 5.2). In two cases, at least one parent was a Western medical doctor. Only one was the offspring of a Chinese doctor, and she had been recruited because, as she told me, one of the vice-presidents had considered her performance during the oral graduation examinations brilliant. She was an exception, and she was not accepted by her Shanghai-trained colleagues who considered her naive.

Senior staff: pillars of the college

In 1989 the Yunnan TCM College had fifty-seven positions for 'associate professors' (*fujiaoshou*), all of them occupied, and eleven for 'professors' (*jiaoshou*), seven of them vacant. Among the seven retired professors some were nationally known; with others who had not survived the Cultural Revolution they had been responsible for the college's good reputation in the 1960s.[14]

In the early 1980s an attempt had been made to improve the quality of the teaching staff. Though generally overlooked in the Western literature, it may not have been coincidence that the 'movement against spiritual pollution' (*fandui jingshen wuran*) of 1982–3 occurred in the year in which the first lot of students who had passed the university entrance exams graduated and had to be assigned positions. During that period the college also recruited experienced doctors from all over the province by offering them associate professorships. Three of the four associate professors, who were considered among the best teachers and therefore allowed to give tuition to a foreigner, had accepted this offer: one had worked as a doctor in an industrial centre, another had been head of an acumoxa and massage department in the capital of an autonomous perfecture, and the third had been an English teacher in a rural high school.[15] In the streets of Kunming I encountered two private practitioners, both of whom had held important cadre positions before the Cultural Revolution, who claimed to have been offered such positions as well. They had declined the offer and instead established thriving private practices building on networks with the government cadres they had known earlier in their careers.

It is not insignificant that the three associate professors were women while the two in private practice were men. China's 'Revolution Postponed' (Wolf 1985) has been reinforced for Chinese doctors, at least through the reforms of the 1980s. In all the private practices that I saw, women were wives or employees. Private practices, like small-scale business, are conducted at the level of households, and household representatives tend to be male. As we have seen, a doctor's reputation depends

[14] Among them were three of Kunming's four 'famous senior Chinese doctors' (*ming laozhongyi*): Wu Peiheng (1888–1971), Dai Lisan (1901–68), and Kang Chengzhi (1899–1970). For short biographies of all professors, see Zhang (1989:151–222).

[15] It was most unusual to hire an associate professor from such a low-status position and such a remote area (where she had been sent after graduation from 1969 to 1984, because of her family background). Her father was a retired professor at the college. One could speak of nepotism, but this would not do justice to the situation, which was very complex. Sometimes negotiable norms allow for an appropriate handling of particular cases.

on 'experience' (*jingyan*), which has more to do with popularity than with skills. Experience was obviously more readily attributed to grey-haired men than to capable women.

The above women all complained that an associate professor had very heavy responsibilities and very little pay or prestige. They taught courses for which younger teachers were not qualified, supervised assistant teachers, performed administrative work, and were often successful clinicians. 'There is a huge gap in the teaching staff between us and the teachers, who have had hardly any work experience, and we have to fill it.'

Associate professors were, moreover, expected to perform clinical research. The year before, an associate professor and one of the assistant teachers had produced a research proposal in the field of 'experimental acumoxa' (*shiyan zhenjiuxue*), examining the effects of different needling procedures at the same acu-points (*xuewei*)[16] on the pulse, blood pressure, and body temperature of rabbits. Their proposal was rejected because the college administration preferred research which promised immediate financial benefits, such as a research project that was aimed at developing a cigarette which contained, apart from the famous Yunnan tobacco, Chinese medical herbs with soothing effects on a sore throat. However, the main research performed by the college staff was neither experimental nor clinical but consisted of writing and revising TCM textbooks.

Summary

As the college authorities pointed out, only the best students and the politically sound were kept at the college as teachers. Their employment had to be approved by the province's Ministry of Education, while TCM doctors in hospitals were approved by the Ministry of Health. Almost all were offspring of cadres, and several were Party members. This meant that TCM teachers were generally not recruited from the offspring of senior Chinese doctors,[17] who were bound to have witnessed in their childhood the efficacy of 'superstitious' (*mixin*) medical practice. The teachers who produced the TCM knowledge, and modified and reproduced the textbooks were not bound to family

---

[16] *Xue* means 'opening' or 'cavity', therefore its translation as *foramen* (Porkert 1974:199), *locus* (Sivin 1987:258–64), and Hole (Unschuld 1988b:71/76). In TCM, there was a tendency to conceive of the 'position of the cavities' (*xuewei*) as a point on the body surface for inserting needles; therefore, it is rendered here as acu-point, following Lu and Needham (1980:13). The term *shuxue* which invoked the classical meaning of acu-points, are rendered as acumoxa *loci*.

[17] Cf. Farquhar (1994a:207, n. 10): 'Many "old Rightists" were deprived of opportunities to teach from the mid-1950s to the 1970s.'

tradition and were likely to be more open to 'scientific' (*kexuehuade*) innovation in medical doctrine.

The students

There are many issues worth exploring with regard to the standardised mode of transmitting knowledge and practice, among them the recruitment of students, students' commitment to their studies, and their prospects of employment after graduation. In contrast to a disciple like Qiudi or a follower like Zhangdi, the students at the college were not recruited on grounds of kin relations or personal character, and they did not have to prove their commitment to their master or mentor in everyday life. Students were placed in a passive mode, and this made the question of their commitment to their studies the more salient.

Recruitment

The ideal for recruitment was equal opportunity for everyone. This was implemented by a quantitative assessment of qualifications, namely, examination marks at high school graduation.[18] More than a hundred students were recruited annually, and the sheer numbers seeking instruction demanded that the mode of transmission be depersonalised and the period of learning limited – five years for regular TCM students, four years for regular students in Traditional Chinese Pharmacy, and three years for acumoxa and massage specialists.[19]

Students were recruited from high school graduates in the natural sciences. This policy made university studies in TCM a field of studies like biomedicine, for which knowledge of mathematics, physics, and chemistry was believed to be indispensable. However, most acumoxa and massage freshmen said that, having been trained in the natural sciences, they found it difficult to grasp the style of knowing Chinese medicine, which is grounded in 'experience' (*jingyan*) and 'virtuosity' or, as TCM teachers put it, 'flexibility' (*linghuo zhangwo*). 'In high school I learnt how to apply principles "mechanically" (*siban*). Now, I

[18] In Yunnan, in the 1980s, 'elementary school' (*xiaoxue*) took five years, 'middle school' (*zhongxue*) took three years of secondary school and three years of high school. 'Secondary school' (*chuzhong*) was completed with graduation exams equivalent to O-levels. At the end of 'high school' (*gaozhong*), which emphasised the study of three subjects, came exams equivalent to A-levels.

[19] 'Research students' (*yanjiusheng*) for a 'doctorate degree' (*boshi*) could not be accepted at the Yunnan TCM College. Postgraduate studies of three years to attain the equivalent of a 'master's degree' (*shuoshi*) could be pursued with only one professor, who left the college in 1992, Prof. Zeng Yulin.

still have not managed to master the flexibility required for following the course of the *Fundamentals* ((*Zhongyi*) *jichu lilun*).'

When I asked teachers and students why high school graduates of the arts and literature were not recruited, many of the younger teachers said that they had never thought of this alternative, and some welcomed it because they had encountered these difficulties themselves. Others insisted on the importance of biomedical knowledge for any medical practitioner. One of them spoke of a pilot project in another province in which TCM students were recruited from among high school graduates in the arts as well as the natural sciences. The senior teachers, by contrast, evaded my question or decisively objected to this thought. They were acutely aware of the policy to make Chinese medicine scientific; the foundations of Chinese medicine as a science were the Western natural sciences.

Whereas TCM students were recruited from all parts of the province, biomedical students, I was told, came mostly from the provincial capital. The Yunnan TCM College was an institution of the provincial government, and the Kunming Western Medical College was run by the city. This seemed to indicate that, in Yunnan, TCM education was for providing health care in rural and peripheral areas and Western medical education for the capital. However, the teachers at the college saw no significance in this institutional division. They explained that high school graduates from urban areas had higher examination scores than those from the periphery and rural areas (although the latter often received bonus points),[20] and that admission to studies in Western medicine required higher marks than for TCM.

The college administrator attributed this institutional division of responsibilities for medical education between the city and the province more to historical accident than to medical policy. In the early 1980s, he said, TCM students had also been recruited from Kunming, and as graduates they had quickly filled the available positions in all the hospitals of Kunming city. In 1986 the government had introduced the policy of 'directed recruitment and job assignment' (*dingxiang zhaosheng*, *dingxiang fenpei*), similar to that during the Cultural Revolution, 'the commune you come from is the commune you go to' (*she lai she qu*).[21] Its intention was, on the one hand, to prevent the exodus of intellectuals from the periphery and rural areas and, on the other, to protect intellectuals from the city from being assigned jobs in rural areas. Therefore,

---

[20] Students were given bonus points if their parents had been 'volunteers to go to the border areas' (*zhiyuan bianjiang*), if they were of a 'minority nationality' (*shaoshu minzu*), or if their parents were 'overseas Chinese' (*huaqiao*) immigrants, for example, from Indonesia.

[21] It was implemented from 1983 onward (Bastid 1984:214).

the Yunnan TCM College accepted only two undergraduates from Kunming in 1988 and 1989 (one of whom was the son of the head of the TCM Department). Even if young people from Kunming achieved the necessary scores and wished to study TCM, they had little hope of being accepted (interview with college administration, December 1989). The majority of the students I interviewed, recruited between 1984 and 1988, came from the periphery of the province, and about half of the students' parents were not 'cadres' (*ganbu*) or 'intellectuals' (*zhishifenzi*), but 'peasants' (*nongmin*) or 'workers' (*gongren*) (see table 5.3). The college was, moreover, open to physically handicapped students who were not accepted at other universities, for instance, students who suffered from impaired vision or limped because of childhood polio.[22]

Thus TCM colleges can be seen as institutions which were supposed to narrow the gaps between the classes, between centre and periphery, between urban and rural areas, and (implicitly) between the healthy and the disabled. Given that TCM studies at university level were open to students who came from a low-class background, the province's periphery, and rural areas, it may not be surprising that government cadres and urban intellectuals tended to consider them of 'low cultural level' (*wenhua shuiping bu gao*). Since they continued to view TCM practitioners in this light, even after completion of five years of university study, the poor reputation of TCM knowledge may partly come from the low status ascribed to the people proficient in it and not merely from the particularities of the knowledge itself.

Commitment to studies

Students were assigned their subjects of study, their teachers, and their jobs. Being placed in this passive position naturally had an impact on their morale. I observed much boredom, disillusionment, indifference, and lethargy among TCM undergraduates.[23] Whereas personal commitment is a *sine qua non* for the secret and personal transmission of knowledge and practice, at the college only compliance with the work rulings could be implemented and controlled.

---

[22] Elementary and high school teachers were expected to be mentally and physically fit; therefore the Teachers' Training College accepted no physically handicapped students. This policy applied even at the university level: a TCM graduate who limped was 'kept at the college' (*liuxiao*) because he was considered very capable but not recruited as a teacher; he worked as a doctor at the college's annex clinic. On health conditions that disqualify an individual from college admission, see Pepper (1984:55).

[23] Acumoxa and massage specialists were, by contrast, much more committed to their studies; acumoxa and massage was in several cases the study of their own choice, and they often had clear plans for future employment.

Table 5.3. Recruitment of TCM students entering the college in 1984, 1986, 1987 and acumoxa students of 1988

Year of Entry	Number	Nationality			Parents' Occupation*								Parents' Residence	
		Han	Other	No answer	TCM Doctor	WBM Doctor	Peasant (nongmin)	Worker (gongren)	Cadre (ganbu)	Intellectual (zhishifenzi)	Other	No answer	Centre (Kunming)	Periphery
1984	6 f	2	0	4	0	0	1	0	1	2	2	0	0	6
**	5 m	4	1	0	2 × 0.5	0	2 × 0.5	0	1	1	0	1	1	4
1986	7 f	6	1	0	0	0	3	2 + 1 × 0.5	0	2 × 0.5	1 × 0.5	0	0	7
	8 m	6	0	2	0	0	4 + 1 × 0.5	1 + 1 × 0.5	0	2 × 0.5	1	0	0	8
1987	6 f	5	1	0	0	0	3 + 2 × 0.5	1 + 1 × 0.5	0	1 × 0.5	1 × 0.5	0	0	6
	7 m	2	2	3	0	0	0	1 + 1 × 0.5	1 × 0.5	0	0	5	2	5
1988	11 f	9	1	1	2 × 0.5	1 + 3 × 0.5	0	0	2 + 2 × 0.5	1	1 × 0.5	3	1	10
	7 m	6	0	1	0	1	3	3	0	1	0	0	1	6
Total	57	40	6	11	4	5	19	12	7	10	6	9	5	52

* 1 = both parents, 0.5 = father or mother
** 1985 in clinical training at various hospitals

The college's work rulings required students to prepare for, attend, and review classes, and to take examinations twice a semester. Generally speaking, students attended classes regularly; the teachers recorded absences (at university level). Almost all students took notes; most students learning a speciality used separate booklets, while others, particularly the regular undergraduates, wrote the teacher's comments in the textbook. Homework consisted mainly of learning textbook passages by heart and sometimes of written replies to standard questions at the end of a chapter.

Most students 'prepared' (*yuxi*) and 'reviewed' (*fuxi*) the lectures by reciting them loudly in the mornings and got to the classroom ten minutes before the first lecture started; one or two were regularly late. Students usually answered the two or three questions at the beginning of each lecture to the teacher's satisfaction, but several times the teacher had to ask a third or fourth student. Students were not expected to recite a long textbook passage; their answers often consisted of a short and standard phrase.

One might have thought that compliance with work rulings would be considered sufficient, but teachers and tutors did make an effort to effect an incorporation of staff standards among the studentship.[24] After the mid-term exams for first-year acumoxa and massage students, which were taken in strict silence under the supervision of two teachers, the teachers expressed extreme disappointment and deep concern about the students' performance. In the following class in political instruction, the students were asked to write essays on their scholarly performance. These essays consisted mostly of repentance and promises to be more conscientious. Standard confessions were: 'I amused myself too much' (*wan de tai duo*); 'I thought I understood without understanding' (*si dong fei dong*); 'I did not prepare and review classes conscientiously' (*fuxi bu renzhen*); 'Success is a matter of personal effort' (*shi zai ren wei*). Some expressed difficulties with adjustment to university conditions and mentioned insomnia, imbalance of their emotional life, boredom, and difficulty in learning by rote memorisation. Having specialised in the natural sciences during the last three years of high school, they were now required to memorise one classical text after another.[25] I never learnt whether the performance of this class had been particularly poor or whether the practice of confession belonged to the routine

---

[24] See Freidson (1970:106), who speaks of an incorporation of 'colleague standards' among physicians in North America.
[25] Two students stood out by writing in verse form about their explorations in the city during their spare time. One student stated that he refused to write anything about personal matters.

Table 5.4. *Students' first choice of studies on the preference forms at high school graduation*

Year of entry	Number	TCM		Western Biomedicine		Other	No answer
		Own wish	Family's	Own wish	Family's		
TCM							
1984	6 f	0	2	0	1	2	1
	5 m	1	2	0	2	0	0
1986	7 f	1	0	0	0	6	0
	8 m	1	0	1	0	6	0
1987	6 f	0	0	3	1	2	0
	7 m	5	0	0	0	1	1
Total	**39**	**8**	**4**	**4**	**4**	**17**	**2**
Acumoxa and massage							
1988	11 f	5	0	2	0	4	0
	7 m·	2	0	0	0	4	1
Total	**18**	**7**	**0**	**2**	**0**	**8**	**1**
Total	**57**	**15**	**4**	**6**	**4**	**25**	**3**

initiation of students at the college. Examinations at the end of term were met with much anxiety and more conscientious preparation.

TCM studies were generally an unpopular choice. When asked informally, many students admitted to having had the wish to study engineering, physics, education or, of course, Western biomedicine, but they said that their exam marks had not been good enough. However, when I asked them what subject they had indicated on the forms they were sent at high school graduation, I found that several had, nevertheless, put TCM as their first choice of studies (see table 5.4). In response to this, students explained how difficult it was to fill out the preference forms before high school graduation, what risks one had to anticipate and what choices were likely to be realised. If they intended to be accepted for university studies at all, it was sometimes more prudent to indicate as first choice a subject at an institution that was not one of the most popular ones. For instance, a student who had wanted to study engineering at the Kunming College of Engineering, which enjoyed a nationwide reputation, had not even considered indicating this on the preference form.[26]

[26] On the difficulties and dangers of completing the preference forms, see Pepper (1984:59–67).

So, instead of asking: 'What was your first choice on the preference forms', I should perhaps have asked: 'What did you wish to study?' Indeed, I had asked this of the first group of students, only to find that they considered it difficult to answer. Some appeared to have difficulty talking about past wishes, and some simply did not understand my question. Therefore, instead of asking: 'What were you wishing in the past?' I asked 'What have you done?' but this led to the problem just described: what students indicated as first choice of studies in the preference forms did not necessarily reflect their own wish. More often than not, they had followed their parents' advice and claimed that it was their own. In fact, whether it was the students' wishes, their parents' wishes adopted as their own, or their obligations to their parents, as either 'filial piety' or straightforward 'obedience' (*xiao*), simply seemed to miss the point. Commitment to one's studies was considered not to depend on private wishes – certainly not on one's wishes at the time the forms were completed. Despite the lack of clarity about what their 'own wishes' meant, only eight of the thirty-nine regular students claimed that TCM was their first choice of studies; for the other four-fifths TCM was not their choice.[27]

In response to the question of whether they liked their studies twenty-six out of thirty-nine wrote that they did; as few as eight wrote that they disliked them and five indicated indifference. On paper the majority of the students seemed to have a positive attitude towards their studies, whereas I had observed widespread disillusionment, particularly among TCM undergraduates. The only way I could explain this discrepancy between what they said and what I thought they felt was that their answers reflected language use that accommodates to social expectations.

A student who wrote that he 'liked' his studies explained: 'You have to like what you do; I am not very interested in Chinese medicine, but I want to learn it well.' He seemed to express what most students who said they 'liked' their studies felt. If 'to like' meant to comply with work rulings or possibly even to be committed to one's studies but not 'to be interested' in them, this would explain why two of them could say simultaneously that they 'liked' their studies and that they wished to change professions.

To like one's studies was the proper thing to do, an unmarked expression; to express dislike was offensive. It is noteworthy that among those eight who openly expressed dislike, five spoke of a concrete altern-ative: one wanted to open a Chinese herbal pharmacy, three planned to

---

[27] The ratio among acumoxa and massage specialists accepted in 1988 was significantly better, seven out of eighteen had put acumoxa and massage as their first choice.

establish private practices, one wished to study TCM theory, and one was studying for exams to be accepted as a 'research student' (*yanjiusheng*) in Chinese philosophy. Those who had the courage to express dislike had alternatives in mind and, rather than being uncommitted, were among the most enterprising students. Those who were completely disillusioned would say instead that they 'had no opinion' (*meiyou yijian*). Much as talking about a bad marriage as 'the usual sort of thing' (*yibande*) avoided stigma (Potter and Potter 1990:192), and actually saying that it was bad would call for intervention, expressing dislike called for proposal of alternatives. The idea of 'changing professions' (*gaihang*) avoided stigma, possibly because it was common practice after the reforms in the 1980s; I took it as a reliable indicator of dislike for the studies. Among the five who expressed 'indifference' (*wusuowei*), several spoke of changing professions. Did indifference stand for disillusionment and dislike?

The third question that related to the students' commitment concerned their plans for the future. In response to this question about half of the students (twenty-six out of fifty-seven) said: 'To become a good doctor' (*dang hao yisheng*). Even students who had expressed indifference replied with this phrase. Thus, this answer could not be used to distinguish committed from uncommitted students. When I insisted that what I was interested in was not stereotyped phrases, but their 'own' (*benrende*) wishes, one of the students exclaimed: 'Of course, we all have the wish to go abroad, of course, each of us wants to open a private practice and be his own master, but you know that there is no sense in making such a statement!' I understood this to mean that he disliked wasting time on hopes that were bound to be disappointed. In this case, the students' attitude did not arise from lack of imaginative thinking, but rather from a reluctance to express in public personal wishes that they considered unrealistic.[28]

The students' unwillingness to talk about unrealistic personal wishes doubtless had to do with their perception of the self and the importance they attached to the self. The notion 'of a private existence within a public world' (Lukes 1973:59), which implies that behind closed doors one may do and think as one wishes without taking the surrounding environment into account, may allow the European to have unrealistic personal wishes – wishes that are 'real' in that limited private sphere. This detached-from-the-environment thinking seems contradictory to common sense and everyday behaviour in China. Things become

---

[28] Psychological tests with Chinese and Polish students have been interpreted to indicate that Chinese are reluctant to *think* of improbable conditions (Gawlikowski 1982); the above finding calls for reconsideration of such interpretations.

Table 5.5. *Graduates' answer to question: Do you like your profession?*

	Year and Programme		
Choice of Answers Given in the Questionnaire	Acumoxa and Massage 1986–8	1987–9	TCM 1985–9
Letters sent out	30	30	60
Letters containing a response to this question	19	18	22
I always liked TCM	12	5	2
I started to like it in the first or second year	3	4	5
I started to like it during clinical training	3	5	11
I started to like it after job assignment	0	0	1
I never liked TCM	0	2	3
I started to dislike it in the first or second year	0	0	2
I started to dislike it during clinical training	0	1	2
I started to dislike it after job assignment	3	2	3

significant not so much because of their existence in this world as because of their relationship with other things. How can a private wish, separated from any context, be considered 'real' at all? 'Becoming a good doctor' was more 'real' and therefore an acceptable response.

Whereas difficulties in evaluating the students' questionnaire answers were endless, the utterances that they volunteered in everyday life situations were much easier to interpret. It was striking to observe, while participating in the clinic, how many students were fascinated by the success they achieved: 'Illness management is unique' (*zhibing dute*); 'Every time I can cure a sick person, it makes me happy.' It was obvious that TCM undergraduates became more interested in their studies during their year of clinical training (see also table 5.5). Some students eventually became more positive: 'In the beginning I did not like Chinese medicine, but eventually I became very interested in it.' 'The teachers have considerably influenced me in this process.' There were, however, also students who were initially interested in Chinese medicine and later became disillusioned. The answers to the letter questionnaires indicated that this was the case, particularly among newly employed graduates (see table 5.5 last line).

Job assignment

The learning process at the TCM college was conspicuously disrupted between April and June 1989, when excitement lay in the air where otherwise indifference predominated. It may not be coincidence that outbreaks of the kind took place precisely in institutions in which knowledge and practice were standardised. While the Western press and overseas Chinese have emphasised the prodemocracy aspect of the movement and no doubt, 'democracy' (*minzhu*) and whatever it implied was an issue for the organisers of the movement, most students at the college knew more clearly what it meant to be against 'corruption and nepotism' (*guandao*) than for democracy.[29] My seventeen to nineteen year old classmates marched out of the college gates on 17, 18, 19 May and on 5 and 6 June, knowing that all of the nation's students were in the streets. In scorching heat, which had melted parts of the asphalt, they followed their fellows carrying their banners and shouting their slogans and found it all very exciting. Compared with the masses of students from other universities, the TCM college was poorly represented in the peaceful and silent crowd on Kunming's main square, but the few who joined with fervour gave way to a deep-rooted anger. 'The more chaos the better', one of the more active ones exclaimed while painting this phrase in beautiful calligraphy onto a strip of cloth that he later tied round his head. He knew about the threat of spies and police and the risk that 'accounts will be settled after the harvest' (*qiuhou suanzhang*),[30] but simply declared: 'We have nothing to lose.' Exactly this attitude has repeatedly assigned twentieth-century Chinese university students the role of rebellion (Schwarcz 1986). Other urban dwellers had employment, flats, and families; they had not much, but something to lose. Teachers could not demonstrate in the streets without the danger of being punished, though they were at least among the spectators, implying support (see also Pieke 1996:186–7). And, of course, students did really have something to lose, namely, the prospects of their future employment. Hanging their heads after the crackdown, they gathered around a tavern table towards midnight with sad looks, and one of the graduates' explained: 'You know the slogan "down with corruption and nepotism" (*dadao guandao*), possibly, you shouted it yourself. Do you know what you were shouting for?! Our concerns are concrete: job assignment; that's what it is all about.'

I slowly came to realise the desperation with which students faced their job assignments. Most took the jobs they were given, but I

---

[29] For a social anthropologist's account of the movement in Beijing, see Pieke (1996:180–252).

[30] He was later assigned a job not at the 'prefecture' (*zhou*) or 'county' (*xian*) level but at a village (*xiangcun*) 'medical station' (*yiliaozhan*). It was not said whether this assignment was related to his activities or not.

remember one graduate who was doing all she could to stay in Kunming: 'The problem of job assignment causes the most headaches' (*fenpei wenti zui touteng*). She suffered from a stomach ulcer and sometimes even had to leave her practical training early on account of it. I met her by chance six months later in the Number Two City Hospital. She was no longer pale and grey in the face, but had proved to be one of the few who 'had a method' of succeeding (*you banfa*). She had managed to stay not as a TCM doctor but as a biomedical paediatric, apparently without 'entering through the backdoor' (*zou houmen*).[31] She was, however, an exception. 'Once a cadre is assigned to a work unit, she is sentenced to lifelong death', explained a graduate who had refused to 'obey job assignment' (*fucong fenpei*) and became an entrepreneur: 'The government's means of control is the "household register" (*hukou*).[32] The household register binds you to a place, a work unit, a village, a street in the city, and this makes you immobile. It guarantees that you are provided with the amount of cereals and rice you need every month for only 6 *yuan*. These days, this costs you 30 *yuan* on the free market. Moreover, in many regions of our country these commodities are just not sold, they are scarce and rationed. For those who engage in small-scale business 30 *yuan* is not much, but imagine someone who gets a job offer from a work unit in Beijing and cannot change her household register to Beijing – tell me, how can she survive if half of her salary is used for buying rice?'

Job assignment has gone through many stages of administrative re-consideration. In 1988 the policy of directed recruitment and directed assignment was standard. A committee of the college arranged a job for a graduate by contacting a hospital representative in the 'prefecture' (*zhou*) or 'county town' (*xian*) the graduate came from. These contacts were easily made because the latter were usually graduates of the college. The college committee's proposal had to be approved by a Committee of the Provincial Parliament which reportedly approved about 70–80 per cent of the proposals; college representatives spoke of 'complications' (*wenti fuza*), students and graduates of corruption and nepotism: 'My aunt is on that committee; that's why I can stay in this city.'

In the mid-1980s a policy of 'mutual selection' (*shuangxiang xuanze*) had been introduced which was, in view of the general discouragement

---

[31] This is another example of negotiable norms which need not imply corruption and nepotism.
[32] See also Yeh and Xu (1990:46).

of individual initiative, truly innovative.[33] It enabled enterprising students
to arrange for job offers from hospitals which they themselves chose to
contact. If hospital and graduate reached agreement, they had to ask
for approval from the college and the committee of the provincial parliament. One college teacher had earlier arranged for a position at a
hospital in another province, but the parliament 'refused to release her
household register' (*zhuazhu hukou bufang*).[34]

The right to work is a Socialist principle, and until the late 1970s the
government guaranteed job assignment to every high school and university graduate (Gold 1991). After interviewing the college teachers, I
realised that they ascribed very explicit advantages to the Socialist system of job assignment. The prospect of the 'iron rice bowl' (*tiefanwan*)
after graduation was an important incentive to endure the hardships
of university studies.[35] The problem of unemployed youth and the
huge 'proletariat' is more than a widely acknowledged problem in the
Chinese and Western literature: it is a reality for every high school and
soon possibly every university graduate. In the late 1970s, the officially
reported number of unemployed young people was disguised by the
fact that high school graduates who refused to go down to the countryside were classified as 'youths awaiting job assignment' (*daiye qingnian*).
These teenagers waited for years, mostly in their parents' flats, with
or without part-time occupations. Then, in the early 1980s, the policy
changed, and high school graduates were no longer guaranteed job
assignment. And, in the late 1980s the Chinese press frequently addressed the topic of relaxing the government's responsibility for job
assignments after university graduation. Only those with the equivalent
of a 'master's degree' (*shuoshi*) or a 'doctorate' (*boshi*) were to enjoy
this privilege.

Students and graduates had mixed feelings. On the one hand, they
wanted the Socialist right of job assignment and spoke of its abolition
as a sign that the value of university degrees was decreasing. On the
other hand, stories abounded of mismanagement of job assignment due
to one's 'political situation' (*zhengzhi tiaojian*), 'family background'
(*jiating wenti*), and so-called 'moral conduct' (*daode wenti*).

---

[33] This is a remarkable change when compared with practices even of the early 1980s
(Henderson and Cohen 1984:39): 'For the ordinary Chinese citizen, then, job assignment and transfer are seldom products of individual initiative. In fact, individual
initiative may instead reflect abuse of the system.'

[34] 'In this sense, the criticism that units "own" their staff is justified' (Henderson and
Cohen 1984:36).

[35] 'Iron rice bowl' is an expression for a position in a work unit with pension. Cadres
cannot be dismissed – the rice bowl cannot break.

Summary

The standardised transmission of knowledge placed the students in a passive role. Since learning demands an active commitment from the students, the question immediately arose of how actively involved they were with their studies. Observation showed that they generally complied with work rulings and that tutors and teachers made an effort to have them adopt staff standards. In conversation many claimed indifference towards or even disillusionment with their studies and hardly anyone was actively trying to change the situation. On the contrary, some who claimed to dislike their studies were among the students with most initiative.

From the questionnnaires it became clear that no one (neither parents nor teachers nor administrators) asked students about their personal wishes, likes, and hopes and that, if they had any the students themselves were unwilling to talk about them. I got the impression that wishes, likes, and hopes were seen as forms of personal 'impulse' or 'will' (*zhi*) and people driven by impulse were considered immature. There was a general assumption that 'doing' engendered 'liking to do'. Indeed, several claimed to have become more positive about their studies as they got more involved with them. In particular, the year of practical training changed the attitude of many students to their subject of learning. Exploration of the curriculum may highlight why.

The curriculum

The curriculum of a TCM regular student comprised 3,733 hours of lectures over four years (see appendix) and a year of full-time practical training in various clinics and hospitals.[36] Of these, 950 hours (25.5 per cent) were reserved for courses on Party history, Marxism and Leninism, foreign languages, and physical training. Of the remaining 2,783 hours, 70 per cent were courses in TCM and 30 per cent courses in biomedicine. Of the 1,948 hours in TCM, 510 hours were reserved for lectures on the medical classics. Aspects of the curriculum discussed here include the introductory courses, which have given rise to a TCM theory; the clinical courses, which point to a continuity with the past; and practical training, which calls for a flexible application of written standards.

---

[36] For acumoxa and massage students it consisted of two and a half years of classroom teaching and six months of practical training.

Table 5.6. *TCM subjects for regular TCM students*

Course Title (identical to Textbook Title)	Lessons (2hrs)/week	Semester
TCM Fundamentals (*Zhongyi jichu lilun*)	3	1st
Traditional Chinese Pharmaceutics (*Zhongyaoxue*)	2	1st, 2nd
TCM Diagnostics (*Zhongyi zhenduanxue*)	3	2nd
Formularies (*Fangjixue*)	3	3rd
Acumoxa (*Zhenjiuxue*)	2.5	3rd
Qigong	1	4th
Massage (*Tuinaxue*)	1.5	4th, 5th
TCM Internal Medicine (*Zhongyi neike xue*)	2	5th
TCM Gynaecology (*Zhongyi fuke xue*)	1.5	5th
TCM Ophthalmology (*Zhongyi yanke xue*)	2	6th
TCM Paediatrics (*Zhongyi erke xue*)	2	7th
TCM External Medicine (*Zhongyi waike xue*)	2.5	8th
TCM Traumatology (*Zhongyi shangke xue*)	2	8th

The introductory courses and the rise of a TCM theory

The course work in the classroom was divided into 'theoretical courses' (*lilun ke*) and 'clinical courses' (*linchuang ke*) (see table 5.6). The theoretical courses were introductory courses that were delivered during the first two years. As 'courses on the basics' (*jichuke*) they were specific to TCM training: they comprised course work recorded in the textbooks *TCM Fundamentals* (*Zhongyi jichu lilun* (Yin 1984)) in the first semester and *TCM Diagnostics* (*Zhongyi zhenduanxue* (Shanxi zhongyi xueyuan 1988)) in the second. The *TCM Fundamentals* discussed basic medical concepts under separate headings, while the *TCM Diagnostics* interrelated them in the context of medical intervention. The introductory courses in pharmaceutics followed the same pattern: in the first-year course based on the textbook *Traditional Chinese Pharmaceutics* (*Zhongyaoxue* (Ling 1984)) each drug was separately presented; the second year was devoted to the combination of drugs in *Formularies* (*Fangjixue*).

Unlike the disciple or follower working under a master or mentor in a medical practice, who learns to break down observed complexities, TCM students were first exposed to one concept after another, each detached from the other, and then expected to put these elements together into a whole. This was called 'systematic' (*xitonghuade*) learning. There was a TCM theory that was systematic, and this theory had to be learnt before students were exposed to medical practice.

The forum for this newly established theory was the classroom. TCM teachers saw many advantages in classroom teaching; a disciple or follower who engaged in medical practice from the beginning would not learn how to reason deductively, they said. Having learnt by imitation, he or she would be perplexed if confronted with a new illness condition. One may question these convictions but easily agree that a teacher could elaborate on a coherent system of medicine in the classroom without being forced to deal with the incongruencies of medical practice. Textbooks provided another forum, on paper, for neat tables of the standardised interrelations between different aspects of the body ecologic. These descriptive statements that set up systems of standardised correlations formed the basis of a 'theory'. It is true that in classical medical writings such as the *Basic Questions*, which was a standard examination text for recruiting medical officials during the Tang dynasty (Yamada 1979), we find lists of systemic correspondences as well. However, although the modern mind inadvertently tends to read them as descriptions, these standard correspondences were probably meant to be read as normative or prescriptive.

As we have seen in the context of Zhang's seminars (chs. 3–4), the relation between medical doctrine and practice is not the same as that between theory and practice. Phrases of the medical classics are generally memorised without being entirely understood, and medical practice is indispensable to the meaning-making process of textual knowledge. A medical doctrine is intricately related to medical practice, the relationship of textual knowledge to practice being determined by the senior doctor's 'virtuosity' (*linghuo*) in applying it. In contrast, the descriptions of TCM texts which make sense in the classroom may be contradicted by a doctor's own experience in medical practice. Descriptions of medical practice give rise to a theory, and medical practice may or may not coincide with them. There is a notorious gap between descriptive medical theory and clinical practice, a gap that does not exist between prescriptive doctrine and practice.

The tendency towards developing a TCM theory seems to be modelled on Western biomedicine. In the set of TCM textbooks published in 1988 the theoretical subjects were multiplied by dividing the course on the *TCM Fundamentals* into four: *TCM Instructions* (*Zhongyixue daolun* (Luzhou yixueyuan)), *Organ Clusters* (*Zangxiangxue* (Yunnan zhongyi xueyuan)), *TCM Etiology and Pathogenesis* (*Zhongyi bingyin bingjixue* (Chengdu zhongyi xueyuan)), and *Outline of TCM Preventive Health Care* (*Zhongyi fangzhixue zonglun* (in press)). It looked as if the introductory courses were designed to constitute something like the 'TCM basic sciences', just as the biomedical sciences are basic to biomedicine: 'Science is the point of entry into medicine, and however restricted the science courses are from the perspective of faculty or Ph.D. students in those disciplines, it is made profoundly clear that learning medicine during the first two years is above all learning the biomedical sciences' (Good and Good 1993:89–90). One may feel inclined to speak of TCM as assimilating Western biomedical standards, but this may not do justice to the processes that are inherent in any standardisation of the transmission of medical knowledge and practice. Insofar as the classroom is a place for standardised instruction of a coherent medical system and textbooks are the predominant genre of medical instruction, the very process of standardisation provides the basis for theory building.

The clinical courses and the continuity with the past

The clinical courses included internal medicine and gynaecology, pae-diatrics, ophthalmology, otorhinolaryngology, acumoxa, traumatology, and external medicine. They were generally taught from the third year (fifth semester) onwards.[37] A comparison with the Chinese medical subjects recognised by the Imperial Court points to a continuity with the past. The clinical courses, in contrast to the introductory courses, are given on subjects that were taught in Imperial times, and detailed longitudinal studies will be needed to show to what extent they have grown out of subjects known since the Song dynasty (see table 5.7).[38]

Practical training, touch, and flexibility in the application of standards

Practical training was the source of discontent that the teachers men-tioned most frequently. They expressed their students' and their own need for more clinical experience. Some teachers deplored the restriction of practical training to the last year of instruction. Since it awakened students' interests in TCM, they proposed that students have access to the clinic as early as the first year.

---

[37] The clinical courses in acumoxa, massage, and *qigong* were taught already in the third and fourth semesters.
[38] Unschuld (1986b) provides a longitudinal study of the commentaries on the *Nan jing*; Despeux & Obringer (1990) of the nosological entity *kesou* (cough), but so far none has been done on a subdiscipline of Chinese medicine.

Table 5.7. *TCM subjects in historical perspective*

Subjects of Chinese Medicine at the Imperial Court,[39] Song Dynasty (960–1279)	TCM Subjects at TCM Colleges, PRC (1949–)
Disorders of adults (*da fang ke*)	Internal medicine (*zhongyi neikexue*)
	Gynaecology (*zhongyi fukexue*)[40]
Disorders related to wind (*feng ke*)	
Disorders of children (*xiao fang ke*)	Paediatrics (*zhongyi erkexue*)
Obstetrics (*chan ke*)	
Disorders of the eyes (*yan ke*)	Ophthalmology (*zhongyi yankexue*)[41]
Mouth, teeth, pharynx, throat (*kou chi yan hou ke*)	Otorhinolaryngology (*zhongyi erbihouke xue*)
Sore, swollen, broken, wounded (*chuang zhong zhe yang ke*)	Traumatology (*zhongyi shangkexue*) External medicine (*zhongyi waikexue*)
Acupuncture and moxibustion (*zhen jiu ke*)	Acumoxa (*zhenjiuxue*)
Inner lesions and incantations (*jin yang shu jin ke*)	——

Practical training took place in a fairly relaxed atmosphere, at least in the acumoxa wards.[42] Students would appear around 9 a.m. and leave at noon. For lack of clientele, they were not expected to return in the afternoon. While waiting for patients they chatted, read novels, smoked (if men), and sometimes joked with the doctor in charge. One of the chief goals of practical training was to learn how to write up case records.[43] There were printed forms for this on which students

[39] These nine subjects were established after the Yuanfeng period (1078–85). Before that, Chinese medicine was divided into three subcategories (*da fang ke, zhen ke,* and *jin yang*) and thirteen subjects (Si and Gong 1988:238).

[40] *TCM Gynaecology* (Meng 1986) discusses pregnancy and postpartum disorders of the woman but not childbirth; Furth (1986:50), rather than translating *fuke* as gynaecology, suggests 'women's department of medicine'. 'Textbooks both argue and demonstrate that *fuke* is basically the same as . . . "internal medicine" (*neike*)' (Farquhar 1991:375).

[41] Here the same word is rendered differently, in approximation of the speaker's understanding in the Song dynasty and in a twentieth-century TCM course.

[42] In Yunnan province, doctors in acumoxa wards at hospitals and clinics were generally not very busy. At the Provincial TCM Hospital, for instance, a ward of two doctors with three to four students saw ten to twenty-five patients a morning.

[43] See also Farquhar (1992). Writing up cases is also central to training American students in biomedicine (see Good 1994:76–83).

only had to fill in the details.[44] Yet case records were rarely presented to the assembly of colleagues as in American hospitals (Anspach 1988); they were individually supervised by the doctor–teacher, and therefore practical training was much more personal than classroom instruction.

One of the students' first reactions to the clinic was to point out the difference between theory and practice: 'This is what is written in the textbook, but here it is all different', or: 'Gynaecology is easy to learn (*fuke hao xue*), but in the clinic everything is different from the theory.' It was not that classroom learning was altogether dismissed as useless, but, as the doctors in the clinic liked to put it, the textbooks contained generalities, while the problems in medical practice demanded a detailed knowledge of the particular; for them the latter was clearly the crucial knowledge. This knowledge of the particular was grounded in a mode of perception that was very different from that in the classroom: touch. To establish a 'diagnosis' (*zhenduan*) the Pulse (*mai*) had to be taken. It is noteworthy that 'Pulse diagnostics' (*maizhen*), said to be the most important means of learning about a patient's condition in Chinese medicine, is grounded in touch. Pulse diagnostics is not simply counting the frequency of beats per minute, but recognising so-called Pulse Images (*maixiang*), experiences of touch which are very particular. Li Shizhen (*c.* 1518–93) had standardised the Pulse Images, limiting them to twenty-eight, and these standard Pulse Images were taught in the course on *TCM Diagnostics* (Deng 1984:66–70). The variety of Pulses students were exposed to in the clinic was, in contrast, overwhelming. Experiences of touch are among the most difficult to standardise. Touch is direct and fairly intimate and, possibly, therefore particularly apt for perceiving individual variability.

Not only the Pulses but also the complaints of the patients and the manifestations of disorders plunged the student into problems that could not be dealt with in a standardised way. In the clinic one could not mechanically apply the standardised knowledge learnt in the classroom, and the learning process relied on different (audiovisual versus tactile) modalities of perception. TCM theory was, unlike other theories of the natural sciences, meant to be related to medical practice not with rigour but with 'flexibility' (*linghuo*). In this respect, the relationship between TCM theory and practice seemed to be modelled on the application of Chinese medical doctrine to medical practice that senior

---

[44] This process is faithfully recorded in the seventeen case histories of Ots (1987: 101–35). For other published case histories, see Farquhar (1991; 1992; 1994a: 46–55).

doctors would master with 'virtuosity' (*linghuo*).[45] TCM doctors called it a 'dialectical' relationship between theory and practice. Students were no longer in the passive role of reproducing knowledge, but actively engaged in medical practice. Sometimes they even found that their therapies had a positive effect, which encouraged and empowered them. These experiences may well explain why, as we have seen, many students became more committed to their studies during the year of practical training.

Standards and their variation

From the above it is clear that the standardised transmission of TCM knowledge referred to a wide spectrum of different standards. The curriculum included standards that had been newly established (theoretical courses), standards that had historically evolved from earlier standards (clinical courses), standards that had nationwide[46] or regional validity,[47] standards that varied according to type of educational institution,[48] and standards that were local.[49]

A mind trained in the Western sciences may find it puzzling that TCM teachers spoke of all these processes, directed towards establishing a standard at these many different levels, as a standardisation of the transmission of Chinese medical knowledge. Confronted with this orchestra of different standards, how can one speak of a standardisation of the whole? We have seen that Chinese medical doctrine, rather than assigning well-being to a single cause, conceives of a harmonious *chorus*

[45] The term *linghuo* is rendered as virtuosity with regard to senior doctors' handling of a doctrine and as flexibility with regard to TCM professionals' application of a theory. The respective translations highlight these doctors' different attitudes to textual knowledge: virtuosity refers to medical expertise that values personal mastery, while flexibility implies that practitioners accept generally valid standards and apply them flexibly.

[46] In 1988–9 and 1989–90, classroom teaching built on the 1984 edition of textbooks adopted nationwide.

[47] In 1985, during a meeting organised by the Central Health Ministry on experiences with the reforms of higher TCM education, the decision was taken to write regional textbooks (five regions: the Northwest, the North, the South, the Centre, and the West). The textbooks were printed in 1988/9. They were used for short-term and brush-up course instruction but, as I learnt during a visit in 1996, not for regular TCM undergraduates.

[48] TCM colleges fall into three types, emphasising either 'research' (*yanjiuxing*), 'clinical practice' (*linchuangxing*), or 'the integration of Western and Chinese medicine' (*zhongxiyi jiehe xing*) (interview with City Health Bureau, December 1989). The curriculum at the Yunnan TCM College stressed training in clinical practice; the students were not expected to pursue university careers. Most students said they 'wanted' to work as practitioners after graduation; only four of fifty-seven expressed the wish to become research students.

[49] For instance, the Yunnan TCM College used the above-mentioned set of regional textbooks for 'evening courses' (*yeban*).

of *qi*. We can also observe an aesthetics throughout the various Chinese scientific doctrines that favours explanations with many levels of meaning. As Unschuld (1988a) points out, this aesthetics is very different from that of a culture shaped by the values of a monotheistic religion. The claim that the diverse processes in TCM institutions are directed towards standardising the transmission of Chinese medicine is grounded in an aesthetics that acknowledges that standardisation may include a broad spectrum of different standards.

The assertions of the people with whom social scientists work need of course not coincide with the categories they use, but in this case it seems perfectly acceptable to speak of a process of standardisation from the observer's point of view as well. Regardless of whether implementing one single standard or many different ones, the standardisation of the curriculum has led to a separation between classroom teaching (where standards are easily established) and training in the clinic (where they are not as easily implemented).

Goals of teaching

When I asked the assistant teachers about their goals in classroom instruction, most admitted to not having thought about it. One of them said: 'The teachers teach, the students listen. The students have no initiative and are not conscientious in their studies. A teacher should awaken a student's interest. Only if a teacher is interested in his subject can he awaken that in his students.' Another one said that apart from transmitting information to the students, a teacher should teach them a 'way of life' (*shenghuo fangfa*). His comment may have reflected the Party's former device of being 'red and expert' (*hongzhuan*), which, having been seriously misused, was not even mentioned by college administrators during the era of Deng's reforms. Indeed, in other contexts of Chinese medical learning acquiring a certain way of life was the premise for being accepted by master or mentor. Within an institution in which knowledge is transmitted in a standardised fashion, one would think that knowledge would be regarded as public property while ways of life were to a certain extent private affairs. However, the aim of transmitting knowledge as well as a way of life is not only a device of the Chinese Communist Party; it has many parallels in other cultures.[50]

---

[50] The portals of the Töchternschule Zürich proclaimed: '*Non scholae, sed vitae discimus*' (a misquotation of the Roman poet Ovid which stands for humanist ideals), and the Cambridge graduation ceremony contains the clause: 'Most worthy Sir . . . I present to you these men, whom I know to be suitable "both in character and learning" (*tam moribus quam doctrina*)'.

I learnt about the teachers' goals of instruction only indirectly,[51] through comments made in passing: (1) You have to explain and let the students understand what they are learning by heart; (2) You have to teach a student a method, not only knowledge; (3) You have to provide more practical training for the students. Evidently, some of the principles they advocated were those of post-Enlightenment knowledge: (1) 'explanation' (*jieshi*) and (2) 'method' (*fangfa*). The need of (3) 'practical training' (*shixi*) appeared to have arisen from the recent emergence of a theory. These principles imply certain assumptions about knowledge.

Explanation is supposed to open up access to knowledge – to make knowledge accessible not only to those who are predestined for it or those whose personalities are compatible with that of the mentor, but to everyone. Belief in the didactic value of explanations is based on the assumption that explicating ('unfolding') packages of meaning yields insight. The complexities of knowledge are divided into basic and advanced knowledge. This is reflected in the structuring of the TCM curriculum into introductory and clinical courses and, among the introductory courses, into courses that present the basic elements separately and those that discuss different combinations of those basic elements.

Explanation also makes the learning process less lonely. It provides guidance, step by step. Gradually, one building block is placed on another. This hierarchical order of teaching may result in a hierarchical structure of knowledge: 'Natural hierarchy is replicated as the implicit order of teaching . . . A slide of low magnification cell structure is followed by an electron micrograph, and from this level to diagrams of molecular structure and genetic expression. A slide at one level is often followed by one just above or below this hierarchy . . .' (Good 1994:75). It would be worth investigating to what extent learning through explanation and hierarchically ordered knowledge are interrelated.

Method, generally mentioned in the context of standardising and systematising Chinese medicine, was always linked to the speeding up of the process of learning. It was also spoken of in a sense reminiscent of explanation. When discussing the relevance of lectures on the medical classics, a teacher said: 'One should learn the method of reading a text, not just learn text after text by heart.' This teacher emphasised the need for understanding what one had learnt. His conviction stood in blatant contradiction with that of a *qigong* healer like Qiu, who did not have to understand the incantations he recited for them to be effective, or a mentor like Zhang, who believed that the meaning of memorised texts would only become apparent in their application to medical practice.

[51] On officially expressed goals of teaching, see H. F. Chen (1984:357–60).

College authorities spoke of applying the method of 'exemplary learning' to lectures on the medical classics. According to this method, originally developed for teaching the natural sciences, definitions of terms were explained by referring to one 'exemplary' experiment only (instead of endlessly repeating experiments of a similar kind). Applied to lectures on the classical literature, this method required students to memorise only short text passages instead of whole books or chapters. While explanation invokes a structure of knowledge, the method of exemplary learning demands a focus on what is considered central. An utterance or an activity is reduced to one crucial point. Exemplary learning demands that the student focus on what is considered central to the message, while a follower like Zhangdi would read the same text with the intention of gaining a sensitivity to a more general kind of pattern recognition.

The fact that the teachers stressed the need for more practical training points up the importance attributed to classroom instruction at TCM colleges. The process of standardising the transmission of Chinese medical knowledge has given rise to a theory, and with it, to an ever increasing gap between theory and practice.

The standardised mode of transmission

The space occupied by the college was clearly bounded, separating 'the populace' (*minjian*) from the world of TCM learning. Work units had been constructed with functionally distinct compartments each of which constituted a separate whole. It was in these newly created spaces of work units that the standardised transmission of knowledge took place. It implied the ideal of equal opportunity for everyone, a quantitative assessment of scholarly qualification in examinations, accommodating a large number of students for only a limited time period of learning, and a relation between teachers and students that was not personal or intimate. The ideal was to treat everyone in the same standard way.

Standards were not always as rigorously implemented as one might expect. In a Socialist work unit colleagues at work were neighbours at leisure. They would know each other for decades within a limited space and under the pressure of scarce resources. Avoidance of personal friction and the matching and balancing of human resources often took precedence over thematic and intellectual demands. That norms were negotiable was not always a sign of nepotism and corruption, being sometimes referred to as pragmatism. A flexible handling of standards was possible because standards were often made up of components that were readily added or subtracted in recognition of a particular situation.

The networks among the staff were intentionally kept rather loose. Staff members had come together only after university graduation, and few were bound by comradeship in their youth. They had gone through various experiences of each other in extreme situations of political unrest, and in anticipation of future upheavals they were not eager to reveal much about themselves to others. These loose networks may well have provided a context within which government policies could be implemented with relative ease. In such a context, the efforts at transforming ethical and other values that a standardisation of the transmission of medical knowledge and practice brings with it were likely to encounter fewer obstacles than in the tightly knit networks of an urban neighbourhood, where interactions between households went back for decades if not generations.

The standardised transmission of knowledge is based on the belief that the complexities of knowing can be 'explained' and that there is a 'method' of learning. Knowledge is conceived of as having a structure and messages as having a point. Textbooks in modern Chinese, explicit and descriptive, have emerged as the predominant genre of medical writing. The classroom provides the space in which the standards they convey are elaborated in a coherent way, for teachers need not deal with the inconsistencies of medical practice. The standardised transmission of Chinese medical knowledge has thus laid the groundwork for building up a theory of TCM.

It remains to be seen whether transmission by means of 'explanation' is bound to give rise to a hierarchical structure of knowledge and whether 'method' inevitably leads to a focused vision resulting, for instance, in focusing on one particular form of interrelation, say a causal one, to the neglect of others. Are interrelations between concepts of TCM theory generally more hierarchical than those in Chinese medical doctrine? Is there a tendency towards a more focused vision in TCM than in conceptualisations of the body ecologic referred to in classical Chinese medical writings? The following chapter addresses these questions.

6   Teaching from TCM texts

TCM teachers claimed to be 'standardising' (*guifanhua*), 'modern-ising' (*xiandaihua*), 'making scientific' (*kexuehua*), and 'systematising' (*xitonghua*) Chinese medical knowledge and practice. Notably, they did not express the aim of 'Westernising' (*xifanghua*) it, but the importance of the West – on a technological, institutional, and ideological level – cannot be overlooked. It is not merely the practice of biomedicine in China which has had an impact on TCM, but also Western scientific thought and practice in general and other ideologies of modernity such as nationalism, Marxism, and materialism. A close look at classroom teaching will reveal both the ways in which these ideologies have led to a reinterpretation of ancient concepts like *yinyang*, the Five Phases (*wuxing*) and the Five Organs (*wuzang*), Essence (*jing*), Breath (*qi*), Blood (*xue*), Liquids and Fluids (*jinye*), and the implications of neglecting the notion of Spirit (*shen*). One may wonder why basic TCM concepts – so extens-ively discussed in the Western literature on Chinese medicine – are once again presented here. The value of this contribution is primarily ethnographic. It intends to show how students learnt about these con-cepts in contemporary China.

A focal point for this examination will be the classes conducted by teacher Tao, one of the best at the college. Tao enjoyed lecturing and had more than twenty years of teaching experience, and his classes, spiced with jokes and anecdotes, were entertaining. His rhetoric was overwhelming as he inundated the students with a flow of idioms from medical practice, expressions from daily life, and phrases from the Party. He said that he prepared each lecture early in the morning and learnt them all by heart. Tao was head of a 'teaching and research office' (*jiaoyanshi*) which comprised twelve teachers. He was an influential 'associate professor' (*fujiaoshou*) in the TCM Department, a college representative on several committees of the Provincial Bureau for Educa-tion, a member of the editorial board of the 1988–9 textbook editions, and chief editor of one of those textbooks. A reliable Party member, he could claim to have lectured throughout the people's movement in May and June 1989 without interruption – admittedly, I was told, once in the presence of only two students. Although nationwide regulations bound Tao to teach the 1984 edition of TCM textbooks, he had enough authority to diverge from a word-for-word reproduction of their contents. Almost every lecture contained a diagram or definition based on his own ideas or ideas contained in the forthcoming editions (to which he had contributed). Other senior staff also substantiated the textbook contents with their personal experiences from medical practice, and they would stress, slightly modify, and occasionally even criticise the textbook contents, but none of them would draw elaborate diagrams on the blackboard as Tao did.[1]

The classes that Tao delivered were based on the textbook *TCM Fundamental Theory*, hereafter *TCM Fundamentals* (*Zhongyi jichu lilun* (Yin 1984)). Comparisons will be made with its more recent editions in 1988–9, namely the *TCM Instructions* (*Zhongyixue daolun* (Luzhou yixueyuan)), *Organ Clusters* (*Zangxiangxue* (Yunnan zhongyi xueyuan)), *TCM Etiology and Pathogenesis* (*Zhongyi bingyin bingjixue* (Chengdu zhongyi xueyuan)), and *Outline of TCM Preventive Health Care* (*Zhongyi fangzhixue zonglun* (in press)). Comparisons will also be made with what my research has led me to consider its precursors (so far not acknowledged as such in the Western literature): the *Canon of Categories*, hereafter *Categories* (*Leijing*), published in 1624 by Zhang Jiebin (1563–1640), the *Essentials of the Inner Canon*, hereafter *Essentials* (*Neijing zhiyao*), published in 1642 by Li Zhongzi (1588–1655), and the TCM textbook of the *Interpretation of the Inner Canon*, hereafter *Interpretation* (*Neijing jiangyi* (Cheng 1984)).

Teacher Tao did not deliver all the classes discussed here; he taught 'acumoxa and massage specialists' (*zhenjiu tuina zhuankesheng*) the *TCM Fundamentals*, and another teacher, Tian, taught second-year 'TCM regular students' (*zhongyi benkesheng*) the *Interpretation*. Tian was a lecturer who belonged to a younger generation than Tao and considered himself a victim of the 'ten chaotic years' (*shinian dongluan*), the Cultural Revolution (1966–76). He declared he had no ambitions and was not a Party member, and the difference between his classes and Tao's showed that the standardised mode of transmission is not always entirely uniform (see also Farquhar 1995).

The college classrooms had four to six rows of wooden tables and benches and two blackboards, one for the teachers and the other, on a side or back wall, for the students. Every few months two students were

---

[1] Tao's presentations were in this respect somewhat exceptional and reminiscent of a 'senior Chinese doctor's' (*laozhongyi*) creative mode of interpretation.

expected to be creative and to fill the latter blackboard with colourful drawings, poems, and personal opinions. The rooms were unheated and, particularly in winter, a cold draught came in through broken windows. Tao stood in front of forty students with the eleven female students in the first two rows, Tian in front of a class of similar size with fewer female students spread throughout the classroom. Tao usually managed to capture his students' attention with his eloquence and liveliness, but Tian was unable to do so and various, somewhat disruptive activities took place on the benches.

Lesson one: China's cultural heritage

The semester began with an instruction by the tutor (usually junior staff) assigned to the class for the entire length of studies. She exhorted the students to attend classes regularly, and to get into the habit of 'preparing' (*yuxi*) and 'reviewing' (*fuxi*) them in the classroom ten minutes before class. Then the teacher, dressed in a white lab coat, began his lecture. In this first lesson, Tao told his students that they would be learning knowledge that was two thousand years old: 'This knowledge is the heart of Chinese medicine; it is at the heart of our culture.' He did not mention Mao's 1955 speech (Lampton 1977:63) or his declaration that Chinese medicine was a 'treasure house' (*baoku*), but he did refer to Mao's nationalistic justification for promoting Chinese medicine within the first five minutes of the lesson.

In all introductory lessons, an outline of the compilations and authors of the Chinese medical literature was given. The teacher lecturing on *Classical Chinese for Medics* (*Yiguwen*) mentioned the *Treatise of Cold Damage Disorders* (*Shang han lun*),[2] essential for Chinese medical practice, and the *Yellow Emperor's Inner Canon* (*Huang di nei jing*), the classic of Chinese medicine.[3] She spoke of Li Shizhen who had compiled the most comprehensive *materia medica*,[4] namely the *Hierarchical Systematisation of the Materia Medica* (*Ben cao gang mu*), and cited a poem attributed to Wang Bing, the editor of the *Basic Questions* (*Su wen*).[5] This teacher had completed university studies in classical Chinese rather than in Chinese medicine, and therefore the titles and names she

---

[2] Attributed to Zhang Ji, Zhongjin (*c.* 150–219), but lost by the end of third century AD and later recomposed, see Sivin (1987:460); translated by Despeux (1985).

[3] The *Yellow Emperor's Inner Canon* consists of two books, the *Basic Questions* (*Su wen*) and the *Divine Pivot* (*Ling shu*); see Yamada (1979), Ren (1982), Keegan (1988), and Sivin (1993). On the reception of the *Inner Canon* in China in comparison with that of the *Treatise of Cold Damage Disorders* in Japan, see Agren (1986).

[4] For details on Li Shizhen, Dongbi (*c.* 1518–1593), see Anon. (1988:227–8).

[5] Wang Bing (eighth century); see Anon. (1988:24).

mentioned were those commonly known among Chinese 'intellectuals' (*zhishi fenzi*) and laypersons.
The *TCM Fundamentals* (Yin 1984:1–2), however, set standards for the professional to which Tao made only a few amendments in his lecture. He spoke of the 'four great canons' (*sidajing*),[6] and then of Hua Tuo,[7] Wang Shuhe,[8] Huangfu Mi,[9] and Sun Simiao.[10] He pointed to compilations such as the *Treatise on the Origins and Symptoms of Disorders* (*Zhu bing yuan hou lun*)[11] and the *Revised Materia Medica* (*Xin xiu ben cao*).[12] He briefly discussed the 'four great and famous physicians' (*sida mingyi*) of the Song and Yuan dynasties with reference to their different geographic origins.[13] Then he mentioned those who had developed the 'doctrine of the Gate of Life' (*mingmenxue*) in the Ming (1368–1644) and Qing dynasties (1644–1911) and mentioned, apart from Zhang Jinyue[14] and Zhao Xianke[15] (who both figured in the textbook), Li Yan.[16] He dwelt on Li Shizhen and spoke of the authors of the doctrine, which stressed the Warmth Factor in certain Disorders (*wenbing xue*), as 'the four in and around Jiangsu province', namely

---

[6] This expression was not used in the textbook, and Tao explained that the four were either the *Nei jing*, the *Nan jing*, the *Shang han lun*, and the *Jin gui yao lüe* [*fang lun*] (*Essentials* [*and Discussions of Prescriptions*] *in the Golden Casket*) or the three former ones and the *Shen nong ben cao jing* (*Divine Husbandman's Materia Medica*). Notably, the *Shen nong ben cao jing* was not mentioned in the introduction of the *TCM Fundamentals* (Yin 1984:1–2).

[7] Tao: 'Hua Tuo (? *c.* 203) is nowadays celebrated and known because of his surgical interventions, but little is known of this largely legendary figure.' See Anon. (1988:120).

[8] Tao mentioned Wang Shuhe (third century) as the compiler of the *Mai jing* (*Canon of the Pulse*; *c.* 280), see Anon. (1988:50).

[9] Huangfu Mi, Shi'an (215–82), was mentioned as the compiler of the *Zhen jiu jia yi jing* (*Systematic Canon of Acumoxa*; 256/82), see Anon. (1988:449–50) and Sivin (1987: 453–4).

[10] Sun Simiao (*c.* 581–682) was mentioned as the author of the *Bei ji qian jin yao fang* (*Essential Prescriptions Worth a Thousand, for Urgent Need*; 650/659). Students and teachers esteemed Sun as essential for the development of *qigong*. For biographical details, see Anon. (1988:181).

[11] Compiled by Chao Yuanfang (sixth/seventh century) in 610, see Anon. (1988:586–7). Tao's comment on it was: 'This is a most interesting book! It contains about 1,700 articles on different disorders, partly with up-to-date information.'

[12] Compiled by Su Jing, Gong (seventh century) in 650/9, see Unschuld (1986a:45–50). Not a single *materia medica* was mentioned in the textbook of the *TCM Fundamentals*. Tao mentioned three in class: the *Shen nong ben cao*, *Xin xiu ben cao*, and *Ben cao gang mu*.

[13] Namely, Liu Wansu, Shouzhen (*c.* 1110 – *c.* 1200); Li Gao, Mingzhi, later known as Dongyuan (1180–1251); Zhang Congzheng, Zihe (*c.* 1156–*c.* 1288); Zhu Zhenheng, Yanxiu (1281–1358), see *Zhongyi gejia xueshuo* (Ren 1986: 37–47, 54–64, 72–83, 84–91).

[14] Zhang Jiebin, Huiqing and Jinyue, (1562–1639), ibid. 126ff.

[15] Zhao Xianke, Yangkui, (1573–1644), ibid. 116ff.

[16] Li Yan, Jianzhai, (sixteenth century), wrote *Yi xue ru men* (*Introduction to Medicine*) in 1575, see Anon. (1988:214).

Wu Youke,[17] Xue Shengbai,[18] Ye Tianshi,[19] and Wu Jutong.[20] Finally, he gave a lively description of how Wang Qingren[21] came to write *Correcting the Errors of Physicians* (*Yi lin gai cuo*). Tao presented the history of Chinese medicine as a history of scientific progress. He characterised an early period by pointing to outstanding personalities of the Han dynasty (206 BC – AD 220) who were often partly legendary, such as Hua Tuo. Then he named seminal works that were compiled shortly before and during the Tang (618–906), which he said constituted, with the installation of the Imperial Medical College (*Tai yi yuan*), the formative period of Chinese medicine. He characterised Chinese medical history from the Song dynasty (960–1279) onwards by referring to various traditions and schools of thought. His historical outline differed significantly, however, from one of a history of science in that he began with canons, the four great canons, that remain the authoritative texts, even today.

In the course on the *Tracts and Links* (*Jingluoxue*)[22] for acumoxa and massage freshmen, the list of compilations and writers in the textbook (Li 1984:19–20) was extensive but the teacher mentioned only a few of them in class. The course itself consisted of text excerpts from the very early medical literature: two fragments of the Mawangdui manuscripts, the 'Moxibustion Canon on the Eleven Foot and Arm Vessels' (Zubi shiyimai jiujing) and the 'Moxibustion Canon on the Eleven Yin and Yang Vessels' (Yinyang shiyimai jiujing),[23] were systematically compared with passages in chapters 10–13 of the *Divine Pivot* (*Ling shu*). The *Canon of Difficult Issues* (*Nan jing*),[24] the coloured diagrams of the Tracts in Sun Simiao's *Essential Prescriptions Worth a Thousand* (*Qian jin fang*),[25]

---

[17] Wu Youxing, Youke (*c.* 1582–1652), ibid. 150ff.

[18] Xue Xue, Shengbai (1681–1770), ibid. 168ff.

[19] Ye Gui, Tianshi (*c.* 1666–1745), ibid. 159ff.

[20] Wu Tang, Jutong (1736–1820), ibid. 174ff.

[21] Wang Qingren, Xunchen (1768–1831), ibid. 260ff.

[22] Sivin (1987:249) speaks of the 'circulation tract system' (*jingluo*), the main lines of which are called 'cardinal tracts' (*jing*), and the branch lines 'reticular tracts' (*luo*). He partly follows Lu and Needham (1980:24ff.) who coined the term 'tracts and channels' as translation for *jingmai*, and partly Porkert's (1974:197, 199) rendering of *jingluo* as 'conduits' or 'sinarteries', more precisely *sinarteriae cardinales et reticulares*. *Luo* are here translated as Links because *luo* means 'to link'. A link is primarily defined by its function of linking but can also be a 'thing' located in space. *Jing* are rendered as Tracts in conformity with the existing terminology. 'Passages' is another term that I find suitable, for *jing* can refer to a 'passage' in time as well as one in space; moreover, the word 'passage' nicely reflects the meaning of *jing* (to pass on).

[23] Buried in 168 BC, excavated from tomb No. 3 at Mawangdui in 1972 (MWD 1985).

[24] Compiler anonymous, probably second century AD; translated by Unschuld (1986b).

[25] The longer title *Bei ji qian jin yao fang* is mentioned in the author's preface, compiled 650/9; translated by Despeux (1987).

Li Shizhen's *Investigation of the Eight Odd Vessels* (*Qi jing ba mai kao*),[26] and Yang Jizhou's *Great Compendium on Acumoxa* (*Zhen jiu da cheng*)[27] were the only other texts the teacher mentioned in class. In the course on *Acumoxa* (*Zhenjiuxue*) for regular TCM undergraduates, the teacher talked about the same compilations in her introductory lesson, although the textbook itself contained no outline of the history of acumoxa (M. Qiu 1985). It is noteworthy that she did not mention the *Canon of Difficult Issues*. When I asked her why, she said that she had simply forgotten. According to Unschuld ((1980)1985:13), the *Canon of Difficult Issues* represents the apex of the 'medicine of systematic correspondence', but had fallen into disregard for several centuries before being revived in the twentieth (Unschuld (1980)1985:46–53). It was only occasionally mentioned in the textbook but during the course the teacher referred to it twice as providing additional information.[28]

The historical outline in the *Organ Clusters* (Yunnan zhongyi xueyuan 1988:3–4), as volume II of the 1988 edition of the *TCM Fundamentals* was called, included several writers and compilations known from the 1984 edition on *Acumoxa* in addition to those mentioned in the 1984 *TCM Fundamentals*. This may be interpreted as a form of official recognition of acumoxa by mainstream TCM scholars due to the therapeutic success of, in particular, acupuncture analgesia (Hsu 1995). If one considers that acumoxa describes the human body in terms which can be fairly easily approximated by biomedical anatomy (Farquhar 1994a:82–4), one can also interpret this as an indication that the editors of the 1988 *Organ Clusters* were emphasising anatomical and material aspects of the body and including more works on acumoxa accordingly.

The students easily remembered the nationalistic motive of their studies: Chinese medicine was their cultural heritage. Some readily identified with their role of perpetuating ancient Chinese culture; some, acumoxa specialists in particular, spoke proudly of learning a medicine that was being exported to the West. Others remarked how useful it would be to learn Western medicine instead: 'If I open a private practice in the county town and know no Western medicine, I won't have any patients. Most people believe in Western medicine; Chinese

---

[26] Compiled in 1572, Anon. 1988:228. Porkert (1974:273) translates *qi* as 'odd'.
[27] Compiled in 1601; see *Gejia zhenjiu xueshuo* (Wei 1987:81).
[28] Once she discussed the notion *shi dong ze bing*, which she proposed interpreting as: 'If this [Vessel] comes into motion then [the following] disorders arise', and the notion *suo chan bing*, interpreted as: 'The disorders produced by [the Vessel]', which were not mentioned in the textbook; and once she gave a detailed account of 'needling techniques' (*cifa*) that were only briefly mentioned in the textbook.

medicine is generally considered "superstition" (*mixin*).[29] Whether the
Chinese heritage was considered 'just as good as the Western', 'so good
that even the West seeks it', or 'not as good as the Western', the
Western was always considered good. That the knowledge they learnt
was age-old was for some students and staff a matter of pride, but for
others an obstacle to China's progress towards a modern state.[30]

The classes on the *Interpretation* were poorly attended. Even during
the mid-term examination there was whispering, and printed textbooks
containing standard exam questions and answers circulated along the
benches. 'These lectures are boring', a student explained. 'It's not that
the classical texts themselves are boring, but the way they are taught
here. This is superficial.' Classes on the *Treatise of Cold Damage Disorders* were, by contrast, a favourite of many students, and not only
because of their reportedly excellent teacher: third-year TCM undergraduates simultaneously attended the clinic once a week and frequently
expressed how intrigued they were to find its ancient 'formulae' (*fangji*)
scarcely altered in application today.

Students learning acumoxa, who generally were not interested in the
canonical literature, nevertheless expressed an interest in buying the
Great Compendium of Acumoxa, but it was not available in any book-
shop. Although they showed little interest in the *Inner Canon* and the
Canon of Difficult Issues, when an itinerant bookseller displayed booklets
with excerpts of these classics in modern Chinese several students were
eager to buy them, disregarding the opinion of others on any contemporary reinterpretation of the classics as: 'All they contain is politics.' A
graduate assigned a post in a 'township hospital' (*weishengyuan*) would
have no access to the medical classics except for the excerpts in the
TCM textbooks. In rural areas, medical books from late Imperial times
would sometimes still be in circulation but not the medical classics.
The responses to the letter questionnaire sent to graduates showed that
about two-thirds had consulted medical classics in their new workplace,
but the literature they listed was very limited (see table 6.1).

Apart from a few retired professors, most members of the staff
had been trained at a TCM college, mainly in the four great canons,

---

[29] This student's comment was accurate insofar as private practitioners often provide
primary health care which has largely adopted and integrated biomedical practices.
However, I encountered hardly any biomedical doctors in private practice. I found
that the main income of a private practitioner comes from highly priced skills in a
traditional or popular speciality like *qigong*, Chinese drug therapies, bone setting, and
the like, with which the costs of the minor interventions of primary health care are
financed.

[30] On the history of the ambivalent attitude towards the West that nationalism created
among Chinese medical doctors, see Croizier (1968).

Table 6.1. *Preferred canonical medical works consulted by graduates*

Subject of graduation	Acumoxa and massage		TCM
College enrolment	1986–8	1987–9	1985–9
Total number of responses	21	19	22
Consulted number of classics	4	5	6
Inner Canon (*Nei jing*)	11	7	4
Treatise of Cold Damage Disorders (*Shang han lun*)	2	4	6
Essentials in the Golden Casket (*Jin gui yao lüe*)	0	1	3
Great Compendium of Acumoxa (*Zhen jiu da cheng*)	4	2	0
Warmth Factor Disorders (*Wen bing xue*)	0	0	3
Systematic Canon of Acumoxa (*Zhen jiu jia yi jing*)	1	0	0

and they were fairly familiar with the medical classics. Several spoke of themselves as adherents of the 'party of the canonical formulae' (*jingfangpai*).[31] Senior teachers all emphasised the importance of memorising canonical texts. This does not of course mean that they took every word of the canons at face value. Some distanced themselves from the phrases they quoted from the classics by saying: 'The ancients (*guren*) say' or 'The ancients did not know'. Although I found that the Ming commentary by Zhang Jiebin (1563–1640) rather than the Tang commentary by Wang Bing (eighth century) tended to be cited in the TCM textbook *Interpretation*, it would be wrong to conclude that more recent interpretations were always considered more refined and accurate. Opinions diverged particularly on the accuracy of modern interpretations of the classics which accorded with biomedical models. Tao was convinced of their scientific value, while others were very sceptical.

Opinions among the younger staff members were most diverse, particularly among the Shanghai-trained acumoxa and massage teachers: 'The introductory course on *Classical Chinese for Medics* is indispensable.' 'The course in *Classical Chinese for Medics* was good and necessary, and so were those on the *Interpretation of the Inner Canon* and the *Selected Writings of Acumoxa* (*Zhenjiu jixuan*).' 'Shanghai is far more progressive, with more courses on Western medicine; here there is more emphasis on the four great canons.' 'Reading the four great canons was a pure

---

[31] They indicated that the Japanese and also certain colleges in the Jiangsu area belonged to the 'party of the fashionable formulae' (*shifangpai*). Certain teachers who had experienced the Japanese occupation during World War II (1937–45) expressed open resentment of the Japanese, even in class, but the young acumoxa staff showed much admiration for Japan, particularly for the Japanese biomedical research on TCM.

Table 6.2. *Courses on canonical medical texts for TCM students*

Textbook	Number of Hours/Semester	Number of Lessons (2hrs)/Week	Semester
Classical Chinese for Medics (*Yiguwen*)	142	2	1st, 2nd
Interpretation of the Inner Canon (*Neijing jiangyi*)	108	3	4th
Treatise of the Cold Damage Disorders (*Shanghanlun*)	108	2	5th, 6th
Essentials in the Golden Casket (*Jingui yaolüe*)	72	2	7th
Warmth Factor Disorders (*Wenbingxue*)	72	2	7th
Summaries of Different Chinese Medical Doctrines (*Zhongyi gejia xueshuo*)	108	3	8th
Total	610	14	

waste of time.' 'We only studied the *Inner Canon*; we should have learnt more of the four great canons.' 'The *Canon on Difficult Issues* is most important for the clinic, but no college offers any courses on it.' Apart from one teacher who advocated the elimination of courses on the four great canons altogether, most of these teachers did not question the general opinion that the medical classics were important for TCM, although most denied their usefulness in the clinic: 'The "ancient books" (*gushu*) provide no guidance for clinical work – for that we have the TCM textbooks on clinical courses – but they are necessary for deeper insights.'

According to the national standard, about one-quarter of the time in courses for regular students was devoted to the Chinese medical canons (see table 6.2), but local authorities felt free to modify these standards. For instance, the introductory course on *Classical Chinese for Medics* was in 1988–9 shortened for those acumoxa and massage students who specialised in massage to 1 semester of 72 hours instead of 2 semesters of 56 hours each, and classes on the *Interpretation* were in 1989 reduced for TCM regular students from 108 hours to 72 hours only.[32] A teacher

---

[32] In the late 1950s, there were daily classes on the *Inner Canon* over two years (Zhang, p.c.).

commented: 'The "party of the TCM colleges" (*xueyuanpai*) emphasises Western biomedicine. It wants to abolish the study of the ancient books and is not serious about the *Inner Canon*.' The college authorities themselves expressed the aim to train students in the reading of canonical medical texts by means of 'examplary learning'. However, if this method reduces the number of examples too much, the claim that the college is transmitting knowledge of China's ancient heritage may become vacuous.

Lesson two: Mao's dialectics

In the second hour Tao started lecturing on the *TCM Fundamentals*. 'I am not a philosopher and not a political scientist, but medicine and philosophy cannot be separated. Their foundations are *yinyang* and the Five Organs.'[33] He then gave an account of the textbook's contents. He spoke of the 'materialist aspect' (*weiwuguan*) and its implications for 'views of life' (*shengmingguan*), for interrelating 'Form and Spirit' (*xingshenguan*) and for the 'inspection of illness' (*jibingguan*). Then he spoke of 'the dialectical approach' (*bianzhengguan*) and stressed 'contradiction' (*maodun*), 'holism' (*zhengti guannian*), and 'the inherent propensity to motion' (*yundongxing*) in all 'material things' (*shiwu*). During the private tutorial in the afternoon, Tao conceded that the notions of contradiction and struggles came from political slogans: 'In this country politics is quite important.' It was natural for him to use idioms of 'materialist dialectics', particularly when he discussed the notion of *yinyang* in class.

With regard to *yinyang*, Tao followed the textbook (*TCM Fundamentals* (Yin 1984:12–15)) in pointing out that the interaction of *yin* and *yang* had four principal aspects: Control through Opposition (*duili zhiyue*), Mutual Reliance and Mutual Use (*hugen huyong*), Equilibrium of Waxing and Waning (*xiaozhang pingheng*), and Mutual Transformation (*xianghu zhuanhua*). Tao wrote these terms on the blackboard, adding his own definitions and examples (see fig. 6.1).

Tao followed the textbook in distinguishing four kinds of opposition, but from the examples that he wrote on the blackboard it was not clear what the difference was between the four kinds of opposition that the four aspects of *yinyang* described. It was, for instance, not immediately intelligible what the difference between 'Heaven checks Earth and

---

[33] The usual expression is *yinyang* and *wuxing* (Five Phases). I was surprised to hear Tao replace the notion of Phases with the notion of Organs. Considering the increasing prominence of *wuzang* (Five Organs) in TCM, it is possible that his saying *wuzang* instead of *wuxing* was intentional.

No. 1. Control through Opposition (*duili zhiyue*):
Fire checks Water, Water checks Fire
Heaven checks Earth, Earth checks Heaven
left checks right, right checks left

No. 2. Mutual Reliance and Mutual Use (*hugen huyong*):
teacher and student
man and woman
Heaven and Earth

No. 3. Equilibrium of Waxing and Waning (*xiaozhang pingheng*):

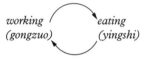

working   *eating*
(gongzuo)   *(yingshi)*

No. 4. Mutual Transformation (*xianghu zhuanhua*):
function and energy (gongneng)

nourishment (yingyang)

Figure 6.1   The Four Aspects of *yinyang* in TCM Teachings

Earth checks Heaven' and 'Heaven and Earth' was. Likewise, the only difference between 'eating and working' and 'nourishment and energy' seemed to be that in one case the arrow was horizontal and in the other vertical.[34]

Recourse to Cruse's *Lexical Semantics* (1986) promised some clarification. According to Cruse (1986:197–264), opposites in English describe four major kinds of opposition: (1) mutually exclusive opposites, here called 'complementaries', which characteristically stand in an either–or relation to each other; (2) 'antonyms', which stand in a gradable relation to each other; (3) 'directional opposites', which describe contrary motions; and (4) 'pseudo-opposites', in which one word has several opposites (see table 6.3). This allows us to reformulate our initial question and ask to which kind of opposition the four aspects of *yinyang* referred.

Naturally, the lexical semantic analysis calls for caveats. Cruse (1986) analysed the English vocabulary and not the Chinese, and this is important in that opposites are recognised as such on the basis of convention.

---

[34] Tao used rounded arrows for describing processes leading to the Equilibrium and the Mutual Transformation of *yinyang* but straight lines and vectors for TCM physiological and biomedical diagrams.

Table 6.3. *Opposites according to Lexical Semantics*
(based on Cruse 1986)

Term for the Opposition	Description of the Relation	Examples in English
1 Complementaries	either–or	dead-alive, open-shut
2 Antonyms	gradable	
2.1 Polar antonyms	objectively descriptive	fast-slow, heavy-light
2.2 Overlapping antonyms	evaluative	good-bad, polite-rude
2.3 Equipollent antonyms	subjective	sweet-sour, nice-nasty
3 Directional Opposites	contrary motion	
3.1 Directions	'potential paths'	up-down, north-south
3.2 Antipodals	extremes	centre-periphery
3.3 Counterparts	balanced irregularities in a uniform shape	convex-concave, male-female
3.4 Reversives	motions in opposite directions	rise-fall, enter-leave, pack-unpack
3.5 Conversives	relation in converging direction	before-after, predator-prey, guest-host, teacher-pupil
4 Pseudo-opposites	opposition of one to several opposites	thin-thick/fat, old-new/young

For instance, Western United Nations bureaucrats tend to oppose 'working time' to 'leisure time', and not working to eating as Tao did. The analysis is, moreover, rendered difficult because the concepts Tao referred to stood out for their 'multivocality' (Turner (1960)1967:48–58). Water, for instance, may refer to what flows in rivers and has depth in lakes, to the stuff we drink and urinate, something cold or salty, sometimes dark and sometimes clear, to the supple and weak, and to the vigour which makes plants pliant.

Nevertheless, the lexical semantic analysis does provide some clarification. Seen in opposition to Fire, the use of Water for extinguishing a Fire and, conversely, the use of Fire to turn the Water with Form (*you xing*) into vapour without Form (*wu xing*) could be meant. In that case, *Water and Fire* could be understood as mutually exclusive opposites that stand in an either–or relation to each other, 'complementaries' in Cruse's terms: if one is alive, the other is not (see table 6.3, section 1). If, in contrast, one were to view *Water and Fire* as indicators of the Cold (*han*) and Hot (*re*), they would probably point to an opposition comparable to that of warmth and coldness on a gradable scale of temperature. In terms of lexical semantics they would be 'polar antonyms' if they were considered objectively descriptive or 'equipollent antonyms', since

Chinese medical concepts often refer to the subjectively felt (table 6.3, sections 2.1 and 2.3). However, in ancient Chinese philosophy *Water and Fire* described yet another kind of opposition. If one consults one of the most frequently cited text passages on the Five Phases from the chapter of the 'Great Plan' (*Hong fan*) in the *Book of Documents* (*Shang shu*), one finds that: 'Water means soaking downward; Fire means flaming upward' (Karlgren 1950:30). *Water and Fire* are here conceived of as 'directional opposites', and thus best classified as 'reversives' (table 6.3, section 3.4).

The examples Tao wrote on the blackboard to illustrate Control through Opposition and Mutual Reliance and Mutual Use can all be understood as 'directional opposites' (table 6.3, section 3): *Heaven and Earth*, like *man and woman*, may be seen as 'counterparts' (Cruse 1986:225), but *man and woman* has, particularly in Chinese, also the connotation of the 'conversive' husband and wife (p. 232). *Teacher and student* constitute another example of 'conversives', and *left and right* indicate, according to Cruse, 'directions' (p. 223). Without being conscious of it, Tao cited examples which emphasised a conception of the universe that Zhang had already stressed: he conceived of it in terms of directional categories (see p. 110). Much as Zhang stressed the Five Directions (*wuwei*), Tao raised examples of 'directional opposites', a finding that makes perfect sense in the light of the ancient conception of the universe as being in constant flow and flux. Flows and changes inherently have a directionality.[35]

Lexical semantics has helped us to recognise what Tao's examples on the blackboard had in common, namely, 'directional opposition', but it has not helped us to distinguish between the four aspects of *yinyang*. The information Tao provided in the classroom proved insufficient to identify the four different forms of opposition that *yinyang* are supposed to describe, and recourse to the textbook gave an equally muddled picture. From the textbook passages on *yinyang* it was impossible to compare and contrast the four aspects of *yinyang* systematically because of the unsystematic choice of citations from the medical classics,[36] the inconsistent interpretation of certain citations,[37] the lack of citations in certain paragraphs,[38] a failure to indicate that a sentence in modern

---

[35] For a more comprehensive analysis, see Hsu (1998).

[36] For instance, a quote describing the Equilibrium of *yinyang* was cited in the paragraph of Control through Opposition (*TCM Fundamentals* (Yin 1984:12)).

[37] For instance, another quote interpreted to refer to the Equilibrium was cited in the paragraph Control through Opposition (ibid: 13).

[38] For instance, in the paragraph on the Equilibrium only a citation describing Control through Opposition was repeated (ibid:13–14).

Chinese was, in fact, a quotation from the classics,[39] and the inclusion of examples from medical practice in one paragraph but not in all the others.[40] Much later I found that Mao's essay 'On Contradiction' clarified the issue (Mao 1961, 1975b). Two of the four aspects attributed to *yinyang* in TCM textbooks were derived from Mao's writings, namely, Control through Opposition and Mutual Transformation. Mao's concept of the Unity of Opposites (*duili tongyi*) was used for reinterpreting the meaning of *yinyang* in the paragraph on Control through Opposition. The textbook compilers may also have borrowed the wording 'mutual transformation' (*huxiang zhuanhua*) from Mao's writings. In this case, however, the reinterpretation of the interaction between *yin* and *yang* was not adjusted to Mao's notion of mutual transformation. Since the textbook contained citations from the medical classics and examples from medical practice, it became apparent that there was a discrepancy between the connotations of the label borrowed from Mao's writings and the classical Chinese medical conception of *yinyang*.

The unity of opposites and the necessity of struggle

'Unity of opposites' (*duili tongyi*) was a favourite phrase of teacher Tao's when he spoke of *yinyang*, and it is also at the core of Mao's essay 'On Contradiction':[41] 'The principle of contradiction within things, that is, the principle of the unity of opposites, is the basic principle of materialist dialectics' (Mao 1961:287). The 'unity of opposites' highlights in Mao's writings not only contradiction within things but also the necessity of struggle. Mao (1975b:341–2) cites Lenin: 'The unity . . . of opposites is conditional, temporary, transitory, relative. The struggle of mutually exclusive opposites is absolute, just as motion and development are absolute.'

Mao (1975b:337) claims 'that the contradictory aspects in every process exclude each other, struggle with each other, and are in opposition to each other'. Opposites may be simultaneously 'one and the same' (*tongyi*) because each is a condition for the other's existence – 'Without life, there would be no death; without death, no life' (p. 316) – and because 'in certain conditions, each of the contradictory aspects within

---

[39] Ibid: 13.
[40] Ibid: 16. The argumentation was obviously muddled in the paragraph of the *TCM Fundamentals* concerned with *yinyang*, but this does not apply to all TCM writings.
[41] On Mao's notion of 'contradiction' (*maodun*), see Soo (1981:46ff.). For a more comprehensive version of the essay 'On Contradiction', originally entitled 'The Law of the Unity of Opposites', and its history, see Knight (1990).

a thing transforms itself into the contrary; it changes its position to that of its opposite' (p. 316). Mao (1975b:338–9) gives as an example the 'revolution of the proletariat': 'The ruled are transformed into the rulers, while the bourgeoisie, the erstwhile ruler, is transformed into the ruled and changes its position to that originally occupied by its opposite.' This means that in materialist dialectics opposites transform themselves into each other. Mao maintains that there are 'two states of motion in all things, that of relative rest and that of conspicuous change' (p. 342). The unity of opposites refers, thus, in terms of lexical semantics, to mutually exclusive opposites, 'complementaries' in Cruse's terms (table 6.3, section 1). It also implies an understanding of change wherein struggle results in unity and, because of the contradiction within things, unity leads necessarily to opposition. It is an idiom which contains a revolutionary message: struggle!

To my surprise, the message to struggle was contained in the discussion of *yinyang* in the *TCM Fundamentals* (Yin 1984:12): '*Yinyang* are opposites; they are also one and the same. That they become one is the result of opposition. In other words, "opposition" (*duili*) is the aspect of the "contrary" (*xiangfan*) between the two; "unity" (*tongyi*) is the aspect of the "complementary" (*xiangcheng*) between the two. If there is no opposition, there is no unity; if there is no contrary, there is no complementary.'[42]

The affinity of this rhetoric with Mao's writings springs to mind. For instance, the Chinese saying 'Opposites are complementary'[43] has become conditional: 'If there is no contrary, then there is no complementary.' The conditional is a grammatical construction that frequently occurs in Mao's writings, but in the above context it makes no sense. A person (an event, or a thing) can complement something without necessarily being its contrary. *Yin* and *yang* need not necessarily be each other's contrary to be complementary.

For interpreting the phrase '*yang* engenders and *yin* causes growth' (*yang sheng yin zhang*), one may emphasise that *yang* is the contrary of *yin*: *yang* engenders and *yin* does not. From a linguistic point of view, *yang* is then the opposite of *yin*; *yang* differs from *yin* 'along only one dimension of meaning' (Cruse 1986:197). In contrast, we could interpret this phrase as emphasising two potentialities which are not very different and certainly not primarily opposites, as my translation 'to engender' and 'to cause growth' suggests. The reduction of *yang* to

---

[42] Here 'complementary' (*xiangcheng*) mean to complement the other, and is not to be confused with Cruse's usage (table 6.3, section 1).

[43] Derived from a phrase in the *History of the Former Han* (*Han shu*); see Mao (1961:326, n. 23). Initially it did not have universal implications (Knight 1990:51).

something that *yin* is not and vice versa becomes irrelevant. *Yin* and *yang* describe two different aspects of becoming. They need not be opposites, just like *bian* and *hua* were not opposites, but described change from different viewpoints. By reducing *yin* and *yang* to contraries, one stresses only one possible interpretation.

The discussion of Control through Opposition in the *TCM Fundamentals* not only reduces *yinyang* to contraries, but also reflects an understanding that unity arises after struggles during a previous period of opposition. *Yin* and *yang* are viewed as struggling with each other and thereby checking and balancing each other. This understanding of *yinyang* cannot be reconciled with others such as, for instance, Zhang's view when commenting on *yinyang* in the *Book of Changes* (see pp. 125–6).

The difference between the Unity of Opposites in materialist dialectics and the unity in the opposition of *yin* and *yang* became the focus of political debate in China's recent past. The Yang Xianzhen campaign was over the interpretation of 'One divides into two' (*yi fen wei er*) and 'Two unites into one' (*er he wei yi*) (Goldman 1981:95–101). In the early 1960s Mao used the expression 'One divides into two' to emphasise a struggle between two mutually exclusive opposites and insisted on a continuation of class struggle during the period of Socialist construction. Yang Xianzhen, in contrast, spoke of 'Two uniting into one' and, applying it to politics, advocated an economy that tolerated collective and private ownership. Yang Xianzhen was a Marxist theoretician who had spent more than twenty years in the Soviet Union, but his views were firmly grounded in the Chinese tradition. He pointed to Chinese concepts like *yinyang*, in which harmony was found in two aspects participating in a single event, just as 'breathing' (*huxi*) was composed of 'exhaling' (*hu*) and 'inhaling' (*xi*). This view made it possible for him to tolerate diversity (Goldman 1981:97–8). Yang was a convenient target for the anti-Soviet campaigns which diverted attention from other tensions in the Party, and was removed from his position in 1964 (Goldman 1981:101). This anecdote is not directly relevant to the observation that Mao's dialectics have since been used even for interpreting *yinyang* in the medical context, but it does highlight how different the ancient and the Maoist understandings of *yinyang* are and how far-reaching the implications of this can be.

Mutual transformation: two different notions of change

The aspect of the interaction between *yinyang* that was labelled Mutual Transformation (*xianghu zhuanhua*) concerned a notion of change into one's opposite. The wording *xianghu zhuanhua* is strikingly similar to one of materialist dialectics, *huxiang zhuanhua* (Mao 1961:318), and it is quite likely that TCM textbook writers borrowed it from Mao's writings.

As a revolutionary, Mao was confronted with problems of changing the social and political conditions in which China found itself at the beginning of the twentieth century. He strongly opposed what he called 'metaphysical doctrines', which he characterised as building on the assumption that things were 'discrete and static'. Moreover, he did not agree that only a change in the environment could effect change; this kind of change he considered quantitative and not qualitative (Mao 1961:296ff.). Mao's (1961:318) notion of change built on Lenin's: '"Dialectics is a teaching which investigates how opposites 'become one' (*tongyi*) (how they change into one) – in which conditions they 'transform themselves into one another' (*huxiang zhuanhua*) and become one."'

Roughly speaking, dialectical change was the union of two antitheses into a synthesis: 'The old unity with its constituent opposites yields to a new unity with its constituent opposites, whereupon a new process emerges to replace the old' (Wakeman 1973:298). Wakeman remarks, however, that 'On Contradiction' did not explain how this change occurred and points to the many examples 'drawn from history to illustrate opposites transforming into each other, but how those changes took place was not actually explained. One stage simply succeeded the next, like a before-and-after still photograph without intermediate motion' (p. 298). To describe change by presenting before-and-after still photographs of two different states is indeed characteristic of 'On Contradiction', but it is not unique to Mao. In the Chinese medical literature processes whereby *yang* is transformed into *yin* or vice versa are often described in terms of before-and-after still photographs.

TCM teachers would readily point to further similarities between Mao's dialectics and the 'dialectics of the *yinyang* school of thought'. Sometimes they would simply state that the precursors of materialist dialectics were, in fact, Chinese. Compared with a monocausal explanation of change which builds on an imagery derived from mechanics and consists of excluding many factors in favour of one conceivable cause–effect sequence along a unidirectional vector of time (as is often the case for assessing biomedical processes), 'materialist dialectics' and '*yinyang* dialectics' have much in common.

Consider, for instance, Mao (1961:318) quoting Lenin: '"Why should the human mind take these opposites not as something dead and rigid, but as something living, conditional, and ever changing, things transforming themselves into one another?"' That things are considered 'living' or, rather, 'ever changing', that they are mutually transformed into each other, that this force for change is within the things themselves, and that each thing is special and particular – features which are found in Mao's understanding of dialectical change – have much in common with the idea that the universe is *yin* and *yang* in constant flux (in the sense of transformation).

However, the difference between the goals of a twentieth-century revolutionary and the ancient Chinese worldview inherent in the notion of *yinyang* is crucial. In the *TCM Fundamentals* (Yin 1984:14), Mutual Transformation is explained in terms of several citations from the *Inner Canon*. One of them is from *Basic Questions*, chapter 66: 'When things are born, one calls it "transformation" (*hua*), and when things reach their extremes, one calls it "transition" (*bian*).' Another is from *Basic Questions*, chapter 5: 'If the cold reaches its extreme, this gives birth to the hot; if the hot reaches its extreme, this gives birth to the cold.' This is illustrated with an example from medical practice: 'In certain acute warmth and heat factor disorders . . . in the condition of high heat (fever), a rapid drop in temperature may suddenly occur, the Complexion becomes Pale (*se cangbai*), the Four Limbs Numb (*sizhi jueleng*), the Pulse Faint (*wei*) and likely to to be Severed (*jue*), etc. This dangerous phenomenon in which the *yangqi* suddenly casts off, this kind of change of Pattern, belongs to those in which a *yang* Pattern "is transformed" (*zhuanhua*) into a *yin* Pattern.' The two citations from the *Inner Canon* and the description of a change in a Distinguishing Pattern (*bianzheng*) point to a kind of change that occurs when an observer sees a boundary being reached and trespassed and a shift to its opposite or, as proposed earlier, a *bian*-change into another entity (see pp. 112–16). This aspect of *yinyang* is labelled Mutual Transformation, the term that stands for dialectical change in Mao's writings. However, the textbook does not stress the necessity of struggle. *Zhuanhua* change is not postulated to occur because of the 'synthesis' (*tongyi*) of two antitheses. Although the word *zhuanhua* occurs both in Mao's essay 'On Contradiction' and in the *TCM Fundamentals*, it has significantly different meanings in these two texts.[44]

In summary, Unity of Opposites is an idiom of materialist dialectics, and in the textbook paragraph entitled Control through Opposition (no. 1) *yinyang* is interpreted to describe dialectical change. The wording

---

[44] It is not my intention to complicate the issue, but the term *zhuanhua* also occurs in the *Inner Canon*, with still another meaning: 'Therefore, if a disorder endures, then it is transformed (*zhuanhua*), the upper and lower parts are out of balance and even a good doctor cannot cure it' (*Basic Questions* 3). *Zhuanhua*, to transform, also refers to processes of digestion (e.g. *Basic Questions* 11). See Ren (1986:1422; 13, 37).

Mutual Transformation (no. 4) has also been borrowed from materialist dialectics, but the interpretation of *yinyang* in this paragraph has not
been adjusted to it.[45]

Lesson three: being systematic

Lesson three began with the students rising from their seats to greet the
teacher (as usual) and continued with their whispering on the benches
as soon as they were seated again (as usual). Throughout the lecture
the teacher stood at the blackboard, spoke in a monotonous voice, and
turned only when the antagonism of the students became unbearably
loud. This lesson was not Tao's, but teacher Tian's third lesson. It was
on the *Interpretation of the Inner Canon* (1984). The *Interpretation* and
the *TCM Fundamentals* have more or less the same thematic structure,
as is easily seen from their table of contents (see table 6.4). A former
edition of the *Interpretation* constituted the introductory course in the
early 1960s, and a former edition of the *TCM Fundamentals* replaced it
from the 1970s onwards.

At the core of the *Interpretation* are whole chapters or parts of chapters from the *Inner Canon*. In accordance with the textual tradition of
Imperial times, the *Interpretation* consists of the 'original text' (*yuanwen*),
followed by a number of 'footnotes' (*zhuci*). And like most texts edited
during the Republican period, the original text is presented in compact
paragraphs (of two to seven lines) and not interspersed with one or
several comments after every phrase of the original text. The interpretive additions by the TCM textbook compilers of the Socialist period
consist merely of introductory remarks at the beginning of each chapter
and 'notes' (*anyu*) at the ends of certain paragraphs, both written in
standard modern Chinese.

The *TCM Fundamentals*, by contrast, are written in standard modern
Chinese and contain only short citations from the *Inner Canon* (and a
few other medical works). In the early 1960s a series of essays that had
apparently been published in the journal called *Fujian Chinese Medicine*
(*Fujian zhongyiyao*) was compiled to form a textbook entitled *The Study
of TCM Fundamentals* (*Zhongyi Jichuxue* (Zhao 1963:1)). Although this
textbook had been printed before the Cultural Revolution, it was pro-
mulgated on a nationwide scale only in the early 1970s. Wicked ton-
gues have spoken of such courses on the *TCM Fundamentals* as easily
digested convenience food for soldier-peasant-worker students, others

---

[45] Possibly, TCM textbook compilers decided for this reason to speak of *xianghu zhuanhua*
instead of *huxiang zhuanhua*.

Categories (1624) (*Lei jing*) 12 Categories in 32 Chapters	*Essentials* (1642) (*Nei jing zhi yao*) 8 Chapters	*Interpretation* (1984) (*Neijing jiangyi*) 9 Chapters and 1 Appendix	*TCM Fundamentals* (1984) (*Zhongyi jichu lilun*) 8 Chapters	1988 editions replacing the *TCM Fundamentals* 4 Volumes
1 *she sheng lei* Self-cultivation	1 *dao sheng* Self-cultivation	1 Introduction	1 Introduction	1 *Zhongyixue daolun* TCM Instruction
2 *yin yang lei*	2 *yin yang*	2 *yinyang wuxing xueshuo* yinyang Five Phases	2 *yinyang wuxing* yinyang Five Phases	
3–4 *zang xiang lei* Hidden and Apparent	5 *zang xiang* Hidden and Apparent	3 *zangxiang xueshuo* Organ Clusters 3.1 *zangfu xueshuo* Organs and Bowels 3.2 *jing qi shen* Essence *qi* Spirit	3 *zangxiang* Organ Clusters	2 *Zangxiangxue* Organ Clusters
			4 *qixue jinye* *qi* Blood Liquids Fluids	
5–6 *mai se lei* Pulse and Complexion	3 *se zhen* Examination of the Complexion 4 *mai zhen* Examination of the Pulse	7 *zhenfa* Methods of Diagnosis		
7–9 *jing luo lei* Tracts and Links	6 *jing luo* Tracts and Links	4 *jingluo xueshuo* Tracts and Links	5 *jingluo* Tracts and Links	
10 *biao ben lei* Ramifications and Roots		5 *bingyin bingji xueshuo* Illness Factors and Illness Triggers	6 *bingyin yu fa bing* Illness Factors and Onset of Illness	3 *Zhongyi bingyin bingjixue* TCM Etiology and Pathogenesis
11 *qi wei lei* *qi* and Flavour				
12 *lun zhi lei* Discussion and Treatment	7 *zhi ze* Principles of Treatment	8 *zhize zhifa* Maxims and Methods of Treatment	7 *bingji* Illness Triggers	
13–18 *ji bing lei* Illnesses	8 *bing neng* Illness Conditions	6 *bingzheng* Illness Patterns	8 *fangzhi yuanze* Principles of Prevention and Treatment	4 *Zhongyi fangzhixue zonglun* Outline of TCM Preventive Medicine
19–24 *zhen ci lei* Needling		9 *yangsheng xueshuo* Self-cultivation		
25–28 *yun qi lei* Phase Energetics		Appendix: *yunqi xueshuo* Phase Energetics		
29–32 *hui tong lei* Congruences				

Table 6.5. *Comments of graduates on TCM textbooks*

	Acumoxa and massage		TCM
TCM textbooks are . . .	1986–8	1987–9	1985–9
Systematic, contain basic knowledge	7	7	10
Useful only for general guidance	5	5	4
(Very) helpful	5	3	5
No comment	2	2	3

of Mao's educational scheme of indoctrination. For anthropologists and historians (e.g. Sivin 1987) it is of utmost interest not least because Chinese medical concepts are discussed in it in a fairly explicit and more readily intelligible way than in classical Chinese.[46] The editors of the *TCM Fundamentals* were not merely commentators, but composers of a coherent text. This opened up a forum for innovation.

Teacher Tian, who taught the course on the *Interpretation*, was not concerned with making Chinese medical concepts fit with Mao's dialectics. Rather, he was preoccupied with a 'systematic' (*xitonghua*) analysis of the medical classics. In his view, the *Inner Canon* was an accumulation of contradictory citations, a real hotchpotch. Students needed systematic guidance, he said. Like other TCM teachers, he emphasised that the systematic presentation of knowledge was the strength of TCM college education and, indeed, college graduates characterised TCM textbooks primarily as systematic (see table 6.5). 'Master–disciple relations had led to the innumerable "lineages of different doctrines" (*xuepai*) of Chinese medical knowledge', one teacher told me during an interview. In his view this was a defect. 'Being systematic is a necessary condition for the standardisation of knowledge, and this is crucial for the survival of Chinese medicine in the future.' The success of Western science came, in his opinion, from its being systematic.

Tao had also been a very articulate spokesman for a systematic approach to knowledge. When I tried to arrange my studies as a combination of classroom and clinical experience, he objected: 'Only the knowledge acquired in the classroom is systematic. If you insist on clinical experience from the very beginning, I won't care a bit about

---

[46] It would be wrong to say that one language (modern Chinese) was more concise than another (classical Chinese), but because of the register in which textbooks are written in modern Chinese the statements are less vague and polysemous.

your training.' Six months later, when I was tired of looking up the rich and flowery and almost poetic vocabulary of *TCM Diagnostics* and wishing I could skip this course altogether, the word intended to force me back into the classroom was 'systematic'. Without a systematic knowledge of diagnostics, how would a doctor learning only from 'experience' (*jingyan*) be able to recognise any as yet unseen disorder in practice? The 'senior doctor' and his 'experience' were the target of TCM polemics, and the attack was launched with the notion 'systematic'.

Tao claimed to be convinced of the therapeutic efficacy of Chinese medicine, but this did not keep him from carrying a stethoscope, generally considered an emblem of biomedicine.[47] He was aware of the manifold contradictions in the medical canons and was able nevertheless to take them as a guide for medical practice. He readily admitted that Chinese medical concepts were vague and context-specific, that norms were negotiable, and that the standard formulae of prescriptions were easily modified. He claimed that all this was precisely the strength of Chinese medicine, but this did not prevent him from emphasising how important it was to be systematic. Being systematic meant being analytic, he said – dividing the whole into separate themes. TCM doctors were generalists; that was the problem. 'The great Western medical discoveries in the last century were made not by generalists but by specialists in ophthalmology, bacteriology, and the like.' The future for TCM was the division of TCM theory into different courses for training specialists.[48] Being systematic, in Tao's opinion, implied specialisation as well as standardisation.

TCM teachers were by no means the first in Chinese medical history to emphasise the need to systematise medical knowledge. Wang Bing's explicit aim to order medical knowledge by editing the *Basic Questions* in AD 762 is well known. The comparison of the *Grand Basis* (*Taisu* (Yang 1981)) with the *Basic Questions* (Anon. 1956) shows that the editor had split up (analysed) the former (or a related text) and rearranged parts of it; apparently, in Wang Bing's case being systematic meant being thematic.[49] About a thousand years later, Zhang Jiebin found

---

[47] Since the stethoscope magnified sounds produced by defective structures in the body (Reiser 1978:23–44), it enabled the doctor to learn about the inside of the body by performing an examination on its surface. This procedure is remarkably similar to Pulse diagnostics, and insofar as the stethoscope underlines the Chinese ethic of being non-invasive, it can also be viewed as an emblem of modern Chinese diagnostics.

[48] This is precisely what the TCM editors of 1988 did, making four books out of one.

[49] Wang Bing's edition is no longer extant. In the Song dynasty edition (1078), the main editors, Gao Baoheng (eleventh century) and Lin Yi (eleventh century), remark that they compared many different editions and 'corrected' more than six thousand words and amended more than two thousand comments (Anon. 1956:3).

Wang Bing's thematic organisation of the *Basic Questions* unintelligible and asserted in his introduction to the *Categories* (*Lei jing* (1624)1985:1–8) that he had considered it necessary to regroup the contents of the entire *Inner Canon* (see also Klein 1987:64–74).[50] In the *Categories* (1624) he did away with the division between the *Basic Questions* and the *Divine Pivot*, thematically ordered chapters and extracts of chapters from both, and regrouped them into twelve different 'categories' (*lei*), thirty-two chapters in all (see table 6.4).

Zhang Jiebin's concept of *lei* (categories), which enabled him to re-structure the *Inner Canon*, deserves further scrutiny. In this context all that can be said about it is that the categories seem to have been phrased in terms of pairs of complementary aspects if one translates *she sheng lei* as the 'Category of Beholding and Giving Birth', *yin yang lei* as the 'Category of *yin* and *yang*', *zang xiang lei* as the 'Category of the Hid-den and the Apparent', *mai se lei* as the 'Category of Pulse and Com-plexion', *jing luo lei* as the 'Category of the Tracts and Links', *biao ben lei* as the 'Category of Ramifications and Roots', *qi wei lei* as the 'Category of the *qi* and Flavour [of Drugs]', and *lun zhi lei* as the 'Category of Treatment and Discussion'. *Ji bing lei* may have meant the 'Category of Complementary *ji*- and *bing*- Morbid Conditions', and *zhen ci lei* the 'Category of Complementary *zhen*- and *ci*- Needling in Acupuncture'. *Yun qi lei* probably meant the 'Category of the Five Circulatory Phases and the Six Seasonal Influences [of Phase Energetics]', and *hui tong lei* is possibly best translated as the 'Category of Congruences'.[51]

Zhang Jiebin's work has had an enduring impact: most of the above twelve categories figure in the introductory TCM textbooks (see table 6.4): the contents discussed in the category *she sheng* of the *Categor-ies* (1624) correspond with those in the chapter on 'Self-cultivation' (*yangsheng xueshuo*) in the *Interpretation* and the 'Principles of Pre-ventive Health Care' (*fangzhi yuanze*) in the *TCM Fundamentals*, though the position of these chapters in the respective works has changed (see

---

[50] Unschuld ((1980)1985:220) therefore proposes to speak of the *Lei jing* as the *Classic Arranged According to Topics*.

[51] The exact meaning of these terms is still subject to further research. The translation of *zang xiang* as 'the hidden and apparent' in Zhang Jiebin's work is somewhat daring; it is derived from the general pattern of the category names. It is consciously rendered as Organ Clusters in TCM textbooks to underline the change in connotation of this term. Porkert (1974:112) relates *xiang* to the Greek *eikon* (icon or image). With regard to the *Yi jing*, Wilhelm ((1923)1981:5) translates *xiang* as Images, which reflects nicely the idea that *xiang* are apparent to the onlooker: 'One observes images' (*guan xiang*). Peterson (1982:80–1) suggests 'figures' as the translation: 'A figure is an image or likeness, but it is also a form or shape, a design or configuration or pattern, and a written symbol.' The translation of *xiang* as 'figures' or 'configurations' comes close to that of 'clusters'.

below); the category *yin yang* corresponds with the chapter on *yinyang wuxing* in the *Interpretation* and the *TCM Fundamentals*; the category *zang xiang* is called the same in the respective chapters of the *Interpretation* and the *TCM Fundamentals*; the category *mai se* corresponds with the chapter 'Methods of Diagnosis' (*zhenfa*) in the *Interpretation*;[52] the category *jing luo* is called the same in the *Interpretation* and the *TCM Fundamentals*; the category on *biao ben* corresponds with the chapters on etiology (*bingyin bingji xueshuo* and *bingyin yu fa bing*) in the *Interpretation* and the *TCM Fundamentals*; the category on *qi wei* is not discussed in the introductory courses to TCM, but it figures in the introductory textbook *Traditional Chinese Pharmaceutics* (*Zhongyaoxue* (Ling 1984)); the category on *zhi lun* corresponds with the chapter on 'Maxims and Methods of Treatment' (*zhize zhifa*) in the *Intepretation* (1984);[53] and the category *ji bing* corresponds with that on 'Patterns of Illness' (*bingzheng*) in the *Interpretation* and 'Illness Triggers' (*bingji*) in the *TCM Fundamentals*. Notably neither the category on *zhen ci* nor that on *hui tong* is mentioned in these two TCM textbooks, and the phase energetics are discussed only in the appendix of the *Interpretation*.

Having established these correspondences, the question naturally arises of why the chapter headings in 1984 TCM textbooks correlate with Zhang Jiebin's categories. Historical considerations led me to investigate the *Essentials* (1642), an introductory reader of the Qing dynasty (1644–1911) and Republican period (1911–49) (Tao, p.c.). It is apparent from a comparison of the chapter headings that the *Essentials* (1642) laid the groundwork for the introductory TCM courses (see table 6.4). Published shortly after the *Categories* (1624), in 1642, the *Essentials* condensed it and largely retained its overall structure (while omitting the five categories *biao ben, qi wei, zhen ci, yun qi,* and *hui tong*).

Was it only the category names and chapter headings that corresponded with each other, and not the chapter contents? I examined the *zangxiang* category with this question in mind. Detailed analysis of its choice of text excerpts from the *Inner Canon* shows that the *Essentials* (1642) did indeed reproduce condensed contents of the *Categories* (1624). In the *Interpretation*, the text excerpts from the *Inner Canon* were, within a certain range, the same as those of its precursors, but the reproduction of the classical text clearly derived from an informed study of the

---

[52] It does not figure in the *TCM Fundamentals* because a new course had been set up: *TCM Diagnostics* (Deng 1984). Considering the importance Western biomedicine attributes to diagnostics, it may not be coincidence that TCM textbook compilers found it necessary, already in the 1960s, to set up a separate course on diagnostics.

[53] Notice that it is left out of the *TCM Fundamentals*, devoted to TCM *theory* only.

Table 6.6. *Excerpts from the* Inner Canon *in the* zangxiang *category of the* Categories, *compared with the* Essentials *and the* Interpretation

Categories (1624) All 32 excerpts of the zang xiang lei (in chapters III and IV)	Essentials (1642) corresponding excerpts on page numbers as in Qin 1985	Interpretation (1984) corresponding excerpts in chapters 2.1–9.1
III.1 *Su wen* 8 (entire text)	p. 38 (extract)	3.2 (identical extract)
III.2 *Su wen* 9 (extract)	p. 39 (identical extract)	3.1 (identical extract)
III.3 *Ling shu* 3 (tiny extract)	p. 41 (identical extract)	3.7 (identical extract)
III.4 *Su wen* 4 (extract)	p. 43 (identical extract)	2.2.3 (entire *Su wen* 4)
III.5 *Su wen* 5 (extract)	p. 44 (identical extract)	2.1.3 (entire *Su wen* 5)
III.6 *Su wen* 67 (second half of chapter)	p. 49 (tiny extract at end)	
III.7 *Su wen* 29 (tiny extract)		3.8 (entire text)
III.8 *Su wen* 10 (beginning of chapter)		
III.9 *Ling shu* 8 (entire text)		3.16 (entire text)
III.10 *Ling shu* 8 (entire text)	p. 47 (identical extract)	3.16 (entire text)
III.11 *Su wen* 11 (extract last part)		
III.12 *Su wen* 21 (extract)	p. 48 (identical extract)	3.9 (identical extract)
III.13 *Su wen* 1 (extract last part)		9.1 (entire text)
III.14 *Ling shu* 54 (entire text)		3.4 (entire text)
III.15 *Ling shu* 6 (last part)		
III.16 *Ling shu* 71 (extract)		
III.17 *Ling shu* 65 (extract last part)		
IV.18 *Ling shu* 59 (latter half)		
IV.19 *Ling shu* 40 (entire text)		
IV.20 *Ling shu* 4 (tiny extract)		
IV.21 *Ling shu* 50 (entire text)		
IV.22 *Ling shu* 53 (entire text)		6.6 (entire text)
IV.23 *Su wen* 11 (extract last part)		3.3 (identical extract)
IV.24 *Su wen* 19 (extract middle part)		
IV.25 *Ling shu* 30 (entire text)	p. 50 (extract)	3.12 (entire text)
IV.26 *Ling shu* 31 (entire text)		
IV.27 *Ling shu* 32 (entire text)		
IV.28 *Ling shu* 47(entire text)		3.17 (extract)
IV.29 *Ling shu* 29 (latter half)		
IV.30 *Ling shu* 72 (entire text)		
IV.31 *Ling shu* 64 (entire text)		
IV.32 *Ling shu* 65 (first part)		

Inner Canon itself.[54] There were visible alterations in the choice of the text excerpts and in their sequencing (see table 6.6). TCM textbook compilers were, like Zhang Jiebin and Li Zhongzi, systematic by being thematic. TCM teachers claimed that systematising meant making scientific. In discussing *yinyang*, for example, Tian applied in his third lesson a schema which reflected his understanding of scientification:

(a) the meaning of *yinyang*
(b) the characteristics of *yinyang*
(c) the evidence for *yinyang*
(d) the application of *yinyang*
(e) the interrelations of *yinyang*
(f) the effects of the transformations of *yinyang* in the body
(g) the pathological changes of *yinyang*

The components of this idiosyncratic schema were a definition (a), an 'objective' description (b), a proof (c), an application (d), and a discussion of the interrrelations of this entity with other entities (e–g). 'The definition of *yinyang*' in section (a) was given in standard Chinese, 'the characteristics of *yinyang*' (b) were rendered with short quotes in classical Chinese (three from p. 22 of the *Interpretation*, one from another chapter), and 'the evidence for *yinyang*' (c) consisted of another quote in classical Chinese (from p. 30). For 'the application of *yinyang*' (d) different interpretations of one classical Chinese quote (from p. 21) were given. The discussion of 'the interrelations of *yinyang*' (e) was divided into three subsections, citing phrases from p. 30, p. 24, and p. 21. The discussion of 'the effects of the transformation of *yinyang* in the body' (f) contained a phrase from p. 23, and only the discussion of 'the pathological changes of *yinyang*' (g) dealt with two paragraphs of the textbook in a more coherent way (on pp. 24–5). Tian was attempting to be systematic and scientific, but he did not rigorously apply any method of text analysis. Rather, he grouped together short phrases that he considered relevant for explaining *yinyang*. Again, his presentation was thematic rather than systematic.

---

[54] The work these TCM textbook compilers performed is remarkable for its philological precision. In the two chapters of the *Interpretation* on *yinyang wuxing* and *zangxiang*, I found only a few characters which deviated from those in a Ming print of the Song edition of the *Basic Questions* (Anon. 1956). The reproduction of the excerpts from the *Inner Canon* in the *Categories* was with a few more exceptions reliable too. The *Essentials*, by contrast, reproduced the texts of the *Inner Canon* by consistently omitting the introductory question and the concluding phrases of a paragraph. Moreover, whole paragraphs of a chapter or several phrases in a paragraph were frequently omitted, often those which are not immediately intelligible to a twentieth-century reader, nor possibly to a reader in the Late Ming.

Notably, teacher Tian did not confront the students with a text. For him the classical Chinese text was raw and had to be prepared for the students' consumption. The textbook editors had already done preliminary work on the text by adding comments and notes to it. TCM teachers like Tian, in conscientiously preparing their lectures, continued this interpretive work. As we have seen, Tian cut up the text into brief phrases taken from very different parts of it, and served the students a kind of textual 'chop-suey'.

In other lessons, Tian would begin by writing a list of Chinese characters on the blackboard, each equated with a modern Chinese word. Only then would he present a sentence in classical Chinese made up of all these characters. Thus the students saw a list of incoherent words suddenly come together in a phrase that immediately made sense. Instead of experiencing the 'multivocality' or polysemy of lexical items which is notorious for anyone who confronts a Chinese medical text, they experienced reliable guidance from their teacher, whose vision of things to come paralleled that of the mentor on the brink of omniscience as, for example, when Zhang engaged in the authoritative mode of interpretation (see pp. 114–18).

Western scholars have criticised this approach as one that transforms a 'treasure house' into a 'quarry' (Porkert 1982:569). Indeed, considering the respect for the golden age of the past, one wonders how its reverence is reconciled with what seems to the outsider a serious violation of its integrity. Here we would do well to recall Zhang's justificatory mode of interpretation which made use of the text to support his personal medical practice – preparing the raw text of the past to fit the needs of the present. What may seem a mutilation to the philologist may be virtuosity to the senior doctor or being systematic to the TCM teacher.

Returning to the four aspects of *yinyang* identified by Tao in his second lesson, let us consider the citations from the *Inner Canon* with which Tian illustrated the aspects called Mutual Reliance and Mutual Use (no. 2) and the Equilibrium of Waxing and Waning (no. 3). Mutual Reliance and Mutual Use he called an 'application of *yinyang*':

1. *yang* engenders, *yin* grows, *yang* kills, *yin* conceals
   (*yang sheng yin zhang, yang sha yin cang*)
2. *yang* is transformed into *qi* and *yin* becomes Form
   (*yang hua qi, yin cheng xing*)

The implications of these citations (from *Basic Questions*, chapter 5) are difficult to assess. Tian wrote several different interpretations on the blackboard. The first was remarkably similar to the one which we encountered in the first paragraph of *Basic Questions*, chapter 66: 'When [the Spiritual] is in the Sky, it is *qi*, and when it is on Earth, it takes Form.' The second was similar to others mentioned in our exploration of *bian* and *hua*. The third was similar in kind. The interaction between *yin* and *yang* dubbed Mutual Reliance and Mutual Use was thus illustrated with citations from the classics similar to those discussed during Zhang's seminars.

The Equilibrium of Waxing and Waning, which was mentioned as the third aspect of *yinyang* in the *TCM Fundamentals*, was not discussed during the introductory lessons on the *Interpretation*. Tian discussed it several weeks later, when the notion of Protective *qi* (*weiqi*) was discussed in the chapter entitled 'Disease Factors and Disease Triggering' (*bingyin bingji xueshuo*). This suggests that the occurrence of the concept of Waxing and Waning (*xiaozhang*) was, in the *Inner Canon* at least, limited to the context of the Nourishing and Protective (*yingwei*).

The text passage Tian used to explain the notion of Waxing and Waning was an extract from *Basic Questions*, chapter 3 (cited in the *Interpretation* (Cheng 1984:90)): 'Therefore the *yangqi*, during daylight, governs the outer sphere [of the body]; at dawn the Human *qi* (*renqi*) is generated, at noon the *yangqi* is thriving, and at sunset the *yangqi* is already depleted, and the Gates of *qi* (*qimen*) close. Therefore, at dusk, one should retire, one should not disturb muscles and bones, and one should not experience mist and dew; if the reverse happens at the above three moments, the body becomes tired and fragile.'

When I asked the young TCM staff what Waxing and Waning meant in comparison with the transformation called *zhuanhua*, they explained that the main difference between the two concepts was probably the rate at which change took place, Waxing and Waning referred to gradual change and *zhuanhua* to sudden change.[55] However, the above citation suggests that the concepts of *zhuanhua* in modern Chinese (comparable to *bian* in classical Chinese) and Waxing and Waning may also differ with regard to the notion of the time in which the changes take place. *Zhuanhua*, when used in the sense of *bian*, is best understood in terms of a polar conception of time, while Waxing and Waning is change with regard to time conceived of as circular; it is used to describe the changes of the attributes to *qi* at dawn, noon, and dusk; the changes of the moon in a month; or those of the seasons in a year.

In summary, the four aspects of *yinyang* provided a recent reinterpretation of *yinyang* which every TCM student had to memorise:

---

[55] The term *xiaozhang bianhua* was a standing expression in the vocabulary of TCM teachers for 'change' in general.

1. Control Through Opposition (*duili zhiyue*) is frequently explained with reference to the Unity of Opposites (*duili tongyi*), a key concept in Mao's essay 'On Contradiction'. It postulates a stage of opposition and absolutely necessary struggles between opposites. In the *TCM Fundamentals*, this notion of necessary struggles is attributed to *yinyang*.
2. Mutual Reliance and Mutual Use (*hugen huyong*) describes different views of change already known to us from Zhang's seminars with little reinterpretation.
3. Equilibrium of Waxing and Waning (*xiaozhang pingheng*) is, in the *TCM Fundamentals*, an aspect of *yinyang* in general. In the *Inner Canon*, by contrast, Waxing and Waning describes change with reference to a circular conception of time in very particular contexts.
4. Mutual Transformation (*xianghu zhuanhua*) seems to be a phrase borrowed from materialist dialectics. In Mao's writings it points to a change that consists of a synthesis of two antitheses. In the *TCM Fundamentals*, however, it is a label for change well known from the Chinese medical literature, sometimes delimited by the term *bian*. Mutual Transformation refers to a change into the opposite that is visible to the observer and takes place when a boundary is reached and transgressed. It designates, for instance, the course of a Distinguishing Pattern changing into another one.

Evidently, TCM definitions built on many different ways of reinterpreting *yinyang*. Control through Opposition referred to an innovative reinterpretation of *yinyang*, conceiving the interaction as dialectical change arising from struggle. Mutual Reliance and Mutual Use referred to rather indeterminate views of mutual interaction as known from the canons. The Equilibrium of Waxing and Waning referred to the generalisation of the comparatively narrow sense of a term known from classical writings. Mutual Transformation was a new label for an age-old concept of change.

Table 6.7. *The course on the* Interpretation, *February–June 1989*

Date	Textbook Chapter	*Nei jing* Chapter	Contents of Lecture
27 Feb.	1	–	Introduction
1 March	1	–	Introduction
4 March	2.1	*Su wen* 5: *Yin yang ying xiang da lun*	*yinyang* Five Phases
6 March	2.1	*Su wen* 5	*yingyang* Five Phases
8 March	2.1	*Su wen* 5	*yinyang* Five Phases
11 March	2.1.4	*Su wen* 4	Seasonal Winds, homework
	3.1	*Su wen* 9: *Liujie zangxianglun*	Organ Clusters
13 March	3.1	*Su wen* 9	Organ Clusters
15 March	3.3	*Su wen* 11: *Wu zang bie lun*	Organ Clusters
18 March	*	?	?
20 March	3.9	*Su wen* 21: *Jing mai bie lun*	Stomach and digestion Prognosis of death and life

Table 6.7. *(cont'd)*

Date	Textbook Chapter	*Nei jing* Chapter	Contents of Lecture
22 March	3.10	*Ling shu* 17: *Mai du*	*he*-Associates of the Organs
	3.11	*Ling shu* 80: *Da gan lun*	End of lesson: short exam
25 March	3.12	*Ling shu* 30: *Jue qi*	Different aspects of *qi*
27 March	3.12	*Ling shu* 30	Different aspects of *qi*
	3.13	*Ling shu* 18: *Ying wei sheng hui*	Protective and Nourishing *qi*
29 March	3.13	*Ling shu* 18	Protective and Nourishing *qi*
2 April	3.14	*Ling shu* 36: *Wu long jin ye bie*	Liquids and Fluids
4 April	3.16	*Ling shu* 8: *Ben shen*	Spirit
6 April	3.16	*Ling shu* 8	Spirit
9 April	5.1	*Su wen* 3: *Sheng qi tong tianlun*	Illness Factors and Triggers
11 April	5.1.2	*Su wen* 3	The importance of *yangqi*
13 April	*	?*Su wen* 3	?
16 April	5.1	*Su wen* 3	Illness Factors, Illness Triggers, and Illness Transitions
18 April	5.2	*Ling shu* 46: *Wu bian*	The Five Transitions
	5.4	*Ling shu* 58: *Zei feng*	Noxious *qi*
20 April	*	?*Ling shu* 58	?Noxious *qi*
23 April	5.3	*Ling shu* 66: *Bai bing shi sheng*	Origin of the Hundred Disorders
25 April	5.3	*Ling shu* 66	Patterns of Accumulations
	5.5	*Su wen* 39: *Zu tong lun*	Congestions
27 April	*	?*Su wen* 39	?Congestions
1 May		no classes	
3 May	5.6	*Su wen* 74: *Zhi zhen yao da lun*	Etiology and Pathogenesis
5 May	*	?*Su wen* 74	?Etiology and Pathogenesis
8 May	5.6	*Su wen* 74	Etiology and Pathogenesis
10 May		?*Su wen* 33: *Ping re bing lun*	?Warmth Factor Disorders
12 May	*	?*Su wen* 33	?Warmth Factor Disorders
15 May	6.2	*Su wen* 33	Warmth Factor Disorders
17 May	6.4	*Su wen* 38: *Ke lun*	Cough
19 May	*	?*Su wen* 38	?Cough
22 May	6.4	*Su wen* 38	Cough
24 May	6.4	*Su wen* 38	Cough
	6.10	*Su wen* 44: *Wei lun*	Limpness
26 May	*	?*Su wen* 44	?Limpness
29 May	6.10	*Su wen* 44	Limpness
31 May	6.8	*Su wen* 43: *Bi lun*	Obstructions
2 June	*	?*Su wen* 43	?Obstructions
5 June	6.5	*Su wen* 39: *Zu tong lun*	Enduring Pain
7 June		students on demonstration	
21 June	9.1	*Su wen* 1: *Shang gu tian zhen lun*	Stages of ageing

* fieldworker absent, attending practical training in the clinic

Table 6.8. *The course on the* TCM Fundamentals,
September 1988 – January 1989

Date	Topic of Lecture
13th Sept.	Historical background
15th Sept.	Holism and dialectics
20th Sept.	*yinyang*
22nd Sept.	*yinyang*
27th Sept.	*yinyang*
29th Sept.	*yinyang*
4th Oct.	Five Phases (*wuxing*)
6th Oct.	Five Phases (*wuxing*)
11th Oct.	Five Phases (*wuxing*)
13th Oct.	Five Phases (*wuxing*)
18th Oct.	Five Organs (*wuzang*): Heart (*xin*)
20th Oct.	Five Organs (*wuzang*): Heart (*xin*)
25th Oct.	Five Organs (*wuzang*): Lungs (*fei*)
27th Oct.	Five Organs (*wuzang*): Lungs (*fei*), Spleen (*pi*)
1st Nov.	Five Organs (*wuzang*): Spleen (*pi*)
3rd Nov.	Five Organs (*wuzang*): Spleen (*pi*), Liver (*gan*)
8th Nov.	Five Organs (*wuzang*): Liver (*gan*)
10th Nov.	Five Organs (*wuzang*): Liver (*gan*), Kidneys (*shen*)
15th Nov.	Five Organs (*wuzang*): Kidneys (*shen*)
17th Nov.	Six Bowels (*liufu*): Stomach (*wei*), Small Intestine (*xiaochang*), Large Intestine (*dachang*), Gallbladder (*dan*), Bladder (*pangguang*)
22nd Nov.	Six Bowels (*liufu*): Triple Burner (*sanjiao*); Odd Palaces (*qiheng zhi fu*)
24th Nov.	Mid-term examination
29th Nov.	Breath (*qi*)
1st Dec.	Blood (*xue*), Liquids and Fluids (*jinye*)
6th Dec.	Tracts and Links (*jingluo*)
8th Dec.	Tracts and Links (*jingluo*)
13th Dec.	Tracts and Links (*jingluo*)
15th Dec.	Disease Factors (*bingyin*): the Six Disease Factors (*liuyin*)
20th Dec.	The Six Disease Factors (*liuyin*): Wind (*feng*), Cold (*han*), Summer Heat (*shu*), Dryness (*zao*), Fire (*huo*), Heat (*re*)
22nd Dec.	Disease Factors: Phlegm (*tanyin*), Stagnant Blood (*yuxue*)
27th Dec.	Disease Factors: Normal and Noxious *qi* (*zhengqi xieqi*)
29th Dec.	Disease Factors: Normal and Noxious *qi*, preventive medicine
3rd Jan.	'In treating Illness trace the Roots' (*zhi bing qiu ben*)

From the Five Phases to the Five Organs

In the course on the *Interpretation* (see table 6.7), three lectures (six hours) were devoted to the chapter entitled *yinyang* Five Phases (*wuxing*) (4–8 March), five hours dealing with *yinyang* and only one with the Five Phases. The following three lectures were about the Organ Clusters (*zangxiang*) (11–15 March). Other lectures dealt with concepts such as Spirit, Fluids, Nourishing and Protective *qi* (20 March – 6 April). Most of the attention was, however, given to Disease Factors and Disease Triggers (*bingyin bingji*) (9 April – 15 May).[56] Disorders that were discussed were Cough (*ke*), Limpness (*wei*), Obstructions (*bi*), and Enduring Pain (*zutong*) (17 May – 5 June). Notably, the first chapter of the *Basic Questions* that discusses ageing and self-cultivation was read in the very last lesson (on 21 June).

In the course on the *TCM Fundamentals*, four lectures were on *yinyang* (20–9 September), four on the Five Phases (4–13 October), and eleven on the Five Organs (*wuzang*) (18 October – 22 November) (see table 6.8). Here too, self-cultivation, now called 'principles of preventive health care' (*fangzhi yuanze*), was discussed at the very end of the term (on 29 December). That the Five Phases were scarcely discussed in the classes on the *Interpretation* and that discussion of the Five Organs constituted the core of the course on the *TCM Fundamentals* seem to reflect a single process of the standardisation of Chinese medical knowledge. We will see that this process is by no means limited to recent developments in the PRC, and that an increased focus on the human body can be traced at least as far back as the seventeenth century.

The courses on the *Interpretation* and the *TCM Fundamentals* were similarly structured, but they also had interesting differences. One similarity was that self-cultivation, central to Chinese medical thought and practice, was only briefly mentioned at the end. It is certainly no accident that it is discussed in the first chapters of the *Basic Questions*, the *Categories* (1624), and the *Essentials* (1642). However, already in the Qing dynasty (1644–1911) the more learned works with high official sponsorship apparently 'stressed theory and causal patterns more than preventive health' (Furth 1987:10). It is likely that this tendency to emphasise etiology and put preventive health last, has been reinforced by the recent impact of disease-and-therapy-oriented biomedicine.

The *Interpretation* and the *TCM Fundamentals* primarily differed in rigour of presentation and thematic priorities; a comparison of tables 6.7 and 6.8 suffices for an appreciation of the systematic design of the course on the *TCM Fundamentals*. This course, which constituted the introductory course for acumoxa and massage specialists, was mostly about the 'physiology' of the human body. The course on the *Interpretation* was delivered to second-year TCM regular students who were

---

[56] This theme did not figure in the *Essentials* (see table 6.4). The emphasis on etiology in TCM theory has also been observed by Farquhar (1994a:86–91). In Western biomedicine, etiology is an important aspect of diagnosis and TCM theory stresses the importance of diagnostics (see above, n. 52).

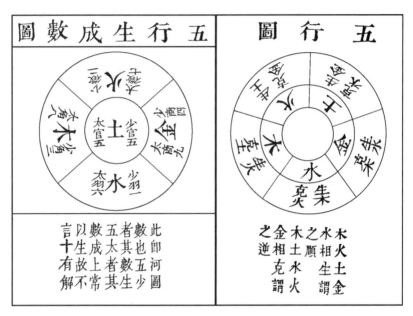

Figure 6.2   Two diagrams of the Five Phases from the chapter
'Phase Energetics' in the *Additional Appendix to the Categories*
(*Lei jing fu yi* (1624)1799:8–9)

familiar with the 'physiology'; hence perhaps its emphasis on 'pathology'. However, the different emphases of these two courses can also be
explained from a historical point of view. We need to remind ourselves
that in the *Inner Canon* only a few chapters are devoted to a systematic
discussion of the Organ Clusters. Many more are concerned with patterns of change and triggers of disorders. The *Interpretation*, which constituted the introductory course in the early 1960s, reflects the contents
of the *Inner Canon* more faithfully than the *TCM Fundamentals* that were
composed later. In other words, the Five Organs have only recently
become fundamental for TCM theory.[57]

It is surprising that even in the course on *Acumoxa*, the Tracts and
Links (*jingluo*) were introduced with emphasis on the Organs and
Bowels (*zangfu*): 'Important are the Five Organs and the Six Bowels
(*liufu*). They generate *qi*, and this is the *qi* that circulates in the Tracts

[57] Compare the textbook contents (table 6.4) with the lectures on the *TCM Fundamentals*
(table 6.7): the centrality of the Five Organs is striking only in the latter. This shows
again that studies of TCM need to combine textual analysis with anthropological
fieldwork.

and Links.'[58] Then, the teacher raised the rhetorical question: 'Why are there exactly twelve Tracts in the body?' and answered it: 'This has to do with the fact that they come from the twelve Organs and Bowels.'[59] His answer further stressed the importance of the Organs and Bowels, although it was from a historical point of view questionable.[60]

Obviously, the Five Organs were more prominent than the Five Phases in theoretical TCM courses. Nevertheless, attempts to eliminate the Five Phases have been in vain (Qiu 1982) – reasoning in terms of the Five Phases remains crucial for medical practice, especially when it comes to 'maxims of treatment' (*zhize*). In discussions with Tao, however, the notion of the Five Phases was largely replaced by the notion of the Five Organs. On one occasion, for instance, I was surprised to find that the Five Phases were only of secondary importance for determining the position of the Five Organs. Confronted with a diagram like the one situating the Five Organs in an orbit (fig. 6.2), I argued that the Earth should be situated at the centre of the four other Phases. As evidence for this, I referred to a text compiled in the Han dynasty (206 BC – AD 220) in which the East was said to be bluegreen, the South red, the West white, the North black, and the top yellow (*Shi ji* 60 (Sima 1959:2115)). Yellow was associated with the Earth and the Earth with the Spleen. Tao was not impressed and responded: 'Sometimes the Heart is the centre, as it is in Western medicine.' As evidence for this, he cited a phrase from *Basic Questions*, chapter 8: 'The Heart has the office of the ruler' (Anon. 1956:23). This anecdote shows not only that the points of view in the canons are varied enough to corroborate two contradictory arguments but also that Tao put the Heart at the centre in both Western biomedical and TCM reasoning. He did not consider the Five Phases central to TCM reasoning when confronted with the question of which was the most central of the Organs.

On another occasion I provoked my teacher by saying that *yinyang* was an earlier concept than the Five Phases.[61] 'This is difficult to tell',

---

[58] Notice that *qi* is supposed to be generated inside the human body, in the Organs. Little attention is given to *qi* that constitutes and permeates both macro- and microcosm.

[59] Namely, the Five Organs and the Pericardium (which counts as the sixth), and the Six Bowels.

[60] In the Mawangdui manuscripts (MWD 1985), the eleven Vessels along the legs and arms do not generally connect with the Five Organs. In *Lingshu* 10 (Ren 1986:299–307), in which these TCM teachings are grounded, each of the six *yin* resp. *yang* Vessels is said to 'belong to' (*shu*) an Organ or a Bowel. Contrary to this teacher's claim, the number of the Organs and Bowels (twelve) probably represents a numerological adjustment to the twelve Tracts.

[61] What I had in mind was Loewe (1982) on the '*Jing fa*' text of the Mawangdui manuscripts: 'The text refers to *yinyang* and alludes to the theory of correspondences (*ganying*), but there is no mention of *wuxing*' (p. 40). However, the issue is very complex and,

was his answer, and he added after a short pause: 'No, first you have the material entities, and then you discuss their interrelations.' He seemed to imply that the Five Phases referred to material entities.[62] I objected and pointed to the 'forms of conduct' or 'processes' (*xing*) (Graham 1989:326) described in the chapter 'Great Plan' in the *Book of Documents*: 'Water means soaking downward; Fire means flaming upward; Wood means bending and straightening; Metal means conforming and changing; Earth means accepting seed and giving crop' (Karlgren 1950:30).[63] Teacher Tao, however, maintained that that text passage was irrelevant to Chinese medicine.[64] In Chinese medicine Water (*shui*), Fire (*huo*), Wood (*mu*), Metal (*jin*), and Earth (*tu*) provided the imagery for *material* entities, and their interrelations were dialectical as assessed by the dialectics of *yinyang*.[65]

Tao defended this view also in his *Newly Edited Manual of Clinical Chinese Medicine* (*Xinbian zhongyi linzheng shouce*): the first section, on 'theoretical characteristics' of TCM, was concerned with the material aspect, the Five Organs, and the second with their interrelations, *yinyang* (Wu et al. 1986:3–6). By replacing the notion of the Five Phases with that of Five Organs, the focus of attention shifts from a preoccupation with change to one with matter. It is not that Tao considered the material aspects of the Five Phases comparable to the four

because of the difficulty of dating the literature, difficult to explore. 'Within this jumble of sources [*Book of Documents*, 'Ten Wings' of the *Book of Changes*, *Spring and Autumn Annals*, etc.] that we cannot place confidently in historical sequence, we find a great many instances of *yinyang* and various fivefold (and other categories) used in quite concrete senses . . . The irreducible uncertainty, inconvenient though it is, is preferable to the delusion of certainty' (Sivin 1995b:3).

[62] Sivin (1987:71), by contrast, points out that in what is possibly the earliest appearance of *wuxing*, the 'Declaration at Gan' (*Gan shi*) preserved in the *Book of Documents*, it refers to moral qualities. Sivin (1995b:5) speaks of 'activities' with regard to the moral categories which the *wuxing* linked to the *Mencius* (*Meng zi*) probably are, and Graham (1986:76) of 'courses of action' in respect of the *wuxing* mentioned in the *Xun zi*.

[63] 'Water: it ought to soak downward, Fire: it ought to flame upward, Wood: it ought to bend and straighten, Metal: it ought to conform and change, Earth: it ought to accept seed and give crop.' If translated in this normative way, the text reads as a prescription rather than a description. Rather than referring to processes, *wuxing* may even in this context have a connotation of normative forms of conduct.

[64] Tao is corroborated by Sivin (1995e:16, n. 20): '*Wu xing* as it appears in this document has little to do with the later Five Phases.' Sivin (1987:71) points out that this passage was extremely influential for two thousand years because of its supposed archaic origin, but is now widely considered a late addition.

[65] This viewpoint seems to be one of a TCM theoretician; no parallels have been found elsewhere. For an authoritative discussion of *wuxing*, in early texts and later, in the medical context, see Sivin (1987:70–80; 1995b:1–19).

TCM Fundamentals (Five Phases in the centre)

自	然			界			五	人			体			
五音	五味	五色	五化	五气	五方	五季	行	五脏	六腑	五官	形体	情志	五声	变动
角	酸	青	生	风	东	春	木	肝	胆	目	筋	怒	呼	握
徵	苦	赤	长	暑	南	夏	火	心	小肠	舌	脉	喜	笑	忧
宫	甘	黄	化	温	中	长夏	土	脾	胃	口	肉	思	歌	哕
商	辛	白	收	燥	西	秋	金	肺	大肠	鼻	皮毛	悲	哭	咳
羽	咸	黑	藏	寒	北	冬	水	肾	膀胱	耳	骨	恐	呻	栗

Organ Clusters (Organ Clusters in the centre)

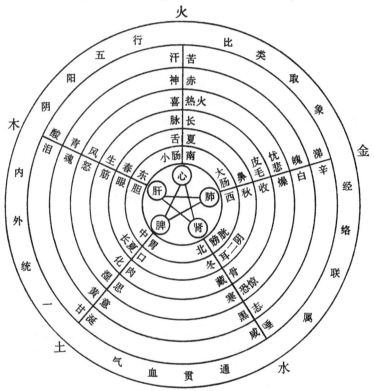

Figure 6.3   Five Phases as represented in the *TCM Fundamentals* (Yin 1984:20) and the *Organ Clusters* (Yunnan zhongyi xueyuan 1988:7)

elements of scholastic medicine, as the Jesuits did,[66] rather, he seemed to associate the Five Phases with the substances to which twentieth-century intellectuals in China generally refer – TCM teachers had all taken courses in chemistry.

Tao was not the only TCM scholar to emphasise the material aspects of the Five Phases. Textbooks on Traditional Chinese Pharmaceutics published since 1970 do not mention a correspondence between the Five Flavours (*wuwei*) and the Five Phases.[67] The interrelations among the Five Phases are discussed in respect to either the Five Organs or the Five Flavours; the Five Phases are simply not mentioned.

A similar tendency becomes evident when one compares the diagrams representing the Five Phases in the *TCM Fundamentals* and in the *Organ Clusters* (fig. 6.3). In the former, the Five Phases are at the centre of the diagram, comprising aspects of the body ecologic inside and outside the human body. In the latter, the Five Organs are at the centre, and the Five Phases on the periphery are hardly noted.

Tao's stress on 'substance' rather than 'force' in classical concepts of 'substance-forces' is also not without precursors. His conception of *yinyang* as a dialectical force and the Five Phases as matter is reminiscent of Zhu Xi's (1130–1200) differentiation between *qi* and substance: '*Yin* and *yang* are *qi*, and the Five Phases are substance. It is through the existence of this substance that phenomenal things were made.' Zhu Xi made a distinction between the material characteristics of *yinyang* and Five Phases, but he maintained simultaneously that: 'It is not true that in addition to *yin* and *yang* there are Five Phases . . .' (cited in Sivin 1987:78). Tao, however, made exactly the mistake that Zhu Xi sought to avoid.

Zhang Jiebin laid the groundwork for the present focus on the Five Organs when he regrouped text passages from the *Inner Canon* into twelve categories. The third category called *zang xiang* (the Hidden and Apparent) put the human body at the centre of attention, and this focus on the body may have prepared the way for later developments

---

[66] Matteo Ricci (1552–1610) considered the Phases to be 'elements' that produced 'all things and phenomena' and considered them, because of the inherent contradictions of the Chinese doctrine, subordinate to the Greek notion of elements. His understanding of the Five Phases has remained predominant far into the twentieth century (Sivin 1987:73–4). Needham (1956:243–4), concerned with questions of science and 'proto-science' in China, proposes to conceive of them less as 'five sorts of fundamental matter' than as 'five sorts of fundamental processes'. Porkert (1974:43–54), who stressed the sequences into which the Phases can be placed, coined the phrase 'Five Evolutive Phases' from which the wording 'Five Phases' is derived.

[67] For example, *Zhongyixue jichu* (Shenyang yaoxueyuan 1978) mentions *yinyang*, but not the Five Phases. *Zhongyaoxue* (Ling 1984:8) mentions the Five Flavours (*wuwei*) but not the Five Phases.

Table 6.9. *Text passages from the* Inner Canon *in the* zangxiang *chapter of the* Interpretation, *compared with their occurrence in the* Categories

Interpretation (1984), chapter 3: Title: Organ Clusters (*zangxiang*)	*Canon of Categories*: (1624)[68]
Subtitle: Organs and Bowels (*zangfu*)	
3.1 *Su wen* 9 (extract)	*Zang xiang* III.2 (identical extract)
3.2 *Su wen* 8 (extract)	*Zang xiang* III.1 (whole)
3.3 *Su wen* 11 (extract)	*Zang xiang* IV.23 (identical extract)
3.4 *Ling shu* 54 (whole)	*Zang xiang* III.14 (whole)
3.5 *Ling shu* 56 (extract)	*Wu wei* XI.2,3 (whole)
3.6 *Ling shu* 33 (whole)	*Jing luo* IX.32 (whole)
3.7 *Ling shu* 2 (tiny extract)	*Zang xiang* III.3 (identical tiny extract)
3.8 *Su wen* 29 (whole)	*Zang xiang* III.7 (tiny extract)
3.9 *Su wen* 21 (extract)	*Zang xiang* III.12 (identical extract)
3.10 *Ling shu* 17 (extract)	*Jing luo* VIII.22 (identical extract)
3.11 *Ling shu* 80 (tiny extract)	*Ji bing* XVIII.81 (entire front part with identical extract)
Subtitle: Essence, Breath, Spirit (*jing, qi, shen*)	
3.12 *Ling shu* 30 (whole)	*Zang xiang* IV.25 (whole)
3.13 *Ling shu* 18 (whole)	*Jing luo* VIII.23 (whole)
3.14 *Ling shu* 36 (whole)	*Ji bing* XVI.58 (whole)
3.15 *Ling shu* 71 (extract)	?
3.16 *Ling shu* 8 (whole)	*Zang xiang* III.9, 10 (whole)
3.17 *Ling shu* 47 (extract)	*Zang xiang* IV.28 (whole)

that made it a material object. Zhang Jiebin did not, however, discuss the body separately from its surroundings. The texts he regrouped under the heading *zang xiang* discussed the resonance of macrocosm and microcosm. The term *zang xiang* itself indicates a holistic view that links the hidden inside the body to the apparent on its surface and outside the body. Numerological rather than material considerations determined the categories: in the texts that were regrouped in the category *yin yang* the number two prevailed, in those of the *zang xiang* the number five.

In the *Interpretation*, the Organs and Bowels and their associations with the Direction-Seasons is no longer recorded in the chapter on *zangxiang*.[69] Now a chapter called '*yinyang* Five Phases' discusses the

[68] Name of the category, chapter (in Roman numbers), text passage quoting the *Inner Canon* (in Arabic numbers).
[69] For example, *Categories* III.4 and III.5 are discussed in the *Interpretation* 2.2.3 and 2.1.3, along with *yinyang* and the Five Phases. See table 6.6.

interrelations between microcosm and macrocosm. The *zangxiang* chapter in the *Interpretation* focuses exclusively on processes inside the body and on entities that appear comparable to those of biomedical anatomy.[70] It contains predominantly texts from the *Divine Pivot*,[71] some of which belong to the 'Category on Tracts and Links' in the *Categories* (1624).[72] In TCM theory the notion of *zang xiang* thus incorporates discussions of the body that used to be relevant mostly to acumoxa.[73]

The human body that has been made the focus of attention by establishing the category *zangxiang* is now approximated to a material entity. In the *Interpretation*, the chapter on *zangxiang* is divided into two sections (see table 6.9), one on *static* entities like the Organs and Bowels and one on Essence, Breath, and Spirit, 'substance-forces' that are said to be in constant flow and motion.[74] *Yinyang* and the Five Phases, discussed in the first chapter, appear now as ordering principles of the universe. Material aspects rather than numerology have become category-determining.

Compartments and Organ Clusters

Having established the centrality of the Five Organs (*wuzang*) in TCM theory, the question arises what exactly they designate. Tao tended to equate the Five Organs – the Heart (*xin*), Lungs (*fei*), Spleen (*pi*), Liver (*gan*), and Kidneys (*shen*) – with the corresponding anatomical entities of biomedicine; therefore I translate them as Organs. Simultaneously, he stressed that they had functions and systemic aspects that were not attributed to them in Western medicine, and therefore I suggest calling them Organ Clusters. The Heart, for instance, is not an anatomical entity alone: 'The Heart governs the Blood (*xue*) and the Pulse (*mai*), it

---

[70] For instance, the third section on the Odd Palaces in the *Interpretation* (3.3) corresponds to the twenty-third in the *Categories* (IV.23). See table 6.9.

[71] In the *Categories*, in chapter III (the first chapter on the category *zang xiang*) ten out of seventeen text passages are from the *Basic Questions*, in the *Interpretation*, in the first section on the *zangxiang* only five out of eleven. In the *Categories*, in chapter IV (the second chapter on *zang xiang*), thirteen out of fifteen text passages come from the *Divine Pivot*, in the *Interpretation* all six passages on *jing*, *qi*, and *shen* are from the *Divine Pivot*.

[72] The 'Category on the Tracts and Links' contains several text passages that can be interpreted as referring to Western anatomical entities and physiological processes. This observation is paralleled by Farquhar (1994b:82): 'The only Chinese medical speciality in which bodies are routinely represented in a form non-specialists find familiar is acupuncture.'

[73] Unschuld (1992:55) stresses the importance of acumoxa for TCM theory. He considers that concepts like *yinyang* and Five Phases have become fundamental to TCM theory because of the increased attention given to acumoxa.

[74] Instead of flow and *flux*; their potential to change is mentioned but not really stressed.

houses the Spirit (*shen*), its Impulse is Enthusiasm (*xi*), its Fluid is Sweat (*han*), its Aperture is the Tongue (*she*), in regard to the body the Heart unites the Pulses, and its Flourishing manifests itself in the Face (*mian*)' (*TCM Fundamentals* (Yin 1984:30−1)).[75] Nor are the interrelations between the different aspects of the Heart systematic: 'to govern' (*zhu*), 'to house' (*cang*), 'to relate to Impulse'[76] (*zai zhi wei*), Fluids (*zai ye wei*), and Apertures (*zai qiao wei*), 'to unite' (*he*), and 'to have a Flourishing at' (*qi hua zai*) a specific area of the body surface.

The systematic presentation of the Organ Clusters in neat tables is welcome as a didactic simplification for an initial grasp of the complexities involved but just as wrong as any neat table of regulations for administrative purposes. Norms are negotiable. Despite the repeated endeavours at systematisation since the formation of the bureaucratic apparatus in China, all Organs and to a lesser degree all Bowels have their particular histories. The ways in which they interrelate are far from systematic. It may therefore be more accurate to speak of their 'systemic' correspondences (which implies interdependence) rather than their 'systematic' correspondences (which has connotations of methodical rigour).

Porkert (1974:108) stresses that Chinese medical reasoning takes place in 'diagrams of *function*' (italics added) and proposed to translate *zang* as 'orbs'. Sivin (1987), in a similar vein, coined the term 'visceral systems of *function*' (italics added) for *zangfu*. These expressions focus on the functional aspects. 'Whereas in anatomy Western medicine, causal and analytic, primarily describes the aggregate of carriers (or substrata) of effects, inductive synthetic Chinese medicine is primarily interested in the fabric of functional manifestations of different body regions.' Porkert (1974:107) opposed the emphasis on function in Chinese medicine to one on structure in biomedical anatomy. However, Porkert's emphasis on the polarity of thinking in terms of either function or structure does not do justice to the functional-structural character of the Organ Clusters in TCM.[77] Unschuld's ((1980)1985:81) translation of *zang* as Depositories (Depots) or Granaries and *fu* as Palaces reflects both their functional and their structural aspects and also highlights

---

[75] An Organ Cluster additionally comprises a 'Bowel on the outside' (*waifu*), in complementarity to the 'Organ inside' (*neizang*). The Bowel corresponding to the Heart, the Small Intestine (*xiaochang*), is briefly mentioned in the following. However, in the *TCM Fundamentals* (Yin 1984:29−43 and 44−7) the Organs (*zang*) and Bowels (*fu*) are discussed separately.

[76] *Zhi* is translated as Impulse in accordance with the observation that wishes, likes, and hopes were generally seen as forms of unrestrained personal 'impulse'.

[77] Likewise the West−East opposition between 'causal−analytic' and 'inductive−synthetic' thinking is, despite its initial value for research in Chinese medicine, highly problematic.

the borrowing of medical terminology from the terminology of administration.[78] But in twentieth-century China no TCM doctor related to the Organ Clusters in terms of their etymology. Biomedical and TCM doctors alike spoke of visceral 'functions' (*gongneng*), 'structures' (*goucheng*), and 'systems' (*xitong*).

As useful as terms like function, structure, and system may be, they do not fully express the imagery underlying the *zangfu*. A *zang* or a *fu* refers, as Unschuld's ((1980)1985:81) translation suggests and as Sivin (1987:183) points out, to a '*guan*, an executive and the office he sits in: an office in a bureaucracy'. This administrative unit is both functionally defined and spatially located. An account of the spatial organisation of 'offices in a bureaucracy', largely determined by function, is not easily rendered. Likewise, it is difficult to account for the *zangfu* in the human body.

The difficulties may well parallel those I encountered when I attempted to describe the spatial organisation of an administrative unit, the compound of the TCM college (see pp. 129–32). The concept that was central to that description was the 'compartment'. Were I to define in retrospect what 'compartment' meant, the same uncomfortable situation would arise for me as for someone confronted with the problem of what a *zangfu* or *zangxiang* is. The work unit compound is, like the human body, as much a spatial unit as a unit which is considered to fulfil certain functions, and the criteria for identifying compartments varied widely. In a parallel way, the different aspects of the Organ Clusters are each determined in terms of very different markers.

The 'compartment' was, like the Depository or Palace, in a spatially definite locality that was, in most cases, defined by its function (e.g. the garage compartment, the administrative compartment, the dormitory compartment). This was, however, not exclusively the case; the sports ground, for instance, had many different functions. In Chinese medicine, likewise, some Organs and Bowels are assigned more specific functions than others.

Some compartments were compact and clearly separated from their surroundings, such as the bicycle lot or the school garden, with fences delineating the boundaries of that space. Other compartments were spatially not as easily recognised as they were on grounds of their function. The printing press brigade, for instance, was clearly defined by its function but spread out among three different buildings. Only

---

[78] Unfortunately, at the period of the formation of what is here called 'the medicine of systemic correspondence', *zang* and *fu* both meant 'storehouse, treasury' (Sivin 1987:121).

after some deliberation did I find spatial features which the three parts of the printing press compartment had in common: they were all on the ground floor. Likewise, the Kidney Cluster is defined functionally more than spatially.

There is still another feature which the *ad hoc* concept of compartment has in common with the notion of *zangfu*: the criteria for identifying one of them may arise in consideration of interrelations with others. One such criterion was a parallel: the uniformed man in the school gate compartment made me see, in an analogous manner, a woman under a bamboo hat as a sign of recognition for the compartment 'showers'. Another such criterion was an opposition: the closed housing equipment compartment was seen in opposition to the open space of the sports ground. During the formative period of Chinese medicine recognition of the Pericardium as the sixth Depository resulted primarily from filling a gap in the conceptual framework; it became the opposite to the Triple Burner which was the sixth Palace (Porkert 1974:147; Sivin 1987:126–9; and, by implication, Unschuld (1980)1985:77, 208). One can continue the comparison by pointing to compartments that were in close proximity, such as the showers and the kitchen because of their shared need of hot water. In the body too, there is a pair of a *zang* and a *fu*, which forms a unique unit in the body: the Spleen and the Stomach.[79]

Compartments in the college compound had a history; some changed location and form over time, some were added, some eliminated. Similarly, each *zang* and *fu* has its own history. This comparison between the compartments of a work unit and the Organ Clusters of the body ecologic may at first glance appear strange, but is intended to highlight how particular and varied the definitions of the Organ Clusters are. Organ Clusters, like compartments, are easy to identify but difficult to define in a systematic way.

Offices and ranks have long been hierarchically ordered in the Chinese bureaucracy, but they are often best dealt with by conceiving of bureaucrats as being clustered (on grounds of a common experience through family ties, native place, school, classroom, or friendship). Likewise, the offices to which the Organs are likened appear as clusters in the body. Clusters are, in cladistics, established to account for observed phenomena of each particular individual, and their identity is established in relation to others in consideration of features chosen at random

---

[79] *Piwei* is a common expression for the unit of Stomach and Spleen in TCM; possibly it was already in the *Basic Questions* conceived of as a unit (see *Basic Questions*, chapter 9, where *pi wei* is mentioned in an enumeration of the Palaces (Ren 1986:1344; 32)).

(Needham 1983).[80] Clusters are integrative and open to incorporate any newcomer, and they are identified on the basis of all kinds of particular interrelations.

From Chinese medical doctrine to TCM theory

Although the Five Phases tended to be replaced by the Five Organs when physiological interrelations and pathological changes were described, the 'maxims for treatment' (*zhize*) continued to be phrased in terms of the Five Phases: 'Blaze the Fire to nourish the soil (Earth)!' (*yi huo bu tu*); 'Drench with Water to restrain the Wood!' (*ci shui han mu*); 'Bank up soil (Earth) to produce Metal!' (*pei tu sheng jin*); 'Bank up soil (Earth) to control Water!' (*pei tu zhi shui*); 'Assist the Metal to level the Wood!' (*zuo jin ping mu*); 'Purge the South and nourish the North!' (*xie nan bu bei*) (*TCM Fundamentals* (Yin 1984:25)). According to the textbook, the Five Phases were used for describing '(1) the "physiology" (*shengli*) and the interrelations of the Organs, (2) the mutual impact of "pathological changes" (*bingbian*) in the Organs and (3) their application in diagnosis and therapy.' The 'physiological' pattern of change was 'giving birth' (*sheng*), and the 'pathological' ones were 'giving birth' and 'insulting' (*wu*), but most prominently the Five Phases were used for formulating therapeutic maxims: giving birth, 'overcoming' (*ke*), and 'multiplying' (*cheng*) (*TCM Fundamentals* (Yin 1984:21–7)).

Reasoning in terms of the Five Phases is indispensable for expressing complex considerations of treatment. In Chinese medicine, therapeutic interventions are not merely based on the principle of opposition or the principle of likeness that are considered characteristic of reasoning in many scholarly medical traditions. Reasoning in terms of the Five Phases is pervasive in the *Basic Questions*, but maxims of treatment in TCM are not limited to this reasoning. They can be formulated in terms of the Eight Rubrics (*bagang*), the Six Disease Factors (*liuyin*), the Four Sectors (*weiqi yingxue*), and the Six Warps (*liujing*) (Farquhar 1994a:76–131), and also the Triple Burner (*sanjiao*). Additionally, there are many other maxims for treatment such as, for instance, 'In treating Illness trace the Roots' (*zhi bing qiu ben*).[81]

---

[80] Cladistics, applied to biosystematics and phylogenetic studies, has come into fashion as a means for overcoming the Linnaean notion of 'species' that is attributed certain ideal characteristics, approximated by a 'type-specimen'. It considers observed phenomena of each individual and establishes their identity in relation to others on account of features chosen at random, which allows for a comparison of any entity with any other and is not restricted to entities which are by convention considered comparable.

[81] These maxims of treatment need to be translated into a range of other concepts that refer to the qualities of specific drugs if one is to write a formulary. Farquhar

To illustrate how the meaning of maxims of medical doctrine is determined by virtuosity in medical practice an example relating to 'Metal gives birth to Water' (*jin sheng shui*) may be helpful. A doctor may, for instance, use it in explaining why he supplements acu-points on the *taiyin*-Lung-Tract, which corresponds to Metal, to treat a dry throat that ultimately results from a Water-Kidney-Depletion: the Lungs govern the *qi* and 'the Kidneys adopt it' (*shen na qi*).[82] By treating the Lungs he supplements the Kidneys. He may mention this maxim in another context too, for instance, when confronted with a patient with swollen extremities. In this context, the phrase 'Metal gives birth to Water' explains the disturbance in the dynamics of the Fluids and implicitly indicates the appropriate treatment. The Lungs regulate the Watercourse (*shuidao*), and the Kidneys govern the Liquids and Fluids: if the disharmony in the Lungs is aggravated, the Kidneys are likely to be affected. After all, 'Metal gives birth to Water', and one of the most likely courses that an illness takes as it grows worse follows the cycle of Giving Birth. Treatment will have to take into account both the Lungs and the Kidneys.

A senior doctor may well say 'This is basic' (*zhe shi jibende*) when he speaks of maxims like 'Metal gives birth to Water', but he is unlikely to say: 'This is in theory so, but not in practice.' Statements of a theory can be contradicted in medical practice but not maxims of a doctrine. Read on their own, maxims tend to be 'empty', vague, or even meaningless; their specific meanings become evident through medical practice.

Here it needs to be interjected that although the maxim 'Metal gives birth to Water' can be attributed distinct and very specific meanings of medical practice, it carries meaning on its own. This is because it evokes an imagery that can accommodate all kinds of phantasies or concrete memories. The phrase *jin sheng shui* (Metal gives birth to Water) reminds me of hearing a Daoist monk say *yan sheng shui* (the rock gives birth to water) as we had entered a granite cave on mount Hua and saw the condensed water droplets on the ceiling; it looked as if the glimmer, which looked like Metal, was producing highly refined Water droplets.[83] Clearly, the maxims of Chinese medical doctrine evoke strong images on their own.

(1994a:205) speaks of different degrees of verbosity, Unschuld (1988c) of 'mediating links' between the concepts of 'basic theory' and the 'empirical categories' of drug effects. Bray (1995) points to different 'levels of causality' in Chinese medical reasoning.

[82] Sivin (1987:228) translates *na* as 'to admit', Farquhar (1994a:95) as 'to accept'; *na* refers to a process of a deep and more fundamental assimilation than that of the Lungs.

[83] I do not mean to imply that the Five Phases are metaphors with a clear historical genealogy of originating in direct observations of nature.

One would be inclined to assume that such maxims formed a system of metaphors, but only the younger teachers I worked with would
speak of them in such terms. Farquhar's (1987:1019) observation with
regard to *yinyang* applies to all the concepts mentioned in the maxims
of Chinese medical doctrine. She reports that an older scholar doctor
reacted angrily to the epistemologically influenced construction that
yinyang were metaphors for natural phenomena. He insisted 'that *yin*
and *yang* were "things" (*dongxi*), not forms of thought'.[84] To many
older scholar doctors, the Five Phases were not merely abstract terms
but often referred to very concrete events. They were not metaphors
either, for in the universe to which they applied one did not make an
ontological distinction that is hierarchical between its different aspects.
The notion of metaphor is grounded in the notion that an idiom has
a primary meaning, and a secondary, metaphoric one. The 'foot' is
primarily a body part, the 'foot' in the phrase 'foot of a mountain' a
metaphor. Yet Wood is as much a thing (*dongxi*) inherent to the body
as a thing inherent to a mountain. In the universe in which the Five
Phases figure, there is no ontological hierarchy of its different aspects.

During the nine months of participant experience in various acumoxa
wards, I rarely heard a doctor mention the above maxims, but I did
occasionally recognise in prescriptions a treatment that was grounded
in them. Obviously, the medical practice persisted while the explanations for it in terms of the Five Phases had been silenced.[85] I took it as
an indication of shifting preoccupations of medical reasoning from maxims of treatment to descriptions of health.

The shift in speech act, from prescription to description, seems to
go hand in hand with a shift in theme of discussion, from 'pathology'
to 'physiology', and in this process, Chinese medical writings have
accommodated many Western biomedical terms and concepts. Already
in the *TCM Fundamentals* the impact of Western biomedical reasoning
is so pervasive that it is impossible to give an exhaustive account of
it. Although language does not directly reflect thought, the linguistic
accommodations evident in the textbook imply important changes in
understanding. These changes occur at the level of choice of vocabulary, for instance, in speaking of 'homeostasis' (*pingheng*) and 'metabolism' (*daixie*) instead of 'harmony' (*tiaohe*); using biomedical instead of
TCM terms such as 'Anus' (*gangmen*) instead of 'gate of the *hun*-soul'

---

[84] Farquhar (1987:1019) continues: 'The system is not applied from without as "theory"
would be to "practice".'
[85] It is likely that rationalisations in a terminology that does not contradict the biomedical
one will increasingly be used for designating those unaltered therapeutic practices.

(*hunmen*); reducing vagueness, for instance, by replacing Blood (*xue*) with 'blood-liquid' (*xueye*), Pulse (*mai*) with 'pulsation' (*maidong*), drug (*yao*) with 'drug-substance' (*yaowu*); and composing hybrids of Chinese and Western medical terms such as 'organ-machine' (*zangqi*). It is also observed on the syntactic level, for instance, by linking two phrases with the conjunction 'because' (*youyu*), which narrows the relation between the two phrases down to a causal or final one, or by transforming a simple indicative phrase into a conditional. On the level of register, textbooks are no longer dialogues but monologues; their rhetoric is so similar to Mao's writings that reading ability in the one facilitates the reading of the other.

On the level of ordering knowledge, Western biomedicine is increasingly taken as a model. In the *Organ Clusters*, for instance, chapters 5–7 bear the titles of chapters in Western biomedical textbooks (see table 6.10). And on the level of the explicit reinterpretation of Chinese medical concepts, conceptions of bodily processes have been interpreted so as not to contradict Western physiology. This last point is illustrated by comparing the *TCM Fundamentals* (Yin 1984:44–9) with the *Organ Clusters* (Yunnan zhongyi xueyuan 1988:33–45) with regard to the term *fu*. In both textbooks the Six Bowels (*liufu*) – the Stomach (*wei*), the Small Intestine (*xiaochang*), the Large Intestine (*dachang*), the Gallbladder (*dan*), the Bladder (*pangguang*), and the Triple Burner (*sanjiao*) – are assigned Western physiological functions of the digestive system: 'intake' (*shouna*),[86] 'digestion' (*xiaohua*), 'assimilation' (*xishou*), and 'excretion' (*paixie*). In both textbooks a separate section has been created for discussing the Odd Palaces (*qiheng zhi fu*). They did not figure prominently in the *Inner Canon*, nor did they appear to have great significance in medical practice, but clearly the Odd Palaces – the Marrow (*sui*) and Bones (*gu*) which cluster with the Kidneys, the Vessels (*mai*) which cluster with the Heart, the Gallbladder (*dan*) which is also one of the Six Bowels, the Brain (*nao*), and the Womb (*nüzibao*) – could be brought into accordance with Western anatomy. Since the majority of the Odd Palaces (*sui, gu, mai, dan*) had been discussed in other contexts, this textbook section only dealt with the Brain and the Womb. Notably, the editors of the *Organ Clusters* additionally dug out a notion from the medical archive that paralleled that of the Womb in the female: the Chambers of Essence (*jingshi*) in the male.[87]

---

[86] This term was not found in any contemporary dictionary and is likely to be the classical term; the following three are all biomedical terms.

[87] Daoist thought takes the female body as basis (Schipper 1978), but apparently Chinese medical doctrine does not (Despeux 1996:107). For incidents of gender transformations in a person, see Furth (1988).

With respect to the notion of *fu*, TCM textbook compilers adjusted the classical doctrine to Western biomedical theory in two ways: by correcting the classical text and by making the commentary on it more precise. Explicit corrections of the classics were very rare, but in an introductory paragraph to the section on the Odd Palaces the editors of the *Organ Clusters* claimed with regard to the Marrow, the Bones, and the Vessels: 'We consider these as 'bodily tissues' (*xingti zuzhi*); they are surely not Organs, and also not Bowels, therefore they do not belong to the category of the Odd Palaces.' Classical texts were usually not corrected so bluntly, but interpreted in a way that did not contradict either the medical canons or Western physiology.

The reinterpretation of the Small Intestine's functions highlights this nicely. According to the *Basic Questions*, chapter 8, 'The Small Intestine is the officer who receives the abundant, it transforms matter and expels it' (cited in *Interpretation* (Cheng 1984:45); *TCM Fundamentals* (Yin 1984:45); *Organ Clusters* (Yunnan zhongyi xueyuan 1988:36)). Zhang Jiebin glosses: 'The Small Intestine resides beneath the Stomach; it receives and ladles out the Watery Grains (*shuigu*) of the Stomach by differentiating between the Clear (*qing*) and the Turbid (*zhuo*). From here, the Watery Fluids (*shuiye*) seep out in the front and the Dregs (*zaopo*) turn to the back. The Spleen by *qi*-Transformations (*qihua*) effects rising while the Small Intestine by Transformation (*hua*) effects descending; therefore one says that it transforms matter and expels it' (cited in *Interpretation* (Cheng 1984:45); *TCM Fundamentals* (Yin 1984:45)). Although Zhang Jiebin's gloss is lengthy, it remains rather unspecific. The one comment which is a bit more precise, 'the Watery Fluids seep out in front', seems to suggest that liquid intake is directly transformed into urine.[88]

Now, Western physiology teaches us that fluids need to be absorbed into the blood and transported to the kidneys before the bladder evacuates them as urine. In the *TCM Fundamentals* the editors' gloss in modern Chinese does not really clarify the issue, but in the *Organ Clusters* the problem has been solved in a most ingenious way. According to Chinese medical doctrine, the Small Intestine separates the Clear from the Turbid. In a second step, the Turbid within the Turbid (*zhuo zhong zhi zhuo*) is directly excreted in the back while the Clear within the Turbid (*zhuo zhong zhi qing*) is absorbed before 'seeping out' as urine. In order to model the functions of the Small Intestine upon those of the small intestine in Western physiology, the textbook compilers had created

---

[88] I have observed this intuitive understanding of urinating even among European biology students.

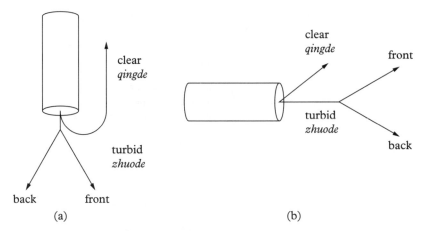

Figure 6.4   Physiology of the Small Intestine (arrow upwards means
absorption, downwards means excretion)
(a) as described in the *TCM Fundamentals* (Yin 1984);
(b) as in the *Organ Clusters* (Yunnan zhongyi xueyuan 1988)

a new pair of categories, very much in the terminology of Chinese
medical doctrine, which allowed them to render the Small Intestine's
functions more accurately (see fig. 6.4).

The precise commentaries on the *Organ Clusters*, often inspired by
Western biomedicine and seldom blatantly contradictory to canonical
doctrine, generally consisted of an altered stress on certain processes.
Jaundice (*huangdan*) has, for instance, been attributed to the Gallbladder, which is the outer aspect of the Liver, instead of the Spleen (Sivin
1987:113), notably, according to my observations in the clinic, without
the need to prove the past wrong: jaundice occurs when the 'Liver
insults the Spleen' (*gan wu pi*). Many TCM reinterpretations consisted
of a modification of Chinese medical reasoning. It would be wrong to
speak of borrowing patchwork from Western biomedicine. The adjustment consisted, in the case of the Small Intestine, of a blow up – a
rather lengthy digression with detailed descriptions of physiological processes on which the canons provided no or only vague information –
and, in the case of jaundice's being attributed to the Liver, of a short-cut.

I have suggested here that phrases in terms of the Five Phases such as
'Metal gives birth to Water' are most significant in the context of providing therapy. They are maxims (in the imperative or optative mood)
rather than descriptions (in the indicative mood), categories that express in shorthand a device for a therapeutic practice. I have proposed

Table 6.10. *Contents of chapters 3–5 in the* TCM Fundamentals *(1984) and the* Organ Clusters *(1988)*

TCM Fundamentals (1984)	Organ Clusters (1988)
Chapter 3 Organ Clusters (*zangxiang*)	Book Title *Organ Clusters* (*zangxiang*)
	Part 1 Introduction
	Part 2 Organs and Bowels (*zangfu*)
3.1 Five Organs (*wuzang*)	2.1 ditto
3.2 Six Bowels (*liufu*)	2.2 ditto
3.3 Odd Palaces (*qiheng zhi fu*)	2.3 ditto
3.4 Their interrelations	
Chapter 4 Breath, Blood, Liquids and Fluids	Part 3 Essence, Breath, Blood, Liquids and Fluids
	3.1 Essence (*jing*)
4.1 Breath (*qi*)	3.2 ditto
4.2 Blood (*xue*)	3.3 ditto
4.3 Liquids and Fluids (*jinye*)	3.4 ditto
4.4 Their interrelations	
Chapter 5 Tracts and Links	Part 4 ditto
5.1 Concept of Tracts and Links and the Composition of the System	4.1 ditto
5.2 Twelve Tracts (*shier jingluo*)	4.2 ditto
5.3 Eight Odd Vessels (*qi jing ba mai*)	4.3 ditto
5.4 Tract Divergents, Diverging Links, Tract Sinews, Cutaneous Regions (*jingbie, bieluo, jingjin, pibu*)	4.4 ditto
5.5 Physiology of the Tracts and Links	4.5 Physiology and Function of the Tracts and Links
	Part 5 The Interrelations within the Body and between the Body and its Environment
	5.1 The Interrelations within the Body (discusses *TCM Fundamentals* 3.4 and 4.4)
	5.2. The Interrelations between the Human Body and its Environment (contains newly added contents)
	Part 6 Holistic View of Vital Activities and Processes
	6.1 Respiration
	6.2 Alimentary Metabolism

Table 6.10. *(cont'd)*

TCM Fundamentals (1984)	Organ Clusters (1988)
	6.3 Metabolism of the Fluids
	6.4 Blood Production and Circulation
	6.5 Growth, Development, and Reproduction
	6.6 Mind, Consciousness, and Thought
	6.7 The Basic Types of Vital Actitity: The Upward and Downward, Outward and Inward Movements
	Part 7 The Constitution
	7.1 The Constitution and its Characteristics
	7.2 Constitutional Types and their Physiological Function
	7.3 Factors that have an Impact on the Constitution

furthermore that much of Chinese medical doctrine consists of sets of such mnemonic maxims rather than a system of propositions that can be deduced from each other. Maxims differ from propositions most decisively with respect to truth value: the value of a maxim is established through success in practice. A maxim is valuable no matter whether it stands in contradiction to others or whether it is self-contradictory, from a 'logical' *(luojixing)* point of view;[89] evidence for its value is given in the practice that corresponds to the maxim. A proposition, by contrast, makes a claim to 'truth' and raises issues of Western philosophy.[90]

[89] I am not speaking of 'logic', a discipline of Western philosophy, but of the understanding of 'logical' as expressed by TCM doctors. 'Logical' designated modes of reasoning that included the explicit recognition of contradictions within one statement or between two statements. The term *luojixing* is a phonetic borrowing of the Greek term, and TCM doctors attributed this mode of reasoning largely to what they considered Western scientific thinking.

[90] Compare with Unschuld (1992:45): 'Recent Chinese and Western publications have overemphasised an allegedly all-pervasive antagonism between modern Western and traditional Chinese medical thought while disregarding some basic epistemological parallels. At the same time, one of the most profound discrepancies separating Chinese and Western cognitive approaches – that is, the attitude towards the truth – appears to have been overlooked.'

The loss of Spirit

The discussion of *yinyang* dialectics, the implications of being systematic, the focused vision giving rise to a body-centred medicine, and the descriptive assessment of TCM physiology have shown that Chinese medical concepts have been adjusted to fit with Marxist dialectics, Western science, and Western biomedicine, all of which have their origins in post-Renaissance, modern Western culture and thought. Significantly, one feature which those traditions of thought have in common, the materialist approach, has led to a neglect of the notion of the Spirit (*shen*) in TCM.

It is not that *shen*, central to Zhang's seminars, was not an issue in TCM textbooks and classes. In the course on the *TCM Fundamentals*, the students learnt about it when the functions of the Heart were discussed, during the first lecture on the Five Organs. In this context, it was taught that *shen* has two senses. In its narrow sense, it indicated a person's state of 'mind' (*jingshen*) and 'consciousness' (*yishi*), 'thinking' (*siwei*), and 'activity' (*huodong*). In its wider sense, similar to Qiu's notion of *shen*, it was 'the outside manifestation of a person's life and activities' (*rende shengming huodong waizai biaoxian*). During mid-term exams students were asked to reproduce this definition.

In *TCM Diagnostics*, *shen* was discussed in the first lesson. It was said to be of primary concern for a 'diagnosis by observation' (*wangzhen*), particularly when inspecting the Complexion (*se*) and the Tongue (*she*): 'Observe Spirit – this is only too important', Tao exclaimed, adding: 'You will grasp its meaning naturally and all by itself, it is not difficult.' Then, he wrote some standard phrases on the blackboard as definitions of the three standard types of *shen*. These were variants of those in the textbook:

The manifestations of Having Spirit (*you shen*) are: the mind is clear, verbal articulation is distinct, vision is bright, vital essences are retained within; complexion is glowing and full, facial expression is rich and natural; responses are nimble and sensitive, movements are agile, body posture is graceful; breathing is smooth and steady, and the muscles are not emaciated.

The manifestations of a Loss of Spirit (*shi shen*) are: the mind is dazed, or the speech is incoherent, or one plucks at one's clothes and strokes the bed, or clutches in the air as if spinning a thread; the eyes are dim and the gaze is distracted, pupils are dull; complexion is grey, facial expression is stiff and listless, responses are retarded, movements are clumsy, posture appears forced; breathing is irregular and the large muscles are already wasting (*TCM Diagnostics* (Deng 1984:10–11)).

The manifestations of the Pseudo-spirit (*jiashen*): teacher Tao described them as marked improvement shortly before death – a well-known phenomenon in medical practice.

Shen in the phrase *you shen* could be understood in its wide as well as narrow sense, while *shen* in *shi shen* was clearly *shen* in its narrow sense, describing certain conditions of mental illness. When these phrases were learnt in juxtaposition, it is therefore quite likely that the students would understand *shen* in *you shen* to be the opposite of *shen* in *shi shen*, and that they would conceptualise it in its narrow sense as the 'mind', with functions of the brain as known from Western biomedicine. Tao, aware of the contradiction this evoked in students who had memorised that 'the Heart houses the Spirit', gave a laconic answer to his own rhetorical question 'Why does the Heart and not the Brain house the Spirit?': 'It is a question of habit' (*xiguan wenti*).

Considering that *shen* was a topic of discussion in the first lesson on the Organ Clusters in the course on the *TCM Fundamentals* (on 10 October 1988) and the first on *TCM Diagnostics* (on 1 March 1989), it was surprising to find that it was hardly ever mentioned in the clinic. Possibly it was so basic that the assessment of the patient's Spirit belonged to tacit knowledge. It was, however, rarely an issue in verbal exchanges on treatment evaluation – this in contrast to Qiu's practice, in which the Spirit indicated a reality more relevant than any technicalities of scientific evidence.

I did hear TCM doctors say: 'His vision is bright' in place of acknowledging that a patient Had Spirit. Or they would say: 'His articulation is distinct, but his movements are not agile.' Substituting explicit and standardised locutions for the vague notion *shen* had several implications for the process of standardising Chinese medicine in medical practice as well. Firstly, an observation such as 'His articulation is distinct' was explicit and easily determined by denotation. One doctor could make such an observation independently of another, and the two could then compare their results. Once an explicit standard was given, one could compare and check one's findings. A TCM doctor's judgement about a patient's condition would thus be controlled by other doctors.

Secondly, statements such as 'The movements have lost agility' and 'The articulation is distinct' pointed to contradictory aspects of a person's condition. Statements of TCM doctors were fairly factual and detached from implications for further social interaction, whereas Having Spirit, *you shen*, in Qiu's practice implied that the treatment had been successful and therefore the patient should pursue it, with its negation implying dissuasion from further treatment. In other words, the replacement of the notion *shen* by statements about distinct observations that could be compared with each other opened up a forum for communication and discussion among experts. Because this terminology was used for gaining authority through recognition by other experts, the doctor's

Table 6.11. *Comparison of the chapter titles in the* Interpretation, TCM Fundamentals, *and* Organ Clusters

Interpretation (1984) (*Neijing jiangyi*) chapter 3.2	*shen jing qi*	Spirit, Essence, Breath
TCM Fundamentals (1984) (*Zhongyi jichu lilun*) chapter 4	*qi xue jinye*	Breath, Blood, Fluids
Organ Clusters (1988) (*Zangxiangxue*) Part 3	*jing qi xue jinye*	Essence, Breath, Blood, Fluids

clients were thereby disempowered. I doubt that the TCM doctors I worked with were aware of these implications. Although the technical terminology they used should have facilitated discussion, I seldom saw them make use of this possibility.

The notion of an all-pervasive *shen* was disappearing not only in medical practice, but in medical theory as well. While the *Interpretation* retained the trilogy *shen-jing-qi*, Spirit-Essence-Breath, which is central to self-cultivation practices (Engelhardt 1987:1), the term *shen* was dropped in later introductory textbooks (see table 6.11).[91] The Spirit was no longer, as in Zhang's seminars, categorised as a 'substance-force' that constitutes and permeates the universe; it had been reduced to a function of the mind, an aspect of the Organ Cluster Heart. Instead, the notion of Liquids and Fluids (short: Fluids, *jinye*)[92] was newly added. Although they had little significance in the clinic, in the *TCM Fundamentals* they have become a superordinate term that subsumes various 'substance-forces' well known from Chinese medical practice, among them Phlegm (*tanyin*).

Phlegm caught my attention because it was the target of TCM polemics. Teachers recited sayings such as: 'Strange diseases are frequently Phlegm' (*guaibing duo tan*), or: 'The hundred diseases come from the haunt of the Phlegm' (*baibing duoyou tan zuo sui*). When teacher Tao introduced the notion of Phlegm in the classroom, he said: 'Go to see a senior Chinese doctor and whatever cough you have, he

---

[91] In the *TCM Fundamentals*, Essence (*jing*) was dropped as well, but, in contrast to *shen*, it figured in the *Revised Outline* (Sivin 1987:237) and reappeared in the *Organ Clusters*.
[92] Despite textbook remarks on *jin* and *ye* (see also Sivin 1987:243–4), the difference between these two concepts is just as inconceivable to most doctors as that between liquids and fluids is in English.

will make Phlegm responsible for it.' Later he continued: 'When a senior doctor speaks of *tanyin* (Phlegm), he does not refer to Zhang Zhongjing's Four Rheums (*siyin*)[93] which I have just presented above. These "old doctors" (*lao yisheng*) know nothing about the above differentiation of *tanyin* and *xuanyin*, and if you ask him what a *xuanyin* is, he can't explain anything to you. All he knows is that the *tanyin* he refers to is that of his master.'

Phlegm had the strength of being extremely vague: it designated (1) symptoms about which a patient complained and (2) visible signs such as 'thick saliva' (*tan*) on the tongue, and it also designated (3) a postulated process in the body with which the doctor explained these signs and symptoms. Tao deplored the popularity that such vague concepts enjoyed among the senior doctors, but instead of ignoring this concept altogether, he devoted an entire lecture to what he considered a systematic discussion of Phlegm, by drawing on the blackboard what looked like elaborate Western physiological charts. Phlegm and also Blood Stasis (*yuxue*)[94] have been among the most controversial themes in recent TCM research.

Phlegm and Blood Stasis referred to a process – a stagnation. Unlike accumulations, which often had Form, and the accumulating *qi* that Qiu saw in the Red Light, stagnations were generally Without Form, invisible. They were postulated processes in the body which were detected by excretions, signs outside the body, such as Phlegm on the tongue or Clots (*kuai*) in the menstrual blood. Since they gave rise to many different disorders, they have recently become classified among the Disease Factors in the *TCM Fundamentals* (Yin 1984:101–2).

Relevant in this context is that the material aspects of 'substance-forces' such as Phlegm were increasingly emphasised. Under the heading 'Breath and Blood, Liquids and Fluids' (*TCM Diagnostics* (Deng 1984:99–106); (Shanxi zhongyi xueyuan 1988:192–9)), Phlegm and Rheum were discussed in the section on the Fluids, Blood Stasis in the section on Blood, and Stagnant *qi* in the section on *qi*. Phlegm, Blood Stasis, and Stagnant *qi* had one process in common, stagnation, but in TCM textbooks they were categorised according to their material aspects and discussed under separate headings. As criterion for the formation of TCM concepts, matter dominated over dynamics.

[93] In the *Jin gui yao lüe* they are *tanyin* (Phlegm Rheum), *xuanyin* (Suspended Rheum), *yiyin* (Spillage Rheum), and *zhiyin* (Propping Rheum) (*TCM Fundamentals* (Yin 1984:101)).

[94] The term *yuxue* was usually not part of the patient's vocabulary. It designated (1) a postulated process inside the body and (2) visible signs such as Clots (*kuai*) of menstrual blood.

The *Organ Clusters* (Yunnan zhongyi xueyuan 1988:123–4) devoted a whole section to the metabolism of the Fluids (section 6.3 in table 6.10). The precision with which their function in respect of each of the Five Organs was described is simply stunning. The source of inspiration evidently being Western physiology, there was nothing here that blatantly contradicted Western biomedicine. *TCM Etiology and Pathogenesis* (Chengdu zhongyi xueyuan 1988:102–5) differentiated between *shui* (Water) and *yin* (Rheum) and between *tan* (Phlegm) and *shi* (Dampness). These notions were systematically presented in the textbook, but such systematics were not really important in medical practice. In the clinic, the process of stagnation constituted the core of medical reasoning for formulating a therapeutic maxim. The fine distinctions between the material aspects of TCM concepts had hardly any relevance in medical practice. This descriptive eloquence reinforced the gap between TCM theory and its application in the practice.

In the *Organ Clusters* (Yunnan zhongyi xueyuan 1988:47–8), the notion *jing* was reintroduced: (1) Essence furthers growth, development, and reproduction; (2) it nourishes and moistens the Organs and Bowels, the Tracts and Links; (3) it transforms into Blood Liquid; and (4) it fills and nourishes the Brain Marrow (*naosui*). As a 'substance-force' considered important for one's genetic constitution, Essence retained its function of transcending a person's Worldly State. However, it was not mentioned as the 'substance-force' that mediates in daily meditation between the body ecologic's two states of being, the Worldly and the Primordial State. The materialist stance in TCM theory had thus led not only to a tendency to neglect the Spiritual and to take a static view of processes, but also to experience time in the linear way in which materials age, thereby disregarding the possibilities of resilience and regeneration that Chinese medical doctrine ascribes to the body ecologic.

The lessons usually ended with the teacher designating certain text passages for the students to memorise. For classroom instruction teachers advocated the didactics appropriate for teaching a theory: explanation and method. For homework, in contrast, the didactic method was rote learning. TCM teachers thereby unwittingly provided the students with the means to learn about the Spiritual. We may be reminded here of Zhang's conviction that memorising texts in combination with experience in medical practice would eventually lead to 'revelations' (*wu*) (see p. 103). Learning by heart was the key to the way of knowing that Zhang considered profound knowledge – the profound knowledge grounded in the Spiritual.

The reinterpretation of Chinese medicine in TCM standards

TCM teachers considered Chinese medical concepts 'coarse' (*cucao*) and based on a 'primitive understanding' (*pusu renshi*). Following Mao's slogan 'The new supersedes the old' (*xin chen fa xie*), these concepts had to be rendered more 'fashionable' (*shimaode*). To 'make the best' of them (*jiangjiu*), they had to be 'modernised' (*xiandaihua*). The foremost goal was therefore 'to standardise' (*guifanhua*) and make Chinese medicine 'systematic' (*xitonghua*); this would render it more 'scientific' (*kexuehua*).

The standardised transmission of Chinese medical knowledge has gone hand in hand with a nationalistic reinterpretation of China's cultural heritage, a Maoist reinterpretation of philosophical concepts like *yinyang*, a body-centred focus on the body ecologic which has led to a shift in emphasis from the Five Phases to the Five Organs, a reinterpretation of prescriptive maxims in a hitherto unknown descriptive precision inspired by Western physiology, and a materialist reinterpretation of the 'substance-forces' constituting and permeating the universe. This has led to a static view of processes, a disregard of the body's resilience, and a neglect of the Spiritual.

It needs to be borne in mind that the process of standardising the transmission of Chinese medical knowledge is not simply an adjustment to Western biomedicine. To reinterpret concepts such as *yinyang* in terms of dialectics has little affinity with Western biomedical theory, nor is materialism specific to Western biomedicine. Moreover, several observations that I recorded seemed to depend more on accidents of history than on any change in styles of knowing induced by the standardised transmission of knowledge.

With regard to whether the mode of teaching by means of 'explanation' and 'method' had any impact on the general understanding of Chinese medical concepts, an increased focus on the physical body is apparent, but the interrelations between Chinese medical concepts do not seem to have become more hierarchical and continue to be placed in relation with each other as clusters.

It is striking that the efforts at standardising the transmission of medical knowledge and practice have produced considerable tension between theory and practice, strict control in classroom instruction and a *laissez-faire* attitude in practical training, indifference in daily life at the college and excitement during the movement against nepotism and corruption, a technical terminology that invites factual discussion and no signs of experts wishing to become involved in discussion, classroom instruction that models itself on the didactics of teaching the natural sciences and homework that consists of the rote learning which is basic to the secret and personal modes of transmitting knowledge. Efforts at standardising the transmission of knowledge and practice seem bound to give rise to a divergence between the proclaimed standards and their implementation.

Discussion: styles of knowing

How do styles of knowing interrelate with ways of learning? The question with which we began cannot be answered conclusively, but the data presented throw some light on the issue. Concepts become 'socialised'. If learnt in different social contexts, they tend to be understood in different ways – they have different meanings, uses, and 'performative significances' in social interaction. Modes of (verbal) reasoning and styles of (non-verbal) knowing have been shown to vary in different social contexts of learning Chinese therapeutics.

Secret knowing

Qigong was veiled in secrecy. It was attributed great powers and often supposed to have immediate effects. Access to these powers was fraught with danger, and the disciple needed guidance. A master would accept a person as a disciple only if this person had extraordinary moral qualities, loyalty to the master and his family, the 'predestined fate' (*yuanfen*) 'just to remember', and perseverance and patience, which, in light of the necessary self-castigation, could only be achieved with composure. A Daoist was to be 'cheerful' (*kailang*).

Verbal reasoning in *qigong* was not elaborate. Words were powerful, verses simple and short. Verses were often recited without knowing their meaning; to be effective, they need not be understood, but correctly pronounced. Knowing *qigong* was marked by an ostensive secrecy. In Qiu's case secrecy was not only an attribute that enhanced his and his family's prestige but also, in the secret society to which he belonged, a weapon of the weak and a form of protection. On the one hand, strategic considerations of flexibility in an environment that is considered hostile may have encouraged the simplicity, brevity, and limited number of the spells and rituals Qiu employed. On the other hand, there is a particular aesthetics to the condensation of value in small commodities like simple words, short verses, and potent gestures seemingly pregnant with a meaning that remains concealed. A healer can, by not entirely revealing the concealed, also adorn himself with these words, verses, and gestures.

To a certain extent, all three traditions of Chinese therapeutics revealed the concealed in forms that were intelligible only to the initiated. Technical terminology and specialised skills draw a boundary between laypersons and those who have access to them. But Qiu kept his knowledge and practice secret while the senior doctor Zhang and the TCM teachers claimed that access to their knowledge was basically open to everyone. Considering that Qiu's verses and gestures could be learnt by imitation, control over the distribution of *qigong* knowledge and practice was an issue. Since verses were said to be effective only if correctly pronounced, they could not be learnt outside a relationship of oral transmission, even if they had been recorded on paper. The master therefore had a means to control the distribution of knowledge.

It is not a paradox that precisely the knowledge that was considered easy to reproduce was most veiled in secrecy. A secret is often very banal, and secrecy a means of social control. If knowledge and practice are believed to be not as easily reproduced, as for instance expertise in Chinese medicine, control over the distribution of knowledge is guaranteed in that it is built into the process of learning.

Personal knowing

The senior Chinese doctor Zhang was the offspring of the fourth generation of a family of Chinese doctors. Brought up in a Catholic convent and compelled to leave after only two years of joining the workforce as a young doctor at the Yunnan TCM College, he did not participate in the 'socialist reconstruction' of the Chinese nation. He was a marginal like Qiu in the modern nation-state, but unlike Qiu, who he saw as belonging among the 'petty people' (*xiaoren*), he considered himself a 'gentleman' (*junzi*) and cultivated relations with intellectuals and high-status officials. Among his followers, he was mostly praised for his Confucian ethics and his 'sensitive concern for others' (*ren*).

One might have been inclined to include Zhang's ways of learning among those of secret knowledge, particularly in light of his emphasis on morals, his need to impress, his control over his disciples, and his emphasis on the Spiritual (*shen*). But Zhang's reasoning, observed also among other senior doctors, was flowery and verbose and could easily be distinguished from Qiu's. His modes of interpretation, which were 'indirect', 'authoritative', 'justificatory', 'creative', and 'achieved by recourse to everyday life', may well have reflected attitudes and practices of the traditional elite. We may assume that the scholar officials in

Imperial China had developed a style of knowing distinct from that of ordinary people.

Knowing Chinese medicine meant acquiring profound knowledge by memorising the 'experience' (*jingyan*) of the ancients in the text and combining it with one's own experience in medical practice. To attain 'profound' (*shen'ao*) knowledge, one had to immerse oneself in learning verses and patiently to assist in therapy. The mentor would comment on certain situations by reciting a phrase that the follower knew by heart without having grasped its meaning. Applied to a particular situation, flowery verses were given down-to-earth meanings. Since the mentor would recite the same verse on different occasions, words and phrases became increasingly polysemous. Over time, the follower would fill the rhythmical rhymes with contents that arose from experience in medical practice.

Although it was claimed that profound knowledge could not be acquired by explication, a mentor was expected to make exegeses of the classical texts. Zhang did not aim at a literal translation of the text; rather, he used the text for conveying his own conviction and experience. The relationship between the text and medical practice was not so much one between a theory and practice as one of applying a doctrine with 'virtuosity' (*ling*) to medical practice.

Zhang's text seminars had the effect that the more we read, the more confused we became, swimming in a sea of verses. There was no certainty on which we could build, no rigour which provoked contradiction. Reasoning was embedded in the rhythm of language. The promise was that one day we would know, just know. Zhang spoke of a 'sudden intuition' (*wu*) and thereby perpetuated the idea, widely attested in the literature, that major insights into the profound knowledge of Chinese medicine come through revelations.

Standardised knowing

At the TCM college, old ways of learning persisted. Students at dusk, murmuring textbook passages on the sports ground, seemed to lull themselves with the text. They learnt standard phrases without pondering their exact contents, just as students of earlier centuries had done. The difference was that the rhetoric they memorised was often in modern Chinese and stylistically more like Mao's writings than like classical medical texts.

Obviously, rote learning was at the core of all three traditions of Chinese medical learning. Qiudi learnt short spells, Zhangdi long text passages from the medical canons, and TCM students shorter ones from TCM textbooks. In *qigong*, memorising texts would lead to visions that endowed the healer with extraordinary powers. In the context of reading canonical texts, it would lay the groundwork for revelations that enabled the senior doctor to gain profound insights. At the TCM college, rote learning persisted even though the professed goals of teaching were clearly in contradiction to this method.

Apart from memorising texts, TCM students were taught by the didactic means of post-Enlightenment education. Classroom instruction was supposed to be based on 'explanation' (*jieshi*) and have 'method' (*fangfa*). The teachers frequently paraphrased, explained, and defined clauses of classical Chinese in modern Chinese. They narrowed down polysemous notions of Chinese philosophy to less ambiguous compound words that often sounded like biomedical terms. The texts were written so that students could understand them in class, and some exam questions concerned the students' comprehension of the texts.

There was a tendency towards constructing a TCM theory that was comprehensible on its own, independent of a mentor's pointing out particular conditions that filled the poetic verses of the medical canons with a very specific meaning. In the 1984 *TCM Fundamentals* phrases in terms of the Five Phases were still juxtaposed with phrases describing signs and symptoms and others outlining maxims for treatment. In the corresponding 1988–9 editions, however, this juxtaposition of philosophical speculation, diagnostics, and therapeutics tended to be broken up. Philosophical generalities were stated on their own, which made them sound like general principles or even natural laws.

TCM theory and practice, it seemed, were increasingly separated from each other. Each seemed to gain in autonomy, a process that was reinforced by the administrative division between hospitals, subject to the Ministry of Health, and the college, subject to the Ministry of Education. The doctors in the respective institutions showed reserve towards each other. The educators suspected the hospital doctors of perpetuating 'superstitious' (*mixin*) practices while the doctors pointed to the necessity of political correctness for being employed among college educators.

The formulation of a theory that can be comprehended more or less in isolation from medical practice is among the most important steps in the standardisation of knowledge. In theory, standards are easily established. In medical practice, even if it is institutionalised in clinics and thereby becomes more standardised, the particular problems a practitioner is faced with slow down any process of standardisation. The standardisation of TCM may therefore have been accelerated by widening the gap between a systematic theory and the unpredictabilities of

medical practice. Contemporary Western biomedicine, which acknowledges an enormous gap between theory and practice, represents a model
case of such standardisation.

TCM texts were viewed as theoretical tools indispensable for medical
practice, and medical practice was considered crucial for advancing
TCM theory. This attitude towards the text echoed Mao's (1965) essay
'On Practice'. Knowing TCM meant placing theory and practice in a
dialectical relation. This was not quite the same as making personally
learnt phrases of medical doctrine meaningful by applying them with
virtuosity to medical practice. While personal experience and 'flexibility'
(linghuo) continued to be valued in TCM, standardised theory had
been learnt in the classroom for several years before it was applied in
the clinic. There was a theory, divorced from medical practice, and the
two had to be placed in a dialectical relation.

Some features distinctive to TCM reasoning – the bias towards
materialism, a preference for singling out a focus in discussion (the
premiss for any comparison), and knowledge stated in the indicative –
pointed to the practices of measurement, comparison, and falsifica-
tion, characteristic of the standardisation of knowledge in the modern
Western sciences. Considering the prestige that Western science currently
enjoys in China, this may not be surprising.

One would not, however, do justice to the complexity of these processes if one were to speak of a piecemeal assimilation of the modern
Western sciences. The process by which the knowledge and technology
of the West are being integrated into Chinese medical knowledge and
practice is marked by an active choice of what is considered suitable for
a particular problem. TCM is being forged so as not to contradict the
canons of either Chinese medical doctrine or biomedical theory.

The current efforts at standardisation are reminiscent of earlier ones
in China's past. TCM theory is not simply modelled upon a prestigious
foreign medicine but integrates many different facets of learning, past
and present, Chinese and foreign. Much of the ongoing reinterpretation
is grounded in an effort 'to be systematic' (xitonghua), in which I see a
continuation of age-old efforts to standardise Chinese medical knowledge and practice.

Non-verbal knowing and participant experience

It goes without saying that the above three settings had much in common. Firstly, the technical terminology was very much the same. Secondly, the modes of transmission were not mutually exclusive. Thirdly,

rote learning from written texts was practised in all of them. Perhaps a participant observer would not have felt it necessary to highlight the differences between them as I have; 'participant experience' might have made the researcher more sensitive to verbally unexpressed tendencies that an observer does not immediately perceive. From a methodological point of view, it is worth noting that I became acutely aware of the differences between the three settings precisely because I went through the learning experiences myself and had subjective reactions distinctive to each.

I found the teachings in the TCM classes the most comprehensible, but not interesting. Reading classical texts with the senior doctor Zhang was sometimes exciting, even illuminating, but more often simply frustrating because many statements seemed arbitrary and often inconsistent with others. Qiu's gestures and incantations are to this day a mystery to me. The subjective responses that I experienced may well have been intended to be evoked in every student, follower, and disciple – they may well have been aimed at by teacher, mentor, and master. Didactic clarity was an explicit goal of the TCM textbook compilers; alternation of excitement and frustration calls for subordination to an omniscient and guiding authority; and the lure of the mysterious gave Qiu's healing performances more significance.

With regard to rote learning participant experience also varied with the context: the Daoist spells were short and often rhymed, but Qiu always found something wrong with my recitation – with its speed, its intonation, or its pronunciation – and I soon gave up. After Zhang's seminars I never made a serious attempt to memorise entire text passages from the canons but would occasionally find myself reciting flowery verses – they were so melodic. Rote learning at the college was necessary to pass the exams, but many sentences were so cumbersome that they were difficult to memorise.

My subjective experiences, identified through introspection, were interrelated with behaviour that a participant observer might have noticed: I often challenged teacher Tao in our lively discussions but asked mentor Zhang questions in a soft voice and observed master Qiu in silence. I did occasionally challenge Zhang, but his response was different from Tao's; instead of playfully countering my argument the senior doctor would look surprised, declare that he did not understand my question, and continue to elaborate his sermon on the text, or he would ask me to repeat my challenge so that I would reformulate it as a humble question. Sometimes I would ask Qiu a series of questions, but he simply ignored them. 'Get out of the habit of asking questions', he once muttered.

Tao's answers to my direct questions were elusive, Zhang's pompous, and Qiu's short, often so short as to be unintelligible. Evidently, direct questions were not approved of in any of the three traditions of learning. The person who may ask direct questions is the one with authority, not the student, follower, or disciple. The teacher's, mentor's, and master's responses reflected particular kinds of resistance. Being short or pompous would not be acceptable for Tao, say, in a meeting of self-confession at the college, and Zhang was too much concerned with presenting himself as a gentleman to be short, but Qiu spoke to me in imperatives. This shows that participant experience allowed me to explore some non-verbal aspects of learning: attitudes to different styles of teaching, memorising texts, and asking questions.

Verbal reasoning, word meaning, and social practice

Since this study is an ethnography that ultimately explores Chinese medical terms, some thought has to be given to the methodological approach adopted for doing so. The investigation built on the insights of methods developed for investigating word meaning, such as identifying semantic components of words (Frake 1961), establishing sense relations between them (Lyons 1977:204), drawing out semantic networks (Good 1977), and exploring different kinds of opposition (Cruse 1986:197–264); methods derived from semantics that are directed at attaining an 'emic' understanding.[1] These methods provided an invaluable background but were, except for Cruse's framework of analysis, only implicitly applied.

The research was also informed by pragmatics, which concerns an investigation of language beyond syntax and semantics. Pragmatics is, according to Levinson (1983:7, 9, italics added), 'The study of language from a *functional* perspective, that is, that it attempts to explain facets of *linguistic structure* by reference to non-linguistic pressures and causes'. It is specifically aimed at 'The study of those relations between language and context that are *grammaticalized*, or *encoded in the structure of a language*'. Pragmatics is directed towards explaining language structure in the light of language use.[2] Since the present ethnography treats

---

[1] The notions of 'emic' and 'etic' can be traced to the linguist's distinction between phonemics and phonetics, the former describing the sounds of a language according to the speakers' perception, the latter according to 'objective' criteria of the outsider-linguist (Headland et al. 1990). There are, however, also instances in which 'the domain of interpretive possibilities is continuous between those of the observer and those of the observed' (Csordas 1993:145).

[2] See also Duranti (1988:211–13) for a definition of language use which applies to pragmatics, sociolinguistics, and the ethnography of speech.

events of verbal expression primarily as aspects of social interaction, it goes beyond the scope of pragmatics in that it explores the significance of words in social practice. It investigates how concepts become 'socialised', the effects they have on verbal and non-verbal social interaction, and what I have proposed to call the 'performative significance' of words in social practice.

The study furthermore built on the idea that the learning experience coins word meaning: it approximated Chinese medical terms by investigating the way in which they were learnt. Toren (1993:462) has repeatedly argued that 'Studies of children's cognitive processes [are] essential if we are to understand what adults are doing and saying'. She emphasises the importance of studying the process of 'coming to know' for understanding the 'knowledge' itself. While Toren's study was about children in Fiji learning the meaning of words that express the social hierarchy of adults and how to behave accordingly, this study was about acolytes – disciples, followers, and students – learning words for appropriate behaviour in medical practice. The approach taken was, again, to explore the meaning of specific words as an aspect not only of language or of *parole*[3] but of social practice.

The concepts investigated were not artifacts, nor were they natural kinds, categories widely recognised on the basis of recent studies on concept acquisition in children (see for instance Keil 1986). Perhaps they are best approximated by Boyer's (1993) notion of 'pseudo-natural kinds'. However, terms for natural kinds, artifacts, and pseudo-natural kinds belong, like colour terms, to very specific domains of meaning. Rather than narrowing the investigation of Chinese medical terms down to research that emphasises the referential aspects of meaning,[4] this study intended to open it up. It treated technical terms like ordinary words, which are often meaningful because of their sense and connotation, and not primarily their reference.

Chinese medical terms seem to have some affinity with words like *bobility* and *baraka* which have proven socially eminently functional precisely because they lack a clearly defined referential meaning and their referential meaning changes as the contexts in which they are uttered change. 'Nothing is more false than the claim that for a given assertion, *its use is its meaning*. On the contrary, its use may depend on its lack of meaning, its ambiguity, its possession of wholly different and

[3] De Saussure ((1916)1967:91) distinguishes between *langage*, an idealised object of study, and *parole*, which speakers speak.
[4] 'Reference' concerns the relationship between language and the world, and is often opposed to 'sense', which is established through the relationship of a linguistic item to others (Lyons 1977:177–206).

incompatible meanings in different contexts, and on the fact that, at the same time, it as it were emits the impression of possessing a constituent meaning throughout – on retaining, for instance, the aura of justification valid only in one context when used in quite another' (Gellner (1958)1970:45). The crucial divergence between the different meanings of a word in the different contexts in which it is uttered is, according to Gellner, often essential for the workings of society.

If one accepts that key concepts of Chinese medicine can be likened to words like *bobility* and *baraka*, there is definitely a difference between categories of the Western sciences in the twentieth century and those of Chinese medical terminology. The former are defined with the aim of being as unambiguous as possible, while the latter are often useful for therapeutic intervention precisely because of their vagueness and polysemy.

Scientific terms are ideally unambiguous in order to assess reality descriptively. This scientific description is bound to lead the researcher to an alienation from the subject he or she describes, the alienation between researcher and researched being intrinsic to the activity of being descriptive. The researcher is meant to set up or refine scientific 'theories' that are descriptive of reality (in the indicative mood). They are not meant to interact with reality as, for instance, does a command (in the imperative mood) and are, in this sense, meant to be detached from reality. It is a commonplace among scientists that there is a gap between theory and practice. A theory is by definition separate from practice. But it is, ultimately, validated by practice: it is modified or abandoned when better ways of manipulating reality are found.

There are several ways of manipulating reality. The detour one takes by describing reality and thereby alienating oneself from it in order, ultimately, to intervene with and manipulate it is just one of them. There are ways in which one can manipulate reality without alienating oneself from it to the same degree as the descriptive scientist. If one makes use of a terminology that is sometimes vague and sometimes polysemous, one can stay actively engaged with reality and often manipulate it successfully. Yet a scholarly discipline grounded in a vague and polysemous terminology is easily decried as 'unscientific'.

Chinese medical terminology is often vague and polysemous, but, as I have shown, it was in ancient times hardly meant to be used to construct a 'theory'. I have approached what is generally called 'Chinese medical theory' as a 'medical doctrine'. The relation between medical doctrine and medical practice differs decisively from that between medical theory and practice: between doctrine and practice there is no gap. The technical terms in Chinese medical doctrine made sense when read on their own, but their relevance for intervening in reality became evident only when applied to particular situations of medical practice. They were hardly coined with the objective of being useful for description alone. Although certainly in some sense descriptive, they were more than that.

There is no doubt that the doctors who intended to manipulate reality often successfully made use of this vague and polysemous terminology in Chinese medical doctrine or, rather, a variety of doctrines. A doctrine was, like a theory, ultimately validated by medical practice: it was modified or abandoned when better ways of performing therapeutic interventions were found. In the sense that the texts of the various Chinese medical doctrines were meant to be useful for manipulating reality and that these doctrines were validated by medical practice, one could say that Chinese medicine was a 'science' long before TCM promoters made it scientific. This kind of 'science' depended on a completely different way of relating textual knowledge to practice.

In summary, by taking word meaning as an aspect of social practice and writing an ethnography that explored word meaning, reasoning with a vague and polysemous terminology has been shown to be extremely functional for the scholar who wishes to assess and influence reality without going through the process of alienation which descriptive scientists are prone to do. This ethnography has shown that Chinese medicine uses word meaning to manipulate reality in a very different way from that of the twentieth-century Western sciences. It has also highlighted that it is controversial, to say the least, to dub the Chinese medical approach 'unscientific'.

Key concepts of Chinese medicine and *qigong*

Different contexts of social practice have been shown to modify the connotation, pragmatic use, and performative significance of Chinese medical terms. The same word uttered in different contexts need not refer to the same concept. Use of the same medical terminology need not be taken as a sign that the same therapeutic practice is being performed. This has far-reaching consequences for the standardisation of any traditional or alternative medicine.

Qi *and its connotations*

The notion of *qi* was central to medical reasoning in all the three contexts. While healers and doctors related to *qi* in similar ways, there were some striking differences. In particular, the notion of *qi* in Qiu's *qigong* differed in several respects from that of the Chinese medical doctors. A first difference was that Qiu could perceive *qi* in the Red Light, he could palpate the surface of the body with his hands and feel whether the 'accumulating *qi*' (*qiji*) inside was 'soft' or not. Chinese medical doctors had no such direct access to the *qi* changes in the body; they had no ability to perceive *qi* visually or to sense its hardness. They gained information on the movements of *qi* by palpating the Pulse (*mai*), which indirectly informed them about postulated processes in the body, or they inferred internal stagnations of *qi* from the inspection of excreta such as Clots in the menstrual blood or secreta such as Phlegm in the body's Apertures. According to Zhang's indirect mode of interpretation, *qi* was Formless (*wu xing*).

There was a second striking difference between Qiu's understanding of *qi* and *qi* in Chinese medical reasoning: Qiu's conception of therapy largely built on the notion that Bad *qi* (*xieqi*) had to be extracted from the patient by/through the healer, who led it to the ground, and Primordial *qi* (*yuanqi*), with its enlivening qualities, had to be taken up from the universe by/through the healer and transferred to the patient. Primordial *qi* and Bad *qi* were by definition good or bad.[5] *Qi* could trespass boundaries such as the boundary between the inside of the body and the outside that was seen as in opposition to it. This conception of *qi* was most conspicuous in Qiu's *qigong* practice, which does not mean that Qiu would not simultaneously speak of harmonising the energies of the body. He sometimes also referred, as did Chinese medical doctors, to the 'body ecologic': *qi* was, in this context of medical reasoning, assigned different qualities mostly in respect of its location or position in the rubrics of the time–space that Chinese medical doctrine recognises. It was a concept marked by uniformity and simultaneously great diversity.

In the body ecologic *qi* was generally not assigned either good or bad qualities; it was the chorus of mutually resonating *qi*, perceived as analogous in micro- and macrocosm, that would give rise to disorders. The notion of the body ecologic builds on the awareness that contemporary concepts of the natural environment have a history and have evolved through complex historical processes. Certain aspects of those terms are best explained by investigating the history of the conceptualisations of the natural environment in the societies from which these medical practices evolved. A more comprehensive understanding of the contemporary notion of *qi* is thus achieved by contextualising it in terms of the

---

[5] The notions Bad *qi* and Primordial *qi* with either inherently enlivening or life-endangering qualities also figured in Chinese medical practice but not as conspicuously as in Qiu's *qigong*.

understanding people had of nature when *qi* became predominant for Chinese medical doctrine.

A third difference was that the *qigong* healer Qiu conceived of lumps coming from tumours, swellings in the lymphatic nodes, and muscle thickenings as 'accumulating *qi*', irrespective of their material aspects. It was important to find out whether *qi* was 'expanding' (*zhang*) or 'softening' (*nen*) – for Qiu *qi* was not only in constant flow but also in constant flux (in the sense that it constantly transformed its qualities and appearances). The senior Chinese doctor Zhang conceived of *qi* in constant flow and flux as well, though he stressed the flow of its circulation more than its transformative fluxes. In TCM there was much talk of *qi* as in constant flow and motion, mostly with regard to its circulation, while it was generally overlooked that *qi* was in constant flux (in the sense of being constantly transformed): *qi* tended to be presented in juxtaposition with Blood (*xue*) and increasingly also with the Liquids and Fluids (*jinye*); its material aspects of being 'pneumatic' were thereby more emphasised than its potential as the 'stuff' (see Sivin 1987:46–7) that is in constant flux and transforms and triggers processes.

In summary, the *qigong* healer Qiu and the Chinese doctors all spoke of *qi*. Their notions of it were in many respects comparable, although the word had subtle differences in connotation in the different contexts of Chinese therapeutics. This analysis of the connotations of a single technical term, *qi*, together with the ethnographic data provided in the previous chapters, gives rise to the interpretation that Qiu's *qigong* healing is grounded in a 'logic of transference'.[6] It is in many respects the same as that of a ritual performance in which enlivening and/or endangering powers are transferred across boundaries. I therefore proposed to view Qiu's *qigong* as a therapy distinct from the many strands of Chinese medicine, even though they use the same technical terms.

Yinyang *and its pragmatics*

Yinyang was on everyone's lips. It consolidated the common-sense truths of everyday life. More precisely, it seemed to reify Mao's notion of materialist dialectics. By saying that a process was one of *yinyang* dialectics, a TCM doctor was not only applying the wisdom of China's cultural heritage but also restating the 'truth' of materialist dialectics.

One could say that *yinyang* had nationalistic and Marxist overtones and attribute this to a change in an idiom's sense and connotations.

---

[6] Lambert (1992:1074) makes a similar distinction between the 'logic of transference' for healing in popular therapeutics and the notion of re-establishing harmony in Ayurveda.

This would imply that the semantics of *yinyang* have changed, which indeed they have in respect to at least one aspect of *yinyang* in TCM teachings. However, the frequent mention of *yinyang* among TCM doctors may well represent a case in which the pragmatics of 'relevance' played a role. It seemed as if Grice's maxim of relevance were being exploited. The answer to the unspoken but ever-present question 'Do you still adhere to Marxist-Socialist thought?' was given by saying that all processes were subject to the materialist dialectics of *yinyang*.[7]

Even in the era of Dengist reforms, reasoning that could be traced to Mao's dialectics pervaded so many domains of everyday life that it went unnoticed by the anthropologist at the time.[8] Newspapers, television, and political study sessions continued to produce slogans along these lines. They were, from autumn 1989 onwards, emitted from the loud-speakers in front of the canteen at breakfast, lunch, and dinner time for staff and students to ingest along with the food from their enamel bowls. Naturally, the dialectics of everyday life were not quite the same as those that the scholar identifies after studying the original sources. Yet the dialectics of everyday life became apparent in the definitions of technical terms in the classroom, in diagnoses of patients' conditions in the clinic (particularly among acupuncturists), in the 'dialectics' of scholarly discussions, in the way in which life histories were communicated to me, and in the way life was generally experienced. There was an awareness of the advantages and disadvantages of everything and anything, a general understanding that the good and the bad together make a whole, a strong conviction of the interdependence of medical theory and practice, an accepting attitude towards contradictory statements, and a general feeling that life was one struggle growing out of another and that in the end it was all just one and the same. *Yinyang* was often mentioned in these connections. It consolidated an everyday-life dialectics that seemed to be derived from Mao's.[9]

Not only did the pragmatics of *yinyang* display conformism to a politically motivated everyday-life philosophy but one aspect of their semantics also suited Mao's dialectics. The first of the four characteristics

[7] The maxim of relevance can explain a wide range of implicatures. The inference works roughly as follows: 'Assume B's utterance is relevant; if it is relevant, then given that A asked the question [Do you still adhere to Marxist-Socialist thought?], B should be providing an answer [All processes are subject to the materialist dialectics of *yinyang*]' (Levinson 1983:107). See Horn (1988:130-3) for a critical review of Grice's original framework.
[8] I therefore have not had the opportunity to elucidate TCM doctors' opinions on the interpretation given in what follows.
[9] Everyday-life dialectics were often a far cry from Mao's, but they may well have been born of an attempt to conform to Marxist-Socialist thought.

attributed to *yinyang* in the *TCM Fundamentals*, Control through Opposition (*duili zhiyue*), reflects the teachings of materialist dialectics in that it sees unity resulting from struggle between two contraries during a previous period of opposition – an understanding of *yinyang* that is not given in classical writings.

Yinyang *and different conceptions of change*

The discussion of the four characteristics attributed to *yinyang* in the *TCM Fundamentals* showed that the process of making these age-old concepts more 'fashionable' (*shimaode*) is grounded in a subtle reinterpretation of the canons. *Yinyang* can be understood to designate dialectic change, indicating a continuous struggle between two contraries. It can also refer to other notions of change, such as the kind that is implied by the phrase that '*yang* engenders and *yin* causes growth', the cyclic Waxing and Waning of the moon or, sometimes, a polar alternation, comparable to the notion of *bian*-change in the 'Commentary' to the *Book of Changes*.

It is a truism that a word can have many connotations. I emphasise it in this context to highlight that the interrelation between words and concepts is very complex. In the case of *yinyang*, we have one idiom that refers to at least four different conceptions of change.[10] The usefulness of such an idiom lies in its capacity to help actors negotiate their positions, to claim authority, express conformity, mask disagreement, and the like – without being confrontational or blatantly contradictory.

The Five Phases and the mood and modality of an utterance

There is a tendency to replace the notion of the Five Phases (*wuxing*) with that of the Five Organs (*wuzang*) in TCM and with that of the Five Flavours (*wuwei*) in Traditional Chinese Pharmaceutics, but reasoning in terms of the Five Phases continues to be prominent, if not indispensable, in assessing postulated processes and formulating maxims of treatment. Maxims of treatment, like *pei tu sheng jin*, are notably not formulated in the indicative mood but in another one approximated in English by the imperative: 'Bank up Earth to produce Metal!' In modern Chinese mood is generally indicated by certain particles at the end of a clause, but in classical Chinese some changes in mood and often also in modality need not be linguistically encoded.

---

[10] The *yinyang* case also highlights different ways in which semantic change can occur: by adding new connotations to already existing connotations of a term, by generalising the sense of a term, and by replacing an old term with a new one.

One can therefore not be entirely sure about the mood and modality of clauses like *jin sheng shui*: it can be understood to mean 'Metal gives rise to Water', but also 'Metal ought to give rise to water' or 'May Metal give rise to Water.' It may well be that reasoning in terms of the Five Phases, particularly in the *Inner Canon*, is prescriptive rather than descriptive. Linguistic form gives us no clue. We have, however, seen that there is a tendency in TCM to shift one's attention from maxims of treatment, which are prescriptive, to descriptions of health in the indicative mood. The shift in mood is one aspect of the ongoing trans-formation of Chinese medical doctrine – the indeterminacy of mood being yet another characteristic of personal knowing – into standardised TCM theory.

Spirit and its performative significance

The term Spirit (*shen*) as used in the three contexts provides perhaps the most striking illustration of possible variations in the performative significance of an idiom.[11] Spirit occurred first in the context of Qiu's treatment of Bao's liver cancer where it figured in determining whether or not Bao would continue treatment. Indicative of a client's general condition and spiritual well-being, it was considered more important than any measurable sign of biomedicine. Spirit was, however, notori-ously vague. To Have Spirit (*you shen*) was an idiom of everyday lan-guage that one used with reference to people who looked healthy and happy, but this hardly applied to Bao in his terminal condition. Whether Bao had Spirit, implying that he should continue treatment, was deter-mined by the group of people present in Qiu's practice. It is quite likely that it was the very vagueness of the term that allowed the clients and healers to reach consensus that Bao had Spirit.

Spirit was also of primary importance in the context of the personal transmission of knowledge. It was mentioned four times in the two opening paragraphs of chapter 66 of the *Basic Questions*, glossed as 'the normal phenomena of nature', 'the changes of things', 'the seasonal changes of nature and different kinds of materials', and 'that in which the application of Heaven becomes evident'. Evidently, its meaning varied according to the specific phrase in which it was mentioned – it was polysemous. The senior doctor Zhang made no attempt whatso-ever to try to reconcile these different meanings.

In the context of the standardised transmission of knowledge, Spirit was discussed only during the theoretical courses in the classroom. In

---

[11] The study of language use in pragmatics is intended to explain language, while the investigation of the performative significance of words explores social practice.

the clinic it was rarely mentioned. The manifestations of Having Spirit, Losing Spirit (*shi shen*), and Pseudo-spirit (*jia shen*) were explained to the students by replacing the vague notion of Spirit with phrases, like, for Having Spirit, 'articulation is distinct', 'movements are agile', and 'breathing is smooth and steady'. The meanings of these phrases were much easier to determine than that of the vague notion of Spirit in the *qigong* healer's practice or in Zhang's text-reading seminars, and TCM doctors tended to speak in terms of these phrases which referred to specific aspects of a condition easily identified in the clinic.

Obviously, the same technical term 'Spirit' had a completely different performative significance in each of these contexts. In the *qigong* healer's practice, 'Spirit' was the word that empowered patients and their fellow patients to take part in the process of healing. In the senior doctor Zhang's seminars, its polysemy allowed the scholar doctor to display his authority in front of his followers. And in the secular institution of the TCM college, while expounded in the classroom, it had hardly any significance in social interaction during the clinical encounter.

If one accepts that the performative significance of such technical terms varies in different social settings, one has to recognise that the standardisation of traditional and the professionalisation of alternative medicines may well preserve the technical terminology of those medicines but not their performative significance. As a result, a therapy that may have empowered clients to take part actively in the healing process may, if standardised, be performed in a way that disempowers them. This may, in turn, have important consequences for the success of the therapy.

Ways of learning and styles of knowing

Technical terms have more than just referential meaning. Their connotations, pragmatics, and performative significances vary in different social contexts, as do the mood and modality of the utterances in which they are mentioned. This has been shown by investigating ways in which these terms are transmitted from one generation to the other and by exploring styles of knowing in social practice rather than contents of knowledge in texts.

As has been emphasised throughout this study it is only this kind of investigation that can illuminate the subtle differences between alternative therapies grounded in the same technical terminology. Use of the same terminology need not be taken as a sign that the same therapeutic practice is being performed. This book underlines the importance of the learning experience in its entirety for acquiring expert knowledge and practice.

Appendix: Curriculum for TCM regular students and acumoxa and massage specialists at the Yunnan TCM College in 1988–9

Subject for TCM Regular Students	Lectures of 2 hrs	Subject for Acumoxa and Massage Specialists	Lectures of 2 hrs
1st semester			
TCM Fundamentals	3	TCM Fundamentals	1.5
zhongyi jichu lilun		*zhongyi jichu lilun*	
Traditional Chinese	2	Traditional Chinese	2
Pharmaceutics		Pharmaceutics	
zhongyaoxue		*zhongyaoxue*	
Classical Chinese for Medics	2	Classical Chinese for Medics	2.5
yiguwen		*yiguwen*	
History of China's Revolution	1	History of China's Revolution	1
zhongguo gemingshi		*zhongguo gemingshi*	
Physical Education	1	Physical Education	1
tiyu		*tiyu*	
Japanese or English	2	English	2
riyu huo yingyu		*yingyu*	
History of Medicine	1		
yishi			
Computing for Beginners	1		
jisuanji jichu			
		Anatomy and Embryology	4
		jiepou zupeixue	
Total	13	Total	14
2nd semester			
TCM Diagnostics	3	TCM Diagnostics	2
zhongyi zhenduanxue		*zhongyi zhenduanxue*	
History of China's Revolution	1	History of China's Revolution	1
zhongguo gemingshi		*zhongguo gemingshi*	
Physical Education	1	Physical Education	1
tiyu		*tiyu*	
Japanese or English	2	English	2
riyu huo yingyu		*yingyu*	
Classical Chinese for Medics	2		
yiguwen			

241

Subject for TCM Regular Students	Lectures of 2 hrs	Subject for Acumoxa and Massage Specialists	Lectures of 2 hrs
Anatomy and Embryology *jiepou zupeixue*	4		
Traditional Chinese Pharmaceutics *zhongyaoxue*	2	Formularies *fangjixue*	2.5
Biology for Medics *yiyong shengwu*	1		
Experimental Biology (laboratory) *shengwu shiyan*	0.5		
		Tracts and Links *jingluoxue*	2
		Acumoxa *loci* *shuxue*	2
		Introduction to Chemistry for Medics *yihua jichu*	1
		Computing for Beginners *jisuanji jichu*	1
Total	16.5	Total	14.5
3rd semester			
Physiology *shenglixue*	3	Physiology *shenglixue*	2.5
Formularies *fangjixue*	3	Formularies *fangjixue*	1
Introduction to Chemistry for Medics *yihua jichu*	1.5	Introduction to Chemistry for Medics *yihua jichu*	1
Experimental Chemistry *yihua shiyan*	1	Experimental Biochemistry for Medics *yihua shanghua shiyan*	1
Japanese or English *riyu huo yingyu*	1	English *yingyu*	1.5
Principles of Marxism and Leninism *malie zhuyi yuanli*	1	Politics and Economics *zhengzhi jingjixue*	1
Physical Education *tiyu*	1	Physical Education *tiyu*	1
Acumoxa *zhenjiuxue*	2.5	Acumoxa *loci* *shuxue*	1.5
		Biochemistry *shengwu huaxue*	1
		Massage *tuinaxue*	2

Subject for TCM Regular Students	Lectures of 2 hrs	Subject for Acumoxa and Massage Specialists	Lectures of 2 hrs
		Needling and Moxa Techniques *zhenfa jiufaxue*	1.5
		Medical Statistics *yixue tongji*	1
		Basics of Computing *jisuanji jichu*	1
Total	14	Total	17

4th semester

Subject for TCM Regular Students	Lectures of 2 hrs	Subject for Acumoxa and Massage Specialists	Lectures of 2 hrs
Microbiology *weishengwu*	1.5	Microbiology *weishengwu*	0.5
Parasitology *jishengchong xue*	0.5	Parasitology *jishengchong xue*	0.5
Practical in Microbiology and Parasitology *weishengwu jichengchong shiyan*	1	Practical in Microbiology and Parasitology *weishengwu jichengchong shiyan*	0.5
Japanese or English *riyu huo yingyu*	2	Technical English *zhuanye yingyu*	1
Principles of Marxism and Leninism *malie zhuyi yuanli*	1		
Physical Education *tiyu*	1		
Biochemistry *shengwu huaxue*	1.5		
Practical in Biochemistry *shenghua shiyan*	1		
Massage *tuinaxue*	1		
qigong	1		
Interpretation of the *Inner Canon* *Neijing jiangyi*	3		
		Pathology *binglixue*	1.5
		Experimental Pathology (laboratory) *bingli shiyan*	1
		TCM Internal Medicine *zhongyi neikexue*	2.5
		Visit to the Clinic for TCM Internal Medicine *zhongyi neike jianxi*	0.5
		TCM Traumatology *zhongyi shangkexue*	1.5

Subject for TCM Regular Students	Lectures of 2 hrs	Subject for Acumoxa and Massage Specialists	Lectures of 2 hrs
		Visit to the Clinic on TCM Traumatology *zhongyi shangke jianxi*	0.5
		Acumoxa Therapy *zhenjiu zhiliaoxue*	2.5
Total	14.5	Total	12.5
5th semester			
TCM Gynaecology *zhongyi fukexue*	1.5	TCM Gynaecology *zhongyi fukexue*	0.5
TCM Internal Medicine *zhongyi neikexue*	2	TCM Paediatrics *zhongyi erkexue*	0.5
Visit to the Clinic for TCM Gynaecology and TCM Internal Medicine *zhongnei zhongfu jianxi*	1		
Japanese or English *riyu huo yingyu*	1	Technical English *zhuanye yingyu*	1
Socialist Construction *shehui zhuyi jianshe*	1		
Physical Education *tiyu*	1		
Pathology *binglixue*	1.5		
Microbiology and Parasitology *weishengwu jishengchong xue*	2.5		
Massage *tuinaxue*	1.5		
Cold Damage Disorders *Shanghanlun*	2		
		Summary of Surgery *xiwai zonglun*	2.5
		Introduction to Internal Medicine *xinei jichu*	2
		Lectures on Genetics *yichuan jiangzuo*	2
		Acumoxa Therapy *zhenjiu zhiliaoxue*	2
		Experimental Acumoxa (laboratory) *shiyan zhenjiuxue*	2
		Acumoxa Doctrines *zhenjiu gejia xueshuo*	1
		Selected Writings on Acumoxa *zhenjiu yixiangxuan*	1.5
Total	15	Total	15

Subject for TCM Regular Students	Lectures of 2 hrs	Subject for Acumoxa and Massage Specialists	Lectures of 2 hrs
6th semester			
Pathology	3		
binglixue			
TCM Ophthalmology	2		
zhongyi yankexue			
Visit to the Clinic for	1		
TCM Ophthalmology			
zhongyi yanke jianxi			
Technical English or Japanese	1		
zhuanye yingyu huo riyu			
Socialist Construction	2		
shehui zhuyi jianshe			
Medical Statistics	1		
yixue tongji			
Cold Damage Disorders	2		
Shanghanlun			
Practical on	1		
Cold Damage Disorders			
Shanghan shixi			
Total	13		
7th semester			
Western Biomedical Diagnostics	3		
xiyi zhenduanxue			
Pathology	1.5		
binglixue			
Pharmacology	1.5		
yaolixue			
Politics and Economics	1		
zhengzhi jingjixue			
TCM Paediatrics	2		
zhongyi erkexue			
Warmth Factor Disorders	2		
wenbingxue			
Essential Prescriptions in the	2		
Golden Casket			
Jingui yaolüe			
Technical English	1		
zhuanye yingyu			
Total	14		
8th semester			
Internal Medicine	2		
neikexue			
Frequent Casualties	1.5		
changjian jizhen			

Subject for TCM Regular Students	Lectures of 2 hrs	Subject for Acumoxa and Massage Specialists	Lectures of 2 hrs
Medical Research Methods *yixue keyan fangfa*	1		
Politics and Economics *zhengzhi jingjixue*	1		
TCM External Medicine *zhongyi waikexue*	2.5		
TCM Traumatology *zhongyi shangkexue*	2		
TCM Doctrines *zhongyi gejia xueshuo*	3		
Total	13		

Glossary of medical and philosophical terms

This glossary provides a synopsis of the Chinese medical terms mentioned in this book with the alternative translations by Manfred Porkert, Paul Unschuld, and Nathan Sivin, and where appropriate other researchers in the field. It also contains some relevant philosophical and other terms encountered during ethnographic work. The initial letter of those Chinese medical terms that need to be understood in a special sense is capitalised (e.g. *xue* Blood), but if the term is frequently used colloquially or biomedically, in different senses, it is given in the lower case (e.g. *shimian* insomnia). The first term provided is the preferred translation; if no other author is given, it is my own. To improve comprehension, some Chinese medical or philosophical categories are given together with their component concepts (e.g. Three Poles: -Heaven, -Earth, and -Man).

P.74 = Porkert 1974, S.87 = Sivin 1987, U.88 = Unschuld 1988b, W.90 = Wiseman 1990

aizheng	癌症	cancer (biomedical)
anmo	按摩	massage; pressing and rubbing
bafeng	八風	Eight Winds (from the eight cardinal directions)
bagang	八綱	Eight Rubrics
yin	陰	*yin*
yang	陽	*yang*
shi	實	Repletion (S.87, U.88, W.90); P.74
xu	虛	Depletion (S.87, U.88); Vacuity (W.90); Inanitas (P.74)
biao	表	Outer (S.87); Exterior (W.90); Outside (U.88); Species (P.74)
li	裡	Inner (S.87); Interior (W.90); Inside (U.88); Intima (P.74)
han	寒	Cold (S.87, U.88, W.90); Algor (P.74)
re	热	Hot (S.87, U.88, W.90); Calor (P.74)

247

bagua	八卦	eight trigrams (Wilhelm (1923)1981:16)
zhen	震	Thunder, the Arousing
xun	巽	Mild Wind, the Gentle
li	離	Fire or Flame, the Clinging
kun	坤	Earth, the Receptive
dui	兌	Lake, the Joyous
qian	乾	Heaven, the Creative
kan	坎	Water, the Abysmal
gen	艮	Mountain, Keeping Still
baiguang	白光	White Light, Bright Light (*qigong* term)
bei		Grief, cf. *qiqing*
bi	痺	Obstruction (accumulated stuff; Blockage; Localised Pain Disorder (S.87); Bi (U.88, W.90)
bian	變	to transgress, transition
bianzheng	辯証	Distinguishing Pattern (Kaptchuk 1983); Manifestation Type Determination (S.87), Pattern Identification (W.90); Syndrome (Farquhar 1994a)
biao		Outer, cf. *bagang*
bing	病	disorder (S.87); illness, sickness (U.88); disease (W.90); sometimes rendered as 'disease' in Eisenberg's (1977:1) sense: 'doctors diagnose and treat disease, traditional healers also redefine illness as disease.'
bingbian	病變	pathological changes
bingji	病機	Disease Triggering, Pathogenesis
bingyin	病因	Disease Factor (W.90), cf. *liuyin*
bu	補	to invigorate; to replenish (S.87); to supplement (U.88, W.90)
bu pi	補脾	to invigorate the Spleen
bu qi	補氣	to invigorate the *qi*
buyao	補藥	invigorating drugs
bu qi	布氣	to diffuse *qi* (Schipper 1982:102)
cang	藏	to house, to store
caoyao	草藥	herbal drugs

caoyi	草醫	herbal medicine
chan ke	產科	department of obstetrics (p.161)
cheng	乘	to multiply cf. *wuxing guanxi*
chuan	喘	asthma
chuang zhong zhe yang ke	疮肿折瘍科	dept. for the sore, swollen, broken, wounded (p.161)
chunyang	純陽	Complete *yang* (*qigong* term)
cifa	刺法	needling techniques
ci shui han mu	滋水涵木	'drench with Water to restrain the Wood' (p.210)
dachang		Large Intestine, cf. *liufu, taiyin*
dachang shu	大肠俞	Large Intestine *shu*-acu-point (W.90)
da fang ke	大方科	department for disorders of adults (p.161)
daixie	代谢	to metabolise
dan		Gall Bladder, cf. *qiheng zhi fu, liufu, jueyin*
danjieshi	胆结石	gallstones
dantian	丹田	Cinnabar Field
shang dantian	上丹田	Upper Cinnabar Field, located at the acupoint *yintang*
zhong dantian	中丹田	Middle Cinnabar Field, at the acupoint *danzhong*
xia dantian	下丹田	Lower Cinnabar Field, about a hand's breadth below the navel
danzhong	膻中	Chest Centre acupoint (W.90)
dao	道	Way, Path
daoyin	道引	to guide and lead (the *qi*), internal conduction (Li & McMahon 1992:145)
di		Earth, see *sanji*
di	締	a Knot which cannot be untied (Harper 1985), cf. *jie, niu*
dianxian	癲癇	convulsions, colloquially equated with epilepsy
dong	動	to come into motion, to move, to be irritated
donggong		meditation by movement, cf. *qigong*
duyao	毒藥	toxic drugs, potent drugs
dui		Lake, cf. *bagua*
duili tongyi	对立统一	unity of opposites (Mao 1961)
duili zhiyue	对立制約	Control through Opposition, cf. *yinyang*

erlong	耳聾	to be deaf, hardness of hearing
erming	耳鳴	to have ringing ears
erzhen	耳针	ear acupuncture
fa guang	發光	to emit Light (*qigong* term)
fa hongguang	發紅光	to emit Red Light
fa huangguang	發黄光	to emit Yellow Light
fa qingguang	發青光	to emit Bluegreen Light
fa qi	發氣	to emit *qi*
fang	方	direction, place; see also *fangji*
fangji	方劑	formula (W.90), prescription
fei		Lungs, cf. *wuzang*
feiqi		Lung *qi*, cf. *qi*, *wuzang*
feng		Wind, cf. *bafeng*, *liuyin*
feng ke	風科	Department of Disorders related to Wind (p.161)
fengqi		Wind *qi*, cf. *qi*, *liuyin*
fenghan	風寒	Wind and Cold
fenghan ganmao	風寒感冒	common cold of the Wind Cold type
fengshibing	風湿病	rheumatism
fu		Bowels, cf. *liufu*
fu	符	sign; a Daoist sign of charm (Schipper 1982:287)
fu	浮	to levitate
fu ke	妇科	Women's Department of Medicine (Furth 1986) (p.161) Gynaecology
fu tong	腹痛	stomach ache
gan		Liver, cf. *wuzang*
ganqi		Liver *qi*, cf. *qi*, *wuzang*
gan wu pi	肝侮脾	the Liver insults the Spleen
ganmao	感冒	common cold
gangmen	肛門	anus
gang ji	纲纪	principle, cf. *ji gang*
gaoxueya	高血压	high blood pressure
gen		Mountain, cf. *bagua*
gongfa	功法	effect of *qigong*, efficiency of *qigong*, *qigong* method, technique of being efficacious
gu		Bones, cf. *qiheng zhi fu*
guzhi zengsheng	骨質增生	hyperosteogeny
guqi		*qi* of the Grains, cf. *qi*
gua	卦	trigram or hexagram
guai bing duo tan	怪病多痰	'strange diseases are frequently due to Phlegm'

guan	官	Senses; an official and the office he sits in
guanjie	關節	joints, articulators (W.90)
guan xiang	观象	to observe Images (Wilhelm 1981)
guang	光	Light, Glow (*qigong* term)
han		Cold, cf. *bagang*, *liuyin*
hanqi		Cold *qi*, cf. *qi*, *liuyin*
han	汗	to sweat, cf. *tu*, *xia*
he	合	to unite
he	合	*he*-acupoint where the *qi* is united (at the elbows and knees) one of five *shu*-acupoints; Uniting Point, Sea Point (W.90); Associate
hongguang	紅光	Red Light, Red Glow
houtian	後天	Wordly State; Postnatal Vitalities (S.87); Later Heaven, Acquired Constitution, Postnatal Constitution (W.90), cf. *xiantian*
hugen huyong	互根互用	Mutual Reliance and Mutual Use, cf. *yinyang*
hua	化	to transform, transformation
hua zheng yi ye	化徵易也	'transformation is the distinguishing marks of one thing changing to the distinguishing marks of another' (Graham 1978:295)
huantiao	環跳	Jumping Round acu-point (W.90)
huangdan	黃疸	jaundice
hun men	魂門	gate of the *hun* soul (to leave the body at death); anus
huo		Fire, cf. *liuyin*, *wuxing*
huoguan	火罐	cupping jar
huo sheng tu	火生土	'Fire gives birth to Earth'
ji	積	Accumulation (W.90)
jichuke	基础科	courses on the basics (introductory courses)
ji gang	纪纲	web without a weaver, cf. *gang ji*
jijie	季節	season
jiju	積聚	Accumulations and Gatherings
jia	瘕	Conglomeration (W.90); Concentration Ills (U.88)

jiaju	瘕聚	Conglomerations and Gatherings (W.90)
jiashen	假神	pseudo-Spirit, cf. *shen*
jian guang	見光	to experience the Light, to see the Light (*qigong* term)
jianzhouyan	肩周炎	periarthritis of the shoulder
jie	結	Knot, cf. *di, niu*
jin		Metal, cf. *wuxing*
jin sheng shui	金生水	'Metal gives birth to Water'
jinshi	近視	short-sightedness
jin yang shu jin ke	金瘍书禁科	Dept. of Inner Lesions and Incantations (p.161)
jinye	津液	Liquids and Fluids; Fluids (W.90); Liquids (U.88); Dispersed Body Fluids (S.87); Active and Structive Fluids (P.74)
jing		Fright, cf. *qiqing*
jing	精	Semen, Essence (S.87, U.88, W.90); Unattached Structive Energy, Structive Potential (P.74)
jing	经	Tracts; to pass through, to pass on, to tradit; Tracts; Cardinal Tracts (S.87); *sinarteriae cardinales* (P.74); cf. *liujing, jingluo*; canon (or classic (S.87, U.88))
jingfangpai	经方派	party of the canonical formulae cf. *shifangpai*
jinggong		meditation in tranquillity, cf. *qigong*
jingluo	经络	Tracts and Links (idiom modelled on that of Tracts and Channels for *jingmai*); Circulation Tract System (S.87), Main Conduits and Network Vessels (U.88); Channels and Connecting Vessels (W.90); Sinarteries, Energetic Conduits, Cardinal and Recticular Conduits (P.74); cf. *liujing*
jingmai	经脉	Tracts and Channels (Lu and Needham 1980); Circulation Vessels (S.87); Channel (W.90), cf. *jingluo*
jingyan	经验	experience

jingshen	精神	Mind; Essence-Spirit (W.90); Vitalities and Spirits (S.87)
jingshi		Chambers of Essence, cf. *qiheng zhi fu*
jiu	灸	moxibustion (i.e. cauterisation with Artemisia leaves)
ju	疽	Abscess; Boil, in TCM with *yin* aspects; deep-seated Abscess (U.88); *ju* (W.90)
jueyin		attenuated *yin* (S.87), cf. *liujing*
kan		Water, cf. *bagua*
ke		to overcome, cf. *wuxing guanxi*
kesou	咳嗽	cough
kong		fear, cf. *wuzhi qiqing*
kou chi yan hou ke	口齒咽喉科	Dept. of Mouth, Teeth, Pharynx, Throat (p.161)
kuai	塊	lump, clot
kun		Earth, cf. *bagua*
lao yisheng	老医生	old doctor
laozhongyi	老中医	senior Chinese doctor
li		Fire, cf. *bagua*
li		Inner, cf. *bagang*
lilunke	理论科	theoretical courses
linbajie	淋巴結	lymphatic nodes
linchuangke	临床科	clinical courses
linggui bafa	靈龜八法	eight methods of the Divine Turtle
linghuo	靈活	virtuosity, flexibility
liu	瘤	Tumour, tumour
liufu	六腑	Six Bowels (U.88, W.90); Palaces (U.88); *yang* Visceral Systems of Function (S.87); *yang* Orbs (P.74), cf. *liufu*, *zangfu*
dan	膽	Gall Bladder (U.88, W.90); Gall Bladder system (S.87); *orbis felleus* (P.74)
xiaochang	小肠	Small Intestine (U.88, W.90); Small Intestine system (S.87); *orbis intestini tenuis* (P.74)
wei	胃	Stomach (U.88, W.90); Stomach System (S.87); *orbis stomachi* (P.74)
dachang	大肠	Large Intestine (U.88, W.90); Large Intestine system (S.87), *orbis intestini crassi* (P.74)

pangguang	膀胱	Bladder (U.88, W.90); Urinary Bladder System (S.87); *orbis vesicalis* (P.74)
sanjiao	三焦	Triple *jiao*; Triple Burner (U.88, W.90); Triple *jiao* System (S.87); *orbis tricaloris*; (P.74); corresponds to Pericardium (*xinbaoluo*)
liujing	六经	Six Tracts or Six Warps (S.87); Six Channels (W.90)
yangming	陽明	*yang* Brightness (S.87, W.90); *yang* Brilliance (U.88); *splendor yang* (P.74)
taiyang	太陽	Mature *yang* (S.87); *yang maior* (P.74); Great *yang* (U.88); Greater *yang* (W.90)
shaoyang	少陽	Immature *yang* (S.87); Minor *yang* (U.88); Lesser *yang* (W.90); *yang minor* (P.74)
taiyin	太陰	Mature *yin* (S.87); *yin maior* (P.74); Greater *yin* (W.90)
shaoyin	少陰	Immature *yin* (S.87); Minor *yin* (U.88); Lesser *yin* (W.90); *yin minor* (P.74)
jueyin	厥陰	Attenuated *yin* (S.87); Ceasing *yin*; Inverting *yin* (W.90); *yin flectens* (P.74)
liuyin	六因	Six Disease Factors; sometimes *liuyin*
feng	風	Wind (S.87, U.88, W.90)
han	寒	Cold (S.87, U.88, W.90)
shi	濕	Damp (U.88, W.90); Moist (S.87)
shu	暑	Heat (S.87); Summer-heat (W.90, U.88)
zao	燥	Dry (S.87, U.88, W.90)
huo	火	Fire (S.87, U.88, W.90)
liuyin	六淫	Six Excesses (S.87), Six Environmental Excesses (W.90); sometimes *liuyin*
lüguan	櫚關	Gate Pass (Qiu's term), cf. *sanguan*
luo	絡	Links; Reticular Tracts (S.87); *sinarteriae reticulares* (P.74); Connecting Vessel (W.90); cf. *jingluo*

mai	脉	(1) Vessels (U.88, W.90); Sinarteries, Energetic Conduits (P.74); Circulation Tract system (S.87); (2) Pulse; Movement in the Vessels (U.88); see also *qiheng zhi fu*
maidong	脉動	pulsation
mai jue	脉绝	the Pulse is severed; cut off (U.88); expire (W.90)
mai wei	脉微	the Pulse is faint, mild (W.90); subtle (S.87); feeble (U.88)
maixiang	脉象	Pulse Images
maizhen	脉診	Pulse diagnostics; cf. *sizhen*
meihe	梅核	Plum Pit (W.90); *globus hystericus* (Ou 1988:28)
mingmen	命門	Gate of Life
mingmen xue	命門學	doctrine of the Gate of Life
ming laozhongyi	名老中医	famous senior Chinese doctor
mingyi	名医	famous doctor
mu		Wood, cf. *wuxing*
na	納	to adopt, to admit (S.87); to accept (Farquhar 1994a)
nao		Brain, cf. *qiheng zhi fu*
naosui	腦髓	Brain Marrow
neidan	內丹	inner alchemy
neiyanggong		Inner Nurture *qigong*, cf. *qigong*
neiqi		Inner *qi*, cf. *qi*
neiyin	內因	Internal Disease Factor (W.90); Inner Cause (S.87)
neizang	內臟	Inner Organs, cf. *wuzang*
nen	嫩	to soften (Qiu's term)
niu	紐	a Knot which can be untied, cf. *di, jie*
nu		Anger, cf. *wuzhi, qiqing*
nüzibao		Womb, cf. *qiheng zhi fu*
paixie	排泻	excretion
pangguang		Bladder, cf. *liufu*
pei tu sheng jin	培土生金	'Bank up Soil to produce Metal' (p.210)
pei tu zhi shui	培土制水	'Bank up Soil to control Water' (p.210)
pi		Spleen, cf. *wuzang*
pi houtian zhi ben	脾後天之本	'the Spleen is the Basis of the Worldly State'

piqi		temper (colloquial); Spleen *qi*, cf. *qi*, *wuzang*
piwei	脾胃	Spleen and Stomach
pingheng	平衡	equilibrium, homeostasis
qi	氣	Breath; Energy, Energetic Configuration, Configurational Energy (P.74); Vapour, Influences (U.88); Basic Stuff; mist, fog; air, vapour and other pneumatic stuff; energies, vitalities; stuff that makes things happen, stuff in which things happen (S.87)
feiqi	肺氣	Lung *qi*, cf. *wuzang*
fengqi	風氣	Wind *qi* cf. *liuyin*
ganqi	肝氣	Liver *qi* cf. *wuzang*
guqi	穀氣	*qi* of the Grains; Grain *qi* (W.90); Alimentary *qi* (P.74)
hanqi	寒氣	Cold *qi*, cf. *liuyin*
jingqi	精氣	prenatal endowment of vitality, Seminal Essence (S.87); Essential *qi* (W.90); (1) Free ('Unattached') Structive Potential, (2) Potentialised Configurational Energy of Undefined Quality, (3) Structive and Active Energy (P.74); Seminal *qi* (Lu and Needham 1980)
neiqi	內氣	Inner *qi* (*qigong*), cf. *waiqi*
piqi	脾氣	Spleen *qi*, cf. *wuzang*
renqi	人氣	*qi* of man's activity; Human *qi* (P.74)
shenqi	腎氣	Kidney *qi*, cf. *wuzang*
shiqi	濕氣	Moist *qi*, cf. *liuyin*
waiqi	外氣	Outer *qi* (*qigong*), cf. *neiqi*
weiqi	胃氣	Stomach *qi*, cf. *liufu*
weiqi	衛氣	Protective *qi* (U.88); Defensive *qi* (P.74, S.87), cf. *yingqi*
xieqi	斜氣	Bad *qi*, Noxious *qi*, Sinister *qi* (as opposed to the Right *qi*); Heteropathic *qi* (P.74, S.87); Evil *qi* (U.88); Pathogenic *qi* (W.90), cf. *zhengqi*
xinqi	心氣	Heart *qi*, cf. *wuzang*
yangqi	陽氣	*yangqi*, *qi* with *yang* qualities, cf. *yinqi*

yinqi	陰氣	*yinqi*, *qi* with *yin* qualities, cf. *yangqi*
yingqi	营氣	Nourishing *qi*; Constructive *qi* (P.74, S.87, U.88), cf. *weiqi*
yuanqi	元氣	Primordial *qi* (P.74, S.87); Original *qi* (U.88, W.90)
yuanqi	原氣	Original *qi* (P.74); Source *qi* (W.90), often synonym to Primordial *qi*
yuzhou zhi qi	宇宙之氣	the *qi* of the universe (Qiu's term)
zaoqi	燥氣	Dry *qi*, cf. *liuyin*
zhenqi	真氣	True *qi* (P.74, S.87, U.88, W.90); inborn vitality (S.87)
zheng qi	正氣	Regular *qi*; Correct *qi* (P.74, W.90); Orthopathic *qi* (S.87), cf. *xieqi*
zhongqi	中氣	Medial *qi* (S.87); Centre *qi* (W.90)
zongqi	宗氣	Gathering *qi*, Ancestral *qi* (W.90); Genetic *qi* (P.74, S.87); the most important *qi* (U.88)
qi dong ze yu	氣動則憂	'if *qi* comes into motion, then there is Anxiety'
qigong	氣功	practice of Breath control (S.87); workings of the Breath (Farquhar 1994a)
donggong	動功	meditation by movement
jinggong	静功	meditation in tranquillity
neiyanggong	內养功	Inner Nurture *qigong*
ruan qigong	軟氣功	soft *qigong*, strengthens one's Inner *qi* (*neiqi*); often associated with *jinggong*, should lead to healing abilities
teyi qigong	特異氣功	extraordinary *qigong*, comprises telepathy, clairvoyance, psychokinesis, and other abilities which may result from *qigong* meditation, depending on one's constitution (*xiantian*)
yinggong	硬功	synonymous to *ying qigong*
ying qigong	硬氣功	hard *qigong*, strengthens one's Outer *qi* (*waiqi*); often associated with *donggong*, and exercises for unarmed combat (*wushu*)

yuan qigong	遠氣功	far-away-effect *qigong*, simultaneous *jinggong* of sender and receiver
qigong jiangzuo	氣功讲座	*qigong* meetings in auditoria or sport stadiums
qigong shi	氣功师	*qigong* master
qi hua	氣化	*qi*-Transformations
qi ji	氣積	*qi* accumulates (lit.); accumulating *qi* (Qiu's term)
qimen	氣門	Gates of *qi*, i.e. acu-points
qi ni	氣逆	*qi* is counterflowing; *qi* Backflow (S.87); *qi* Counterflow (W.90)
qixue butiao	氣血不調	'Breath and Blood are not in harmony'
qi zhi	氣滯	*qi* is stagnant (lit.); Stagnant *qi*, *qi* Stasis (S.87); *qi* Stagnation (W.90)
qiheng zhi fu	奇恆之腑	Odd Palaces; Paraorbs (P.74); auxiliary *yang* systems of function (S.87); Curious Organs (W.90)
nao	腦	Brain (P.74, U.88, W.90); Cerebral system (S.87)
sui	髓	Marrow (P.74, U.88, W.90); Medulla (P.74); Medullary system (S.87)
gu	骨	Bones (P.74, U.88, W.90); Bony system (S.87)
mai	脉	Vessel (P. 74, U.88, W.90); Sinarteries (P.74); Circulation Tract system (S.87)
dan	膽	Gall Bladder (P.74, U.88, W.90); Gall Bladder system (S.87)
nüzibao	女子包	Womb (P.74, W.90); Womb system (S.87); Uterus (W.90)
jingshi	精室	Chambers of Essence; Testicles
qi hua zai	其華在	to have a Flourishing at; its Outward Manifestation is (P.74)
qi jing ba mai	奇经八脉	Eight Odd Vessels; Eight Odd Conduits (P.74); Eight Extraordinary Tracts (S.87); Eight Extraordinary Vessels (W.90)

qian		Heaven, cf. *bagua*
qie mai	切脉	to take the Pulse, to palpate the Pulse
qing	清	Clear
qiqiao	七竅	Seven Apertures Orifices (S.87, U.88); Opering (P.74, U.88); Portals (W.90)
yan	眼	eyes
er	耳	ears
bikong	鼻孔	nostrils
kou	口	mouth
qiqing	七情	Seven Emotions, cf. *wuzhi*
nu	怒	Anger (P.74, S.87, U.88, W.90)
xi	喜	Enthusiasm; Joy (S.87, U.88, W.90); Pleasure (P.74)
si	思	Worry (S.87, W.90); Cogitation (P.74); Thought (W.90); Preoccupation, Ratiocination (S.87)
you	憂	Sorrow (P.74, S.87); Mourning (U.88); Anxiety (W.90)
kong	恐	Fear (P.74, U.88, W.90); Apprehension (S.87)
bei	悲	Grief (S.87, U.88); Sorrow (W.90)
jing	驚	Fright (U.88, W.90); Fear (S.87)
qishan	七疝	Seven Amassments (not standardised)
re		Hot, cf. *bagang*
ren	人	Man, mankind, microcosm, cf. *sanji*
renqi	人氣	Human *qi*, cf. *qi*
renshen	人參	ginseng
ruyi	儒医	scholar doctor
ruan qigong		soft *qigong*, cf. *qigong*
sanbao	三宝	three treasures:
shen	神	Spirit, cf. *shen*
jing	精	Essence, Semen, cf. *jingqi*
xue	血	Blood, (P.74; S.87; U.88; W.90)
sancai	三材	three geniuses, synonymous to *sanji*

sanguan	三關	the Three Narrow Passes (*qigong* term)
weilüguan	尾櫚關	Caudal Pass
jia ji guan	夾脊關	Tightened Spine Pass
yuzhenguan	玉枕關	Jade Pillow Pass
sanguang	三光	Three Lights
ri	日	sun
yue	月	moon
xing	星	stars
sanji	三极	Three Poles:
tian	天	Heaven, Sky, Nature, macrocosm
di	地	Earth
ren	人	man, microcosm
sanjiao	三焦	Triple *jiao*, cf. *liufu*
shangjiao	上焦	upper *jiao*
zhongjiao	中焦	middle *jiao*
xiajiao	下焦	lower *jiao*
se	色	Complexion
se cang bai	色蒼白	the Complexion is pale
shan	疝	Amassment; Accumulation Ill (Unschuld 1985); *shan* (W.90)
shang dantian		Upper Cinnabar Field, cf. *dantian*
shaoyang		Lesser *yang*, cf. *liujing*
shaoyin		Lesser *yin*, cf. *liujing*
she sheng	攝生	to preserve one's life
she	舌	Tongue
she dan bai	舌淡白	the Tongue is pale
shen		Kidneys, cf. *wuzang*
shen	神	Spirit (U.88, W.90); spiritual force, the body's governing vitalities, divine forces (S.87); Divinity (W.90); (1) a manifest Configurative Force, (2) the active aspect of a Configurative Force (P.74); cf. *sanbao*
jia shen	假神	pseudo-Spirits; Fallacious Spirit, False Spiritedness (W.90)
shi shen	失神	Loss of Spirits; Spiritlessness (W.90)
you shen	有神	to have Spirits
shenjing shuairuo	神经衰弱	neurasthenia
shen ming zhi fu	神明之府	the abode of the Spiritual and Bright

shen na qi	腎納氣	'the Kidneys adopt *qi*,' cf. *na*
shenyan	腎炎	nephritis, kidney infection
sheng	聖	sagacity
sheng	生	to engender, to give rise to, raw, cf. *zhang, wuxing guanxi*
shengli	生理	physiology
shi		Repletion, cf. *bagang*
shi	時	timespan of two hours; season
shi		Damp, Moist, cf. *liuyin*
shiqi		Moist *qi*, cf. *qi, liuyin*
shifangpai	時方派	party of the fashionable formulae
shi dong ze bing	是動則病	'if this comes into motion, then disorders arise'
shi mian	失眠	insomnia
shi shen		Loss of Spirits, cf. *shen*
shoufa	手法	skills of handling the needle
shouna	收納	intake
shu	屬	to belong to
shu	暑	Summer-heat, cf. *liuyin*
shuxue	俞穴	acumoxa *loci*
shui		Water, cf. *wuxing*
shuidao	水道	Watercourse
shuigu	水穀	Watery Grains, i.e. fermenting food (S.87); Grain and Water (W.90)
shui hua wei qi	水化為氣	Water is transformed into *qi*
shuiye	水液	Watery Fluids, Water (W.90)
shuiyin	水飲	Water Rheum (W.90), see also *siyin*
shuizhong	水肿	Oedema
si		Worry, cf. *wuzhi, qiqing*
siyin	四飲	Four Watery Mucus (S.87); Four Rheums (W.90)
tanyin	淡飲	Phlegm Rheum (W.90)
xuanyin	懸飲	Suspended Rheum (W.90)
yiyin	溢飲	Spillage Rheum (W.90)
zhiyin	支飲	Propping Rheum (W.90)
sizhen	四诊	four diagnostic examinations
maizhen	脉诊	Pulse diagnostics
she zhen	舌诊	diagnostics by inspecting the Tongue
wang zhen	望诊	diagnostics by observation (of Complexion)
wen zhen	闻诊	diagnostics by listening and smelling

sizhi jueleng	四肢厥冷	the Four Limbs are numb and cold
suantong	酸痛	sore and painful
sui		Marrow, cf. *qiheng zhi fu*
suo chan bing	所產病	'disorders produced by the Vessel'
taiyang		Greater *yang*, cf. *liujing*
taiyin		Greater *yin*, cf. *liujing*
tan	淡	Phlegm (S.87, U.88, W.90); Mucus (S.87)
tanyin	淡飲	Phlegm; Phlegm Rheum (W.90), cf. *siyin*
teyi qigong		extraordinary *qigong*, cf. *qigong*
tian	天	Heaven, Sky, Nature, cf. *sanji*
tiaohe	調和	harmony, to harmonise (W.90)
tinggong	听宮	Auditory Palace acu-point (W.90)
toushi	透視	to have a penatrating vision or X-ray vision, to see
touteng	头痛	headache, to have a headache
touxuan	头眩	dizziness, to feel dizzy
tu	吐	to vomit, see also *han*, *xia*
tu		Earth, cf. *wuxing*
tu ke shui	土克水	'Earth overcomes the Water'
tuina	推拿	massage; pushing and pulling
waiqi		Outer *qi*, cf. *qi*
waiyin	外因	External Disease Factor (W.90); Outer Cause (S.87)
wangjiang	王浆	royal jelly
wangzhen	望診	diagnostics by observation, cf. *sizhen*
wei	痿	Limpness
wei		Stomach, cf. *liufu*
weiqi		Stomach *qi*, cf. *qi*; *liufu*
weikuiyang	胃潰瘍	stomach ulcer
weiqi		Protective *qi*, cf. *qi*
wei qi ying xue	衛氣营血	Four Sectors (S.87): Protective *qi* Sector, *qi* Sector, Nourishing *qi* Sector, Blood Sector
weizhong	委中	Bend Middle acu-point (W.90)
wenbingxue	溫病學	Warmth Factor doctrine
wu		to insult, cf. *wuxing guanxi*
wu	悟	revelation

wuqi	五氣	Five *qi*, Five Seasonal Influences, cf. *liuyin* (without *huo*)
wushan	五疝	Five Amassments (not standardised)
wushu	武術	unarmed combat (Lu and Needham 1980)
wuwei	五位	Five Directions (four cardinal directions and centre)
wuwei	五味	Five Flavours (U.88, W.90); Sapours (P.74, S.87)
suan	酸	Sour (S.87, U.88, W.90)
ku	苦	Bitter (S.87, U.88, W.90)
gan	甘	Sweet (S.87, U.88, W.90)
xin	辛	Pungent (S.87); Acrid (U.88, W.90)
xian	鹹	Salty (S.87, U.88, W.90)
wuxing	五行	Five Phases (P.74, S.87, U.88, W.90); Five Evolutive Phases (P.74); Five Activities (S.87); Five Courses of Action (Graham 1986:76); Five Processes (Graham 1989:326); Five Courses of Materials (Graham 1986:77)
mu	木	Wood (P.74, S.87, U.88, W.90)
huo	火	Fire (P.74, S.87, U.88, W.90)
tu	土	Earth (P.74, S.87, W.90); Soil (U.88, W.90)
jin	金	Metal (P.74, S.87, U.88, W.90)
shui	水	Water (P.74, S.87, U.88, W.90)
wuxing xianghu guanxi		Interelations between the Fire Phases
sheng	生	to give birth (physiological and pathological pattern of change and therapeutic device)
wu	侮	to insult (pathological pattern of change); to violate (P.74)
ke	克	to overcome (therapeutic device); to check (P.74)
cheng	乘	to multiply (therapeutic device); to accroach (P.74)
wu yun liu qi xue shuo	五運六氣學説	phase energetics (P.74)

wuzang	五臟	Five Organs, Five Depositories (U.88 *zang*: 'Depot', storage unit); Five *yin* Orbs, *orbes horrealis* (P.74); Five *yin* Visceral Systems of Function (S.87); Five Viscera (U.88, W.90)
gan	肝	Liver (U.88, W.90); Hepatic System (S.87); *orbis hepaticus* (P.74)
xin	心	Heart (U.88, W.90); Cardiac Visceral System (S.87); *orbis cardialis* (P.74)
pi	脾	Spleen (U.88, W.90); Splenetic System (S.87); *orbis linealis* (P.74)
fei	肺	Lungs (U.88, W.90); Pulmonary System (S.87); *orbis pulmonalis* (P.74)
shen	腎	Kidneys (U.88, W.90); Renal System (S.87); *orbis renalis* (P.74)
wuzang buhe	五臟不和	'the Five Organs are not united'
wuzang zhengjie	五臟癥結	Concretions and Knots in the Five Depositories
wuzhi	五志	Five Impulses; 'will', psychic reactions (P.74); Intent (S.87); Mind (U.88); orientation (emotion) (W.90)
nu	怒	Anger, cf. *qiqing*
xi	喜	Joy, cf. *qiqing*
si	思	Worry, cf. *qiqing*
you	憂	Sorrow, cf. *qiqing*
kong	恐	Fear, cf. *qiqing*
wu xing		Without Form, cf. *xing*
xi		joy, cf. *wuzhi*, *qiqing*
xinbaoluo	心包絡	Pericardium (W.90); Cardiac Envelope Junction (S.87); Heart Enclosing Network (U.88); *orbis pericardialis* (P.74); cf. *liufu*, *shaoyang*
xishou	吸收	assimilation; absorption
xiyi	西醫	Western biomedicine
xia dantian		Lower Cinnabar Field, cf. *dantian*

xia	下	to purge, cf. *han, tu* (known as the three basic treatments)
xiantian	先天	Primordial State, Constitution; Prenatal Vitalities (S.87); Earlier Heaven, Congenital Constitution (W.90); previous to one's existence, transmitted by one's parents (U.88), cf. *houtian*
xiang	象	Image, Figure, Configuration, written symbol
xiang	香	to smell pleasant
xianghu zhuanhua	相互轉化	Mutual Transformation, cf. *yinyang*
xiang tu	想吐	to feel nauseous, to wish to vomit (colloquial)
xiaochang		Small Intestine, cf. *liufu, shaoyin*
xiao fang ke	小方科	department for disorders of children (p.161)
xiaohua	消化	digestion
xiaozhang bianhua	消長變化	change, growth and decline
xiaozhang pingheng	消長平衡	Equilibrium of Waxing and Waning, cf. *yinyang*
xiaozhoutian	小周天	Minor Cosmic Circulation
xiaozhoutian tong	小周天通	the Minor Cosmic Circulation is connected
xie nan bu bei	泻南补北	'purge the South and supplement the North' (P.210)
xieqi		Bad *qi*, Noxious *qi*, cf. *qi*
xieshi	斜濕	Malignant Dampness
xin		Heart, cf. *wuzang, shaoyang*
xinqi		Heart *qi*, cf. *qi, wuzang*
xing	形	Form
you xing	有形	it has Form
wu xing	無形	it has no Form, without Form
xingti zuzhi	形體組织	bodily tissues
xiushen	修身	self-cultivation
xu		Depletion, cf. *bagang*
xuanyin		Suspended Rheum, cf. *siyin*
xue		Blood, cf. *sanbao*
xue	穴	*foramen*, a cavity or an opening (P.74); acupuncture *locus* (S.87); hole, insertion point (U.88); acupuncture point, hole (W.90)

xuewei	穴位	acu-point; acupuncture point (W.90)
xue xu sheng feng	血虛生風	'Blood Depletion gives rise to Wind'
xueye	血液	Blood; Blood-Liquid
xun		Mild Wind, cf. bagang
yan ke	眼科	Department for Disorders of the Eyes, Ophthalmology (p.161)
yang		yang, cf. *yinyang, bagang*
yangming		yang Brightness, cf. *liujing*
yangqi		yang qi, cf. *qi*
yang sha yin cang	陽殺陰藏	'*yang* kills *yin* conceals'
yangsheng	养生	nurture one's life
yang sheng yin zhang	陽生陰長	'*yang* engenders and *yin* causes growth'
yangxing	养性	to nurture one's Nature
yao	父	line of a hexagram
yao	藥	drug
yaowu	藥物	drug substance
ye	液	Fluids, cf. *jinye*
yi huo bu tu	益火补土	'blaze the Fire to supplement the Soil' (p.210)
yinian	意念	imagination, to imagine, to do by the force of the mind
yisheng	医生	doctor, referential term and polite address
yishi	医士	regular practitioner (lowest grade)
yiyao	医药	medicine
yiyuan	医院	hospital
yiyin		Spillage Rheum, cf. *siyin*
yin		yin, cf. *yinyang, bagang*
yin		Rheum, cf. *siyin*
yintang	印堂	Hall of Impression (W.90) (acu-point between eyebrows)
yin cheng xing	陰成形	yin becomes Form
yinqi		yinqi, cf. *qi*
yinqi wei dong, yangqi wei san	陰氣未動 陽氣未散	'*yinqi* has not yet come into motion, *yangqi* is not yet dispersed'
yinyang	陰陽	yinyang
duili zhiyue	对立制約	Control through Opposition (TCM phrase)
hugen huyong	互根互用	Mutual Reliance and Mutual Use (TCM phrase)
xiaozhang pingheng	消長平衡	Equilibrium of Waxing and Waning (TCM phrase)

xianghu zhuanhua	相互轉化	Mutual Transformation (TCM phrase)
yinyang bujiao	陰陽不交	'*yinyang* have no intercourse'
yin zui shen	陰最深	'*yin* is at its deepest, i.e. fullest'
yinggong		hard *qigong* cf. *ying qigong*
ying qigong		hard *qigong*, cf. *qigong*
yingwei	营衞	the Nourishing and Protective, cf. *qi, wei qi ying xue*
yong	癰	Boil, in TCM associated with *yang* aspects; Welling Abscess (U.88); a *yong* (W.90), cf. *ju*
you shen		to have Spirit, cf. *shen*
you xing		it has Form, cf. *xing*
you		Sorrow, cf. *wuzhi, qiqing*
yuzhou zhi qi		*qi* of the universe, cf. *qi*
yuxue	瘀血	Blood Stasis; Coagulation of Blood (S.87); Stagnating Blood (U.88); Static Blood (W.90)
yun	運	rotation, Circulatory Phase
yunqi sueshuo	運氣学说	phase energetics (abbrev.)
yuan	元	origin, basis, root, cf. *yuanqi*
yuanqi		Original *qi*, cf. *qi*
yuanqi		Primordial *qi*, cf. *qi*
yuan qigong		far-away-effect *qigong*, cf. *qigong*
zai zhi wei	在志為	to relate to Impulse
zai ye wei	在液為	to relate to Fluids
zai qiao wei	在窍為	to relate to Apertures
zang	臟	Organs, Orbs, cf. *wuzang, zangfu, zangxiang, zangqi*
zangfu	臟腑	Organs and Bowels, Organs; Visceral Systems of Function (S.87); Viscus-Bowel (W.90), cf. *wuzang, liufu*
zangqi	臟器	Organs (biomedical and TCM term), cf. *zang, zangfu, zangxiang*
zangxiang	臟象 or 藏象	Organ Clusters, the Hidden and the Apparent; Orbiscon (P.74), cf. *zangfu*
zangxiangxue	臟象學 or 藏象學	Orbisiconography (P.74); Visceral Manifestation Theory (W.90); cf. *zangfu*
zao		Dry, cf. *liuyin*
zaopo	糟粕	Waste, Dregs
zaoqi		Dry *qi*, cf. *qi*

zhang	長	to grow, to distend, cf. *sheng*
zhen		Thunder, cf. *bagua*
zhenduan	診斷	to diagnose, cf. *sizhen*
zhenqi		True *qi*, cf. *qi*
zhenjiu	针灸	acupuncture and moxibustion, acumoxa
zhen jiu ke	针灸科	Department of Acumoxa (p.161)
zheng1	征 = 徵	Evidence (U.88); Signs of Illness (Farquhar 1994a)
zheng2	症	Complex of Complaints; (1) Illness, Complaint, Symptoms, (2) Pathocondition (U.88); Individual Symptoms (S.87); Disease (W.90); Symptoms of Illness (Farquhar 1994a)
zheng3	证 = 證	Patterns; Manifestation Type (S.87); Evidence, Symptoms (U.88); Sign, Pattern (W.90); Illness Syndromes (Farquhar 1994a), cf. *bianzheng*
zheng4	癥	Concretion (W.90)
zhengji	癥積	Concretions and Accumulations (W.90)
zhengjia	癥瘕	Concretions and Conglomerations (W.90)
zhengqi		Regular *qi*, cf. *qi*
zhi	痔	Piles, Haemorrhoids (W.90)
zhi	志	Will, Impulse; cf. *wuzhi*
zhi bing qiu ben	治病求本	in treating illness trace the Roots
zhize	治則	maxims of treatment, therapeutic maxims
zhongchengyao	中成药	ready-made Chinese medical drugs
zhongxiyi jiehe	中西医結合	integrated Chinese and Western medicine
zhongyao	中藥	Chinese medical drugs, Traditional Chinese Pharmaceutics
zhongyi	中醫	Chinese medicine, TCM
zhong dantian		middle Cinnabar Field, cf. *dantian*
zhu	主	to govern
zhuo	濁	Turbid
zhuo zhong zhi qing	濁中之清	the Clear within the Turbid
zhuo zhong zhi zhuo	濁中之濁	the Turbid within the Turbid

zi	子	11p.m.–1a.m., when *yin* is at its deepest (1st of 12 *shi-hours*)
zongqi		gathering *qi*, cf. *qi*
zuo jin ping mu	佐金平木	'assist the Metal to level the Wood' (p.210)
zuo yuezi	坐月子	to go into confinement
zuogu shenjing tong	坐骨神经痛	sciatic pain

References

Agren H. 1986: Chinese Traditional Medicine: Temporal Order and Synchronous Events. In J. T. Fraser et al. (eds.) *Time, Science, and Society in China and the West.* Amherst: University of Massachusetts Press, 211–18.

Anderson E. N. 1988: *The Food of China.* New Haven: Yale University Press.

Andrès G. 1980: *Principes de la Médecine selon la Tradition.* Paris: Dervy Livres.

Andrews B. J. 1996: The Making of Modern Chinese Medicine, 1895–1937. Ph.D. thesis, University of Cambridge.

Anspach R. R. 1988: Notes on the Sociology of Medical Discourse: The Language of Case Presentation. In J. Colombotos (ed.) *Continuities in the Sociology of Medicine.* Special Issue. *Journal of Health and Behaviour* 29: 357–75.

Austin J. L. 1962: *How to do Things with Words.* Oxford: Clarendon.

Bastid M. 1984: Chinese Educational Policies in the 1980s and Economic Development. *China Quarterly* 98: 189–219.

Bates D. (ed.) 1995: *Knowledge and the Scholarly Medical Traditions.* Cambridge: Cambridge University Press.

Beattie J. H. M. 1980: On Understanding Sacrifice. In M. F. C. Bourdillon and M. Fortes (eds.) *Sacrifice.* Bristol: Academic, 29–44.

Bellman B. L. 1975: *Village Curers and Assassins: on the Production of Fala Kpelle Cosmological Categories.* The Hague: Mouton.

1984: *The Language of Secrecy: Symbols and Metaphors in Poro Ritual.* New Brunswick: Rutgers University Press.

Benedict C. 1996: *Bubonic Plague in Nineteenth-Century China.* Stanford: Stanford University Press.

Bian Y. 1994: *Work and Inequality in Urban China.* Albany: State University of New York Press.

Blacker C. 1975: *The Catalpa Bow: a Study of Shamanistic Practices in Japan.* London: Allen & Unwin.

Bodde D. 1957: Evidence for 'Laws of Nature' in Chinese Thought. *Harvard Journal of Asiatic Studies* 20: 709–27.

1979: Chinese 'Laws of Nature': a Reconsideration. *Harvard Journal of Asiatic Studies* 39: 139–55.

Boehmer T. 1977: Taoist Alchemy: a Sympathetic Approach through Symbols. In M. Saso and D. W. Chappell (eds.) *Buddhist and Taoist Studies* I. Honolulu: University Press of Hawaii, 55–78.

Boyer P. 1986: The 'Empty' Concepts of Traditional Thinking: a Semantic and Pragmatic Description. *Man* 21: 50–64.

1990: *Tradition as Truth and Communication: a Cognitive Description of Traditional Discourse*. Cambridge: Cambridge University Press.

1993: Pseudo-natural Kinds. In P. Boyer (ed.) *Cognitive Aspects of Religious Symbolism*. Cambridge: Cambridge University Press, 121–41.

Bray F. 1995: A Deathly Disorder: Understanding Women's Health in Late Imperial China. In D. Bates (ed.) *Knowledge and the Scholarly Medical Traditions*. Cambridge: Cambridge University Press, 235–50.

Bühler K. (1934)1982: *Sprachtheorie*. Stuttgart: Fischer.

Chao Y. L. 1995: Medicine and Society in Late Imperial China: a Study of Physicians in Suzhou. Ph.D. dissertation in History, University of California, Los Angeles.

Chen H. F. (ed.) 1984: *Chinese Health Care: a Comparative Review of the Health Services in the People's Republic of China*. Modern Chinese Medicine 3. Lancaster: MTP Press.

Chen N. N. 1995: Urban Spaces and Experiences of *qigong*. In S. D. Davis et al. (eds.) 1995: *Urban Spaces in Contemporary China: the Potential for Autonomy and Community in Post-Mao China*. Washington, D.C.: Woodrow Wilson Center Press and Cambridge: Cambridge University Press, 347–61.

Connerton P. 1992: Bakhtin and the Representation of the Body. *Journal of the Institute of Romance Studies* 1: 349–62.

Cooper E. 1980: *The Wood-Carvers of Hongkong: Craft Production in the World Capitalist Periphery*. Cambridge: Cambridge University Press.

Cordier G. 1925: L'Enseignement en Chine. *Revue Indo-Chinoise* 11–12: 387–432.

Creery J. L. 1973: The Symbolism of Popular Taoist Magic. Ph.D. dissertation in Anthropology, Cornell University.

Croizier R. C. 1968: *Traditional Medicine in Modern China: Science, Nationalism, and the Tensions of Cultural Change*. Cambridge, Mass.: Harvard University Press.

1976: The Ideology of Medical Revivalism in Modern China. In C. Leslie (ed.) *Asian Medical Systems: a Comparative Study*. Berkeley: University of California Press, 341–55.

Croll E. 1981: *The Politics of Marriage in Contemporary China*. Cambridge: Cambridge University Press.

Cruse D. A. 1986: *Lexical Semantics*. Cambridge: Cambridge University Press.

Csordas T. 1993: Somatic Modes of Attention. *Cultural Anthropology* 8: 135–56.

Cullen C. 1993: Patients and Healers in Late Imperial China: Evidence from the *Jinpingmei*. *History of Science* 31: 99–150.

D'Andrade R. 1995: *The Development of Cognitive Anthropology*. Cambridge: Cambridge University Press.

Davis S. 1996: The Cosmobiological Balance of the Emotional and Spiritual Worlds: Phenomenological Structuralism in Traditional Chinese Medical Thought. *Culture, Medicine and Psychiatry* 20: 83–123.

Day C. B. 1969: *Chinese Peasant Cults*. New York: Altai.

De la Robertie C. 1986: *De la Signification des Mutations en Médecine*, Yi yi yi: *Traduction d'un Chapitre du* Lei jing fu yi *(1624)*. Rennes: Cercle Sinologique de l'Ouest.

Despeux C. 1985: *Shanghanlun: Traité des 'Coups de Froid'*. Paris: Edition de la Tisserande.

1987: *Préscriptions d'Acuponcture Valant Mille Onces d'Or: Traité d'Acuponcture de Sun Simiao du VIIe Siècle*. Paris: Guy Trédaniel.

1988: *La Moëlle du Phénix Rouge: Santé et Longue Vie dans la Chine du XVIe Siècle*. Paris: Guy Trédaniel.

1994: *Taoïsme et Corps Humain: Le* Xiuzhentu. Paris: Guy Trédaniel.

1995: L'Expiration des Six Souffles d'après les Sources du Canon Taoïque: Un Procédé Classique du *qigong*. In J.-P. Diény (ed.) *Hommage à Kwong Hing Foon. Etudes d'Histoire Culturelle de la Chine*. Paris: Collège de France, Institut des Hautes Etudes Chinoises, 129–63.

1996: Le Corps, Champ Spatio-temporel, Souche d'Identité. *L'Homme* 137: 87–118.

forthcoming: The System of the Five Circulatory Phases and the Six Seasonal Influences (*wuyun liuqi*), a Source of Innovation in Medicine under the Song. In E. Hsu (ed.) *Chinese Medicine: Innovation, Convention and Controversy*. Cambridge: Cambridge University Press.

Despeux C. and Obringer F. 1990: Conceptualisation d'un État Pathologique dans la Médecine Chinoise Traditionelle, Exemple de la Toux. *Revue d'Histoire des Sciences* 43 (1): 36–56.

Dissanayake W. 1993: Body in Social Theory. In T. P. Kasulis et al. (eds.) *Self as Body in Asian Theory and Practice*. Albany: State University of New York Press, 21–36.

Doumer P. 1902: *Situation de l'Indo-Chine 1897–1901*. Hanoi: F. H. Schneider.

Duden B. (1987)1991: *The Woman beneath the Skin: a Doctor's Patients in Eighteenth-Century Germany*. Cambridge, Mass.: Harvard University Press.

Dunstheimer G. 1972: Religious Aspects of Secret Societies. In J. Chesneaux (ed.) *Popular Movements and Secret Societies in China 1840–1950*. Stanford: Stanford University Press, 23–8.

Duranti A. 1988: Ethnography of Speaking: Towards a Linguistics of Praxis. In F. Newmeyer (ed.) *Language: the Socio-cultural Context*. Linguistics: the Cambridge Survey IV. Cambridge: Cambridge University Press, 210–28.

Eisenberg L. 1977: Disease and Illness: Distinctions between Professional and Popular Ideas of Sickness. *Culture, Medicine and Psychiatry* 1: 9–33.

Elman B. A. 1984: *From Philosophy to Philology: Intellectual and Social Aspects of Change in Late Imperial China*. Cambridge, Mass.: Harvard University Press.

Elvin M. 1985: Between the Earth and Heaven: Conceptions of the Self in China. In M. Carrithers et al. (eds.) *The Category of the Person: Anthropology, Philosophy, History*. Cambridge: Cambridge University Press, 156–89.

Engelhardt U. 1987: *Die Klassische Tradition der Qi-Uebungen (Qigong). Eine Darstellung anhand des Tang-zeitlichen Textes* Fu qi jing yi lun *von Sima Chengzhen*. Stuttgart: Franz Steiner.

Evans-Pritchard E. E. 1937: *Witchcraft, Oracles and Magic Among the Azande*. Oxford: Clarendon.

1956: *Nuer Religion*. Oxford: Oxford University Press.

Fabrega H. and Silver D. B. 1973: *Illness and Shamanistic Curing in Zinacantan: an Ethnomedical Analysis*. Stanford: Stanford University Press.

Fairbank J. K. and Liu K. C. 1980: *The Cambridge History of China: Late Ch'ing 1800–1911*. Cambridge: Cambridge University Press.

Farquhar J. 1986: Knowledge and Practice in Chinese Medicine. Ph.D. dissertation in Anthropology, University of Chicago.

1987: Problems of Knowledge in Contemporary Chinese Medical Discourse. *Social Science and Medicine* 24 (20): 1013–21.

1991: Objects, Processes, and Female Infertility in Chinese Medicine. *Medical Anthropology Quarterly* 5 (4): 370–99.

1992: Time and Text: Approaching Chinese Medical Practice through Analysis of a Published Case. In C. Leslie and A. Young (eds.) *Paths to Asian Medical Knowledge*. Berkeley: University of California Press, 62–73.

1994a: *Knowing Practice: the Clinical Encounter of Chinese Medicine*. Boulder: Westview.

1994b: Multiplicity, Point of View, and Responsibility in Traditional Chinese Healing. In A. Zito and T. E. Barlow (eds.) *Body, Subject and Power in China*. Chicago: University of Chicago Press, 78–99.

1995: Rewriting Traditional Medicine in post-Maoist China. In D. Bates (ed.) *Knowledge and the Scholarly Medical Traditions*. Cambridge: Cambridge University Press, 251–76.

1996a: Market Magic: Getting Rich and Getting Personal in Medicine after Mao. *American Ethnologist* 23 (2): 239–57.

1996b: 'Medicine and the Changes are One': an Essay in Divination Healing with Commentary. *Chinese Science* 16: 107–34.

Favret-Saada J. (1977)1980: *Deadly Words: Witchcraft in the Bocage*. Cambridge: Cambridge University Press and Paris: Editions de la Maison des Sciences de l'Homme.

Fei H. T. and Chang C. I. 1949: *Earthbound China: a Study of Rural Economy in Yunnan*. London: Routledge and Kegan Paul.

Fleck L. (1935)1980: *Entstehung und Entwicklung einer wissenschaftlichen Tatsache. Einführung in die Lehre von Denkstil und Denkkollektiv*. Frankfurt: Suhrkamp.

Foucault M. (1976)1990: *The History of Sexuality: an Introduction*. Harmondsworth: Penguin.

Frake C. O. 1961: The Diagnosis of Disease Among the Subanun of Mindanao. *American Anthropologist* 63: 113–32.

Frankel S. and Lewis G. 1989: Patterns of Continuity and Change. In S. Frankel and G. Lewis (eds.) *A Continuing Trial of Treatment: Medical Pluralism in Papua New Guinea*. Dordrecht: Kluwer, 1–33.

Frankenberg R. 1993: Anthropological and Epidemiological Narratives of Prevention. In S. Lindenbaum and M. Lock (eds.) *Knowledge, Power, and Practice: the Anthropology of Everyday Life*. Berkeley: University of California Press, 219–42.

Freedman M. 1967: *Rites and Duties, or: Chinese Marriage*. London: Bell.

Freidson E. 1970: *The Profession of Medicine: a Study of the Sociology of Applied Knowledge*. New York: Dodd, Mead and Company.

Fung Y. L. 1953: *A History of Chinese Philosophy*, II. Princeton: Princeton University Press.

Furth C. 1986: Blood, Body and Gender: Medical Images of the Female Condition in China, 1600–1800. *Chinese Science* 7: 43–66.

1987: Concepts of Pregnancy, Childbirth, and Infancy in Ch'ing Dynasty China. *Journal of Asian Studies* 46 (1): 7–35.

1988: Androgynous Males and Deficient Females: Biology and Gender Boundaries in Sixteenth- and Seventeenth-Century China. *Late Imperial China* 9 (2): 1–31.

Furth C. and Ch'en S. Y. 1992: Chinese Medicine and the Anthropology of Menstruation in Contemporary Taiwan. *Medical Anthropology Quarterly* 6 (1): 27–48.

Gawlikowski K. 1982: Two National Ways of Reasoning: Interpretation of the Cause–Effect Relationship by Chinese and Polish University Students. A Psychological Study. In W. Eberhard et al. (eds.) *East Asian Civilizations, I: Ethnic Identity and National Characteristics*. Federal Republic of Germany: Simon and Magiera, 82–131.

Gellner E. (1958)1970: Concepts and Society. In B. R. Wilson (ed.) *Rationality*. Oxford: Blackwell, 18–49.

1977: Patrons and Clients. In E. Gellner and J. Waterbury (eds.) *Patrons and Clients*. London: Duckworth, 1–6.

Gernet J. 1972: *Le Monde Chinois*. Paris: Armand Colin.

Giles L. (ed. and transl.) 1948: *A Gallery of Chinese Immortals: Selected Biographies*. London: John Murray.

Goffman E. (1961)1975: *Asylums: Essays on the Social Situation of Mental Patients and Other Inmates*. Harmondsworth: Penguin.

Gold T. B. 1989: Guerilla Interviewing Among the Getihu. In P. Link et al. (eds.) *Unofficial China: Popular Culture and Thought in the PRC*. Boulder: Westview, 175–92.

1991: Youth and the State. *The Individual and the State in China*. Special Issue. *China Quarterly* 127: 594–612.

Goldman M. 1981: *China's Intellectuals: Advise and Dissent*. Cambridge, Mass.: Harvard University Press.

Good B. J. 1977: The Heart of What's the Matter: the Semantics of Illness in Iran. *Culture, Medicine, and Psychiatry* 1: 25–58.

1994: *Medicine, Rationality, and Experience: an Anthropological Perspective*. Cambridge: Cambridge University Press.

Good B. J. and DelVecchio Good M.-J. 1993: Learning Medicine. In S. Lindenbaum and M. Lock (eds.) *Knowledge, Power, and Practice: the Anthropology of Medicine and Everyday Life*. Cambridge: Cambridge University Press, 81–107.

Goody E. N. 1978: Towards a Theory of Questions. In E. N. Goody (ed.) *Questions and Politeness*. Cambridge: Cambridge University Press, 17–55.

Goody J. 1977: *The Domestication of the Savage Mind*. Cambridge: Cambridge University Press.

1987: *The Interface between the Written and the Oral*. Cambridge: Cambridge University Press.

1990: *The Oriental, the Ancient and the Primitive: Systems of Marriage and the Family in the Pre-Industrial Societies of Eurasia*. Cambridge: Cambridge University Press.

Gould Martin K. 1975: Medical Systems in a Taiwan Village: Ong-Ia-Kong, the Plague God as a Modern Physician. In A. Kleinman et al. (eds.) *Medicine in Chinese Cultures: Comparative Studies of Health Care in Chinese and Other Societies*. Washington D.C.: Geographic Health Studies, 115–41.

Graham A. C. 1978: *Later Mohist Logic, Ethics and Science*. Hongkong: Chinese University Press.

1986: *Yin-Yang and the Nature of Correlative Thinking*. Singapore: Institute of East Asian Philosophies.

1989: *Disputers of the Tao: Philosophical Argument in Ancient China*. La Salle, Ill.: Open Court.

Granet M. 1934: *La Pensée Chinoise*. Paris: La Renaissance du Livre.

Griaule M. (1948)1966: *Dieu d'Eau: Entretiens avec Ogotemmêli*. Paris: Fayard.

Haar B. J. ter 1992: *The White Lotus Teachings in Chinese Religious History*. Leiden: Brill.

Hacking I. 1992: 'Style' for Historians and Philosophers. *Studies in the History and Philosophy of Science* 23 (1): 1–20.

Hall D. L. and Ames T. A. 1987: *Thinking Through Confucius*. Albany: State University of New York Press.

Hammes M. and Ots T. 1996: *33 Fallbeispiele zur Akupunktur aus der Volksrepublik China*. Stuttgart: Hippokrates.

Hanson M. forthcoming: Awaken Physicians with a Stick: Creating a New Canon in Nineteenth-Century China. In E. Hsu (ed.) *Chinese Medicine: Innovation, Convention and Controversy*. Cambridge: Cambridge University Press.

Harper D. 1985: A Chinese Demonography of the Third Century B.C. *Harvard · Journal of Asiatic Studies* 45: 459–541.

1990a: The Conception of Illness in Early Chinese Medicine, as Documented in Newly Discovered 3rd and 2nd Century B.C. Manuscripts (Part I). *Sudhoffs Archiv* 74 (2): 210–35.

1990b: Technical Knowledge in Ancient China: Analysis of a Teaching on Physical Cultivation from the Ma-wang-tui Medical MSS. Conference paper, American Association of Asian Studies, Chicago.

(transl. and study) 1998: *Early Chinese Medical Literature: the Mawangdui Medical Manuscripts*. London: Routledge.

Harrison's 1987: *Harrison's Principles of Internal Medicine*. E. Braunwald et al. (eds.). 11th edition, 2 Vols. New York: McGraw-Hill.

Hayley A. 1980: A Communal Relationship with God: the Nature of the Offering in Assamese Vaishnavism. In M. F. C. Bourdillon and M. Fortes (eds.) *Sacrifice*. Bristol: Academic, 107–25.

Headland T. N., Pike K. L. and Harris M. (eds.) 1990: *Emics and Etics: the Insider/Outsider Debate*. Newbury Park, Calif.: Sage.

Hebel J. and Schucher G. 1991: From Unit to Enterprise? The Chinese *Tanwei* in the Process of Reform. *Issues & Studies* 27 (4): 24–43.

Henderson G. E. and Cohen M. S. 1984: *The Chinese Hospital: a Socialist Work Unit*. New Haven: Yale University Press.

Henderson J. B. 1991: *Scripture, Canon, and Commentary: a Comparison of Confucian and Western Exegesis*. Princeton: Princeton University Press.

Heusch L. de 1985: *Sacrifice in Africa: a Structuralist Approach*. Manchester: Manchester University Press.

Horn L. R. 1988: Pragmatic Theory. In F. Newmeyer (ed.) *Linguistic Theory: Foundations*. Linguistics: The Cambridge Survey I. Cambridge: Cambridge University Press, 113–45.

Hsu E. 1992a: Transmission of Knowledge, Texts and Treatment in Chinese Medicine. Ph.D. thesis in Social Anthropology, University of Cambridge.

1992b: The Reception of Western Medicine in China: Examples from Yunnan. In P. Petitjean et al. (eds.) *Science and Empires*. Dordrecht: Kluwer, 89–101.

1994: Change in Chinese Medicine: *bian* and *hua*. An Anthropologist's Approach. In V. Alleton and A. Volkov (eds.) *Notions et Perceptions de Changement en Chine*. Paris: Institut des Hautes Etudes Chinoises, Collège de France, 41–58.

1995: The Manikin in Man: Cultural Crossing and Creativity. In G. Aijmer (ed.) *Syncretism and the Commerce of Symbols*. Göteborg: Institute for Advanced Studies in Social Anthropology, 156–204.

1996a: Innovations in Acumoxa: Acupuncture Analgesia, Scalp Acupuncture and Ear Acupuncture in the PRC. *Social Science and Medicine* 42 (3): 421–30.

1996b: The Polyglot Practitioner: Towards Acceptance of Different Approaches in Treatment Evaluation. In S. Gosvig Olesen and E. Hoeg (eds.) *Studies in Alternative Therapy* III. *Communication in and about Alternative Therapies*. Odense: Odense University Press, 37–53.

1996c: Acumoxa in Yunnan: a Case Study of Standardising Chinese Medicine at a Medical College of the PRC. *Southwest China Cultural Studies* 1: 217–48.

1998: *Yinyang* and Mao's Dialectics in Traditional Chinese Medicine. In J. Helbling (ed.) *Asia in Swiss Anthropology*. Special Issue, *Asiatische Studien* 52 (2): 419–44.

in press: Spirits (*shen*), Styles of Knowing, and Authority in Chinese Medicine. *Culture, Medicine, and Psychiatry*.

forthcoming: Das Konzept der Einverleibung: 'Embodiment'. In C. E. Gottschalk-Batschkus et al. (eds.) *Grundlagen der Ethnomedizin*. Berlin: Springer.

Hsu F. L. K. 1983: *Exorcising the Trouble Makers. Magic, Science, and Culture*. Westport: Greenwood.

Hubert H. and Mauss M. (1898)1964: *Sacrifice: its Nature and Function*. Chicago: University of Chicago Press.

Hutchins E. 1980: *Culture and Inference: a Trobriand Case Study*. Cambridge, Mass.: Harvard University Press.

Hymes R. P. 1987: Not quite Gentlemen? Doctors in Sung and Yuan. *Chinese Science* 8: 9–76.

Janzen J. M. 1978: *The Quest of Therapy in Lower Zaire*. Berkeley: University of California Press.

Kaptchuk T. J. 1983: *Chinese Medicine: the Web that has no Weaver*. London: Rider.

Karlgren B. 1950: *The Book of Documents*. Museum of Far Eastern Antiquities, Stockholm, Bulletin 22.

Keegan D. J. 1988: *The 'Huang-Ti Nei-Ching': the Structure of the Compilation; the Significance of the Structure*. Ph.D. dissertation in History, University of California, Berkeley.

Keil F. C. 1986: The Acquisition of Natural Kind and Artifact Terms. In W. Demopoulos and A. Marras (eds.) *Language Learning and Concept Acquisition*. Norwood, N.J.: Ablex, 133–53.

Kempson R. M. 1977: *Semantic Theory*. Cambridge: Cambridge University Press.

Klein H. 1987: *Les Théories Hermétiques de la Médicine Traditionelle en Chine. Recherches sur la Vie et l'Oeuvre de Chang Chieh-Pin Médecin-Philosophe de l'Epoque des Ming*. Paris: Dervy.

Kleinman A. 1980: *Patients and Healers in the Context of Culture: an Exploration of the Borderland between Anthropology, Medicine and Psychiatry*. Berkeley: University of California Press.

1986: *Social Origins of Distress and Disease: Depression, Neurasthenia, and Pain in Modern China*. New Haven: Yale University Press.

Knight N. 1990: *Mao Zedong on Dialectical Materialism: Writings in Philosophy, 1937*. Armonk: Sharpe.

Kohn L. (ed.) 1989: *Taoist Meditation and Longevity Techniques*. Ann Arbor: Center for Chinese Studies, University of Michigan.

Kuhn P. A. 1990: *Soulstealers: the Chinese Sorcery Scare of 1768*. Cambridge, Mass.: Harvard University Press.

Kuriyama S. 1987: Pulse Diagnosis in the Greek and Chinese Traditions. In Y. Kawakita (ed.) *History of Diagnostics*. Osaka: Taniguchi Foundation, 43–67.

1993: Concepts of Disease in East Asia. In K. F. Kiple (ed.) *The Cambridge World History of Human Disease*. Cambridge: Cambridge University Press, 53–9.

1994: The Imagination of Winds and the Development of the Chinese Conception of the Body. In A. Zito and T. E. Barlow (eds.) *Body, Subject and Power in China*. Chicago: University of Chicago Press, 23–41.

1995: Visual Knowledge in Classical Chinese Medicine. In D. Bates (ed.) *Knowledge and the Scholarly Medical Traditions*. Cambridge: Cambridge University Press, 205–34.

Laderman C. 1981: Symbolic and Empirical Reality: a New Approach to the Analysis of Food Avoidances. *American Ethnologist* 3: 468–93.

Lambert H. 1992: The Cultural Logic of Indian Medicine: Prognosis and Etiology in Rajasthani Popular Therapeutics. *Social Science and Medicine* 34 (10): 1069–76.

Lampton D. M. 1977: *The Politics of Medicine in China: the Policy Process 1949–1977*. Boulder: Westview.

Landy D. 1977: Role Adaptation: Traditional Curers under the Impact of Western Medicine. In D. Landy (ed.) *Culture, Disease and Healing*. New York: Macmillan, 468–81.

Lau D. C. 1963: *Lao Tzu, Tao Te Ching*. Harmondsworth: Penguin.

1979: *Confucius, The Analects (Lun yü)*. Harmondsworth: Penguin.

Leach E. 1961: Two Essays Concerning the Symbolic Representation of Time. In *Rethinking Anthropology*. London: Athlone, 124–36.

Leslie C. (ed.) 1976a: *Asian Medical Systems: a Comparative Study*. Berkeley: University of California Press.

Leslie C. 1976b: The Ambiguities of Medical Revivalism in Modern Inida. In C. Leslie (ed.) *Asian Medical Systems: a Comparative Study*. Berkeley: University of California Press, 356–67.

Leslie C. and Young A. (eds.) 1992: *Paths to Asian Medical Knowledge*. Berkeley: University of California Press.

Lévi-Strauss C. (1958)1963: The Sorcerer and his Magic. In *Structural Anthropology*. Harmondsworth: Penguin, 167–85.

Levinson S. C. 1983: *Pragmatics*. Cambridge: Cambridge University Press.

Lewis G. 1976: A View of Sickness in New Guinea. In J. B. Loudon (ed.) *Social Anthropology and Medicine*. London: Academic, 49–103.

1980: *Day of Shining Red*. Cambridge: Cambridge University Press.

1986: The Look of Magic. *Man* 21: 414–37.

Lewis M. E. 1990: *Sanctioned Violence in Early China*. Albany: State University of New York Press.

Li H. L. 1991: *Die Grundstruktur der chinesischen Gesellschaft: vom traditionellen Clan System zur modernen Danwei Organisation*. Opladen: Westdeutscher Verlag.

Li L. and McMahon K. 1992: The Contents and the Terminology of the Mawangdui Texts on the Arts of the Bedchamber. *Early China* 17: 145–85.

Lloyd G. E. R. 1991a: Galen on Hellenistics and Hippocrateans: Contemporary Battles and Past Authorities. In *Methods and Problems in Greek Science: Selected Papers*. Cambridge: Cambridge University Press, 398–416.

1991b: The Invention of Nature. In *Methods and Problems in Greek Science: Selected Papers*. Cambridge: Cambridge University Press, 417–34.

1995: Epistemological Arguments in Early Greek Medicine in Comparative Perpective. In D. Bates (ed.) *Knowledge and the Scholarly Medical Traditions*. Cambridge: Cambridge University Press, 25–40.

1996: *Adversaries and Authorities: Investigations into Ancient Greek and Chinese Science*. Cambridge: Cambridge University Press.

Lock M. M. 1980: *East Asian Medicine in Urban Japan*. Berkeley: University of California Press.

Loewe M. A. N. 1982: The Manuscripts from Tomb Number Three Mawang-tui. In R. P. Kramers (ed.) *China: Continuity and Change*. Zürich: Hausdruckerei der Universität, 29–55.

Lu F. 1989: *Dan wei* – a Special Form of Social Organisation. *Social Sciences in China* 10 (3): 100–22.

Lu G. D. and Needham J. (1966)1970: Medicine and Chinese Culture. In J. Needham et al. (eds.) *Clerks and Craftsmen in China and the West*. Cambridge: Cambridge University Press, 263–93.

1980: *Celestial Lancets: a History and Rationale of Acupuncture and Moxa*. Cambridge: Cambridge University Press.

Lucas A. E. 1982: *Chinese Medical Modernisation: Comparative Policy Continuities, 1930s – 1980s*. New York: Praeger.

Luhrmann T. M. 1989: *Persuasions of the Witch's Craft: Ritual, Magic, and Witchcraft in Present-day England*. Oxford: Blackwell.

Lukes S. 1973: *Individualism*. Oxford: Blackwell.

Lyons J. 1977: *Semantics*. 2 vols. Cambridge: Cambridge University Press.

Mao Z. D. 1975a: On Practice. In Committee for the Publication of the *Selected Works of Mao Tse-tung*, Central Committee of the Communist Party of China (eds.) *Selected Works of Mao Tse-tung* I. Beijing: Foreign Language Press, 295–309.

1975b: On Contradiction. In Committee for the Publication of the *Selected Works of Mao Tse-tung*, Central Committee of the Communist Party of China (eds.) *Selected Works of Mao Tse-tung* I. Beijing: Foreign Language Press, 311–47.

Mauss M. 1950: *Essai sur le Don*. Paris: Presses Universitaires de France.

McGuire M. B. 1983: Words of Power: Personal Empowerment and Healing. *Culture, Medicine and Psychiatry* 7: 221–40.

McMullen D. 1988: *State and Scholars in T'ang China*. Cambridge: Cambridge University Press.

Miura K. 1989: The Revival of *Qi*: *Qigong* in Contemporary China. In L. Kohn (ed.) *Taoist Meditation and Longevity Techniques*. Ann Arbor: Center for Chinese Studies, University of Michigan, 331–62.

Morris B. 1990: Thoughts on Chinese Medicine. *Eastern Anthropologist* 42: 1–33.

Naquin S. 1976: *Millenarian Rebellion in China: the Eight Trigrams Uprising of 1813*. New Haven: Yale University Press.

Needham J. 1956: *Science and Civilisation in China* II. *History of Scientific Thought*. Cambridge: Cambridge University Press.

Needham R. 1983: Polythetic Classification. In *Against the Tranquility of Axioms*. Berkeley: University of California Press, 36–65.

Oberländer C. 1996: *Zwischen Tradition und Moderne: Die Bewegung für den Fortbestand der Kanpô-Medizin in Japan*. Stuttgart: Franz Steiner.

Obeyesekere G. 1969: The Ritual Drama of the Sanni Demons: Collective Representations of Disease in Ceylon. *Comparative Studies in Sociology and History* 2: 174–216.

Ohnuki-Tierney E. 1984: *Illness and Culture in Contemporary Japan: an Anthropological View*. Cambridge: Cambridge University Press.

Oppitz M. and Hsu E. (eds.) 1998: *Naxi and Moso Ethnography: Kin, Rites, Pictographs*. Zürich: Völkerkundemuseum.

Ots T. (1987)1990: *Medizin und Heilung in China: Annäherungen an die Traditionelle Medizin*. 2nd edn. Berlin: Reimer.

1990: The Angry Liver, the Anxious Heart and the Melancholy Spleen: the Phenomenology of Perceptions in Chinese Culture. *Culture, Medicine and Psychiatry* 14: 21–58.

Ownby D. 1993: Chinese *hui* and the Early Modern Social Order: Evidence from Eighteenth-Century Southeast China. In D. Ownby and M. Somers Heidhues (eds.) *'Secret Societies' Reconsidered: Perspectives on the Social History of Modern South China and Southeast Asia*. Armonk: Sharpe, 34–67.

Parish W. L. 1990: What Model Now? In R. Y. W. Kwok et al. (eds.) *Chinese Urban Reform: What Model Now?* Armonk: Sharpe, 3–16.

Pepper S. 1984: *China's Universities Post-Mao Enrolment Policies and their Impact on the Structure of Secondary Education: a Research Report*. Ann Arbor: Center for Chinese Studies, University of Michigan.

Peterson W. J. 1982: Making Connections: 'Commentary on the Attached Verbalizations' of the *Book of Change*. *Harvard Journal of Asiatic Studies* 42 (1): 67–116.

Pieke F. 1996: *The Ordinary and the Extraordinary: an Anthropological Study of Chinese Reform and the 1989 People's Movement in Beijing*. London: Kegan Paul.

Porkert M. 1961: Untersuchungen einiger philosophisch–wissenschaftlicher Grundbegriffe und Bezeichnungen im Chinesischen. *Zeitschrift der Morgenländischen Gesellschaft* 110 (2): 422–52.
— 1965: Die energetische Terminologie in den chinesischen Medizinklassikern. *Sinologica* 8 (4): 184–210.
— 1974: *The Theoretical Foundations of Chinese Medicine: Systems of Correspondence*. Cambridge, Mass.: MIT Press.
— 1976: Die sachlichen Prämissen für eine wissenschaftliche Diskussion der Akupunktur. *Deutsches Ärzteblatt – Ärztliche Mitteilungen* 73 (18): 1240–4.
— 1982: The Difficult Task of Blending Chinese and Western Science: the Case of Modern Interpretations of Traditional Chinese Medicine. In G. H. Li et al. (eds.) *Explorations in the History of Science and Technology in China*. Shanghai: Zhonghua wenshi luncong, 553–72.
Potter S. H. and Potter J. 1990: *China's Peasants: the Anthropology of a Revolution*. Cambridge: Cambridge University Press.
Pullum G. K. 1991: The Great Eskimo Vocabulary Hoax. In *The Great Eskimo Vocabulary Hoax and Other Irreverent Essays in the Study of Language*. Chicago: University of Chicago Press, 159–71.
Qiu R. Z. 1982: Philosophy of Medicine in China (1930–1980). *Metamedicine* 3: 35–73.
Reiser S. J. 1978: *Medicine and the Reign of Technology*. Cambridge: Cambridge University Press.
Robinet I. 1989a: Visualization and Ecstatic Flight in Shangqing Taoism. In L. Kohn (ed.) *Taoist Meditation and Longevity Techniques*. Ann Arbor: Center for Chinese Studies, University of Michigan, 159–91.
— 1989b: Original Contributions of *Neidan* to Taoism and Chinese Thought. In L. Kohn (ed.) *Taoist Meditation and Longevity Techniques*. Ann Arbor: Center for Chinese Studies, University of Michigan, 297–328.
Roseman M. 1991: *Healing Sounds from the Malaysian Rainforest: Temiar Music and Medicine*. Berkeley: University of California Press.
Roth H. D. 1990: The Early Taoist Concept of *Shen*: a Ghost in the Machine? In K. Smith (ed.) *Sagehood and Systemizing Thought in Warring States and Han China*. Brunswick, Me.: Asian Studies Program, 11–32.
Ruel M. J. 1990: Non-sacrificial Ritual Killing. *Man* 25: 323–35.
Saussure F., de 1967: *Grundfragen der Allgemeinen Sprachwissenschaft*, 2nd edn. Berlin: De Gruyter.
Schall P. 1965: *Der Arzt in der chinesischen Kultur*. Stuttgart: Fink.
Scheid V. 1998: Plurality and Synthesis in Contemporary Chinese Medicine. Ph.D. thesis in Social Anthropology, University of Cambridge.
Scheper-Hughes N. and Lock M. M. 1987: The Mindful Body: a Prolegomenon to Future Work in Medical Anthropology. *Medical Anthropology Quarterly* 1 (1): 6–41.
Schipper K. 1978: The Taoist Body. *History of Religions* 17: 355–86.
— 1982: *Le Corps Taoïste, Corps Physique – Corps Sociale*. Paris: Fayard.
Schnorrenberger C. C. 1983: *Lehrbuch der chinesischen Medizin für westliche Aerzte: Die theoretischen Grundlagen der chinesischen Akupunktur und Arzneiverordnung*. 2nd edn. Stuttgart: Hippocrates.

Schwarcz V. 1986: *The Chinese Enlightenment: Intellectuals and the Legacy of the Fourth May Movement of 1919.* Berkeley: University of California Press.

Sharma U. 1996: Bringing the Body Back into (Social) Action: Techniques of the Body and the Cultural Imagination. *Social Anthropology* 4 (3): 251–62.

Shaughnessy E. L. 1993: *I ching.* In M. Loewe (ed.) *Early Chinese Texts: a Bibliograpgical Guide.* Berkeley: Society for the Study of Early China and Institute of East Asian Studies, 216–28.

—— 1994: A First Reading of the Mawangdui *Yijing* Manuscript. *Early China* 19: 47–73.

Shweder R. A. 1972: Aspects of Cognition in Zinacanteco Shamans: Experimental Results. In W. A. Lessa and E. Z. Vogt (eds.) *Reader in Comparative Religion: an Anthropological Approach.* 3rd edn. New York: Harper and Row.

Simmel G. 1950: *The Sociology of Georg Simmel.* (Transl., ed., and with an Introduction by K. H. Wolff.) New York: Free Press.

Sivin N. 1987: *Traditional Medicine in Contemporary China: a Partial Translation of* Revised Outline of Chinese Medicine *(1972) with an Introductory Study on Change in Present-day and Early Medicine.* Ann Arbor: Center for Chinese Studies, University of Michigan.

—— 1990: Change and Continuity in Early Cosmology: the Great Commentary and the Book of Changes. *Kyōto daigaku jinbun kagaku kenkyū hōkoku,* 3–43.

—— 1993: *Huang ti nei ching.* In Loewe M. (ed.) *Early Chinese Texts: a Bibliographical Guide.* Berkeley: Society for the Study of Early China and Institute of East Asian Studies, 196–215.

—— 1995a: Comparing Greek and Chinese Philosophy and Science. In *Medicine, Philosophy and Religion in Ancient China: Researches and Reflections.* Aldershot: Variorum, 1–11.

—— 1995b: The Myth of the Naturalists. In *Medicine, Philosophy and Religion in Ancient China: Researches and Reflections.* Aldershot: Variorum, 1–33.

—— 1995c: An Introductory Bibliography of Traditional Chinese Medicine: Books and Articles in Western Languages. In *Medicine, Philosophy and Religion in Ancient China: Researches and Reflections.* Aldershot: Variorum, 1–15.

—— 1995d: Text and Experience in Classical Chinese Medicine. In D. Bates (ed.) *Knowledge and the Scholarly Medical Traditions.* Cambridge: Cambridge University Press, 177–204.

—— 1995e: State, Cosmos, and Body in the Last Three Centuries B.C. *Harvard Journal of Asiatic Studies* 55 (1): 5–37.

Skorupski J. 1976: *Symbol and Theory: a Philosophical Study of Theories of Religion in Social Anthropology.* Cambridge: Cambridge University Press.

Smith R. 1991: *Fortune-tellers and Philosophers: Divination in Traditional Chinese Society.* Boulder: Westview.

Soo F. Y. K. 1981: *Mao Tse-tung's Theory of Dialectic.* Dordrecht: Reidel.

Sturtevant W. C. 1964: Studies in Ethnoscience. In A. K. Romney and R. G. D'Andrade (eds.) *Transcultural Studies in Cognition.* Special Publication. *American Anthropologist* 66 (3), Part 2: 99–131.

Sundararajan K. W. 1990: The *qigong* Healer as a Hypnotist. Ms. 14pp.

Tambiah S. J. 1968: The Magical Power of Words. *Man* 3: 175–208.

—— 1977: The Cosmological and Performative Significance of a Thai Cult of Healing through Meditation. *Culture, Medicine and Psychiatry* 1: 97–132.

Topley M. 1975: Chinese and Western Medicine in Hongkong: some Social and Cultural Determinants of Variation, Interaction and Change. In A. Kleinman et al. (eds.) *Medicine in Chinese Cultures: Comparative Studies of Health Care in Chinese and Other Societies.* Washington, D.C.: Geographic Health Studies, 241–71.

— 1976: Chinese Traditional Etiology and Methods of Cure in Hongkong. In C. Leslie (ed.) *Asian Medical Systems: a Comparative Study.* Berkeley: University of California Press, 243–65.

Toren C. 1993: Making History: the Significance of Childhood Cognition for a Comparative Anthropology of Mind. *Man* 28: 461–78.

Tu W. M. 1993: *Way, Learning, and Politics: Essays on the Confucian Intellectual.* Albany: State University of New York Press.

Turner V. W. 1960: Muchona the Hornet, Interpreter of Religion. In J. B. Casagrande (ed.) *In the Company of Man.* New York: Harper, 333–55.

— (1960)1967: Ritual Symbolism, Morality, and Social Structure among the Ndembu. In *The Forest of Symbols: Aspects of Ndembu Ritual.* Ithaca: Cornell University Press, 48–58.

Unschuld P. U. (1980)1985: *Medicine in China: a History of Ideas.* Berkeley: University of California Press.

— 1982: Der Wind als Ursache des Krankseins: Einige Gedanken zu Yamada Keiji's Analyse der Shao-shih Texte des *Huang-ti Nei-ching.* T'oung-Pao 68: 91–131.

— 1986a: *Medicine in China: a History of Pharmaceutics.* Berkeley: University of California Press.

— 1986b: *Nan-ching: the Classic of Difficult Issues.* (With Commentaries by Chinese and Japanese Authors from the Third through to the Twentieth Century.) Berkeley: University of California Press.

— 1988a: Gedanken zur kognitiven Aesthetik Europas und Ostasiens. In *Akademie der Wissenschaften zu Berlin, Jahrbuch.* Berlin: de Gruyter, 352–66.

— 1988b: *Introductory Readings in Classical Chinese Medicine.* (Sixty Texts with Vocabulary and Translation, a Guide to Research Aids and a General Glossary.) Dordrecht: Kluwer.

— 1988c: Culture and Pharmaceutics: some Epistemological Observations on Pharmacological Systems in Ancient Europe and Medieval China. In S. Van der Geest and S. R. Whyte (eds.) *The Context of Medicines in Developing Countries.* Dordrecht: Kluwer, 179–97.

— 1992: Epistemological Issues and Changing Legitimation: Traditional Chinese Medicine in the Twentieth Century. In C. Leslie and A. Young (eds.) *Paths to Asian Medical Knowledge.* Berkeley: University of California Press, 44–61.

Van der Geest S. 1990: Anthropologists and Missionaries: Brothers under the Skin. *Man* 25: 588–601.

Wakeman F. 1972: Secret Societies in China, 1800–1856. In J. Chesneaux (ed.) *Popular Movements and Secret Societies in China 1840–1950.* Stanford: Stanford University Press, 29–47.

— 1973: *History and Will: Philosophical Perspectives of Mao Tse-tung's Thought.* Berkeley: University of California Press.

Waley A. 1934: *The Way and its Power.* London: Allen and Unwin.

White S. 1993: Medical Discourses, Naxi Identities, and the State: Transformations in Socialist China. Ph.D. dissertation in Medical Anthropology, University of Califormia, Berkeley.

Whorf B. L. (1940) 1956: Science and Linguistics. In J. B. Carroll (ed.) *Language, Thought and Reality: Selected Writings of Benjamin Lee Whorf.* Cambridge, Mass.: MIT Press, 207–19.

Whyte M. K. and Parish W. L. 1984: *Urban Life in Contemporary China.* Chicago: University of Chicago Press.

Wilhelm H. (1943)1960: *Change: Eight Lectures on the Yijing.* London: Routledge and Kegan Paul.

(1951)1977: The Concept of Time. In *Heaven Earth and Man in the Book of Changes.* Seattle: University of Washington Press, 3–28.

Wilhelm R. (1923)1981: *I Ging: Text und Materialien.* Düsseldorf: Diederichs.

Wiseman N. 1990: *Glossary of Chinese Medical Terms and Acupuncture Points.* Brookline: Paradigm.

Wodiunig T. 1992: Von 'Rohen' zu 'Gekochten' zu 'Nationalen' Minderheiten: Ethnische Identität in der Provinz Yunnan. Lizentiatsarbeit, Ethnologisches Seminar Zürich.

Wolf M. 1985: *Revolution Postponed: Women in Contemporary China.* Stanford: Stanford University Press.

Wu Y. Y. 1993–4: A Medical Line of Many Masters: a Prosopographical Study of Liu Wansu and his Disciples from the Jin to the Early Ming. *Chinese Science* 11: 36–65.

Yamada K. 1979: The Formation of the *Huang-ti Nei-ching. Acta Asiatica* 36: 67–89.

Yeh A. G. O. and Xu X. Q. 1990: Changes in City Size and Regional Distribution 1953–1986. In Kwok et al. (eds.) *Chinese Urban Reform: What Model Now?* Armonk: Sharpe, 45–61.

Zimmermann F. (1982)1987: *The Jungle and the Aroma of Meats: an Ecological Theme in Hindu Medicine.* Berkeley: University of California Press.

CHINESE REFERENCES

Anon. [164/139 BC] 1954: *Huainan zi (Writings of the King of Huainan). Zhuzi jicheng* 7. Beijing: Zhonghua shuju chubanshe.

Anon. [762] 1956: *Huang di nei jing su wen (Yellow Emperor's Inner Canon, Basic Questions).* Edited by Wang Bing. Facsimile of Gu Congde's Ming dynasty reprint of the Song edition of 1067. Beijing: Renmin weisheng chubanshe.

Anon. 1988: *Zhongyi renwu cidian (Dictionary of Personages of Chinese Medicine).* Shanghai: Shanghai cishu chubanshe.

Ban Gu [1st century AD] 1962: *Han shu (The History of the Former Han).* Beijing: Zhonghua shuju.

Chen Yuanpeng 1995: Songdai de ruyi – Jianping Robert P. Hymes you guan Song Yuan yizhe diweide lundian (The Scholar Doctors of the Song Dynasty – Evaluating Robert P. Hymes' Argument concerning the Position of the Physicians of the Song and Yuan). *Xinshixue* 6 (1): 179–203.

Duan Yucai [1815] 1981: *Shuo wen jie zi zhu* (*Analytical Dictionary of Characters*). Compiled by Xu Shen in 121. Shanghai: Shanghai guji chubanshe.

Jiangling Zhangjiashan Hanjian zhengli xiaozu (eds.) 1989: Jiangling Zhangjiashan Hanjian 'Mai shu' shiwen (Explanations to the Han Bamboo Slips on the 'Document of the Vessels' from Zhangjiashan in Jiangling), *Wenwu* 7: 72–4.

Li Fang [983] (1960)1985: *Tai ping yu lan* (*Imperial Encyclopedia of the Taiping Reign Period*). Beijing: Zhonghua shuju.

Li Gao [1249] 1976: *Pi wei lun* (*Treatise of the Spleen and Stomach*). Hunansheng zhongyiyao yanjiusuo (eds.). Beijing: Renmin weisheng chubanshe.

Li Zhongzi [1642] (1963)1985: *Nei jing zhi yao* (*Essentials of the Inner Canon*, abbr.: *Essentials*). Beijing: Renmin weisheng chubanshe.

Ma Boying 1994: *Zhongguo yixue wenhua shi* (*A History of Medicine in Chinese Culture*). Shanghai: Shanghai renmin chubanshe.

Ma Boying, Gao Xi, and Hong Zhongli 1993: *Zhongwai yixue wenhua jiaoliu shi – Zhongwai yixue kua wenhua chuantong* (The History of Intercultural Medicine Communication between China and Foreign Countries – The Chinese-Foreign Medicine Cuts across Cultural Traditions). Shanghai: Wenhui chubanshe.

Ma Jiren 1983: *Zhongguo qigongxue* (*The Study of qigong in China*). Xi'an: Shanxi keji chubanshe.

Mao Zedong 1961: Maodunlun (Treatise on Contradiction). In Zhonggong zhongyang Mao Zedong xuanji chuban weiyuanhui (eds.) *Mao Zedong xuanji* I. Beijing: Renmin chubanshe, 287–326.

Matsuda Takatomo 1984: *Zhongguo wushu shilüe* (*Outline of the History of Unarmed Combat in China*). Chengdu: Sichuan keji chubanshe.

Mawangdui Hanmu boshu zhengli xiaozu (eds.) 1980–5: *Mawangdui Hanmu boshu* (MWD) (*Silk Manuscripts of the Han tomb in Mawangdui*), 4 vols. Beijing: Wenwu chubanshe.

Mawangdui Hanmu boshu zhengli xiaozu (eds.) 1985a: Yinyang shiyimai jiujing jiaben (Moxibustion Canon for the Eleven *yin* and *yang* Vessels, manuscript A). In *Mawangdui Hanmu boshu* IV. Beijing: Wenwu chubanshe, 7–13.

Mawangdui Hanmu boshu zhengli xiaozu (eds) 1985b: Zubi shiyimai jiujing (Moxibustion Canon for the Eleven Foot and Arm Vessels). In *Mawangdui Hanmu boshu* IV. Beijing: Wenwu chubanshe, 1–6.

MWD 1985, cf. Mawangdui Hanmu boshu zhengli xiaozu.

Nanjing zhongyi xueyuan yijing jiaoyanzu (eds.) 1961: *Nanjing yishi* (*Interpretation of the Classic of Difficult Issues*). Shanghai: Shanghai keji chubanshe.

Ou Ming (ed.) 1988: *Yinghan zhongyi cidian*. Xianggang: Sanlian shudian youxian gongsi and Guangdong keji chubanshe.

Qin Bowei (1957)1985: *Neijing zhiyao qianjie* (*Superficial Explanations for the Essentials of the Inner Canon*). Beijing: Renmin weisheng chubanshe.

Ren Yingqiu 1982: 'Huangdi neijing' yanjiu shijiang (Ten Lectures on Research on the *Yellow Emperor's Inner Canon*). In Ren Yingqiu and Liu Zhanglin (eds.) *'Neijing' yanjiu luncong*. Wuhan: Hubei renmin chubanshe, 1–99.

Ren Yingqiu (ed.) 1986: *Huangdi neijing zhangju suoyin* (*Index to the Yellow Emperor's Inner Canon*). Beijing: Renmin weisheng chubanshe.

Si Yuanyi and Gong Chun 1988: *Yishixue* (*History of Medicine*). Gaodeng yiyao yuanxiao jiaocai. Wuhan: Hubei kexue jishu chbanshe.

Sima Qian [*c.* 90 BC] 1959: *Shiji* (*Historical Records*). Beijing: Zhonghua shuju.

Sun Simiao [650/659] 1955: *Bei ji qian jin yao fang* (*Essential Prescriptions Worth a Thousand, for Urgent Need*). Facsimile of the Jianghu Medical School's reprint of a Northern Song edition that was reprinted in 1307 by the Meixi Shuyuan. Beijing: Renmin weisheng chubanshe.

Sun Zhensheng (ed.) 1981: *Baihua yijing* (*The Book of Changes in the Vernacular*). Taibei: Xingguang chubanshe.

Sun Zhirang (ed.) (1934)1939: *Mozi xiangu* (*Interpretation of the Mozi*). Attributed to Mo Di and his disciples (4th century BC). Shanghai: Xingfa guanshu yinwushang.

Tian Jinguo 1987: *Yunnan yiyao weisheng jianshi* (*Outline of the History of Medicine and Hygiene in Yunnan*). Kunming: Yunnan keji chubanshe.

Wang Zuyuan [1834] 1956: *Nei gong tu shuo* (*Illustrated Exegesis on Inner Alchemy*). Beijing: Renmin weisheng chubanshe.

Wu Zongbo, Yang Guoxiang, and Zhang Danian 1986: *Xinbian zhongyi linzheng shouce* (*Newly Edited Manual for Clinical Chinese Medicine*). Kunming: Yunnan keji chubanshe.

Xi Yuntai 1985: *Zhongguo wushu shi* (*History of Unarmed Combat in China*). Beijing: Renmin tiyu chubanshe.

Yang Shangshan [666/683] 1981: *Huang di nei jing tai su* (*The Yellow Emperor's Inner Canon, Grand Basis*). Tōyo Igaku Kenkyujo (eds.). Facsimile of the 1168 AD edition kept at Ninnaji. Osaka: Tōyo Igaku Zenpon Sōsho.

Yu Ke (ed.) 1980: *Shanhaijing jiaozhu* (*Commentary on the Classic of Mountains and Lakes*). Shanghai: Shanghai guji chubanshe.

Zhang Dehou 1989: *Yunnan zhongyi xueyuan yuanshi 1960–1988* (*Yunnan TCM College, History of the College from 1960 to 1988*). Kunming: Yunnan keji chubanshe.

Zhang Jiebin [1624] 1799: *Lei jing fu yi* (*Additional Appendix to the Categories*). Jinchang cuiyin tang.

Zhang Jiebin [1624] (1965)1985: *Lei jing* (*Canon of Categories*, abbr.: *Categories*). Beijing: Renmin weisheng chubanshe.

Zhang Shitong (ed.) 1974: *Xunzi jianzhu* (*Commentary on the Xunzi*). Attributed to Xun Qing (298–238 BC). Shanghai: Shanghai renmin chubanshe.

Zhang Zhongjing guoyi daxue shiyong jiaocai (eds) 1985: *Yijing xuandu* (*Selected Readings of the Yijing*). 98 pp.

Zhangjiashan Hanjian Zhenglizu (eds.) 1990: Zhangjiashan Hanjian 'Yinshu' shiwen (Explanations to the Han Bamboo Slips 'Document of Guiding' from Zhangjiashan). *Wenwu* 10: 82–6.

Zhongyi dacidian and Bianji weiyuanhui (eds.) 1987: *Zhongyi dacidian, Neike fence* (*TCM Comprehensive Dictionary of Internal Medicine*). Beijing: Renmin weisheng chubanshe.

Zou Xuexi 1986: *Yixue shijiang* (*Ten Lectures on the Doctrine of the Changes*). Chengdu: Sichuan kexue jishu chubanshe.

TCM TEXTBOOKS

Cheng Shide (ed.) 1984: *Neijing jiangyi* (*Interpretation of the Inner Canon*, abbr.: *Interpretation*). Shanghai: Shanghai kexue jishu chubanshe.

Chengdu zhongyi xueyuan (ed.) 1988: *Zhongyi bingyin bingjixue* (*TCM Etiology and Pathogenesis*). Guiyang: Guizhou renmin chubanshe.

Deng Tietao (ed.) 1984: *Zhongyi zhenduanxue* (*TCM Diagnostics*). Shanghai: Shanghai kexue jishu chubanshe.

Li Ding (ed.) 1984: *Jingluoxue* (*Tracts and Links*). Shanghai: Shanghai kexue jishu chubanshe.

Ling Yigui (ed.) 1984: *Zhongyaoxue* (*Traditional Chinese Pharmaceutics*). Shanghai: Shanghai kexue jishu chubanshe.

Luzhou yixueyuan (eds.) 1987: *Zhongyixue daolun* (*TCM Instructions*). Guiyang: Guizhou renmin chubanshe.

Meng Yuankai (ed.) 1986: *Zhongyi fukexue* (*TCM Gynaecology*). Shanghai: Shanghai kexue jishu chubanshe.

Qiu Maoliang (ed.) 1985: *Zhenjiuxue* (*Acumoxa*). Shanghai: Shanghai kexue jishu chubanshe.

Ren Yingqiu (ed.) 1986: *Zhongyi gejia xueshuo* (*Summaries of Different Chinese Medical Doctrines*). Shanghai: Shanghai kexue jishu chubanshe.

Shanxi zhongyi xueyuan (eds.) 1988: *Zhongyi zhenduanxue* (*TCM Diagnostics*). Guiyang: Guizhou renmin chubanshe.

Shenyang yaoxueyuan (eds.) 1978: *Zhongyixue jichu* (*Basics of the Study of Chinese Medicine*). Beijing: Renmin weisheng chubanshe.

Wei Jia (ed.) 1987: *Gejia zhenjiu xueshuo* (*Summaries of Different Doctrines of Acumoxa*). Shanghai: Shanghai kexue jishu chubanshe.

Yang Changsen (ed.) 1985: *Zhenjiu zhiliaoxue* (*Acumoxa Therapy*). Shanghai: Shanghai kexue jishu chubanshe.

Yin Huihe (ed.) 1984: *Zhongyi jichu lilun* (*Fundamental Theory of TCM*, abbr.: *TCM Fundamentals*). Shanghai: Shanghai kexue jishu chubanshe.

Yunnan zhongyi xueyuan (ed.) 1988: *Zangxiangxue* (*Organ Clusters*). Guiyang: Guizhou renmin chubanshe.

Zhao Fen (ed.) 1963: *Zhongyi jichuxue* (*Study of the Basics of Chinese Medicine*). Beijing: Renmin weisheng chubanshe.

General index

Index of Chinese book titles and chapter headings discussed in text

Book titles are given in italics, chapter headings in quotes. Words in classical Chinese are generally monosyllabic, words in standard modern Chinese can have more syllables.

Index of Chinese personal names

(style name (*zi*), if known, given after comma)